10761

Scanning the Century

THE PENGUIN BOOK OF
THE TWENTIETH CENTURY IN POETRY

Edited by

PETER FORBES

VIKING

IN ASSOCIATION WITH

THE POETRY SOCIETY

VIKING

Published by the Penguin Group

First published 1999
1 3 5 7 9 10 8 6 4 2
This edition published by The Softback Preview, 1999 in association with Penguin Books

Editorial matter copyright © Peter Forbes, 1999

The Acknowledgements on pages 555–569 constitute an extension of
this copyright page

Set in 10.75/13.5 pt Monotype Sabon
Typeset by Rowland Phototypesetting Ltd,
Bury St Edmunds, Suffolk
Printed in England by Clays Ltd, St Ives plc

A CIP catalogue record for this book is available from the British Library

ISBN 0-670-88011-6

Contents

Preface

Scanning the Century tells the story of the twentieth century in poetry – primarily the story of world events and the new moods thrown up by technical and social change. It draws on English poetry from Britain, America and wherever English is spoken, and on poetry in translation, especially from Europe. The book is intended to be readable both as condensed history and as vivid poetry.

There are many possible approaches towards the arrival of the Millennium, from hitching a ride on a comet to a refusal to acknowledge the importance of such an arbitrary milestone. In my case, born in 1947, and with a longstanding fascination for the history of the century and a passion to understand its dynamics, I recognize it as an aid to concentrating the mind. We have become so used to saying, 'this is the twentieth century after all', as if everyone knew what that entailed, that to see this touchstone of modernity start to become just another period of history to be reassessed and, if necessary, cut down to size, is salutary. *Scanning the Century* is my contribution to this process.

The aim of this book is to capture the flavour of the century with something like the tang of newsreel and the zest of popular song. The thirty-nine sections run the gamut of moods, from the deadly serious to the playful. It would be possible to imagine a documentary anthology which concentrated solely on the outward appearance of the century's life, on public events and technical change, but personal emancipation has been such a strong theme of the century that this element is a vital strand of the work. There has been a rash of single-issue anthologies in recent years: on love, death, family relationships, particular wars, etc., but none that brings all of these elements into some sort of relationship, as a newspaper does. As the century ends, a trawl through the papers and media suggests that our lives are dominated by crime, sport, new technology, sex and a dumbed-down Hooray-Hello! cult of celebrity-for-celebrity's sake. No doubt this is a distortion but to ignore these aspects would be to falsify the picture: so crime, big and small, pornography, Match of the Day, e-mail and Monroe, Chaplin, Ali and Princess Diana all have a place here.

The twentieth century invented the concept of lifestyle, and the moods and attitudes that lie behind lifestyles have often found perfect expression in a poem: the desire for pine and white paint that swept through the Western world in the Sixties (Blake Morrison's 'Pine'); Les Murray's 'Dream of Wearing Shorts Forever'; Jenny Joseph's blast for a richer old age in 'Warning'.

This has been a great century of poetry. No other age demonstrates such a flowering of human possibility besides – when the pace of change has precipitated crises – such terrifying oppression and denial of humanity. And the poetry has captured its range and multi-faceted identity. I have not hesitated to include some poems written long after the events they describe, such as Paul Muldoon's 'Truce' (World War I), Donald Davie's 'Remembering the 'Thirties' and Carol Kizer's 'Twelve O'Clock' (Hiroshima). Poetry is not instant reportage but one of the ways by which we remember and commemorate.

The book owes its existence to Tony Lacey at Penguin, who liked the idea in the first place and gave it enthusiasm, practical support and valuable editorial criticism throughout. My editor, Charlie Hartley, sharpened up the final stages, reminding me how much the broad picture still needs its fine tuning; Nick Wetton weathered an unusually wide-ranging permissions list with thoroughness and good humour; and Liz Halsall kept the show on the road with calm efficiency. I am particularly grateful to those who helped me to track down poems I might otherwise never have found, especially Stephen Burt, Antonia Byatt, Hans Magnus Enzensberger, Miroslav Holub, Jerzy Jarniewicz, Glyn Maxwell, Dennis O'Driscoll, Tony Rudolf, Piotr Sommer. Not every lead resulted in a poem in the book – many did – but all such suggestions assisted the process of compilation immeasurably. Michael Hamburger and Ewald Osers undertook translations especially for the book and P. D. Royce provided literal translations of poems under consideration and advice on poems in foreign languages. Help with elucidating particular poems and footnotes came from John Levett, Norman Rose and Clive Wilmer. The bulk of the research was carried out in the two essential libraries for poetry research: the Poetry Library on the South Bank and the British Library. Twentieth-century anthologies are major undertakings and this one would not have been possible without the support of the Poetry Society and its Director Chris Meade and Chair Mary Enright. Jon Stallworthy and Edward Mendelson, literary executors of Louis MacNeice and W. H. Auden, respectively, provided generous and kind assistance with regard to the poets' substantial contributions to this book. The constant reader over my shoulder and sounding board throughout the work has been my partner Diana Reich.

London, September 1998

NOTE: Footnotes after the poems are the editor's unless otherwise indicated.

Introduction

'We are living in an epoch rife with problems and perils, but it is not boring.' Primo Levi spoke as someone with good reason to denounce the age in which he lived: he survived Auschwitz to write the classic of concentration-camp literature *If This is a Man*. But he also wrote many works, in prose and verse, in which, out of his profession of chemist and his boundless curiosity, he mined a vein of fantasy, whimsy and gentle reflection. 'All, all of a piece throughout' – Dryden's verdict on the seventeenth century – cannot be applied to the twentieth, which shows greater swings between horror and vivacity, between the good life and inhumane oppression, than any other.

There is no doubt that, in drawing a line under the century, the horrific scale of its tragedies and their duration loom very large. But there were also long islands of peace in many parts of the world, mostly after 1945, and Harold Macmillan's 1957 remark, that 'most of our people have never had it so good,' was no more than the truth. This anthology tries to balance the claims of war and peace, to celebrate the twentieth century's felicities and to counterpoint them with the starker material.

The phrase 'twentieth century' has often been used as an epithet (as have the decades) as if it implied some agreed set of attributes. (The Australian poet Les Murray has satirized this practice: 'Nor did Cromwell thunder, *After all,/in the bowels of Christ this is the seventeenth century.*') But however loose and tautological, these crude labels do nevertheless mean something. In a secular and highly mobile age, when the timeless repetitions of seasons and religious rites have lost their force, and as an unprecedented welter of innovation, both technical and social, has been unleashed, people need to place some sort of grid over the flux in order to orientate themselves.

In all the arts and sciences, the period 1900–1913 is one of the most extraordinary in history. The turn of the century really did coincide with a radical shift in sensibility – so extreme, in fact, that it took most of the population decades to absorb the implications. This clash between the new ideas and the old order of the nineteenth century was partly responsible for two world wars.

On 14 December 1899, the German physicist Max Planck made the revolutionary discovery that radiation – including light and radio waves – was not a continuous phenomenon as had been thought, but, like matter, could be broken down to a smallest possible unit, an atom of radiation: the quantum. The consequences of this led to quantum theory, a completely new theory of matter, and eventually to nuclear fission. Einstein's Special Theory of Relativity emerged in 1905, radically redefining notions of time and space which had stood unchanged since Newton in the late seventeenth century.

In painting, the revolution begun by the Impressionists led to successive waves of innovation in the early twentieth century: Post-Impressionism, Expressionism, Fauvism, Futurism, Cubism, Dada, Constructivism, Surrealism. In music, the gradual tolerance of increased dissonance which had been a facet of Western music since Mozart suddenly became a torrent of discords and thunderous rhythms.

How did poetry respond to the ferment of Modernism and the new science? At the end of the nineteenth century English poetry was in a bad way. The fustiness, the fly-blown rhetoric, the stilted polite formulations, the pallid invocations of once vigorous myths, the coy apostrophization of women, what MacNeice called 'castrated nature poetry' – the genteel circumlocutions of Edwardian and Georgian poetry had to be swept away. T. S. Eliot did it in 1914, forensically and efficiently, with 'Preludes': 'The winter evening settles down/With smell of steaks in passageways.'

But Eliot's new diction was a cold mandarin voice – it destroyed the old effectively enough but it was too thin and priggish to give a universal voice to the century. A gentler revolution was launched by Robert Frost: updating Wordsworth's revolution of a hundred years before, he brought a new plain vernacular voice into poetry. The emergence of a characteristic twentieth-century vernacular was common to prose and verse, indeed it marked a change in the way people spoke. A clear shift in the English language can be seen by comparing the prose of two writers such as Dickens and E. M. Forster:

Whether this young gentleman (for he was but three-and-twenty) combined with the miserly vice of an old man, any of the open-handed vices of a young one, was a moot point; so very honourably did he keep his own counsel.

(*Our Mutual Friend*)

He waited in his cave a minute, and lit a cigarette so that he could remark on rejoining her, 'I bolted in to get out of the draught,' or something of the sort.

(*A Passage to India*)

Where the Dickens is formal, parenthetical, relishing its overload of clauses, loving the sound of its own voice, the Forster is linear, casual, unostentatious, economical, turned down at the edges ('something of the sort'). Of course, some late-twentieth-century prose stylists could be as flamboyant as Dickens – Saul Bellow, John Updike, Salman Rushdie – but the voice adopted by Forster has done sterling service throughout the century. It was able to accommodate the matter of the twentieth century, however extreme. In writing about totalitarianism, George Orwell aspired to prose 'as transparent as a window pane'. Primo Levi chose the style of 'a factory report' to describe his experience of Auschwitz.

Poets too have had to find strategies for dealing with the scale of the century's tragedies. In the case of the First World War, poets were actually the first to articulate the fact that the war was not what people at home imagined. Both the traditional practice of war and Edwardian rhetoric collapsed on the Western front. The development of automatic weapons and the reluctance of the generals to adopt tank warfare meant that whole platoons of bayonet-and-rifle-wielding men could be simply mown down by machine-gun emplacements. Thousands of years of Homeric stylization of war were also destroyed. The War was a great leveller – officers and men suffered equally and both felt betrayed by the generals and politicians. The War greatly accelerated the decline of deference and the stilted top-hatted formality of the ruling class. Owen felt that to describe what he actually saw itself constituted a form of poetry: 'the poetry is in the pity.' Owen's subject, 'war and the pity of war', was perhaps more influential in shaping the minds of the next generation than was his own poetic practice. Owen was essentially a lush Keatsian lyric poet who encountered the antithesis of Keats' 'warm south' and managed, at the cost of laming his rhymes, to make his subject fit the Keatsian mould. (His principal innovation was para-rhyme, e.g.,

'It seemed that out of battle I *escaped*/down some profound dull tunnel, long since *scooped* . . .' [ed.'s italics.])

However poets have actually written, the public perception of their art has been enormously influenced by a statement Eliot made in 1921, the year before he published *The Waste Land*: 'We can only say that it appears likely that poets in our civilization, as it exists at present, must be *difficult*.' What Eliot said earlier in the same passage has been more important for the way that poetry is actually produced. 'When a poet's mind is perfectly equipped for its work, it is constantly amalgamating disparate experience; the ordinary man's experience is chaotic, irregular, fragmentary. The latter falls in love, or reads Spinoza, and these two experiences have nothing to do with each other, or with the noise of the typewriter or the smell of cooking; in the mind of the poet these experiences are always forming new wholes.' The recipe for subject matter is what was taken up by most poets but it is the notion of 'difficulty' that has been remembered by the potential audience and has helped create an unjustified aura of obscurity around the whole subject of twentieth-century poetry.

But between them, Eliot, Frost and Owen cleared the way for a kind of poetry in which the material of modern life could find a voice commensurate with the speaking voice. There is a connection between hierarchical societies, behaviour and language. The new plain voice accompanied the gradual trend towards informality in behaviour. A poem of John Betjeman's about the death of George V (1936) dramatizes the shift in its final image: 'a young man lands hatless from the air'. This is the Playboy King, Edward VIII, mobile and unadorned in the modern manner.

The vernacular voice consolidated in the 1930s. Poets from 1900 to 1930 often sound slightly dated to our ears, but the poetry written by Louis MacNeice in the Thirties has the voice we still use today:

> Now the till and the typewriter call the fingers,
>   The workman gathers his tools
> For the eight-hour day but after that the solace
>   Of films or football pools
> Or of the gossip or cuddle, the moments of self-glory
>   Or self-indulgence, blinkers on the eyes of doubt,
> The blue smoke rising and the brown lace sinking
>   In the empty glass of stout.   (*Autumn Journal*)

MacNeice called this kind of verse 'impure poetry' – poetry which allowed the sights and sounds of the world to gatecrash its formal enclosure. All of the subject matter of the twentieth century can be accommodated in such verse, and it is not simply a matter of the phenomenon noted with distaste by Virginia Woolf and ambivalence by George Orwell with respect to the novels of James Joyce: both thought that Joyce had simply inverted the old ideals of truth and beauty, by making ugliness the touchstone. MacNeice's image of the brown lace in the glass of stout is a lyric image; it is only surprising that such lyric grace should be inspired by a stolid, unromantic drink. This ability to find beauty in everyday life rather than in conventionally exalted subjects, is one of the glories of the century's poetry.

With regard to English poetry, Auden and MacNeice are the presiding spirits of this anthology. For every Auden poem included here, two more could have been selected. No other poet was so good on so many of the key themes of the century. Until his late, neologizing, maiden-Aunt phase, he kept his eye on the subject and always found the right form. Both Auden and MacNeice answered Eliot's plea for difficulty in a complex age by being not difficult *but various*. When Auden said, in his introduction to the anthology *The Poet's Tongue* (1935), a vastly inclusive collection with folk songs and riddles besides straight poetry, 'A great many people dislike the idea of poetry as they dislike over-earnest people, because they imagine it is always worrying about the eternal verities,' he might have had the anguished Eliot in mind. Auden believed that light verse was particularly suited to the twentieth century and proved it in *Letter to Lord Byron*, almost a mid-twentieth-century anthology in itself.

Louis MacNeice devised a recipe for the modern poet which remains a role model: 'I would have a poet able-bodied, fond of talking, a reader of newspapers, capable of pity and laughter, informed in economics, appreciative of women, involved in personal relationships, actively interested in politics, susceptible to physical impressions.' *Autumn Journal*, several extracts from which appear in the book, captures the soul of modern man, torn between his private obsessions and delights and a world going mad all around him.

This English vernacular voice is, of course, not the only successful poetic strategy of the century. Things developed differently in continental Europe. In Baudelaire, French poetry had already managed to liberate itself from bourgeois stuffiness by the mid-nineteenth century, and movements in poetry followed movements in painting and music. Apollinaire was at the centre of the French artistic ferment during the First World War. In the programme for the ballet *Parade* (1917), with music by Satie and sets by Picasso, he used the term 'surrealism' for the first time. Surrealist poetry, of which André Breton was the leading practitioner, was thus bound up with the other arts from the start. Closely associated with surrealism was Tristan Tzara's Dada movement (a deliberate exploitation of the inconsequential and nonsensical in protest at the absurdity of the War). Apollinaire's 'The Marvels of War' makes a fascinating contrast with Wilfred Owen and the English war poets, and introduces an aspect of poetry that would become a running theme throughout the century, i.e., irony, a deliberate eschewing of a simple 'honest' relationship between words and the world. In the hands of the postmodernist theorists, a complete breakdown between the two was postulated. This is a breach too far, but ironic registers have proliferated as the century has progressed.

A nucleus of European poets – Bertolt Brecht, Hans Magnus Enzensberger, Miroslav Holub, Primo Levi, Czesław Miłosz, Jacques Prévert, Wisława Szymborska – occupies a central place in this book. From their different perspectives, they generally share an interest in the rigour of science as an antidote to absurdity, dogma, and the mayhem generated by irrationalists. Facing up to the worst, they demonstrate a post-religious affirmation and suggest what humanity might be like if it could put aside its murderous childhood.

The work of most of these European poets is in free verse, ideas about which have cast a pall over the century's poetry, with simplistic battle lines being drawn up. In this selection, poems by such diverse figures as Apollinaire, Cummings, Prévert, Ginsberg, Ferlinghetti, Holub and Rosemary Tonks demonstrate the effectiveness of free verse. The movement of the verse enacts the mood of the subject – to formalize these poems would be to straitjacket them. And the jibe against free verse that it is formless clearly does not apply to these poems, which are strongly dramatic and well suited to reading out loud.

But to suggest that the twentieth century *demands* free verse would mean that we would have to lose Auden's 'September 1, 1939', MacNeice's *Autumn Journal*, Larkin's 'Essential Beauty' and many more. Why should we? The franker diction of the twentieth century and the vocabularies of new technical developments, products, lifestyles, movements in art and the media have created fresh possibilities for formal poetry. Polysyllabic technical words take on a new resonance within iambic verse, as John Levett's poem 'SDI' shows, incorporating material such as 'A satellite's remote, panoptic eye' into perfect iambic pentameter.

If public events have posed one challenge for poets during the century, another has come from the authority assumed by science. Early attempts to make connections between the two were misdirected. The American poet William Carlos Williams said:

It may seem presumptive to state that such an apparently minor activity as a movement in verse construction could be an indication of Einstein's discoveries in the relativity of our measurements of physical matter . . . but such is the fact.

And:

Far from being fixed, our prosodic values should rightly be seen as only relatively true.

This was a disastrous mis-reading of the relationship between science and art, and similar errors are still being perpetrated today. Williams assumed that the word 'relative' as it is used in ordinary speech could be easily yoked to the concept of relativity introduced by Einstein. 'Relative' was a word with added value: to use it, however wantonly, was thought to earn instant brownie points. But there is nothing 'relative' about the cornerstone of Einstein's theory: the universality and immutability of the speed of light, 299,792 km per second. Williams' apparent reaching out to science was no more than an attempt to hijack some of its power and glamour.

Nevertheless, science and poetry can have a fruitful relationship. For writers like Primo Levi and Miroslav Holub (both practising scientists), science provides a value system because it is the one domain immune from human sentiment. In his prose work *The Periodic Table*, Levi often uses science as an antidote to the oppressive distortions of racism: 'matter is matter, neither noble nor vile, infinitely transformable, and its proximate origin is of no importance whatsoever.' Similarly, for Holub it is the fact that science gives us images of the world that are 'utterly free from old mythologies and demonology' that is valuable to him as a poet. In Holub's poem 'Žito the Magician', the court magician will perform any trick for the Emperor but when asked to produce a value of 'sine alpha greater than one' he has to say that this at least is impossible: not difficult or not not-possible-at-the-moment, but impossible for all time. By the end of the century, a body of work had been established in which science began to take its place, as Wordsworth, in the Preface to *Lyrical Ballads* (1802), predicted it one day would:

If the labours of Men of science should ever create any material revolution, direct or indirect, in our condition, and in the impressions which we habitually receive, the Poet will sleep then no more than at present; he will be ready to follow the steps of the Man of science, not only in those general indirect effects, but he will be at his side, carrying sensation into the midst of the objects of the science itself.

The science section of the book is one of the longest and richest, as it should be.

The enormities of the Second World War, the Holocaust, the nuclear bomb, and totalitarian oppression posed the greatest challenges of all. Can any words be found to deal with material annihilation and utter dehumanization? The critic Theodor Adorno said that 'to write a poem after Auschwitz is barbarous'. In fact a great deal of very successful poetry has been written on the most terrible themes. Although some poets such as the Pole Tadeusz Różewicz have half-accepted Adorno's injunction and written stark anti-poetry, in practice, a range of techniques has proved viable. Paul Celan's 'Death Fugue' has a mesmeric incantatory quality of quasi-biblical lamentation. Much of the war poetry used the antithetical strategy of Henry Reed's 'Naming of Parts': here is the garden of peace (which we have not got), and here is the weapon you must use. The long years of communist oppression in Eastern Europe were notable for the use of fable and allegory as means to evade the censor, as in Zbigniew Herbert's 'Damastes (Also Known as Procrustes) Speaks' and Marin Sorescu's 'The Glass Wall'.

On one reading, the twentieth century has been one of unprecedented destruction and regression. The Twentieth-Century European Book of the Dead (including Russia) – those who died prematurely through war, man-made famine, political oppression or genocide – amounts to approximately 110 million people (or approximately the current populations of France and the UK combined). But to represent the century entirely or even mainly by poems about these subjects would be to misrepresent an era which has also included a remarkable flowering of creativity, personal mobility and choice. For the first time in history, millions have not been restricted to the culture in which they happened to grow up, rooted in a time and place, but have been able to explore the by now enormous library of recorded music and film, to see other cultures at first hand and the great events of the century on newsreel. Despite the effects of this cultural overload on the production of new art and its tendency towards postmodernist pick-and-mix, at the end of the century it is worth celebrating this bonanza. And more than that, twentieth-century technology and mobile social patterns have encouraged a kind of happy magpie creative opportunism, exemplified by the Beatles, who had no sense of history other than rock 'n' roll history but who plundered musical forms from the Blues to Indian music to Bach, transformed the ephemera of newspapers and TV into art and told us how many holes it takes to fill the Albert Hall. It is this happy opportunism that some sections of the anthology seek to capture: Ferlinghetti grafting the hipster language of bebop on to the Crucifixion story; John Updike's skittering evocation of the life of Fifties film stars; Roger McGough's gentle surrealistic take on office life in 'cosy biscuit'.

For when the twentieth century was not engaged in orgies of mass destruction, the dominant mood was one of vivacity, a classless, unstuffy *joie de vivre* that was present in many key traits of the century: in the rise of rhythm in Latin music, rock and the jazz of the bop era with its delight in turning hackneyed old tunes into chromatic psalms for the modern city; in eclectic late-twentieth-century interior decoration and cuisine; in the knowing *lingua franca* of advertising; in the inexorable rise of colour in colour film, moving and still, colour printing, colour computing; in the intricate and elegant discoveries of science; and simply in a new tempo of informal life. Michael Frayn once captured this mood of a bountiful age in a piece of incidental journalistic prose:

How sweet life can be, living in the cracks and fringes of a wealthy society! This is real riches, voluptuous to the touch – to sit on old basket chairs someone threw out, to work late and early, to run out to the supermarket and buy a 2 litre bottle of wine for 40p [1972] and fall asleep after lunch, to know the children have just disappeared into someone else's garden with 5 of their friends and with any luck won't be back until bedtime. You think Rockefeller had such a life?

This characteristic note of insouciance emerges in disparate personalities and societies throughout the century: in the artists around Picasso in the early century with their sheer exuberance in throwing off the weight of representational dullness; in inventors like Edison who could make electricity talk, or Turing and Von Neumann who turned the abstruse mathematical logic of the nineteenth-century mathematician Boole into a machine that mediates our entire civilization, the computer; and in scientists like Einstein, Rutherford, Watson and Crick who revealed the elegant and sometimes terrifying architecture behind our existence. I have tried to find poems that capture this creative efflorescence. America is the country where this plenitude has its fullest expression and, not surprisingly, American poets – from Howard Nemerov in the Fifties to James Tate and Mark Halliday today – have been most adept in the realm of cornucopia.

Against all this, even in peacetime the twentieth century has some substantial minuses against its account. The persistence of gaping pockets of poverty amidst plenty, drug-related crime, and the large-scale destruction of the natural environment and degradation of the atmosphere, water and soil are problems which were still worsening at the end of the century. Nature, which had been a constant touchstone for every poet from Homer to Hardy, is now something deeply problematical. As far back as 1939, MacNeice could write:

> Sing us no more idylls, no more pastorals,
> No more epics of the English earth;
> The country is a dwindling annexe to the factory,
> Squalid as an afterbirth.

A great deal of nature poetry has been written without addressing MacNeice's contention that both the power and spirit that once resided in hills, groves and the running brooks have been eroded: factory farming, absentee landlords, mechanization, pollution, loss of species, genetic engineering and the leisure industry have piled on the damage since MacNeice wrote. His conclusion, 'squalid as an afterbirth', is no longer true, the mess having been tidied up and the stable fitted out as a leisure complex for townies. Of course, many poems have been written protesting against these changes but the vital centres of twentieth-century life have been in the towns and cities.

But the towns and cities are not well either. Townscapes have been destroyed and architects have shown an inability to create harmonious groups of buildings to cope with twentieth-century living requirements. Surprisingly, in Britain it was a poet who was most successful in focusing attention on the problem: John Betjeman, who uniquely combined a career as a poet with that of architectural gadfly and eye-opener to the nation.

The late twentieth-century got itself into a tangle about art and élitism, popular versus serious culture, tabloid values versus high art, often crystallized in the shorthand slogan 'Keats or Dylan?' It seems a curious dichotomy – Keats being on a different historical shelf of the culture emporium; Auden/Dylan would make more sense, and both are represented here. The best popular art and the most accessible high art meet on the same ground, and it is on this territory that *Scanning the Century* is pitched. The more arid reaches of contemporary art and the braying vulgarity of tabloid culture are distorted caricatures which feed off each other. There is a huge body of work for which the labels 'élitist' and 'populist' are unnecessary travesties – direct, comprehensible, shapely poems that reflect the world we all know, but not slavishly, because that is the job of the journalist and historian, not the poet.

This was the documentary century: full of events and inventions, full of sound and fury signifying we-don't-quite-yet-know-what, and the poems here are chosen to represent its many facets. And yet to present the twentieth century in poetry as an enormous Levi-esque factory report would be to falsify some of the very characteristics that make the century distinctive. Anyone resurrected from the eighteenth or nineteenth century would remark on the persistent strain of surrealism, so persistent we hardly notice it any more. Take Auden's 'Funeral Blues'. Popular because it is so bold, direct and emotive, it also has unobtrusive and extremely effective surreal elements: 'Pour away the ocean and sweep up the wood.'

And the daring leaps and dislocations of early twentieth-century Modernism have similarly become part of our linguistic register. Precedents for these innovations can be found in previous eras, in figures such as Bosch, Lewis Carroll, Blake, but it is only in the twentieth century that these moods have become part of the fabric of existence. When John Lennon published his sub-Joycean/Carrollish musings in 1964 (*In His Own Write* and *A Spaniard in the Works*) no one needed instructions in how to read them. Since the Sixties, American poets such as John Ashbery and Frank O'Hara and, more recently, James Tate and Mark

Halliday, have developed a kind of freewheeling cultural ramble of a poem, reminiscent of the novelistic ploy of stream-of-consciousness, with material supplied by America's overflowing image bank.

Since World War II, poetry has fared rather differently to the other major arts. Painting and music entered new realms of experimentation and increasingly came to be philosophical commentaries on the possible existence of art rather than the thing itself. This alienated much of the audience that had followed Modernism up until that point. In music, the gap was filled by the joyous explosion of jazz, popular and 'world' music, which will come to be seen as the most representative music of these times; in visual art, design, graphics, film, TV and advertising filled the gulf created by the painters' abdication. But poetry shows far more continuity. Auden, for example, wrote many sonnets with which Shakespeare would have felt at home, and at the end of the century the new poets were still learning from him. Even the freest of free verse poets like Ginsberg and Ferlinghetti have roots in the Bible or vernacular speech.

The second half of the century shows an acceleration of a tendency present throughout: towards increasing consciousness and self-consciousness. Everything can now be aired, every corner of the human psyche explored, every dark silent secret brought out into the open and verbalized. At its worst this has become prurience, prying into the bedrooms of the famous, but at its best it has been a necessary stage in the maturation of humankind.

But by the end of the century, something was clearly wrong with self-consciousness, and the problem lurks under the banner of postmodernism. Postmodernism is a philosophy which criticizes the concept of reality, whether in history or science, on the basis of certain paradoxical aspects of language (for example, the ability of a few freakish sentences to contradict themselves, as in the Ancient Greek paradox: 'All Cretans are Liars', which if said by a Cretan is self-contradictory). But science does *not* consist of individual, refutable and sometimes self-contradictory propositions like 'All Cretans are Liars' (philosophy does): science is an interlocking web of predictively effective deductions and operations. As for history, we know from direct experience it is real, and problems of interpretation should not be allowed to deflect us from this knowledge.

Needless to say, the documentary realism of this book is at odds with this postmodern approach to history and reality. What *is* relevant about postmodernism is the idea that the media have become so powerful, and people so attuned to them, that reality is often made subservient to their demands. To a large degree, history is now second-guessed by the media and the cameras are waiting: which is obviously a temptation to create a media diversion while the real action takes place elsewhere. There are many poems in the sections 'Workout in Reality Gym' and 'We Billion Cheered' on the strange collusion between reality and the media.

One of the fascinations of twentieth-century poetry is to see how cultures talk to each other through their poetry. Many Russian poets, for example, have been fascinated by America and have written vividly about that country. Jacques Prévert's bold and sardonic provocations flung in the face of the defeatist and reactionary France of World War II were taken up by the Beats in America in the Fifties and by the Liverpool poets in the Sixties in England. The East European poets of the communist era, writing under duress, were an inspiration for poets in Northern Ireland.

Literature has always been re-energized by bringing it closer to vigorous speech. In a sense, much of the work is done anonymously in everyday life by people who have no idea they are contributing to literature. Their innovations, honed in everyday discourse, are brought into literature by those with the sharpest linguistic antennae. In a mild way, it happened when Wordsworth and Coleridge broke with the stilted diction of eighteenth-century poetry. It happened powerfully in American fiction of the twentieth century when the melting pot brought Jewish, Italian and African idioms into the English language. In poetry, the blues had an important influence, as did the hipster speech associated with bebop jazz. Jazzing the language has also been a feature of the Caribbean. Creole, or Nation Language, is to English poetry in the late twentieth century what Burns's Lallans was to the nineteenth, a highly spiced language that can be appreciated beyond the inner circle of the language's users.

By the end of the century, there were as many good women poets writing as there were men, but in most countries in the first half century female poets were virtually invisible. The great exception was Russia, supposedly the most backward European nation in 1900. Of the group of four so-called Silver Age poets of the twentieth century, two – Marina

Tsvetaeva and Anna Akhmatova – were women (Boris Pasternak and Osip Mandelstam were the men). Great poetry defies socially deterministic explanations.

In America, the most emancipated country, women poets did come through earlier than in Britain – one of the founders of modern American poetry in the nineteenth century was a woman, Emily Dickinson. Marianne Moore was a leading member of the great Modernist generation of American poets in the Twenties and Thirties, and Elizabeth Bishop and Sylvia Plath were amongst the most influential poets of the mid-century.

Women poets had a strong presence in eastern Europe during the Communist era, which suggests that the formal equality of these regimes, however fraudulent they were in other respects, was not entirely a dead letter. In the Nobel-Prize-winning Polish poet Wisława Szymborska, the period produced one of the century's most characteristic poets, equally able to focus on its terrors and its domestic ironies, the long vistas of science and the world in front of her nose. In Britain the real surge in women poets had to wait until the 1980s when the one-track Oxbridge domination of English poetry finally broke down.

The question has to be asked: whose century is this book devoted to? An anthology of twentieth-century poetry from the entire world would be much larger than this book, and almost certainly unmanageable and unfocused. The structure of the book is guided by the fact of twentieth-century life that many events have had global significance. The century's wars were the first to be called world wars. The new technologies of motorcars, aircraft, computers, nuclear power, television, audio and domestic appliances know no frontiers, although their rate of uptake has varied dramatically from region to region. Social changes, popular music and film, and sport have a similarly global reach.

The twentieth century has had a powerful homogenizing effect – those who fought in World War II, from whatever country, encountered the same sort of experience. Those who tried to fight differently, like the Poles in 1939, who still had a cavalry, quickly learned that there was only one way. Similarly, American-style consumerism, modern media and technical education have had the effect that hundreds of millions of people across the globe now share a common sensibility despite their different languages and cultural roots. This homogenization has not destroyed human individuality: every country adds its own accents to the imported product, just as Django Reinhardt took American jazz and added elements from gypsy music and French chanson to create something new, or the Beatles who, steeped in every form of American popular music, nevertheless created something quintessentially English.

Beyond the easily defined territory of the world wars, global technologies and media, I have tried to devise subject headings that allow as many facets of world experience as possible to be represented. Having said that, it is clear that the majority of the poems here come from Europe and America. Whatever is to come, it was the American century and the century of catastrophic European decline. American preeminence, however much it might be resented, is fairly universally accepted. Blinded by decades of American-sponsored affluence since World War II, Europe still has to come to terms with the traumas of two wars and its consequent loss of world influence and moral authority. In 1900, Europe controlled virtually the entire world; in the 1990s, resurgence of conflict in the old European fault line of the Balkans was only brought under control by American intervention (as, to a large degree, were World Wars I and II). That Europeans have not recognized their propensity for self-destruction is obvious from the many pious pronouncements on the wars in Bosnia and Kosovo along the lines that such primitive slaughter is unthinkable in modern Europe. The record of the century suggests that it is only too thinkable and that modern Europe has been the most murderous civilization in recorded history. Great civilizations in decline can often produce magnificent art, and the poetry of the wars and the Holocaust are vital bodies of work for anyone trying to understand how the most developed societies could revert to medieval barbarity at a time when technical progress had made prosperity for all a possibility for the first time in history.

The twentieth century has been much reviled during its progress, even during the most fruitful periods. The journey travelled in terms of self-awareness can perhaps be judged by comparing two poems from this selection. Joseph Brodsky, writing in 1985, burlesques a series of anarchist murders of public figures in 1914 because they, unlike the murder in Sarajevo of the Archduke Franz Ferdinand that triggered World War I, had no wider consequences: 'ah white puffs in the blue acrylic! . . ./There is something pastoral, nay! idyllic/about these murders' (p. 12), whereas Hardy, writing in 1912 of the Titanic, is as ponderous and majestic as the berg itself: 'And as the smart ship grew/

In stature, grace, and hue,/In shadowy silent distance grew the Iceberg too' (p. 8). Between is almost a century's growth of psychological awareness, the loss of certain easy assumptions about our good faith and the inevitability of social progress. The future will make of us what it wants. The best epitaph I can imagine would be a century-wide extrapolation of Donald Davie's poem 'Remembering the 'Thirties':

> A neutral tone is nowadays preferred.
> And yet it may be better, if we must,
> To praise a stance impressive and absurd
> Than not to see the hero for the dust.

Many of the century's most dramatic innovations in art and science were made at the very beginning. The intellectual *élan* of Einstein's Special Theory of Relativity, the developing knowledge of atomic structure, the liberated colour harmonies of Matisse and Derain in their Fauvist period, the space-chopping of Cubism and the prismatic barbarous glory of Stravinsky's *Rite of Spring* might have marked the beginning of a new golden age. But the political culture of Europe lagged behind. Locked into nineteenth-century patterns of secret diplomacy, the jostling of the Great Powers – Germany, France, Russia, Austria-Hungary and Britain – showed no such quantum leap. Despite the emergence of Symbolism on the Continent in the late nineteenth century, and of Whitman's ecstatic free verse in America, poetry written in English was still largely traditional in technique, exemplified by Kipling and Hardy, but the urban anti-lyricism of Eliot's 'Preludes' marked the beginning of Modernism and the sensibility we now recognize as characteristic of the twentieth century. With hindsight, Cavafy's 'Waiting for the Barbarians' and the German poet Alfred Lichtenstein's 'Prophecy' seem to sound the leitmotivs of the century's tragedies.

Joseph Brodsky

From *History of the Twentieth Century*
(A Roadshow)

1901. A swell, modest time.
A T-bone steak is about a dime.
Queen Victoria dies; but then Australia
repeats her silhouette and, *inter alia*,
joins the Commonwealth. In the humid woods
Of Tahiti, Gauguin paints his swarthy nudes.

In China, the Boxers take the rap.
Max Planck in his lab (not on his lap
yet) is studying radiation.
Verdi dies too. But our proud nation,
represented by Mrs Disney, awards the world
with a kid by the name of Walt
who'll animate the screen. Off screen,
the British launch their first submarine.
But it's a cake-walk or a Strindberg play
or Freud's 'Psychopathology of Everyday
Life' that really are not to be missed!
And McKinley's shot dead by an anarchist.

The man of the year is Signore Marconi.
He is an Italian, a Roman.
His name prophetically rhymes with 'Sony':
they have a few things in common.

(GUGLIELMO MARCONI)
'In a Catholic country where the sky is blue
and clouds look like cherubs' vestiges,
one daily receives through the air a few
wordless but clear messages.
Regular speech has its boring spoils:
it leads to more speech, to violence,
it looks like spaghetti, it also coils.
That's why I've built the wireless!'

1902. Just another bland
peaceful year. They dissect a gland
and discover hormones. And a hormone
once discovered is never gone.
The Boer War (ten thousand dead) is over.
Elsewhere, kind Europeans offer
railroad chains to a noble savage.
A stork leaves a bundle in a Persian cabbage
patch, and the tag reads 'Khomeini.' Greeks, Serbs, Croats,
and Bulgars are at each others' throats.

Claude Monet paints bridges nevertheless.
The population of the US
is approximately 76
million: all of them having sex
to affect our present rent.
Plus Teddy Roosevelt's the President.
                    [. . .]
1903. You may start to spy
on the future. Old Europe's sky
is a little dim. To increase its dimness,
the Krupp Works in Essen erect their chimneys.
(Thus the sense of Geld breeds the sense of guilt.)
Still, more smoke comes from London, from a smoke-filled
room where with guile and passion
Bolsheviks curse Mensheviks in Russian.
Speaking of Slavs: the Serbian King and Queen
are done by local well-wishers in.
Painters Whistler, Gauguin, Pissarro are gone.
Panama rents us its Canal Zone.
While bidding their maidens bye-bye and cheerio,
the tommies sail off to grab Nigeria
and turn it into a British colony:
to date, a nation's greatest felony
is if it's neither friend nor foe.
My father is born. So is Evelyn Waugh.

Man of the year, I am proud to say
is two men. They are brothers. Together, they
sport two heads, four legs and four hands – which brings
us to their bird's four wings.

    (THE WRIGHT BROTHERS)
    'We are Orville and Wilbur Wright.
    Our name simply rhymes with "flight"!
    This may partially explain
    why we decided to build a plane.
    Oh there are no men in the skies, just wind!
    Cities look like newspaper print.

Mountains glitter and rivers bend.
But the ultimate plane'd rather bomb than land!'
                    [. . .]
1905. In the news: Japan.
Which means that the century is upon
us. Diminishing the lifespan
of Russian dreadnoughts to nought, Japan
tells *urbi et orbi* it's loathe to lurk
in the wings of geography. In Petersburg
those whose empty stomachs churn
take to the streets. Yet they won't return
home, for the Cossacks adore long streets.
A salesman of the Singer sewing devices greets
in Latvia the arrival of yet another
daughter, who is to become my mother.
In Spain, unaware of this clever ploy,
Pablo Picasso depicts his 'Boy
With Pipe' in blue. While the shades of blonde,
Swedes and Norwegians, dissolve their bond
And Norway goes independent; yet
that's not enough to turn brunette.
Speaking of things that sound rather queer,
E is equated to MC^2
by Albert Einstein, and the Fauvists
(*Les Fauves* is the French for unruly beasts)
unleash Henri Matisse in Paris.
'The Merry Widow' by Franz Lehar is
the toast of the town. Plus Transvaal gets its
constitution called by the natives 'the pits'.
And Greta Garbo, *La belle dame sans*
merci, is born. So are neon signs.

Boxers: a shamanic grass-roots protest movement in China against Western domination
at the turn of the century. The boxers danced themselves into a trance which was
supposed to act as a charm against the power of Westerners.

Max Planck: the German physicist who, on 14 December 1899, proposed that radiation
was not continuous but came in small packets which he called quanta: the beginning
of the quantum revolution in physics.

McKinley: William McKinley was President of the USA from 1897–1901. His assassina-
tion was one of a wave of anarchist outrages at the time: also killed were the President
of France, the King and Queen of Italy and the Empress of Austria.

Bolsheviks and Mensheviks: two opposing factions of communists in pre-Revolutionary Russia. The names (*bolshe* = large, *menshe* = small) echo, no doubt unconsciously, Swift's stock political opponents, the Big-Endians and the Little-Endians. The Bolsheviks ruthlessly defeated the Mensheviks in carrying through the Revolution.

urbi et orbi: all and sundry (literally, 'to the city and the world').

Cossacks: warrior-peasants who lived in communes, especially in the Ukraine, and who served as a cavalry under the Tsar.

$E = mc^2$: Einstein's equation of the century. Energy (E) is related to any particular mass (m) by the square of the speed of light (c). Since the speed of light is enormous (299,792 km per second) the energy potentially realizable in small amounts of matter is correspondingly large.

C. P. Cavafy

Waiting for the Barbarians

What are we waiting for, assembled in the forum?

    The barbarians are due here today.

Why isn't anything going on in the senate?
Why are the senators sitting there without legislating?

    Because the barbarians are coming today.
    What's the point of senators making laws now?
    Once the barbarians are here, they'll do the legislating.

Why did our emperor get up so early,
and why is he sitting enthroned at the city's main gate,
in state, wearing the crown?

    Because the barbarians are coming today
    and the emperor's waiting to receive their leader.
    He's even got a scroll to give him,
    loaded with titles, with imposing names.

Why have our two consuls and praetors come out today
wearing their embroidered, their scarlet togas?
Why have they put on bracelets with so many amethysts,
rings sparkling with magnificent emeralds?

Why are they carrying elegant canes
beautifully worked in silver and gold?

   Because the barbarians are coming today
   and things like that dazzle the barbarians.

Why don't our distinguished orators turn up as usual
to make their speeches, say what they have to say?

   Because the barbarians are coming today
   and they're bored by rhetoric and public speaking.

Why this sudden bewilderment, this confusion?
(How serious people's faces have become.)
Why are the streets and squares emptying so rapidly,
everyone going home lost in thought?

   Because night has fallen and the barbarians haven't come.
   And some of our men just in from the border say
   there are no barbarians any longer.

Now what's going to happen to us without barbarians?
They were, those people, a kind of solution.

Translated from the Greek by
Edmund Keeley and Philip Sherrard.

T. S. Eliot

From *Preludes*

I

The winter evening settles down
With smell of steaks in passageways.
Six o'clock.
The burnt-out ends of smoky days.
And now a gusty shower wraps
The grimy scraps

Of withered leaves about your feet
And newspapers from vacant lots;
The showers beat
On broken blinds and chimney-pots,
And at the corner of the street
A lonely cab-horse steams and stamps.

And then the lighting of the lamps.

II

The morning comes to consciousness
Of faint stale smells of beer
From the sawdust-trampled street
With all its muddy feet that press
To early coffee-stands.

With the other masquerades
That time resumes,
One thinks of all the hands
That are raising dingy shades
In a thousand furnished rooms.

Thomas Hardy

The Convergence of the Twain

(Lines on the Loss of the 'Titanic')

I

In a solitude of the sea
Deep from human vanity,
And the Pride of Life that planned her, stilly couches she.

II

Steel chambers, late the pyres
Of her salamandrine fires,
Cold currents thrid, and turn to rhythmic tidal lyres.

III

Over the mirrors meant
To glass the opulent
The sea-worm crawls – grotesque, slimed, dumb, indifferent.

IV

Jewels in joy designed
To ravish the sensuous mind
Lie lightless, all their sparkles bleared and black and blind.

V

Dim moon-eyed fishes near
Gaze at the gilded gear
And query: 'What does this vaingloriousness down here?' . . .

VI

Well: while was fashioning
This creature of cleaving wing,
The Immanent Will that stirs and urges everything

VII

Prepared a sinister mate
For her – so gaily great –
A Shape of Ice, for the time far and dissociate.

VIII

And as the smart ship grew
In stature, grace, and hue,
In shadowy silent distance grew the Iceberg too.

IX

Alien they seemed to be:
No mortal eye could see
The intimate welding of their later history,

X

Or sign that they were bent
By paths coincident
On being anon twin halves of one august event,

XI

Till the Spinner of the Years
Said 'Now!' And each one hears,
And consummation comes, and jars two hemispheres.

The *Titanic* sank on her maiden voyage on 15 April 1912 with the loss of 1,513 lives.
thrid: thread (archaic).

Rudyard Kipling

The Gods of the Copybook Headings

As I pass through my incarnations in every age and race,
I make my proper prostrations to the Gods of the Market-Place.
Peering through reverent fingers I watch them flourish and fall,
And the Gods of the Copybook Headings, I notice, outlast them all.

We were living in trees when they met us. They showed us each in turn
That Water would certainly wet us, as Fire would certainly burn:
But we found them lacking in Uplift, Vision and Breadth of Mind,
So we left them to teach the Gorillas while we followed the March of
    Mankind.

We moved as the Spirit listed. *They* never altered their pace,
Being neither cloud nor wind-borne like the Gods of the Market-Place;
But they always caught up with our progress, and presently word
    would come
That a tribe had been wiped off its icefield, or the lights had gone out
    in Rome.

With the Hopes that our World is built on they were utterly out of
    touch,
They denied that the Moon was Stilton; they denied she was even
    Dutch.
They denied that Wishes were Horses; they denied that a Pig had
    Wings.
So we worshipped the Gods of the Market, Who promised these
    beautiful things.

When the Cambrian measures were forming, They promised
    perpetual peace.
They swore, if we gave them our weapons, that the wars of the tribes
    would cease.
But when we disarmed, They sold us and delivered us bound to our
    foe,
And the Gods of the Copybook Headings said: '*Stick to the Devil
    you know.*'

On the first Feminian Sandstones we were promised the Fuller Life
(Which started by loving our neighbour and ended by loving his
    wife),
Till our women had no more children and the men lost reason and
    faith,
And the Gods of the Copybook Headings said: '*The Wages of Sin is
    Death.*'

In the Carboniferous Epoch we were promised abundance for all,
By robbing selected Peter to pay for collective Paul;
But, though we had plenty of money, there was nothing our money
    could buy,
And the Gods of the Copybook Headings said: '*If you don't work,
    you die.*'

Then the Gods of the Market tumbled, and their smooth-tongued
    wizards withdrew,
And the hearts of the meanest were humbled and began to believe it
    was true
That All is not Gold that Glitters, and Two and Two make Four –
And the Gods of the Copybook Headings limped up to explain it
    once more.

As it will be in the future, it was at the birth of Man –
There are only four things certain since Social Progress began:
That the Dog returns to his Vomit and the Sow returns to her Mire,
And the burnt Fool's bandaged finger goes wabbling back to the Fire;

And that after this is accomplished, and the brave new world begins,
When all men are paid for existing and no man must pay for his sins,
As surely as Water will wet us, as surely as Fire will burn,
The Gods of the Copybook Headings with terror and slaughter
    return!

Alfred Lichtenstein

Prophecy

Sometimes there comes – I have a premonition –
A deathstorm out of the distant North.
Everywhere the stink of corpses
The great murder begins.

The heart of heaven darkens,
The storm lifts its deadly claws:
The base are hurled to the ground
Actors explode, girls go berserk.

With a crash a stable falls
Not even a fly can save itself.
Beautiful homosexual men
Tumble out of their beds.

Walls of all the houses crack.
Fish are rotting in the streams.
Everything comes to its own sticky end.
Screeching buses are overturned.

1913

Translated from the German by
Peter Forbes and P. D. Royce.

Joseph Brodsky

From *History of the Twentieth Century*

1914

Nineteen-fourteen! Oh, nineteen-fourteen!
Ah, some years shouldn't be let out of quarantine!
Well, this is one of them. Things get raw:
In Paris, the editor of *Figaro*
is shot dead by the wife of the French finance
minister, for printing this lady's – *sans*
merci, should we add? – steamy letters to
– ah, who cares! . . . And apparently it's *c'est tout*
also for a socialist and pacifist
of all times, Jean Jaurès. He who shook his fist
at the Parliament urging hot heads to cool it,
dies, as he dines, by some bigot's bullet
in a cafe. Ah, those early, single
shots of Nineteen-fourteen! ah, the index finger
of an assassin! ah white puffs in the blue acrylic! . . .
There is something pastoral, nay! idyllic
about these murders. About that Irish enema
the Brits suffer in Dublin again. And about Panama
Canal's grand opening. Or about that doc
and his open heart surgery on his dog . . .
Well, to make these things disappear forever,
the Archduke is arriving at Sarajevo;
and there is in the crowd that unshaven, timid
youth, with his handgun . . . (*To be continued*)

Jean Jaurès: French socialist leader (1856–1914) assassinated by a fanatical nationalist during the lead-up to World War I.
'*that unshaven, timid youth*': Gavrilo Princip, a Serbian anarchist, assassinated the Archduke Franz Ferdinand of Austria-Hungary on 28 June 1914 in Sarajevo, the event that precipitated World War I.

WORLD WAR I: 1914–1918

In the First World War, poets were in the forefront of political and moral consciousness. The English poets, exemplified by Wilfred Owen, were the first to tell the truth about a war in which the European powers were attempting to persevere with nineteenth-century techniques of war in the face of new weapons, especially the machine-gun, which made such combat a meaningless slaughter. The artistic response to the War was different in continental Europe: absurdity on the battlefield bred absurdism in art. In 'The Marvels of War', Apollinaire managed to apply surrealist techniques to the War itself, whilst the Romanian Tristan Tzara, in the artistic and political hotbed of neutral Zurich, developed the antipolitical artform Dada. The dislocations introduced at this time remained a feature of the century's poetry, however much tempered by an ostensible return to more formal verse in the 1930s.

Wilfred Owen

The Parable of the Old Man and the Young

So Abram rose, and clave the wood, and went,
And took the fire with him, and a knife.
And as they sojourned both of them together,
Isaac the first-born spake and said, My Father,
Behold the preparations, fire and iron,
But where the lamb, for this burnt-offering?
Then Abram bound the youth with belts and straps,
And builded parapets and trenches there,
And stretchèd forth the knife to slay his son.
When lo! an Angel called him out of heaven,
Saying, Lay not thy hand upon the lad,
Neither do anything to him, thy son.

Behold! Caught in a thicket by its horns,
A Ram. Offer the Ram of Pride instead.

But the old man would not so, but slew his son,
And half the seed of Europe, one by one.

Wilfred Owen

Dulce et Decorum Est

Bent double, like old beggars under sacks,
Knock-kneed, coughing like hags, we cursed through sludge,
Till on the haunting flares we turned our backs
And towards our distant rest began to trudge.
Men marched asleep. Many had lost their boots
But limped on, blood-shod. All went lame; all blind;
Drunk with fatigue; deaf even to the hoots
Of tired, outstripped Five-Nines that dropped behind.

Gas! GAS! Quick boys! – An ecstasy of fumbling,
Fitting the clumsy helmets just in time;
But someone still was yelling out and stumbling,
And flound'ring like a man in fire or lime . . .
Dim, through the misty panes and thick green light,
As under a green sea, I saw him drowning.

In all my dreams, before my helpless sight,
He plunges at me, guttering, choking, drowning.

If in some smothering dreams you too could pace
Behind the wagon that we flung him in,
And watch the white eyes writhing in his face,
His hanging face, like a devil's sick of sin;
If you could hear, at every jolt, the blood
Come gargling from the froth-corrupted lungs,
Obscene as cancer, bitter as the cud
Of vile, incurable sores on innocent tongues, –

My friend, you would not tell with such high zest
To children ardent for some desperate glory,
The old Lie: *Dulce et decorum est*
Pro patria mori.

Dulce et decorum est / *Pro patria mori*: It is noble and fitting to die for one's country.

Guillaume Apollinaire

The Marvels of War

How beautiful those rockets are which fill the dark
They rise to their own level and then lean down to look at us
They are women who dance with an awareness of eyes arms and
    hearts

I recognized your smile and your vivacity

It is also the daily apotheosis of all my Berenices whose flowing hair
    turned into comets' tails
These twice gilded dancers belong to all times and all races
They quickly bear children who only have time to die
How beautiful those rockets are
But it would be more beautiful if there were even more
If there were millions of them which would have a full and relevant
    meaning like the letters of a book
However it is as lovely as if life itself emerged from creatures about
    to die

But it would be more beautiful if there were still more of them
However I watched them like a beauty which presents itself and
    immediately fades away
I seem to be at a feast lighted *a giorno*
The banquet which the earth offers to herself
She is hungry and opens these long pale mouths
The earth is hungry and behold her cannibal Balthasar's feast

Who would have said that one could be anthropophagous to this
    extent
And that it took so much fire to roast human flesh
That is why the air had a slight empyreumatic taste which was not
    bad by god
But the feast would be even better if the sky ate with the earth
It only swallows souls
Which is a manner of not feeding itself
And is content with juggling multi-colored fires

But I have flowed into the sweetness of this war with all my company
    along the trenches
A few cries of flame continually announce my presence
I have dug the bed in which I flow and branch out into a thousand
    little streams which go everywhere
I am in the front line trenches and also everywhere or rather I begin
    to be everywhere
It is I who begin this matter for centuries to come
It will take longer to attain than not the myth of Icarus

I bequeath to the future the story of Guillaume Apollinaire
Who was in the war and could be everywhere
In the happy villages behind the lines
In all the rest of the universe
In those who died tangled in the barbed wire
In women in cannon in horses
At the zenith and the nadir and the four cardinal points
And in the unique intensity of this eve of battle
And without doubt it would be more beautiful
If I could suppose that all the things everywhere in which I reside
Could be also in me
But there is nothing so made in this respect
For if I am everywhere right now there is still only I who can be in
    me

Translated from the French by Roger Shattuck.

a giorno: as if by daylight.
empyreumatic: with a taste or smell of burning flesh.

Edmund Blunden

'Trench Nomenclature'

Genius named them, as I live! What but genius could compress
In a title what man's humour said to man's supreme distress?
Jacob's Ladder ran reversed, from earth to a fiery pit extending
With not angels but poor Angles, those for the most part descending.
Thence *Brock's Benefit* commanded endless fireworks by two nations,
Yet some voices there were raised against the rival coruscations.
Picturedome peeped out upon a dream, not Turner could surpass,
And presently the picture moved, and greyed with corpses and
    morass.
So down south; and if remembrance travel north, she marvels yet
At the sharp Shakespearean names, and with sad mirth her eyes are
    wet.
The Great Wall of China rose, a four-foot breastwork, fronting guns
That, when the word dropped, beat at once its silly ounces with
    brute tons;
Odd *Krab Krawl* on paper looks, and odd the foul-breathed alley
    twisted,
As one feared to twist there too, if *Minnie*, forward quean, insisted.
Where the Yser at *Dead End* floated on its bloody waters
Dead and rotten monstrous fish, note (east) *The Pike and Eel*
    headquarters.
Ah, such names and apparitions! name on name! what's in a name?
From the fabled vase the genie in his cloud of horror came.

quean: impudent or ill-behaved woman (archaic).

Ivor Gurney

The Bohemians

Certain people would not clean their buttons,
Nor polish buckles after latest fashions,
Preferred their hair long, putties comfortable,
Barely escaping hanging, indeed hardly able,
In Bridge and smoking without army cautions
Spending hours that sped like evil for quickness,
(While others burnished brasses, earned promotions)
These were those ones who jested in the trench,
While others argued of army ways, and wrenched
What little soul they had still further from shape,
And died off one by one, or became officers
Without the first of dream, the ghost of notions
Of ever becoming soldiers, or smart and neat,
Surprised as ever to find the army capable
Of sounding 'Lights out' to break a game of Bridge,
As to fear candles would set a barn alight.
In Artois or Picardy they lie – free of useless fashions.

Paul Muldoon

Truce

It begins with one or two soldiers
And one or two following
With hampers over their shoulders.
They might be off wildfowling

As they would another Christmas Day,
So gingerly they pick their steps.
No one seems sure of what to do.
All stop when one stops.

A fire gets lit. Some spread
Their greatcoats on the frozen ground.
Polish vodka, fruit and bread
Are broken out and passed round.

The air of an old German song,
The rules of Patience, are the secrets
They'll share before long.
They draw on their last cigarettes

As Friday-night lovers, when it's over,
Might get up from their mattresses
To congratulate each other
And exchange names and addresses.

Erich Fried

French Soldiers Mutiny – 1917

For years the troops have gone
like lambs to the slaughter

but these are bleating
They are marching through the town

They are marching
and they are bleating like sheep

By bleating they cease to be
a herd of sheep

Translated from the German by
Stuart Hood.

Mutinying French soldiers actually did bleat as a protest. – Author's note.

Ezra Pound

From *E.P. Ode pour L'Élection de son Sépulcre*

IV

These fought in any case,
and some believing,
           pro domo, in any case . . .

Some quick to arm,
some for adventure,
some from fear of weakness,
some from fear of censure,
some for love of slaughter, in imagination,
learning later . . .
some in fear, learning love of slaughter;

Died some, pro patria,
    non 'dulce' non 'et decor' . . .
walked eye-deep in hell
believing in old men's lies, then unbelieving
came home, home to a lie,
home to many deceits,
home to old lies and new infamy;
usury age-old and age-thick
and liars in public places.

Daring as never before, wastage as never before.
Young blood and high blood,
fair cheeks, and fine bodies;

fortitude as never before

frankness as never before,
disillusions as never told in the old days,
hysterias, trench confessions,
laughter out of dead bellies.

V

There died a myriad,
And of the best, among them,
For an old bitch gone in the teeth,
For a botched civilization,

Charm, smiling at the good mouth,
Quick eyes gone under earth's lid,

For two gross of broken statues,
For a few thousand battered books.

Tristan Tzara

total circuit by the moon and colour

the iron eye will change to gold
the compasses have put flowers in our ear-drums
watch for the fabulous prayer sir
tropical
on the eiffel tower's violin and star chimes
the olives swell pac pac and will symmetrically crystalize
everywhere
lemon
the ten sou piece
sundays have brilliantly fondled god dada dance
sharing the cereals
the rain
newspaper
slowly slowly
butterflies five yards long disintegrate like mirrors
like the flight of night rivers climbs with the fire
towards the milky way
the ways of light the hair of irregular rains
and the artificial summer-houses that fly age in your heart
when you think I see
morning

that screams
the cells dilate
bridges stretch and rise up in the air to scream
around magnetic poles the rays arrange themselves like
peacocks' feathers
boreal
and the waterfalls do you see? arrange themselves in their own light
at the north pole a huge peacock will slowly unfurl the sun
at the other pole will be the night of serpent-eating colours
slide yellow
the bells
nervous
to clear it up the reds will march
when I ask how
the deeps shout
lord my geometry

Translated from the French by Lee Harwood.

Philip Larkin

MCMXIV

Those long uneven lines
Standing as patiently
As if they were stretched outside
The Oval or Villa Park,
The crowns of hats, the sun
On moustached archaic faces
Grinning as if it were all
An August Bank Holiday lark;

And the shut shops, the bleached
Established names on the sunblinds,
The farthings and sovereigns,
And dark-clothed children at play

Called after kings and queens,
The tin advertisements
For cocoa and twist, and the pubs
Wide open all day;

And the countryside not caring:
The place-names all hazed over
With flowering grasses, and fields
Shadowing Domesday lines
Under wheat's restless silence;
The differently-dressed servants
With tiny rooms in huge houses,
The dust behind limousines;

Never such innocence,
Never before or since,
As changed itself to past
Without a word – the men
Leaving the gardens tidy,
The thousands of marriages
Lasting a little while longer:
Never such innocence again.

RED DAWN:
THE RUSSIAN REVOLUTION 1917–1921

Although Marx had not seen Russia as a likely candidate for revolution, the disastrously reactionary policies of the Tsar and the chaos of World War I led to one of the great turning points that echoed down the century. Early twentieth-century Russia was blessed with a dazzling array of great poets: Blok, Mayakovsky, Akhmatova, Pasternak, Mandelstam, Tsvetaeva. All except Mayakovsky and, to some extent, Blok were hostile to Communism and suffered at its hands. Blok's 'The Twelve' captures some of the tempestuousness of the times. Terror and civil war followed closely on the Revolution's heels, and by 1921 a pattern of oppression was established in the Soviet Union that was to last for most of the century, with poets and other artists struggling against censorship, intimidation and recruitment as propagandists.

Jacques Réda

October Morning

Lev Davidovitch Bronstein's goatee beard quivers,
His hands quiver, so does his shaggy hair; in a moment he's going to
Pop out of his waistcoat and lose his professorial eyeglasses,
He who talks to the sailors of Kronstadt carved from roughly
Squared Finnish timber and almost as tough as
The rifle butts which make the dirty snow spurt up.
He preaches, Lev Davidovitch, shouts himself hoarse, while
Slowly the turrets of the *Aurora* turn upon the leaden Neva
Towards the Winter Palace's dark frontage.
　　　　　　What a smooth tongue, and what a yellow sky;
What weight of history on the empty bridges where sometimes
A car rumbles, wings bristling with bayonets.

At Smolny, tonight, the beards have grown; eyes
Smarting with tobacco and the light bulbs' glare
Show their whites, Petrograd, facing your silence
Where amid the fierce, attentive Letts,
Lev Davidovitch prophesises, exhorts, threatens, trembles
Too as he feels the centuries' immobile mass
Swing once and for all around, like guns upon their axes,
At the very edge of this October morning.
                                        (And already Vladimir
Ilyitch has secretly reached the capital; he will sleep,
Later, made up for the same part, in a glass coffin,
For ever motionless beneath the bouquets and ovations.
Meanwhile, Lev Davidovitch jerks back his tousled hair,
Clutches his spectacles,
                              – a little blood, a little
Mexican sky will mingle there on his last day, so far
From you, muddy October, rapturous in the wind of the red flags.)

Translated from the French by Edward Lucie-Smith.

Lev Davidovitch Bronstein: the real name of Leon Trotsky, the leading Russian revolu-
tionary alongside Lenin. In 1927 Stalin expelled him from the Party, sent him at first
into internal exile, then, in 1929, deported him. He was murdered on Stalin's orders in
Mexico in 1940.
Kronstadt and *the Aurora*: the naval garrison at Kronstadt, near St Petersburg (then
called Petrograd), supported the Revolution and the *Aurora* fired on the Winter Palace
during its storming on 25 October 1917.
Smolny: an educational institute used by the Bolsheviks as their headquarters during
the Revolution.
Letts: Latvians.
Vladimir Ilyitch: Lenin.

Alexander Blok

From *The Twelve*

I

Darkness – and white
snow hurled
by the wind. The wind!
You cannot stand upright
for the wind: the wind
scouring God's world.

The wind ruffles
the white snow, pulls
that treacherous
wool over the wicked ice.
Everyone out walking
slips. Look – poor thing!

From building to building over
the street a rope skips nimbly,
a banner on the rope – ALL POWER
TO THE CONSTITUENT ASSEMBLY.
This old weeping woman is worried to death,
she doesn't know what it's all about:
that banner – for God's sake –
so many yards of cloth!
How many children's leggings it would make –
and they without shirts – without boots – without . . .

The old girl like a puffed hen picks
her way between drifts of snow.
'Mother of God, these Bolsheviks
will be the death of us, I know!'

Will the frost never lose its grip
or the wind lay its whips aside?

The bourgeois where the roads divide
stands chin on chest, his collar up.

But who's this with the mane
of hair, saying in a
whisper: 'They've sold us down
the river. Russia's down and out'?
A pen-pusher, no doubt,
a word-spinner . . .

There's someone in a long coat, sidling
over there where the snow's less thick.
'What's happened to your joyful tidings,
Comrade cleric?'

Do you remember the old days:
waddling belly-first to prayer,
when the cross on your belly would blaze
on the faithful there?

Translated from the Russian by
Jon Stallworthy and Peter France.

Maximilian Voloshin

Terror

In the night – would gather for work. They would read through
Certificates, cases, reports.
With a hasty hand they signed their decisions.
They yawned. They drank wine.
In the morning they passed out vodka to soldiers;
In the evening by candlelight
They would call out the lists – men and women.
They herded them to the dark yard.
They took off all footwear, underwear, clothing
Which they tied into bundles, then
Loaded onto a cart. And took away.

They divided the watches and rings.
At night they would drive them barefoot and hungry
Over the icy ground.
In the northeast wind, out of town to the fields
They would prod them with gun butts to reach the ravine
Lighted them up with lanterns.
For half-a-minute the machine guns would clatter.
Finished them with bayonets.
Those still alive were shoved into a hole
Which they quickly filled with earth.
And then with a broad Russian song ringing
They returned to the city – home.
And at dawn – dogs, wives and mothers
Stole out for the same ravine.
They dug the ground, fought over bones
And kissed the beloved flesh.

1921

Translated from the Russian by
Vladimir Markov and Merrill Sparks.

Anna Akhmatova

Why is our century worse than any other?

Why is our century worse than any other?
Is it that in the stupor of fear and grief
It has plunged its fingers in the blackest ulcer,
Yet cannot bring relief?

Westward the sun is dropping,
And the roofs of towns are shining in its light.
Already death is chalking doors with crosses
And calling the ravens and the ravens are in flight.

1919

Translated from the Russian by D. M. Thomas.

THE JAZZ AGE: 1920–1929

In 1917, European domination ended and the fate of the century passed largely into the hands of America and Russia. It was also the beginning of a sense of world consciousness and, in President Woodrow Wilson's Fourteen Points for the Peace Settlement, of the idea of a World Order. Despite their irreconcilable differences, the heroic note of newly powerful nations flexing their muscles was similar in Russia and America. So much so that Mayakovsky, a Russian poet who had embraced the Revolution, could also catch the spirit of America in 'Brooklyn Bridge'. The publication of Eliot's *The Waste Land* in 1922 completed the Modernist revolution and effectively rendered obsolete the pallid and genteel brand of poetry known as Georgianism which had tried to cling to nineteenth-century techniques and subject matter.

Vladimir Mayakovsky

Brooklyn Bridge

Hey, Coolidge boy,
make a shout of joy!
When a thing is good
                    then it's good.
Blush from compliments
                    like our flag's calico,
even though you're
                    the most super-united states
                                                    of
America.
Like the crazy nut
                who goes
                        to his church

or retreats
        to a monastery
                simple and rigid –
so I
    in the gray haze
           of evening
humbly
      approach
           the Brooklyn Bridge.
Like a conqueror
        on cannons with muzzles
                    as high as a giraffe
jabbing into a broken
          city besieged,
so, drunk with glory,
          alive to the hilt,
I clamber
      proudly
          upon Brooklyn Bridge.
Like a stupid painter
        whose enamored eyes pierce
a museum Madonna
        like a wedge.
So from this sky,
        sowed into the stars,

I look at New York
        through Brooklyn Bridge.

New York,
      heavy and stifling
           till night,
has forgotten
      what makes it dizzy
           and a hindrance,
and only
      the souls of houses

rise in the transparent
                    sheen of windows.
Here the itching hum
                    of the 'el'
                              is hardly heard,
and only by this
                hum,
                    soft but stubborn,
can you feel the trains
                    crawl
                              with a rattle
as when dishes
                    are jammed into a cupboard.
And when from
                    below the startled river
a merchant
                transports sugar
                                        from the factory bins –
then
        the masts passing under the bridge
are no bigger
                    in size
                              than pins.
I'm proud
                of this
                        mile of steel.
In it my visions
                    are alive and real –
a fight
        for structure
                              instead of arty 'style',
the harsh calculation
                              of bolts
                                        and steel.
If the end
                of the world
                              comes –

and chaos
            wipes out
                        this earth
and if only this
                bridge
                            remains
rearing over the dust of death,
then
        as little bones,
                        thinner than needles,
clad with flesh,
                standing in museums,
                                    are dinosaurs, –
so from this
            bridge
                    future geologists
will be able
            to reconstruct
                        our present course.
They will say:
                – this
                        paw of steel
joined seas,
            prairies and deserts,
from here,
            Europe
                    rushed to the West,
scattering
            to the wind
                        Indian feathers.
This rib here
            reminds us
                        of a machine –
imagine,
        enough hands, enough grip
while standing,
                with one steel leg
                            in Manhattan

to drag
       toward yourself
              Brooklyn by the lip!
By the wires
        of electric yarn
I know this
        is
           the Post-Steam Era.
Here people
        already
            yelled on the radio,
here people
        already
            flew by air.
For some
        here was life
              carefree,
                  unalloyed.
For others
        a prolonged
              howl of hunger.
From here
        the unemployed
jumped headfirst
           into
              the Hudson.
And finally
        with clinging stars
                  along the strings of cables
my dream comes back
           without any trouble
and I see –
        here
           stood Mayakovsky,
here he stood
        putting
           syllable to syllable.

I look,
          as an eskimo looks at a train,
I dig into you,
                    like a tick into an ear.
Brooklyn Bridge.
Yes,
     you've got something here.

Translated from the Russian by
Vladimir Markov and Merrill Sparks.

Coolidge: Calvin Coolidge, President of the USA 1923–29.
el: the elevated rapid transit railways in New York, which pre-dated the first subways in 1904 and ran alongside them for many years, were known as 'els'.

T. S. Eliot

From *The Waste Land*

FROM III. THE FIRE SERMON

At the violet hour, when the eyes and back
Turn upward from the desk, when the human engine waits
Like a taxi throbbing waiting,
I Tiresias, though blind, throbbing between two lives,
Old man with wrinkled female breasts, can see
At the violet hour, the evening hour that strives
Homeward, and brings the sailor home from sea,
The typist home at teatime, clears her breakfast, lights
Her stove, and lays out food in tins.
Out of the window perilously spread
Her drying combinations touched by the sun's last rays,
On the divan are piled (at night her bed)
Stockings, slippers, camisoles, and stays.

I Tiresias, old man with wrinkled dugs
Perceived the scene, and foretold the rest –
I too awaited the expected guest.
He, the young man carbuncular, arrives,
A small house agent's clerk, with one bold stare,
One of the low on whom assurance sits
As a silk hat on a Bradford millionaire.
The time is now propitious, as he guesses,
The meal is ended, she is bored and tired,
Endeavours to engage her in caresses
Which still are unreproved, if undesired.
Flushed and decided, he assaults at once;
Exploring hands encounter no defence;
His vanity requires no response,
And makes a welcome of indifference.
(And I Tiresias have foresuffered all
Enacted on this same divan or bed;
I who have sat by Thebes below the wall
And walked among the lowest of the dead.)
Bestows one final patronising kiss,
And gropes his way, finding the stairs unlit . . .

   She turns and looks a moment in the glass,
Hardly aware of her departed lover;
Her brain allows one half-formed thought to pass:
'Well now that's done: and I'm glad it's over.'
When lovely woman stoops to folly and
Paces about her room again, alone,
She smooths her hair with automatic hand,
And puts a record on the gramophone.

Tiresias: a Theban seer first mentioned in *The Odyssey*. Blind and having experienced a change of sex, he is seen by Eliot as being uniquely wise in sexual matters.

Fernando Pessoa

WRITING AS ÁLVARO DE CAMPOS

From *Triumphal Ode*

Hi there, streets, hi there, squares, hello, *la foule*!
Everything that passes, everything that stops at shop windows!
Merchants; vagrants, dapper *escrocs*;
Obvious members of aristocratic clubs;
Squalid doubtful figures; family men vaguely happy
And fatherly even in the stream of gold running across the waistcoat
From pocket to pocket!
Everything that passes, everything that passes and never passes!
Overemphasised presence of *cocottes*;
Interesting commonplace (and who knows the inside?)
Of middle-class women, mother and daughter mostly.
Walking in the street, going somewhere;
The mincing grace of homosexuals cruising;
And everyone with simple elegance strolling and showing off
And after all having a soul in there!

(Ah, how I would love to be the *souteneur* of it all!)

The marvellous beauty of political corruptions,
Delicious financial and diplomatic scandals,
Political attacks in the streets,
And now and then the comet of a regicide
Lighting with Freak and Fanfare the usual clear
Skies of everyday Civilisation!

Newspaper denials,
Insincerely sincere political articles,
Cheque-book journalism, big-time crimes –
Two columns going over the page!
The fresh smell of printer's ink!
Posters put up recently, still wet!

Yellow *vients-de-paraître* with white wrappers!
How I love you all, all, all,
How I love you in every way,
With my eyes and my ears and my sense of smell
And of touch (what feeling you means to me!)
And with my intelligence like antennae you set quivering!
Ah, how all my senses lust for you!

Fertilisers, steam threshing machines, advances in agriculture!
Agricultural chemistry, and business almost a science!
O showcases of travelling salesmen,
Of travelling salesmen, knights-errant of Industry,
Human extensions of factories and quiet offices!

O farms in shop windows! O mannequins! O latest fashions!
O useless articles everyone wants to buy!
Hey there, big stores with various departments!
Hey there, illuminated signs winking on and off!
Hey there, everything that today is built of, that makes today
     different from yesterday!
Aha, reinforced cement, concrete, from cement, new processes!
Advances in gloriously death-dealing weaponry!
Armour, guns, machine-guns, submarines, aeroplanes!
I love you all, everything, like a wild beast.
I love you carnivorously,
Perversely, curling my eyes
Round you, O big, commonplace, useful, useless things,
O thoroughly modern things,
O contemporaries of mine, the present and nearest form
Of the immediate system of the Universe!
New Revelation, metallic, dynamic, of God!

Translated from the Portuguese by Keith Bosley.

la foule: the crowd.   *escrocs*: crooks.   *cocottes*: tarts.   *souteneur*: pimp.
vients-de-paraître: publications 'just out'.

Langston Hughes

The Weary Blues

Droning a drowsy syncopated tune,
Rocking back and forth to a mellow croon,
    I heard a Negro play.
Down on Lenox Avenue the other night
By the pale dull pallor of an old gas light
    He did a lazy sway . . .
    He did a lazy sway . . .
To the tune o' those Weary Blues.
With his ebony hands on each ivory key
He made that poor piano moan with melody.
    O Blues!
Swaying to and fro on his rickety stool
He played that sad raggy tune like a musical fool.
    Sweet Blues!
Coming from a black man's soul.
    O Blues!
In a deep song voice with a melancholy tone
I heard that Negro sing, that old piano moan –
    'Ain't got nobody in all this world,
        Ain't got nobody but ma self.
        I's gwine to quit ma frownin'
        And put ma troubles on the shelf.'
Thump, thump, thump, went his foot on the floor.
He played a few chords then he sang some more –
    'I got the Weary Blues
        And I can't be satisfied.
        Got the Weary Blues
        And can't be satisfied –
        I ain't happy no mo'
        And I wish that I had died.'
And far into the night he crooned that tune.
The stars went out and so did the moon.
The singer stopped playing and went to bed
While the Weary Blues echoed through his head.
He slept like a rock or a man that's dead.

Galway Kinnell

For the Lost Generation

Oddities composed the sum of the news.
$E = mc^2$
Was another weird
Sign of the existence of the Jews.

And Paris! All afternoon in someone's attic
We lifted our glasses
And drank to the asses
Who ran the world and turned neurotic.

Ours was a wonderful party,
Everyone threw rice,
The fattest girls were nice,
The world was rich in wisecracks and confetti.

The War was a first wife, somebody's blunder.
Who was right, who lost,
Held nobody's interest,
The dog on top was as bad as the dog under.

Sometimes after whiskey, at the break of day,
There was a trace
Of puzzlement on a face,
Face of blue nights that kept bleaching away.

Look back on it all – the faraway cost,
Crash and sweet blues
(O Hiroshima, O Jews) –
No generation was so gay as the lost.

LOW DISHONEST DECADE:
THE THIRTIES

No decade had a more natural span, was framed as neatly, if that is the word, as the Thirties. The collapse of the financial markets in America in 1929, and the consequent worldwide unemployment, brought the manic Twenties to an end. The disruption of world trade, and its concomitant economic nationalism, were powerful factors in the rise of fascism. The Thirties had a peculiar flavour, partly captured, and partly created (in England, at least), by the poets, of whom W. H. Auden was the acknowledged leader. 'Audenland' is a country of the mind, inspired by the new actuality – the ribbon development suburbia which grew up from 1935, with its ocean-liner factories making consumer goods – but it also owed much to Auden's peculiar poetic cast of mind. Auden equated the immaturity of the society he saw around him with the tribal rituals of the English public school. Germany began the decade as the decadent magnet for the curious – a life documented by many visiting writers. The art movement of the decade was surrealism.

Basil Bunting

Aus dem Zweiten Reich

I

Women swarm in Tauentsienstrasse.
Clients of Nollendorferplatz cafés,
shadows on sweaty glass,
hum, drum on the table
      to the negerband's faint jazz.
Humdrum at the table.

Hour and hour
meeting against me,
efficiently whipped cream,
efficiently metropolitan chatter and snap,
transparent glistening wrapper
        for a candy pack.

Automatic, somewhat too clean,
body and soul similarly scented,
on time,
rapid, dogmatic, automatic and efficient,
ganz modern.

'Sturm über Asien' is off, some other flicker . . .
Kiss me in the taxi, twist fingers in the dark.
A box of chocolates is necessary.
I am preoccupied with Sie and Du.
        The person on the screen,
divorced and twenty-five, must pass for fourteen
for the story's sake, an insipidity
contrived to dress her in shorts
and a widenecked shirt with nothing underneath
so that you see her small breasts when she
often bends towards the camera.
Audience mainly male stirs,
        I am teased too,
I like this public blonde better than my brunette,
        but that will never do.
– Let's go,
arm in arm on foot over gleaming snow
past the Gedächtnis Kirche
to the loud and crowded cafés near the Bahnhof Zoo.

Better hugged together ('to keep warm')
under street trees whimpering to the keen wind
over snow whispering to many feet,
find out a consolingly mediocre
neighbourhood without music, varnished faces
bright and sagacious against varnished walls,

youngsters red from skating,
businessmen reading the papers:
no need to talk – much:
what indolence supplies.
'If, smoothing this silk skirt, you pinch my thighs,
that will be fabelhaft.'

II

Herr Lignitz knows Old Berlin. It is near the Post Office
with several rather disorderly public houses.
'You have no naked pictures in your English magazines.
It is shocking. Berlin is very shocking to the English. Are
    you shocked?
Would you like to see the naked cabarets
in Jaegerstrasse? I think there is
nothing like that in Paris.
Or a department store? They are said to be
almost equal to Macy's in America.'

III

The renowned author of
more plays than Shakespeare
stopped and did his hair
with a pocket glass
before entering the village,
afraid they wouldnt recognize
caricature and picturepostcard,
that windswept chevelure.

Who talked about poetry,
and he said nothing at all;
plays,
and he said nothing at all;
politics,
and he stirred as if a flea
bit him
but wouldnt let on in company;
and the frost in Berlin,
muttered: 𝔖𝔠𝔥𝔯𝔢𝔠𝔨𝔩𝔦𝔠𝔥

Viennese bow from the hips,
notorieties
contorted laudatory lips,
wreaths and bouquets surround
the mindless menopause.
Stillborn fecundities,
frostbound applause.

1931

Aus dem Zweiten Reich: 'From the Second Reich'. The Second Reich was the German regime that lasted from unification by Bismarck in 1871 to Hitler's accession in 1933. The First Reich was the medieval German empire.
ganz: quite.
Sturm über Asien: *Storm over Asia*, a film by V. I. Pudovkin.
fabelhaft: gorgeous.
Schrecklich: dreadful.

Bertolt Brecht

From *Late Lamented Fame of the Giant City New York*

XI

What people they were! Their boxers the strongest!
Their inventors the most practical! Their trains the fastest!
And also the most crowded!
And it all looked like lasting a thousand years
For the people of the city of New York put it about themselves:
That their city was built on the rock and hence
Indestructible.

XII

Truly their whole system of communal life was beyond compare.
What fame! What a century!

XIII

Admittedly that century lasted
A bare eight years.

XIV

For one day there ran through the world the rumour of strange
    collapses
On a famous continent, and its banknotes, hoarded only yesterday
Were rejected in disgust like rotten stinking fish.

XV

Today, when the word has gone round
That these people are bankrupt
We on the other continents (which are indeed bankrupt as well)
See many things differently and, so we think, more clearly.

XVI

What of the skyscrapers?
We observe them more coolly.
What contemptible hovels skyscrapers are when they no longer yield
    rents!
Rising so high, full of poverty? Touching the clouds, full of debt?
What of the railroad trains?
In the railroad trains, which resemble hotels on wheels, they say
Often nobody lives.
He travels nowhere
With incomparable rapidity.
What of the bridges? The longest in the world, they now link
Scrapheap with scrapheap.
And what of the people?

XVII

They still make up, we hear, but now
It's to grab a job. Twenty-two year old girls
Sniff cocaine now before setting out
To capture a place at a typewriter.
Desperate parents inject poison into their daughters' thighs
To make them look red hot.

XVIII

Gramophone records are still sold, not many of course
But what do they tell us, these cows who have not learned
To sing? What

Is the sense of these songs? What have they really
Been singing to us all these years long?
Why do we now dislike these once celebrated voices?
Why
Do these photos of cities no longer make the slightest impression on
    us?
Because word has gone round
That these people are bankrupt.

XIX

For their machines, it is said, lie in huge heaps (the biggest in the
    world)
And rust
Like the machines of the Old World (in smaller heaps).

Translated from the German by Frank Jellinek.

C. Day Lewis

From *The Magnetic Mountain. XXXII*

You that love England, who have an ear for her music,
The slow movement of clouds in benediction,
Clear arias of light thrilling over her uplands,
Over the chords of summer sustained peacefully;
Ceaseless the leaves' counterpoint in a west wind lively,
Blossom and river rippling loveliest allegro,
And the storms of wood strings brass at year's finale:
Listen. Can you not hear the entrance of a new theme?

You who go out alone, on tandem or on pillion,
Down arterial roads riding in April,
Or sad beside lakes where hill-slopes are reflected
Making fires of leaves, your high hopes fallen:
Cyclists and hikers in company, day excursionists,
Refugees from cursed towns and devastated areas;
Know you seek a new world, a saviour to establish
Long-lost kinship and restore the blood's fulfilment.

You who like peace, good sorts, happy in a small way
Watching birds or playing cricket with schoolboys,
Who pay for drinks all round, whom disaster chose not;
Yet passing derelict mills and barns roof-rent
Where despair has burnt itself out – hearts at a standstill,
Who suffer loss, aware of lowered vitality;
We can tell you a secret, offer a tonic; only
Submit to the visiting angel, the strange new healer.

You above all who have come to the far end, victims
Of a run-down machine, who can bear it no longer;
Whether in easy chairs chafing at impotence
Or against hunger, bullies and spies preserving
The nerve for action, the spark of indignation –
Need fight in the dark no more, you know your enemies.
You shall be leaders when zero hour is signalled,
Wielders of power and welders of a new world.

Stephen Spender

Unemployed

Moving through the silent crowd
Who stand behind dull cigarettes,
These men who idle in the road,
I have the sense of falling light.

They lounge at corners of the street
And greet friends with a shrug of shoulder
And turn their empty pockets out,
The cynical gestures of the poor.

Now they've no work, like better men
Who sit at desks and take much pay
They sleep long nights and rise at ten
To watch the hours that drain away.

I'm jealous of the weeping hours
They stare through with such hungry eyes
I'm haunted by these images,
I'm haunted by their emptiness.

Louis MacNeice

From *An Eclogue for Christmas*

A. I meet you in an evil time.

B.   The evil bells
   Put out of our heads, I think, the thought of everything else.

A. The jaded calendar revolves,
   Its nuts need oil, carbon chokes the valves,
   The excess sugar of a diabetic culture
   Rotting the nerve of life and literature;
   Therefore when we bring out the old tinsel and frills
   To announce that Christ is born among the barbarous hills
   I turn to you whom a morose routine
   Saves from the mad vertigo of being what has been.

B. Analogue of me, you are wrong to turn to me,
   My country will not yield you any sanctuary,
   There is no pinpoint in any of the ordnance maps
   To save you when your towns and town-bred thoughts collapse,
   It is better to die *in situ* as I shall,
   One place is as bad as another. Go back where your instincts call
   And listen to the crying of the town-cats and the taxis again,
   Or wind your gramophone and eavesdrop on great men.

A. Jazz-weary of years of drums and Hawaiian guitar,
   Pivoting on the parquet I seem to have moved far
   From bombs and mud and gas, have stuttered on my feet
   Clinched to the streamlined and butter-smooth trulls of the élite,
   The lights irritating and gyrating and rotating in gauze –
   Pomade-dazzle, a slick beauty of gewgaws –

I who was Harlequin in the childhood of the century,
Posed by Picasso beside an endless opaque sea,
Have seen myself sifted and splintered in broken facets,
Tentative pencillings, endless liabilities, no assets,
Abstractions scalpelled with a palette-knife
Without reference to this particular life.
And so it has gone on; I have not been allowed to be
Myself in flesh or face, but abstracting and dissecting me
They have made of me pure form, a symbol or a pastiche,
Stylised profile, anything but soul and flesh:
And that is why I turn this jaded music on
To forswear thought and become an automaton.

W. H. Auden

From *Letter to Lord Byron. II*

We're entering now the Eotechnic Phase
    Thanks to the Grid and all those new alloys;
That is, at least, what Lewis Mumford says.
    A world of Aertex underwear for boys,
    Huge plate-glass windows, walls absorbing noise,
Where the smoke nuisance is utterly abated
And all the furniture is chromium-plated.

Well, you might think so if you went to Surrey
    And stayed for week-ends with the well-to-do,
Your car too fast, too personal your worry
    To look too closely at the wheeling view.
    But in the north it simply isn't true.
To those who live in Warrington or Wigan,
It's not a white lie, it's a whacking big 'un.

There on the old historic battlefield,
    The cold ferocity of human wills,
The scars of struggle are as yet unhealed;
    Slattern the tenements on sombre hills,
    And gaunt in valleys the square-windowed mills

That, since the Georgian house, in my conjecture
Remain our finest native architecture.

On economic, health, or moral grounds
    It hasn't got the least excuse to show;
No more than chamber pots or otter hounds;
    But let me say before it has to go,
    It's the most lovely country that I know;
Clearer than Scafell Pike, my heart has stamped on
The view from Birmingham to Wolverhampton.

Long, long ago, when I was only four,
    Going towards my grandmother, the line
Passed through a coal-field. From the corridor
    I watched it pass with envy, thought 'How fine!
    Oh how I wish that situation mine.'
Tramlines and slagheaps, pieces of machinery,
That was, and still is, my ideal scenery.

Hail to the New World! Hail to those who'll love
    Its antiseptic objects, feel at home.
Lovers will gaze at an electric stove,
    Another poésie de départ come
    Centred round bus-stops or the aerodrome.
But give me still, to stir imagination
The chiaroscuro of the railway station.

Preserve me from the Shape of Things to Be;
    The high-grade posters at the public meeting,
The influence of Art on Industry,
    The cinemas with perfect taste in seating;
    Preserve me, above all, from central heating.
It may be D. H. Lawrence hocus-pocus,
But I prefer a room that's got a focus.

Eotechnic Phase: Auden's preferences led him to make a Freudian slip: Lewis Mumford talked of three stages of economic development: the Eotechnic (water and wood); the Palaeotechnic (coal and iron); and the *Neotechnic* (electricity and alloys).
poésie de départ: the poetry of departures; the romance of leave-taking.
chiaroscuro: effects of light and shade in art and nature.

John Betjeman

Sun and Fun

Song of a Night-Club Proprietress

I walked into the night-club in the morning;
   There was kummel on the handle of the door.
The ashtrays were unemptied,
The cleaning unattempted,
   And a squashed tomato sandwich on the floor.

I pulled aside the thick magenta curtains
   – So Regency, so Regency, my dear –
And a host of little spiders
Ran a race across the ciders
   To a box of baby 'pollies by the beer.

Oh sun upon the summer-going by-pass
   Where ev'rything is speeding to the sea,
And wonder beyond wonder
That here where lorries thunder
   The sun should ever percolate to me.

When Boris used to call in his Sedanca,
   When Teddy took me down to his estate
When my nose excited passion,
When my clothes were in the fashion,
   When my beaux were never cross if I was late,

There was sun enough for lazing upon beaches,
   There was fun enough for far into the night.
But I'm dying now and done for,
What on earth was all the fun for?
   For I'm old and ill and terrified and tight.

André Breton

Postman Cheval

We are the birds always charmed by you from the top of these
    belvederes
And that each night form a blossoming branch between your
    shoulders and the arms of your well beloved wheelbarrow
Which we tear out swifter than sparks at your wrist
We are the sighs of the glass statue that raises itself on its elbow
    when man sleeps
And shining holes appear in his bed
Holes through which stags with coral antlers can be seen in a glade
And naked women at the bottom of a mine
You remembered then you got up you got out of the train
Without glancing at the locomotive attacked by immense barometric
    roots
Complaining about its murdered boilers in the virgin forest
Its funnels smoking jacinths and moulting blue snakes
Then we went on, plants subject to metamorphosis
Each night making signs that man may understand
While his house collapses and he stands amazed before the singular
    packing-cases
Sought after by his bed with the corridor and the staircase
The staircase goes on without end
It leads to a millstone door it enlarges suddenly in a public square
It is made of the backs of swans with a spreading wing for banisters
It turns inside out as though it were going to bite itself
But no, it is content at the sound of our feet to open all its steps like
    drawers
Drawers of bread drawers of wine drawers of soap drawers of ice
    drawers of stairs
Drawers of flesh with handsfull of hair
Without turning round you seized the trowel with which breasts are
    made

We smiled at you you held us round the waist
And we took the positions of your pleasure
Motionless under our lids for ever as a woman delights to see man
After having made love.

Translated from the French by David Gascoyne.

Donald Davie

Remembering the 'Thirties

I

Hearing one saga, we enact the next.
We please our elders when we sit enthralled;
But then they're puzzled; and at last they're vexed
To have their youth so avidly recalled.

It dawns upon the veterans after all
That what for them were agonies, for us
Are high-brow thrillers, though historical;
And all their feats quite strictly fabulous.

This novel written fifteen years ago,
Set in my boyhood and my boyhood home,
These poems about 'abandoned workings', show
Worlds more remote than Ithaca or Rome.

The Anschluss, Guernica – all the names
At which those poets thrilled or were afraid
For me mean schools and schoolmasters and games;
And in the process some-one is betrayed.

Ourselves perhaps. The Devil for a joke
Might carve his own initials on our desk,
And yet we'd miss the point because he spoke
An idiom too dated, Audenesque.

Ralegh's Guiana also killed his son.
A pretty pickle if we came to see
The tallest story really packed a gun,
The Telemachiad an Odyssey.

II

Even to them the tales were not so true
As not to be ridiculous as well;
The ironmaster met his Waterloo,
But Rider Haggard rode along the fell.

'Leave for Cape Wrath tonight!' They lounged away
On Fleming's trek or Isherwood's ascent.
England expected every man that day
To show his motives were ambivalent.

They played the fool, not to appear as fools
In time's long glass. A deprecating air
Disarmed, they thought, the jeers of later schools;
Yet irony itself is doctrinaire,

And curiously, nothing now betrays
Their type to time's derision like this coy
Insistence on the quizzical, their craze
For showing Hector was a mother's boy.

A neutral tone is nowadays preferred.
And yet it may be better, if we must,
To praise a stance impressive and absurd
Than not to see the hero for the dust.

For courage is the vegetable king,
The sprig of all ontologies, the weed
That beards the slag-heap with his hectoring,
Whose green adventure is to run to seed.

The Anschluss: Hitler's annexation of Austria on 12 March 1938.
Guernica: the Basque town bombed by German bombers in April 1937 during the
Spanish Civil War.

PRELUDE TO A WAR:
FASCISM V. COMMUNISM 1933–1939

In retrospect, the struggles of the Thirties can be seen as the inevitable clash between an emerging technological consumerist society and the old ideas of blood and soil and a fixed social hierarchy. Nazism was partly a fearful reaction against the new science, art and culture of the cities. Locked in a death struggle, fascism and communism became mirror images, with the same terror directed at the people (often arbitrary in the case of communism, ruthlessly targeted in the case of Nazism); the same intolerance of artistic freedom and insistence on vapid 'naturalistic' art, preferably in a pseudo-heroic mode; the same hostility towards a science that didn't serve the regime and its ideology. Both fascism and communism were enemies of the twentieth century. All poets can do is to warn, and they did: probably in no other era did poets so much feel the need to be politically committed, however much this distorted their natural poetic bent. The Spanish Civil War (1936–9) was the great rallying point. Some, like Mandelstam in Russia and the English poet John Cornford in Spain, paid with their lives.

W. B. Yeats

The Second Coming

Turning and turning in the widening gyre
The falcon cannot hear the falconer;
Things fall apart; the centre cannot hold;
Mere anarchy is loosed upon the world,
The blood-dimmed tide is loosed, and everywhere
The ceremony of innocence is drowned;
The best lack all conviction, while the worst
Are full of passionate intensity.

Surely some revelation is at hand;
Surely the Second Coming is at hand.

The Second Coming! Hardly are those words out
When a vast image out of *Spiritus Mundi*
Troubles my sight: somewhere in sands of the desert
A shape with lion body and the head of a man,
A gaze blank and pitiless as the sun,
Is moving its slow thighs, while all about it
Reel shadows of the indignant desert birds.
The darkness drops again; but now I know
That twenty centuries of stony sleep
Were vexed to nightmare by a rocking cradle,
And what rough beast, its hour come round at last,
Slouches towards Bethlehem to be born?

Spiritus Mundi: the image is from the Prophetic Books of William Blake.

Bertolt Brecht

To Those Born Later

I

Truly, I live in dark times!
The guileless word is folly. A smooth forehead
Suggests insensitivity. The man who laughs
Has simply not yet had
The terrible news.

What kind of times are they, when
A talk about trees is almost a crime
Because it implies silence about so many horrors?
That man there calmly crossing the street
Is already perhaps beyond the reach of his friends
Who are in need?

It is true I still earn my keep
But, believe me, that is only an accident. Nothing
I do gives me the right to eat my fill.
By chance I've been spared. (If my luck breaks, I am lost.)

They say to me: Eat and drink! Be glad you have it!
But how can I eat and drink if I snatch what I eat
From the starving, and
My glass of water belongs to one dying of thirst?
And yet I eat and drink.

I would also like to be wise.
In the old books it says what wisdom is:
To shun the strife of the world and to live out
Your brief time without fear
Also to get along without violence
To return good for evil
Not to fulfil your desires but to forget them
Is accounted wise.
All this I cannot do:
Truly, I live in dark times.

II

I came to the cities in a time of disorder
When hunger reigned there.
I came among men in a time of revolt
And I rebelled with them.
So passed my time
Which had been given to me on earth.

My food I ate between battles
To sleep I lay down among murderers
Love I practised carelessly
And nature I looked at without patience.
So passed my time
Which had been given to me on earth.

All roads led into the mire in my time.
My tongue betrayed me to the butchers.
There was little I could do. But those in power
Sat safer without me: that was my hope.
So passed my time
Which had been given to me on earth.

Our forces were slight. Our goal
Lay far in the distance
It was clearly visible, though I myself
Was unlikely to reach it.
So passed my time
Which had been given to me on earth.

III

You who will emerge from the flood
In which we have gone under
Remember
When you speak of our failings
The dark time too
Which you have escaped.
For we went, changing countries oftener than our shoes
Through the wars of the classes, despairing
When there was injustice only, and no rebellion.

And yet we know:
Hatred, even of meanness
Contorts the features.
Anger, even against injustice
Makes the voice hoarse. Oh, we
Who wanted to prepare the ground for friendliness
Could not ourselves be friendly.

But you, when the time comes at last
And man is a helper to man
Think of us
With forbearance.

Translated from the German by
John Willett, Ralph Manheim and Erich Fried.

Eugenio Montale

The Hitler Spring

The dense white cloud of the mayflies crazily
Whirls around the pallid street lamps and over the parapets,
Spread on the ground a blanket on which the foot
Grates as on sprinkled sugar; the looming summer now
Releases the nightfrosts which it was holding
In the secret caves of the dead season,
In the gardens of Maiano where the sandpits stop.

And soon over the street an infernal messenger passes in flight;
The murderers salute; a mystical gulf, fired
And beflagged with swastikas, has taken and swallowed us;
The shopwindows, humble and inoffensive, are closed
Though armed – they also –
With cannon and toys of war;
The butcher has struck who dresses with flowers and berries
The muzzles of the slaughtered goats.
The ritual of the mild hangman, once innocent of blood,
Is changed to a spastic dance of shattering wings,
The mayflies' tiny deaths whiten the piers' edge
And the water continues to eat at the
Shoreline, and no one is any more blameless.

All for nothing, then? – and the Roman candles
At San Giovanni, which gradually
Blanched the horizon, and the pledges and the long farewells
Strong as a baptism, in the sorrowful expectation
Of the horde, (but a bud striped the air, distilling
On the ice and on the rivers of your country
The messengers of Tobias, the seven, the seeds
Of the future) and the heliotrope
Born of your hands – all burned, sucked dry
By a pollen that cries like fire
And is winged with ice and salt.

O this ulcered
Spring will still be festival, if it can freeze again
In death that death! Observe once more
Up yonder, Clizia, your destiny, you
Preserved through change by a love which does not change
Until the blind sun you carry in you
Blinds itself in that other, and confounds itself
In Him, for all.

Perhaps the sirens and the bells
Which salute the monsters in the night
At their witch's sabbath are already confounded
With the sound which unloosed from heaven descends and
     conquers –
With the breath of a dawn which may yet reappear
Tomorrow, white but without wings
Of terror, to the parched arroyos of the south.

Translated from the Italian by Maurice English.

arroyo: a stream.

Louis MacNeice

From *Autumn Journal*

VI

And I remember Spain
    At Easter ripe as an egg for revolt and ruin
Though for a tripper the rain
    Was worse than the surly or the worried or the haunted faces
With writings on the walls –
    Hammer and sickle, Boicot, Viva, Muerra;
With café-au-lait brimming the waterfalls,
    With sherry, shellfish, omelettes.
With fretted stone the Moor
    Had chiselled for effects of sun and shadow;

With shadows of the poor,
  The begging cripples and the children begging.
The churches full of saints
  Tortured on racks of marble –
The old complaints
  Covered with gilt and dimly lit with candles.
With powerful or banal
  Monuments of riches or repression
And the Escorial
  Cold for ever within like the heart of Philip.
With ranks of dominoes
  Deployed on café tables the whole of Sunday;
With cabarets that call the tourist, shows
  Of thighs and eyes and nipples.
With slovenly soldiers, nuns,
  And peeling posters from the last elections
Promising bread or guns
  Or an amnesty or another
Order or else the old
  Glory veneered and varnished
As if veneer could hold
  The rotten guts and crumbled bones together.
                    [. . .]
And we sat in trains all night
  With the windows shut among civil guards and peasants
And tried to play piquet by a tiny light
  And tried to sleep bolt upright;
And cursed the Spanish rain
  And cursed their cigarettes which came to pieces
And caught heavy colds in Cordova and in vain
  Waited for the right light for taking photos.
And we met a Cambridge don who said with an air
  'There's going to be trouble shortly in this country,'
And ordered anis, pudgy and debonair,
  Glad to show off his mastery of the language.
But only an inch behind
  This map of olive and ilex, this painted hoarding,
Careless of visitors the people's mind
  Was tunnelling like a mole to day and danger.

And the day before we left
   We saw the mob in flower at Algeciras
Outside a toothless door, a church bereft
   Of its images and its aura.
And at La Linea while
   The night put miles between us and Gibraltar
We heard the blood-lust of a drunkard pile
   His heaven high with curses;
And next day took the boat
   For home, forgetting Spain, not realising
That Spain would soon denote
   Our grief, our aspirations;
Not knowing that our blunt
   Ideals would find their whetstone, that our spirit
Would find its frontier on the Spanish front,
   Its body in a rag-tag army.

John Cornford

A Letter from Aragon

This is a quiet sector of a quiet front.

We buried Ruiz in a new pine coffin,
But the shroud was too small and his washed feet stuck out.
The stink of his corpse came through the clean pine boards
And some of the bearers wrapped handkerchiefs round their faces.
Death was not dignified.
We hacked a ragged grave in the unfriendly earth
And fired a ragged volley over the grave.

You could tell from our listlessness, no one much missed him.

This is a quiet sector of a quiet front.
There is no poison gas and no H.E.

But when they shelled the other end of the village
And the streets were choked with dust
Women came screaming out of the crumbling houses,
Clutched under one arm the naked rump of an infant.
I thought: how ugly fear is.

This is a quiet sector of a quiet front.
Our nerves are steady; we all sleep soundly.

In the clean hospital bed my eyes were so heavy
Sleep easily blotted out one ugly picture,
A wounded militiaman moaning on a stretcher,
Now out of danger, but still crying for water,
Strong against death, but unprepared for such pain.

This on a quiet front.

But when I shook hands to leave, an Anarchist worker
Said: 'Tell the workers of England
This was a war not of our own making,
We did not seek it.
But if ever the Fascists again rule Barcelona
It will be as a heap of ruins with us workers beneath it.'

                                                        1936

H.E.: high explosive.

Jaroslav Seifert

Salute to the Madrid Barricades

Covered in quicklime in his native soil
García Lorca, warrior and poet,
lies crouching in the dugout of his grave
without a rifle, lyre, ammunition.
The rug of days on which the Moors now dance

is woven now from pools of tears and blood,
and across Alpine glaciers, Pyrenean heights,
from the ancient stairway leading to the Castle
a poet's speaking to him,
a poet still alive
with his clenched fist sends to that distant grave
a gentle kiss,
the kind that poets save for one another.

Not for murder
but for days of peace
sounds the sweet song
and that soft play, the play of words and rhymes
that we have sought
under our lovers' hearts and under trees in blossom,
to shape a verse
as sonorous and as beautiful
as ringing bells and speech on plain folk's lips.

But when the pen turned into a rifle
who did not flee?

A bayonet, too, can write on human skin,
its letters burning like the crimson leaves
through which I'm wading at this difficult hour.

Yet one thing I do know, dead friend:
along the boulevards of Madrid
workers will march again and they will sing
your songs, dear poet,
when they've hung up the rifles they now lean on,

when they have hung them up in gratitude
as do the lame in Lourdes
their now no longer needed crutches.

Translated from the Czech by Ewald Osers.

García Lorca: Spanish poet murdered by the Fascists in 1936.

Miguel Hernández

The Wounded Man

(for the wall of a hospital in all the gore)

I

The wounded stretch across the battlefields.
And from the long length of these fighters' bodies
a wheatfield of warm fountains springs up,
spreading into raucous jets.

Blood always rains upside down, toward the sky.
And wounds make sounds, just like conch shells
when the rapidity of flight is in them,
the essence of waves.

Blood smells like the sea, tastes like the sea, and the wine cellar.
The wine cellar of the sea, of hardy wine, breaks open
where the wounded man, shivering, goes under,
blossoms, and finds himself.

I am wounded. Look at me: I need more lives.
The one I have is too small for the consignment
of blood that I want to give up through my wounds.
Tell me who has not been wounded.

My life is a wound with a happy childhood.
Ay, the poor man who is not wounded, who never feels
wounded by life, never rests in life,
happily wounded!

If a man goes cheerfully to hospitals,
they change into gardens of half-opened wounds,
of flowering oleanders in front of the operating room
with its bloodstained doors.

II

I bleed for freedom, I fight, I survive.
For freedom I give my eyes and hands,
like a generous and captive tree of flesh,
to the surgeons.

For freedom I feel more hearts
in me than grains of sand: my veins give up foam,
and I enter the hospitals, I enter the bandages
as if they were lilies.

For freedom I sever myself, with bullets,
from those who dumped her statue into the mud.
And I sever myself from my feet, my arms,
my house – from everything.

Because where these empty eye-sockets dawn
she will put two stones that see the future,
and make new arms and new legs grow
from the pruned flesh.

The body's relics that I give up in each wound
will bud again in autumnless flutterings of sap.
Because I am like the cropped tree, and I bud again:
because I still have life.

Translated from the Spanish by Don Share.

Pastor Niemöller

1938

'First they came for the Jews
And I did not speak out –
Because I was not a Jew.

Then they came for the communists
And I did not speak out –
Because I was not a communist.

Then they came for the trade unionists
And I did not speak out –
Because I was not a trade unionist.

Then they came for me –
And there was no one left
To speak out for me.'

Osip Mandelstam

The Stalin Epigram

Our lives no longer feel ground under them.
At ten paces you can't hear our words.

But whenever there's a snatch of talk
it turns to the Kremlin mountaineer,

the ten thick worms his fingers,
his words like measures of weight,

the huge laughing cockroaches on his top lip,
the glitter of his boot-rims.

Ringed with a scum of chicken-necked bosses
he toys with the tributes of half-men.

One whistles, another meouws, a third snivels.
He pokes out his finger and he alone goes boom.

He forges decrees in a line like horseshoes,
One for the groin, one the forehead, temple, eye.

He rolls the executions on his tongue like berries.
He wishes he could hug them like big friends from home.

November 1933

Translated from the Russian by
Clarence Brown and W. S. Merwin.

This poem caused Mandelstam's first arrest, in 1934. He was later released, exiled to the Urals and then Voronezh. In May 1938 he was arrested again, sentenced to five years' hard labour, and died on 27 December 1938 in a transit camp.

Anna Akhmatova

From *Requiem*

No, not under a foreign heavenly-cope, and
Not canopied by foreign wings –
I was with my people in those hours,
There where, unhappily, my people were.

In the fearful years of the Yezhov terror I spent seventeen months in prison queues in Leningrad. One day somebody 'identified' me. Beside me, in the queue, there was a woman with blue lips. She had, of course, never heard of me; but she suddenly came out of that trance so common to us all and whispered in my ear (everybody spoke in whispers there): 'Can you describe this?' And I said: 'Yes, I can.' And then something like the shadow of a smile crossed what had once been her face.

1 April 1957, Leningrad

Dedication

The mountains bow before this anguish,
The great river does not flow.
In mortal sadness the convicts languish;
The bolts stay frozen. There's someone who
Still feels the sunset's glow,
Someone who can still distinguish
Day from night, for whom the fresh
Wind blows. But we don't know it, we're obsessive,
We only hear the tramp of boots, abrasive
Keys scraping against our flesh.
Rising as though for early mass,
Through the capital of beasts we'd thread.
Met, more breathless than the dead,
Mistier Neva, lower sun. Ahead,
Hope was still singing, endlessly evasive.
The sentence! and now at last tears flood.
She'd thought the months before were loneliness!
She's thrown down like a rock.
The heart gives up its blood.
Yet goes . . . swaying . . . she can still walk.
My friends of those two years I stood
In hell – oh all my chance friends lost
Beyond the circle of the moon, I cry
Into the blizzards of the permafrost:
Goodbye. Goodbye.

[. . .]

VIII. To Death

You will come in any case, so why not now?
Life is very hard: I'm waiting for you.
I have turned off the lights and thrown the door wide open
For you, so simple and so marvellous.
Take on any form you like.
Why not burst in like a poisoned shell,
Or steal in like a bandit with his knuckleduster,
Or like a typhus-germ?

Or like a fairy-tale of your own invention –
Stolen from you and loathsomely repeated,
Where I can see, behind you in the doorway,
The police-cap and the white-faced concierge?
I don't care how. The Yenisei is swirling,
The Pole Star glittering. And eyes
I love are closing on the final horror.

Translated from the Russian by D. M. Thomas.

the Yezhov terror: Nikolai Yezhov was head of the Soviet state security police, the NKVD (forerunner of the KGB), from 1936 to 1938. He implemented Stalin's Great Terror of 1937–8, under which, officially, 681,692 persons were executed. Yezhov himself was executed in 1940.
Neva: the river in St Petersburg.
Yenisei: a major river in Siberia.

Louis MacNeice

From *Autumn Journal*

VII

Conferences, adjournments, ultimatums,
    Flights in the air, castles in the air,
The autopsy of treaties, dynamite under the bridges,
    The end of *laissez faire*.
After the warm days the rain comes pimpling
    The paving stones with white
And with the rain the national conscience, creeping,
    Seeping through the night.
And in the sodden park on Sunday protest
    Meetings assemble not, as so often, now
Merely to advertise some patent panacea
    But simply to avow
The need to hold the ditch; a bare avowal
    That may perhaps imply
Death at the doors in a week but perhaps in the long run
    Exposure of the lie.

Think of a number, double it, treble it, square it,
  And sponge it out
And repeat *ad lib.* and mark the slate with crosses;
  There is no time to doubt
If the puzzle really has an answer. Hitler yells on the wireless,
  The night is damp and still
And I hear dull blows on wood outside my window;
  They are cutting down the trees on Primrose Hill.
The wood is white like the roast flesh of chicken,
  Each tree falling like a closing fan;
No more looking at the view from seats beneath the branches,
  Everything is going to plan;
They want the crest of this hill for anti-aircraft,
  The guns will take the view
And searchlights probe the heavens for bacilli
  With narrow wands of blue.
And the rain came on as I watched the territorials
  Sawing and chopping and pulling on ropes like a team
In a village tug-of-war; and I found my dog had vanished
  And thought 'This is the end of the old régime,'
But found the police had got her at St John's Wood station
  And fetched her in the rain and went for a cup
Of coffee to an all-night shelter and heard a taxi-driver
  Say 'It turns me up
When I see these soldiers in lorries' – rumble of tumbrils
  Drums in the trees
Breaking the eardrums of the ravished dryads –
  It turns me up; a coffee, please.
And as I go out I see a windscreen-wiper
  In an empty car
Wiping away like mad and I feel astounded
  That things have gone so far.
And I come back here to my flat and wonder whether
  From now on I need take
The trouble to go out choosing stuff for curtains
  As I don't know anyone to make
Curtains quickly. Rather one should quickly
  Stop the cracks for gas or dig a trench

And take one's paltry measures against the coming
  Of the unknown Uebermensch.
But one – meaning I – is bored, am bored, the issue
  Involving principle but bound in fact
To squander principle in panic and self-deception –
  Accessories after the act,
So that all we foresee is rivers in spate sprouting
  With drowning hands
And men like dead frogs floating till the rivers
  Lose themselves in the sands.
And we who have been brought up to think of 'Gallant Belgium'
  As so much blague
Are now preparing again to essay good through evil
  For the sake of Prague;
And must, we suppose, become uncritical, vindictive,
  And must, in order to beat
The enemy, model ourselves upon the enemy,
  A howling radio for our paraclete.
The night continues wet, the axe keeps falling,
  The hill grows bald and bleak
No longer one of the sights of London but maybe
  We shall have fireworks here by this day week.
                    [. . .]

                    VIII
The night grows purple, the crisis hangs
  Over the roofs like a Persian army
And all of Xenophon's parasangs
  Would take us only an inch from danger.
Black-out practice and ARP,
  Newsboys driving a roaring business,
The flapping paper snatched to see
  If anything has, or has not, happened.
And I go to the Birmingham Hippodrome
  Packed to the roof and primed for laughter
And beautifully at home
  With the ukulele and the comic chestnuts;

'As pals we meet, as pals we part' –
  Embonpoint and a new tiara;
The comedian spilling the apple-cart
  Of *doubles entendres* and doggerel verses
And the next day begins
  Again with alarm and anxious
Listening to bulletins
  From distant, measured voices
Arguing for peace
  While the zero hour approaches,
While the eagles gather and the petrol and oil and grease
  Have all been applied and the vultures back the eagles.
But once again
  The crisis is put off and things look better
And we feel negotiation is not vain –
  Save my skin and damn my conscience.
And negotiation wins,
  If you can call it winning,
And here we are – just as before – safe in our skins;
  Glory to God for Munich.
And stocks go up and wrecks
  Are salved and politicians' reputations
Go up like Jack-on-the-Beanstalk; only the Czechs
  Go down and without fighting.

Uebermensch: the Superman of Nazi doctrine.

Stephen Sherrill

Katyn Forest

I am 1939 and cold air.
I want a cigarette but will make do
with this shovel. This shovel
feels good after stale bread and weeks
in the dark.
To have purpose satisfies.

I am 1939 and too young to smoke.
Don't be absurd.
Joseph Stalin came to dinner and refused
to eat the soup. I have shovel and purpose.
My hands are free only because I do not resist.
I don't scream through sawdust simply because I don't scream.

I am the beginning of a stamp collection:
ten, meticulously affixed to a small card.
I'll be found in a breast pocket, yellowed and peeling.
This place is called Kosygori or Goat Hill.
There are rumors of orchards in the air.
All I ask, really, is that someone forward
our correspondence.

It is 1939 and we are tired.
There is much to be done, but patience
is all we can give. For now I'm content to lie
on the twenty one thousand eight hundred fifty six backs
of my father, press my mouth to the bullet hole
at the base of his skull and hum softly
until my own drum sounds.

Germany and Russia both invaded Poland in September 1939 and the country was partitioned. Stalin ordered the execution of 26,000 Polish officers. When the Germans released evidence for the massacre in 1943 the Russians held the Germans responsible for the crime. For reasons of their own, the Western powers were evasive about the issue for many years. Under Gorbachev and Yeltsin, Russian responsibility was admitted.

W. H. Auden

September 1, 1939

I sit in one of the dives
On Fifty-Second Street
Uncertain and afraid
As the clever hopes expire
Of a low dishonest decade:
Waves of anger and fear
Circulate over the bright
And darkened lands of the earth,
Obsessing our private lives;
The unmentionable odour of death
Offends the September night.

Accurate scholarship can
Unearth the whole offence
From Luther until now
That has driven a culture mad,
Find what occurred at Linz,
What huge imago made
A psychopathic god:
I and the public know
What all schoolchildren learn,
Those to whom evil is done
Do evil in return.

Exiled Thucydides knew
All that a speech can say
About Democracy,
And what dictators do,
The elderly rubbish they talk
To an apathetic grave;
Analysed all in his book,
The enlightenment driven away,
The habit-forming pain,

Mismanagement and grief:
We must suffer them all again.

Into this neutral air
Where blind skyscrapers use
Their full height to proclaim
The strength of Collective Man,
Each language pours its vain
Competitive excuse:
But who can live for long
In an euphoric dream;
Out of the mirror they stare,
Imperialism's face
And the international wrong.

Faces along the bar
Cling to their average day:
The lights must never go out,
The music must always play,
All the conventions conspire
To make this fort assume
The furniture of home;
Lest we should see where we are,
Lost in a haunted wood,
Children afraid of the night
Who have never been happy or good.

The windiest militant trash
Important Persons shout
Is not so crude as our wish:
What mad Nijinsky wrote
About Diaghilev
Is true of the normal heart;
For the error bred in the bone
Of each woman and each man
Craves what it cannot have,
Not universal love
But to be loved alone.

From the conservative dark
Into the ethical life
The dense commuters come,
Repeating their morning vow,
'I *will* be true to the wife,
I'll concentrate more on my work',
And helpless governors wake
To resume their compulsory game:
Who can release them now,
Who can reach the deaf,
Who can speak for the dumb?

All I have is a voice
To undo the folded lie,
The romantic lie in the brain
Of the sensual man-in-the-street
And the lie of Authority
Whose buildings grope the sky:
There is no such thing as the State
And no one exists alone;
Hunger allows no choice
To the citizen or the police;
We must love one another or die.

Defenceless under the night
Our world in stupor lies;
Yet, dotted everywhere,
Ironic points of light
Flash out wherever the Just
Exchange their messages:
May I, composed like them
Of Eros and of dust,
Beleaguered by the same
Negation and despair,
Show an affirming flame.

Linz: Hitler grew up in the Austrian town of Linz. He was forced to leave the Realschule in 1904 before completing his studies because of mediocre results.

WORLD WAR II: 1939–1945

'Where are the war poets?' was the cry in England, and the truth is that English poets found it hard to cope with the idea of remote combat – 'This is a damned inhuman sort of war,' wrote the English poet R. N. Currey. The American poets who served in the US Air Force and Navy – Randall Jarrell and Richard Eberhart – had less difficulty and wrote fine poems of the air war. But this was total war and all poetry written at this time, whether written in the forces or by civilians, was war poetry. The conflict produced a tempering of poetic styles and similar poems were written by poets from such diverse traditions as the English, Russian and French. Louis Aragon, a surrealist in pre-war France, wrote, in 'The Lilacs and the Roses', a classic elegy, twentieth-century in the economy of its language but timeless in its music. By 1945, poets could only wring their hands about a Europe which had apparently tried to commit cultural suicide.

Louis Aragon

The Lilacs and the Roses

O months of blossoming, months of transfigurations,
May without a cloud and June stabbed to the heart,
I shall not ever forget the lilacs or the roses
Nor those the Spring has kept folded away apart.

I shall not ever forget the tragic sleight-of-hand,
The cavalcade, the cries, the crowd, the sun,
The lorries loaded with love, the Belgian gifts,
The road humming with bees, the atmosphere that spun,
The feckless triumphing before the battle,
The scarlet blood the scarlet kiss bespoke
And those about to die bolt upright in the turrets
Smothered in lilac by a drunken folk.

I shall not ever forget the flower-gardens of France –
Illuminated scrolls from eras more than spent –
Nor forget the trouble of dusk, the sphinx-like silence,
The roses all along the way we went;
Flowers that gave the lie to the soldiers passing
On wings of fear, a fear importunate as a breeze,
And gave the lie to the lunatic push-bikes and the ironic
Guns and the sorry rig of the refugees.

But what I do not know is why this whirl
Of memories always comes to the same point and drops
At Sainte-Marthe . . . a general . . . a black pattern . . .
A Norman villa where the forest stops;
All is quiet here, the enemy rests in the night
And Paris has surrendered, so we have just heard –
I shall never forget the lilacs nor the roses
Nor those two loves whose loss we have incurred:

Bouquets of the first day, lilacs, Flanders lilacs,
Soft cheeks of shadow rouged by death – and you,
Bouquets of the Retreat, delicate roses, tinted
Like far-off conflagrations: roses of Anjou.

Translated from the French by Louis MacNeice.

Ruthven Todd

These Are Facts

These are facts, observe them how you will:
Forget for a moment the medals and the glory,
The clean shape of the bomb, designed to kill,
And the proud headlines of the papers' story.

Remember the walls of brick that forty years
Had nursed to make a neat though shabby home;
The impertinence of death, ignoring tears
That smashed the house and left untouched the Dome.

Bodies in death are not magnificent or stately,
Bones are not elegant that blast has shattered;
This sorry, stained and crumpled rag was lately
A man whose life was made of little things that mattered;

Now he is just a nuisance, liable to stink,
A breeding-ground for flies, a test-tube for disease:
Bury him quickly and never pause to think,
What is the future worth to men like these?

People are more than places, more than pride;
A million photographs record the works of Wren;
A city remains a city on credit from the tide
That flows among its rocks, a sea of men.

                                        1941

On 29 December 1940, St Paul's Cathedral miraculously survived a massive air raid.

Henry Reed

From *Lessons of the War*

NAMING OF PARTS

To-day we have naming of parts. Yesterday,
We had daily cleaning. And to-morrow morning,
We shall have what to do after firing. But to-day,
To-day we have naming of parts. Japonica
Glistens like coral in all of the neighbouring gardens,
        And to-day we have naming of parts.

This is the lower sling swivel. And this
Is the upper sling swivel, whose use you will see,
When you are given your slings. And this is the piling swivel,
Which in your case you have not got. The branches
Hold in the gardens their silent, eloquent gestures,
        Which in our case we have not got.

This is the safety-catch, which is always released
With an easy flick of the thumb. And please do not let me
See anyone using his finger. You can do it quite easy
If you have any strength in your thumb. The blossoms
Are fragile and motionless, never letting anyone see
    Any of them using their finger.

And this you can see is the bolt. The purpose of this
Is to open the breech, as you see. We can slide it
Rapidly backwards and forwards: we call this
Easing the spring. And rapidly backwards and forwards
The early bees are assaulting and fumbling the flowers:
    They call it easing the Spring.

They call it easing the Spring: it is perfectly easy
If you have any strength in your thumb: like the bolt,
And the breech, and the cocking-piece, and the point of balance,
Which in our case we have not got; and the almond-blossom
Silent in all of the gardens and the bees going backwards and
    forwards,
    For to-day we have naming of parts.

Keith Douglas

How to Kill

Under the parabola of a ball,
a child turning into a man,
I looked into the air too long.
The ball fell in my hand, it sang
in the closed fist: *Open Open
Behold a gift designed to kill.*

Now in my dial of glass appears
the soldier who is going to die.
He smiles, and moves about in ways

his mother knows, habits of his.
The wires touch his face: I cry
NOW. Death, like a familiar, hears

and look, has made a man of dust
of a man of flesh. This sorcery
I do. Being damned, I am amused
to see the centre of love diffused
and the waves of love travel into vacancy.
How easy it is to make a ghost.

The weightless mosquito touches
her tiny shadow on the stone,
and with how like, how infinite
a lightness, man and shadow meet.
They fuse. A shadow is a man
when the mosquito death approaches.

James Applewhite

News of Pearl Harbor

From the arched Philco with its speaker like a Gothic window
      came news from the sky. Later, newsreels showed the *Arizona*
hulled over, burning. The P-40's and slender-tailed B-17's in
      their peacetime markings lay crumpled in piles. The sky
became accelerator of change – no longer the river with
      its slow hieroglyphic, its evolution from sailing craft
and log raft to steam-huffed packet. Not the railroad
      with its comprehensible, coal-fired engine in its black
piston-shape, not even the new year's models of Chryslers
      and Buicks, but an airborne sound from the distance: Pearl
Harbor, jewel-lustrous, catastrophic syllables. Volunteers
      watched from Forest Service tower and rooftop, with manuals
to aid them, though the middle-aged eyes behind glasses confused one
      aircraft with another. But the boy on the roof of his father's
station recognized each type as by instinct – in the one-room
      house all windows, as he waited for apocalyptic sightings.

He imagined a desperate combat the whole country entered in,
        his somnolent South now wired by the phone line that
began at his own left hand to the military fathers, whose
        planes changed as quickly as the broadcasts: P-38's and
B-17's, the milk-jug P-47's, moving through the new marks,
        with armor and self-sealing tanks, machine guns and
cannon, stabilizer-fins extended. Young men training
        at Seymour Johnson nearby strained to learn control
of a fighter like a winged locomotive. One of these P-47's
        crashed in the edge of his county. He went with his father.
The boulderlike motor had broken from its mounts, an engine
        of two thousand horsepower rolling like the Juggernaut of
wartime, bowling down pine trees, letting in sunlight
        through the central, violated grove, toward the hollow,
frangible body. This Thunderbolt of a technical rhetoric
        in a pastoral accumulated too vividly for scrutiny
illuminated a fuselage broken at the cockpit: a pilot's
        seat stark as an electric chair, where the throne
of this new succession stood jellied with blood.

The Japanese air raid on the US Naval Base at Pearl Harbor, Hawaii, on 7 December
1941, brought America into the war.

Louis Simpson

I Dreamed that in a City Dark as Paris

I dreamed that in a city dark as Paris
I stood alone in a deserted square.
The night was trembling with a violet
Expectancy. At the far edge it moved
And rumbled; on that flickering horizon
The guns were pumping color in the sky.

There was the Front. But I was lonely here,
Left behind, abandoned by the army.
The empty city and the empty square
Was my inhabitation, my unrest.

The helmet with its vestige of a crest,
The rifle in my hands, long out of date,
The belt I wore, the trailing overcoat
And hobnail boots, were those of a *poilu*.
I was the man, as awkward as a bear.

Over the rooftops where cathedrals loomed
In speaking majesty, two aeroplanes,
Forlorn as birds, appeared. Then growing large,
The German *Taube* and the *Nieuport Scout*,
They chased each other tumbling through the sky,
Till one streamed down on fire to the earth.

These wars have been so great, they are forgotten
Like the Egyptian dynasts. My confrere
In whose thick boots I stood, were you amazed
To wander through my brain four decades later
As I have wandered in a dream through yours?

The violence of waking life disrupts
The order of our death. Strange dreams occur,
For dreams are licensed as they never were.

Taube and *Nieuport Scout*: fighter planes of WWI, German and French, respectively.

Jacques Prévert

The New Order

The sun lies on the soil
Litre of spilled red wine
A house has collapsed
Like a drunk on the pavement
And under its still standing porch
A girl is stretched
A man on his knees beside her
Is about to finish her off

In the wound where the sword stirs
The heart doesn't stop bleeding
And the man lets out a war-cry
Like an absurd peacock's cry
And his cry gets lost in the night
Out of life out of time
And the man with face of dust
The lost and ruined man
Stands up and cries 'Heil Hitler!'
In a desperate voice
Facing him in the debris
Of a burnt-out shop
The portrait of a pale old man
Regards him kindly
Stars shine on his sleeve
Others also on his cap
Like the stars shine at Christmas
On the pine tree for the little ones
And the storm-trooper
Before the marvellous colour-photo
Suddenly finds himself at home again
In the very heart of the new order
And puts his dagger back in its sheath
And goes off straight ahead
Automaton of the new Europe
Run wild with homesickness
Adieu adieu Lily Marlene
And his step and his song wander off in the night
And the portrait of the pale old man
Among the debris
Remains alone and smiles
Tranquil in the semi-dark
Senile and sure of himself.

Translated from the French by
Lawrence Ferlinghetti.

The New Order: the collaborationist French government at Vichy.

János Pilinszky

The French Prisoner

If only I could forget that Frenchman.
I saw him, just before dawn, creeping past our quarters
into the dense growth of the back garden
so that he almost merged into the ground.
As I watched he looked back, he peered all round –
at last he had found a safe hideout.
Now his plunder can be all his!
He'll go no further, whatever happens.

Already he is eating, biting into the turnip
which he must have smuggled out under his rags.
He was gulping raw cattle-turnip!
Yet he had hardly swallowed one mouthful
before it flooded back up.
Then the sweet pulp in his mouth mingled
with delight and disgust the same
as the unhappy and happy come together
in their bodies' voracious ecstasy.

Only to forget that body, those quaking shoulder blades,
the hands shrunk to bone,
the bare palm that crammed at his mouth, and clung there
so that it ate, too.
And the shame, desperate and enraged
of the organs embittered against each other
forced to tear from each other
their last bonds of kinship.

The way his clumsy feet had been left out
of the gibbering bestial joy
and splayed there, crushed beneath
the rapture and torture of his body.
And his glance – if only I could forget that!

Though he was choking, he kept on
forcing more down his gullet – no matter what –
only to eat – anything – this – that – even himself!

Why go on. Guards came for him.
He had escaped from the nearby prison camp.
And just as I did then, in that garden,
I am strolling here, among garden shadows, at home.
I look into my notes and quote:
'If only I could forget that Frenchman . . .'
And from my ears, my eyes, my mouth
the scalding memory shouts at me:

'I am hungry!' And suddenly I feel
the eternal hunger
which that poor creature has long ago forgotten
and which no earthly nourishment can lessen.
He lives on me. And more and more hungrily!
And I am less and less sufficient for him.
And now he, who would have eaten anything,
is clamouring for my heart.

Translated from the Hungarian by
Ted Hughes and János Csokits.

Randall Jarrell

A Front

Fog over the base: the beams ranging
From the five towers pull home from the night
The crews cold in fur, the bombers banging
Like lost trucks down the levels of the ice.
A glow drifts in like mist (how many tons of it?),
Bounces to a roll, turns suddenly to steel
And tires and turrets, huge in the trembling light.

The next is high, and pulls up with a wail,
Comes round again – no use. And no use for the rest
In drifting circles out along the range;
Holding no longer, changed to a kinder course,
The flights drone southward through the steady rain.
The base is closed . . . But one voice keeps on calling,
The lowering pattern of the engines grows;
The roar gropes downward in its shaky orbit
For the lives the season quenches. Here below
They beg, order, are not heard; and hear the darker
Voice rising: *Can't you hear me? Over. Over –*
All the air quivers, and the east sky glows.

Richard Eberhart

The Fury of Aerial Bombardment

You would think the fury of aerial bombardment
Would rouse God to relent; the infinite spaces
Are still silent. He looks on shock-pried faces.
History, even, does not know what is meant.

You would feel that after so many centuries
God would give man to repent; yet he can kill
As Cain could, but with multitudinous will,
No farther advanced than in his ancient furies.

Was man made stupid to see his own stupidity?
Is God by definition indifferent, beyond us all?
Is the eternal truth man's fighting soul
Wherein the Beast ravens in its own avidity?

Of Van Wettering I speak, and Averill,
Names on a list, whose faces I do not recall
But they are gone to early death, who late in school
Distinguished the belt feed lever from the belt holding pawl.

Durs Grünbein

Poem on Dresden

For Via Lewandowsky

Town simulating death, baroque wreck on the Elbe
  Floating in a brown solution, developed late
    It emerges from snot and water, a magic picture,
      A puzzle, majestic, with which war
        Defused the horrors of this *world of destruction*
          . . . which took nothing away from these bridges,
            Nor from the skyline, the narrow towers.
Chiavari's swan and the balcony of Europe –
  Sandstone softening everything that grows up here.
    The best depressant is the genius loci
      In a place fattened on memories,
        Dry-rot, prettied up as nostalgia
          Narcotic as psychotropic iambs,
            Anglo-Saxon version of *nevermore*.

Dresden, too, is a work of the painter's apprentice
  With his talent manqué in Vienna
    Who imposed his breach of style on half Europe.
      In this case there arose as if spontaneously
        A technique of blanket rubbing-
          Out by foreign bombers, masters of their métier
            One night in February when the snow was black.
True to the plans of his artist friend Speer
  ('The future, Albert!') what will remain of *architectural substance*
    A thousand years on, glorious in decline,
      Will be the beauty of ruins, their *value as ruin*.
        That's Romanticism turned practical in the hands
          Of engineers. *A total work of art*
          Lauds it under rubble even now.

In the future perfect everything will have fallen silent.

Translated from the German by Raymond Hargreaves.

Dresden was bombed by the RAF on the night of 13/14 February 1945. Firestorms were created and the city almost entirely destroyed. Such bombing raids were the policy – known as Area Bombing – of the Head of Bomber Command, Sir Arthur ('Bomber') Harris.

Ilya Ehrenburg

Retribution

She lay beside the bridge. The German troops had reckoned
To cheapen her by this. Instead, her nakedness
Was like an ancient statue's unadorned perfection,
Was like unspotted Nature's loveliness and grace.
We covered her and carried her. The bridge, unsteady,
Appeared to palpitate beneath our precious load.
Our soldiers halted there, in silence stood bare-headed,
Each transformed, acknowledging the debt he owed.
Then Justice headed westward. Winter was a blessing,
With hatred huddled mute, and snows a fiery ridge.
The fate of Germany that murky day was settled
Because of one dead girl, beside a shaky bridge.

Translated from the Russian by Gordon McVay.

James Dickey

The Performance

The last time I saw Donald Armstrong
He was staggering oddly off into the sun,
Going down, of the Philippine Islands.
I let my shovel fall, and put that hand
Above my eyes, and moved some way to one side
That his body might pass through the sun,

And I saw how well he was not
Standing there on his hands,
On his spindle-shanked forearms balanced,
Unbalanced, with his big feet looming and waving
In the great, untrustworthy air
He flew in each night, when it darkened.

Dust fanned in scraped puffs from the earth
Between his arms, and blood turned his face inside out,
To demonstrate its suppleness
Of veins, as he perfected his role.
Next day, he toppled his head off
On an island beach to the south.

And the enemy's two-handed sword
Did not fall from anyone's hands
At that miraculous sight,
As the head rolled over upon
Its wide-eyed face, and fell
Into the inadequate grave

He had dug for himself, under pressure.
Yet I put my flat hand to my eyebrows
Months later, to see him again
In the sun, when I learned how he died,
And imagined him, there,
Come, judged, before his small captors,

Doing all his lean tricks to amaze them –
The back somersault, the kip-up –
And at last, the stand on his hands,
Perfect, with his feet together,
His head down, evenly breathing,
As the sun poured up from the sea

And the headsman broke down
In a blaze of tears, in that light
Of the thin, long human frame

Upside down in its own strange joy,
And, if some other one had not told him,
Would have cut off the feet

Instead of the head,
And if Armstrong had not presently risen
In kingly, round-shouldered attendance,
And then knelt down himself
Beside his hacked, glittering grave, having done
All things in this life that he could.

Ivan Elagin

'The last foot soldier has already fallen . . .'

The last foot soldier has already fallen;
The last pilot chuted into the sea.
On railroad tracks the piled-up ties are smoking;
The wire of fences withers rustily.

This tank that sticks its steel out of the water,
This broken bridge, kneeling upon its knees . . .
They now are silent – these who saw the horror,
And they forget the fight and war's disease.

But Earth's wakening day is full of labor;
The cranes in harbors start to turn once more,
The houses hoist themselves up on their crutches . . .
The cities treat and heal each open sore.

Here they will build, and break again, rebuilding,
While down the road to his home walks someone.
He'll knock – and his mother will come to open –
She'll open the doors to her gray-haired son.

Translated from the Russian by
Vladimir Markov and Merrill Sparks.

Czesław Miłosz

Dedication

You whom I could not save
Listen to me.
Try to understand this simple speech as I would be ashamed of
  another.
I swear, there is in me no wizardry of words.
I speak to you with silence like a cloud or a tree.

What strengthened me, for you was lethal.
You mixed up farewell to an epoch with the beginning of a new one,
Inspiration of hatred with lyrical beauty,
Blind force with accomplished shape.

Here is the valley of shallow Polish rivers. And an immense bridge
Going into white fog. Here is a broken city,
And the wind throws the screams of gulls on your grave
When I am talking with you.

What is poetry which does not save
Nations or people?
A connivance with official lies,
A song of drunkards whose throats will be cut in a moment,
Readings for sophomore girls.
That I wanted good poetry without knowing it,
That I discovered, late, its salutary aim,
In this and only this I find salvation.

They used to pour millet on graves or poppy seeds
To feed the dead who would come disguised as birds.
I put this book here for you, who once lived
So that you should visit us no more.

Warsaw, 1945

Translated from the Polish by the Author.

Jaime Gil de Biedma

In Mournful Praise and Memory of the French Song

C'est une chanson
qui nous resemble.
– Kosma and Prévert, 'Les Feuilles Mortes'

Europe was a mess: it will come back to you.
I have a whole world of faded images
left from that time, the bomb-gutted
buildings so hard on the eyes.
All over Spain people jammed together at the movies
and central heating didn't exist.

It was peace – after all that blood –
that showed up in tatters, unchanged from the way
we Spaniards had known her those five years.
And a whole continent gone to seed,
rotting away with history and the black market,
was all of a sudden more familiar to us.

Sketches of postwar Europe
that seem to be soaked in silent rain,
drab cities where a train pulls in
filthy with refugees: how many things
of our recent history you brought for us, stirring up
hope and also fear throughout our country.

Even the air then became somehow
suspended, as though asking a question,
and in the rundown corner bars
the losers spoke in low voices . . .
We, the youngest ones, hoped as always
for something definite for everyone.

And it was at that point,
in that time of hope mixed with fear

– so hard to believe – that you suddenly came to be,
O sordid rose, stained
and man-made, shy, grimy and beautiful
French song of my youth.

You were the undreamed-of thing that captures
the imagination, for life is like that;
you who sang of disreputable courage,
the uprisings that broke out like flames,
and the fear of sleeping alone,
the deep feelings that end in heartbreak.

How we all loved you from the start!
Yours was a world of nights, of lovers
standing locked in the shadow of a doorstep,
we heard an echo of ourselves in the
muted sound of your melody, and it filled us
with frustrated longing for rebellion.

And even now, alone, late at night,
a drink in my hand, when I think of my life
your melody comes back
like a goodbye: *sans faire du bruit.*
It's as if it were yesterday again – with a difference.
Today there's no hope of revolution.

Splintered postwar Europe
with the moon looming up through broken windows,
Europe before the German miracle,
bitter image of my lifetime!
We lived through that, and are no longer the same,
though now and then we can still be moved by a song.

Translated from the Spanish by Timothy Baland.

'Les Feuilles Mortes' was written by Jacques Prévert in 1943 but not released till after the War. It was translated into English as 'Autumn Leaves'.
sans faire du bruit: without a noise (from the song).

DEATH FUGUE:
THE HOLOCAUST 1933–1945

The dismal lesson that technical progress and an increase in the power and organization of human societies could *amplify* the consequences of primitive hatreds, rather than ameliorate or end them, lies at the heart of ·the century. Mass genocide occurred several times but the industrial scale of Nazi genocide and the intended total destruction of the European Jews was unique. It was an event that changed world consciousness. The critic Theodor Adorno pronounced: 'after Auschwitz, to write a poem is barbaric'. Some poets such as the Pole Tadeusz Różewicz acted this out by writing anti-poetry. Adorno was wrong, but, after the Holocaust, poets would never again be able to write with the blithe assurance of a Keats, 'Beauty is truth, truth beauty'.

W. H. Auden

From *Ten Songs*

I

Say this city has ten million souls,
Some are living in mansions, some are living in holes:
Yet there's no place for us, my dear, yet there's no place for us.

Once we had a country and we thought it fair,
Look in the atlas and you'll find it there:
We cannot go there now, my dear, we cannot go there now.

In the village churchyard there grows an old yew,
Every spring it blossoms anew:
Old passports can't do that, my dear, old passports can't do that.

The consul banged the table and said:
'If you've got no passport you're officially dead':
But we are still alive, my dear, but we are still alive.

Went to a committee; they offered me a chair;
Asked me politely to return next year:
But where shall we go to-day, my dear, but where shall we go
    to-day?

Came to a public meeting; the speaker got up and said:
'If we let them in, they will steal our daily bread';
He was talking of you and me, my dear, he was talking of you and
    me.

Thought I heard the thunder rumbling in the sky;
It was Hitler over Europe, saying: 'They must die';
We were in his mind, my dear, we were in his mind.

Saw a poodle in a jacket fastened with a pin,
Saw a door opened and a cat let in:
But they weren't German Jews, my dear, but they weren't German
    Jews.

Went down to the harbour and stood upon the quay,
Saw the fish swimming as if they were free:
Only ten feet away, my dear, only ten feet away.

Walked through a wood, saw the birds in the trees;
They had no politicians and sang at their ease:
They weren't the human race, my dear, they weren't the human race.

Dreamed I saw a building with a thousand floors,
A thousand windows and a thousand doors;
Not one of them was ours, my dear, not one of them was ours.

Stood on a great plain in the falling snow;
Ten thousand soldiers marched to and fro:
Looking for you and me, my dear, looking for you and me.

March 1939

Carol Rumens

The Hebrew Class

Dark night of the year, the clinging ice
a blue pavement-Dresden,
smoking still, and in lands more deeply frozen,
the savage thaw of tanks:

but in the Hebrew class it is warm as childhood.
It is Cheder and Sunday School.
It is the golden honey of approval,
the slow, grainy tear saved for the bread

of a child newly broken
on the barbs of his Aleph-Bet,
to show him that knowledge is sweet
– and obedience, by the same token.

So we taste power and pleasing,
and the white wand of chalk lisps on the board,
milky as our first words.
We try to shine for our leader.

How almost perfectly human
this little circle of bright heads bowed before
the declaration of grammatical law.
Who could divide our nation

of study? Not even God.
We are blank pages hungry for the pen.
We are ploughed fields, soft and ripe for planting.
What music rises and falls as we softly read.

Oh smiling children, dangerously gifted ones,
take care that you learn to ask why,
for the room you are in is also history.
Consider your sweet compliance

in the light of that day when the book
is torn from your hand;
when, to answer correctly the teacher's command,
you must speak for this ice, this dark.

Karen Gershon

I Was Not There

The morning they set out from home
I was not there to comfort them
the dawn was innocent with snow
in mockery – it is not true
the dawn was neutral was immune
their shadows threaded it too soon
they were relieved that it had come
I was not there to comfort them

One told me that my father spent
a day in prison long ago
he did not tell me that he went
what difference does it make now
when he set out when he came home
I was not there to comfort him
and now I have no means to know
of what I was kept ignorant

Both my parents died in camps
I was not there to comfort them
I was not there they were alone
my mind refuses to conceive
the life the death they must have known
I must atone because I live
I could not have saved them from death
the ground is neutral underneath

Every child must leave its home
time gathers life impartially
I could have spared them nothing since
I was too young – it is not true
they might have lived to succour me
and none shall say in my defence
had I been there to comfort them
it would have made no difference

In 1938–9 the Red Cross organized the evacuation of about 10,000 Jewish children from Germany and Austria and Eastern Europe. The programme became known as the Kindertransport. Their parents were left behind and mostly perished in the Camps.

Boris Slutsky

About the Jews

Jews don't plant wheat
Jews trade in corner-shops
Jews go bald earlier
More Jews are thieves than cops.

Jews are adventurers,
No good at war.
Ivan fights in the trenches.
Abram mans the store.

I've heard it since my childhood.
Soon I'll be decrepit
Still I can't escape it:
The shout of 'Jews, Jews'.

I've never been in trade.
I've never stolen once.
I carry this damned race
Inside like a disease.

The bullets didn't get me.
This must surely prove
None of the Jews were shot.
They all came home alive.

Translated from the Russian
by Carol Rumens.

Czesław Miłosz

A Poor Christian Looks at the Ghetto

Bees build around red liver,
Ants build around black bone.
It has begun: the tearing, the trampling on silks,
It has begun: the breaking of glass, wood, copper, nickel, silver, foam
Of gypsum, iron sheets, violin strings, trumpets, leaves, balls,
    crystals.
Poof! Phosphorescent fire from yellow walls
Engulfs animal and human hair.

Bees build around the honeycomb of lungs,
Ants build around white bone.
Torn is paper, rubber, linen, leather, flax,
Fiber, fabrics, cellulose, snakeskin, wire.
The roof and the wall collapse in flame and heat seizes the
    foundations.
Now there is only the earth, sandy, trodden down,
With one leafless tree.

Slowly, boring a tunnel, a guardian mole makes his way,
With a small red lamp fastened to his forehead.
He touches buried bodies, counts them, pushes on,
He distinguishes human ashes by their luminous vapor,
The ashes of each man by a different part of the spectrum.
Bees build around a red trace.
Ants build around the place left by my body.

I am afraid, so afraid of the guardian mole.
He has swollen eyelids, like a Patriarch
Who has sat much in the light of candles
Reading the great book of the species.

What will I tell him, I, a Jew of the New Testament,
Waiting two thousand years for the second coming of Jesus?
My broken body will deliver me to his sight
And he will count me among the helpers of death:
The uncircumcised.

Warsaw, 1943

Translated from the Polish by the Author.

Paul Celan

Death Fugue

Black milk of daybreak we drink it at sundown
we drink it at noon in the morning we drink it at night
we drink and we drink it
we dig a grave in the breezes there one lies unconfined
A man lives in the house he plays with the serpents he writes
he writes when dusk falls to Germany your golden hair Margarete
he writes it and steps out of doors and the stars are flashing he
    whistles his pack out
he whistles his Jews out in earth has them dig for a grave
he commands us strike up for the dance

Black milk of daybreak we drink you at night
we drink in the morning at noon we drink you at sundown
we drink and we drink you
A man lives in the house he plays with the serpents he writes
he writes when dusk falls to Germany your golden hair Margarete
your ashen hair Shulamith we dig a grave in the breezes there one lies
    unconfined

He calls out jab deeper into the earth you lot you others sing now
    and play
he grabs at the iron in his belt he waves it his eyes are blue
jab deeper you lot with your spades you others play on for the dance

Black milk of daybreak we drink you at night
we drink you at noon in the morning we drink you at sundown
we drink and we drink you
a man lives in the house your golden hair Margarete
your ashen hair Shulamith he plays with the serpents

He calls out more sweetly play death death is a master from
    Germany
he calls out more darkly now stroke your strings then as smoke you
    will rise into air
then a grave you will have in the clouds there one lies unconfined

Black milk of daybreak we drink you at night
we drink you at noon death is a master from Germany
we drink you at sundown and in the morning we drink and we drink
    you
death is a master from Germany his eyes are blue
he strikes you with leaden bullets his aim is true
a man lives in the house your golden hair Margarete
he sets his pack on to us he grants us a grave in the air
he plays with the serpents and daydreams death is a master from
    Germany

your golden hair Margarete
your ashen hair Shulamith

Translated from the German by Michael Hamburger.

Rachel Korn

Arthur Ziegelboim

When was it sealed, when was it decreed,
Your great, your wonderful deathless deed?
Did it come to you like a child in your dream?
Or did a dark messenger bring you the tale,
In your London exile?

Did the messenger come to your door, and knock,
A woman heavily shrouded in black –
'I come from the Warsaw Ghetto, where the earth is on fire!'
Her clothes in rags, a tattered shroud,
And her lips red with blood?

Then you knocked at doors, and found hearts that were closed.
You tried to rouse them, but they wouldn't be roused.
What people were those who refused to listen,
When children were gassed and flung on the mound?
And no one raised a hand!

You carried round stacks of papers to show.
'You may be right,' they said, 'but how can we know?
We want to believe you. But these are not facts.
And we are bound by conventions and acts.'

You brought out a list of the dead.
'How can you prove they are dead?' they said.
So to convince them, you added your name to the list.
You always gave proofs, like a realist.

One May night, when the orchards ripened in the land,
And Spring walked around with stars, hand in hand,
One window in a London street showed a light.
That was you, sitting down alone, to write.

You wrote your last letters, and your last Testament,
For the dawn to read, before the night was spent.
Then a shot rang out, a single shot
To wipe out the shame of which you wrote.
You died to make the world listen to the cry
From the Warsaw Ghetto, across the sky.

Translated from the Yiddish by
Joseph Leftwich.

Primo Levi

Buna

Torn feet and cursed earth,
The long line in the gray morning.
The Buna smokes from a thousand chimneys,
A day like every other day awaits us.
The whistles terrible at dawn:
'You multitudes with dead faces,
On the monotonous horror of the mud
Another day of suffering is born.'
Tired companion, I see you in my heart.
I read your eyes, sad friend.
In your breast you carry cold, hunger, nothing.
You have broken what's left of the courage within you.
Colorless one, you were a strong man,
A woman walked at your side.
Empty companion who no longer has a name,
Forsaken man who can no longer weep,
So poor you no longer grieve,
So tired you no longer fear.
Spent once-strong man.
If we were to meet again

Up there in the world, sweet beneath the sun,
With what kind of face would we confront each other?

28 December 1945

Translated from the Italian by
Ruth Feldman and Brian Swann.

Buna: the synthetic rubber factory attached to Auschwitz-Birkenau concentration camp in Poland, where the inmates worked as slave labourers.

Andrew Motion

Anne Frank Huis

Even now, after twice her lifetime of grief
and anger in the very place, whoever comes
to climb these narrow stairs, discovers how
the bookcase slides aside, then walks through
shadow into sunlit rooms, can never help

but break her secrecy again. Just listening
is a kind of guilt: the Westerkirk repeats
itself outside, as if all time worked round
towards her fear, and made each stroke
die down on guarded streets. Imagine it –

three years of whispering and loneliness
and plotting, day by day, the Allied line
in Europe with a yellow chalk. What hope
she had for ordinary love and interest
survives her here, displayed above the bed

as pictures of her family; some actors;
fashions chosen by Princess Elizabeth.
And those who stoop to see them find
not only patience missing its reward,
but one enduring wish for chances

like my own: to leave as simply
as I do, and walk at ease
up dusty tree-lined avenues, or watch
a silent barge come clear of bridges
settling their reflections in the blue canal.

Anne Frank Huis: the house in Prinsengracht, Amsterdam, where Anne Frank and her family hid from the Nazis in a secret annexe at the top of the house until they were betrayed in 1944. Anne Frank and her sister Margot died in Bergen-Belsen concentration camp.
Westerkirk: the church close to Anne Frank's House.

Dan Pagis

Draft of a Reparations Agreement

All right, gentlemen who cry blue murder as always,
nagging miracle-makers,
quiet!
Everything will be returned to its place,
paragraph after paragraph.
The scream back into the throat.
The gold teeth back to the gums.
The terror.
The smoke back to the tin chimney and further on and inside
back to the hollow of the bones,
and already you will be covered with skin and sinews and you will
     live,
look, you will have your lives back,
sit in the living room, read the evening paper.
Here you are. Nothing is too late.
As to the yellow star:
it will be torn from your chest
immediately
and will emigrate
to the sky.

Translated from the Hebrew by Stephen Mitchell.

THE NEW APOCALYPSE:
THE ATOMIC BOMB 1945

The greatest single increase in human power in history provides the ultimate test of the ability of human beings to restrain their murderous tendencies. The Atom Bomb seems to have been used at Hiroshima and Nagasaki as if it were simply a bigger bomb than usual rather than something unprecedented (indeed, some conventional bombing raids, such as those on Tokyo, killed as many as the Hiroshima bomb). But the blind annihilating capacity of the Bomb is a challenge to poets greater even than the Holocaust. Poetry lies in the details and the Bomb obliterates all detail. Poetry's small 'affirming flame' has to contend with the prospect of ultimate negation.

Carolyn Kizer

Twelve O'Clock

At seventeen I've come to read a poem
At Princeton. Now my young hosts inquire
If I would like to meet Professor Einstein.
But I'm too conscious I have nothing to say
To interest him, the genius fled from Germany just in time.
'Just tell me where I can look at him,' I reply.

Mother had scientific training. I did not;
She loved that line of Meredith's about
The army of unalterable law.
God was made manifest to her in what she saw
As the supreme order of the skies.
We lay in the meadow side by side, long summer nights

As she named the stars with awe.
But I saw nothing that was rank on rank,
Heard nothing of the music of the spheres,

But in the bliss of meadow silences
Lying on insects we had mashed without intent,
Found overhead a beautiful and terrifying mess,

Especially in August, when the meteors whizzed and zoomed,
Echoed, in little, by the fireflies in the grass.
Although, small hypocrite, I was seeming to assent,
I was dead certain that uncertainty
Governed the universe, and everything else,
Including Mother's temperament.

A few years earlier, when I was four,
Mother and Father hushed before the Atwater-Kent
As a small voice making ugly noises through the static
Spoke from the grille, church-window-shaped, to them:
'Listen, darling, and remember always;
It's Doctor Einstein broadcasting from Switzerland.'

I said, 'So what?' This was repeated as a witticism
By my doting parents. I was dumb and mortified.
So when I'm asked if I would like to speak to Einstein
I say I only want to look at him.
'Each day in the library, right at twelve,
Einstein comes out for lunch.' So I am posted.

At the precise stroke of noon the sun sends one clear ray
Into the center aisle: He just appears,
Baggy-kneed, sockless, slippered, with
The famous ravelling grey sweater;
Clutching a jumble of papers in one hand
And in the other his brown sack of sandwiches.

The ray haloes his head! Blake's vision of God,
Unmuscular, serene, except for the electric hair.
In that flicker of a second our smiles meet:
Vast genius and vast ignorance conjoined;
He fixed, I fluid, in a complicit yet
Impersonal interest. He dematerialized and I left, content.

It was December sixth, exactly when,
Just hours before the Japanese attack
The Office of Scientific R & D
Began 'its hugely expanded program of research
Into nuclear weaponry' – racing the Germans who, they feared,
Were far ahead. In fact, they weren't.

Next night, the coach to school; the train, *Express*,
Instead pulls into every hamlet: grim young men
Swarm the platforms, going to enlist.
I see their faces in the sallow light
As the train jolts, then starts up again,
Reaching Penn Station hours after midnight.

At dinner in New York in '44, I hear the name
Of Heisenberg: Someone remarked, 'I wonder where he is,
The most dangerous man alive. I hope we get to him in time.'
Heisenberg. I kept the name. Were the Germans, still,
Or the Russians, yet, a threat? Uncertainty . . .
But I felt a thrill of apprehension: Genius struck again.

It is the stroke of twelve – and I suppose
The ray that haloes Einstein haloes me:
White-blonde hair to my waist, almost six feet tall,
In my best and only suit. Why cavil? – I am beautiful!
We smile – but it has taken all these years to realize
That when I looked at Einstein he saw me.

At last that May when Germany collapsed
The British kidnapped Heisenberg from France
Where he and colleagues sat in a special transit camp
Named 'Dustbin', to save them from a threat they never knew:
A mad American general thought to solve
The post-war nuclear problem by having them all shot.

Some boys in pristine uniforms crowd the car
(West Pointers fleeing from a weekend dance?),
Youth's ambiguities resolved in a single action.

I still see their faces in the yellow light
As the train jolts, then starts up again,
So many destined never to be men.

In Cambridge the Germans visited old friends
Kept apart by war: Austrians, English, Danes,
'In a happy reunion at Farm Hall.'
But then the giant fist struck – in the still
Center of chaos, noise unimaginable, we thought we heard
The awful cry of God.

Hiroshima. Heisenberg at first refused
To believe it, till the evening news confirmed
That their work had led to Hiroshima's 100,000 dead.
'Worst hit of us all,' said Heisenberg, 'was Otto Hahn,'
Who discovered uranium fission. 'Hahn withdrew to his room,
And we feared that he might do himself some harm.'

It is exactly noon, and Doctor Einstein
Is an ancient drawing of the sun.
Simple as a saint emerging from his cell
Dazed by his own light. I think of Giotto, Chaucer,
All good and moral medieval men
In – yet removed from – their historic time.

The week before we heard of Heisenberg
My parents and I are chatting on the train
From Washington. A grey-haired handsome man
Listens with open interest, then inquires
If he might join us. We were such a fascinating family!
'Oh yes,' we chorus, 'sit with us!'

Penn Station near at hand, we asked his name.
E. O. Lawrence, he replied, and produced his card.
I'd never heard of him, but on an impulse asked,
'What is all this about the harnessing
Of the sun's rays? Should we be frightened?'
He smiled. 'My dear, there's nothing in it.'

So, reassured, we said goodbyes,
And spoke of him in coming years, that lovely man.
Of course we found out who he was and what he did,
At least as much as we could comprehend.
Now I am living in the Berkeley hills,
In walking distance of the Lawrence lab.

Here where Doctor Lawrence built the cyclotron,
It's noon: the anniversary of Hiroshima:
Everywhere, all over Japan
And Germany, people are lighting candles.
It's dark in Germany and Japan, on different days,
But here in Berkeley it is twelve o'clock.

I stand in the center of the library
And he appears. Are we witnesses or actors?
The old man and the girl, smiling at one another,
He fixed by fame, she fluid, still without identity.
An instant which changes nothing,
And everything, forever, everything is changed.

Heisenberg: Werner Heisenberg was one of the discoverers of quantum mechanics in 1925. He was Germany's leading physicist during the War and as such was in charge of Germany's nuclear programme.
cyclotron: a machine that accelerates ions inside a ring of electromagnets to achieve high-speed nuclear collisions. It was invented by the American physicist Ernest O. Lawrence in 1931.

William Stafford

At the Bomb Testing Site

At noon in the desert a panting lizard
waited for history, its elbows tense,
watching the curve of a particular road
as if something might happen.

It was looking at something farther off
than people could see, an important scene
acted in stone for little selves
at the flute end of consequences.

There was just a continent without much on it
under a sky that never cared less.
Ready for a change, the elbows waited.
The hands gripped hard on the desert.

Millen Brand

August 6, 1945

Fred Braun has just leaned out on a low windowsill
that needs painting. There are cracks in it,
but so far they have let no rain through.
They can wait a little longer.
This moment is his to enjoy,
looking at his apple orchard and two small plum trees
and under them a red napkin of bee balm.
It is beautiful and peaceful. His wife
is troweling a flower bed
along the house wall. He hears
the thud of an apple falling, part
of the nice lethargy of the day. And today
across the world
behind a plane, the Enola Gay, there floats in the air, slowly
    descending,
a hardly visible thin tube
with a small fuse at one end
that will fire one of two parts at the other end
and explode this almost unnoticeable filament
with a light brighter than the sun. Below,
in the wooden city of Hiroshima
can it not be that a man

has just rolled back one of his living-room shutters
and is looking out on his garden, thinking,
The morning glories on their bamboo sticks,
the blue sky,
how beautiful everything is! Let me enjoy it.
I should be painting shutters,
but they can wait.
The rain does not yet come through.

Tōge Sankichi

The Shadow

Cheap movie theaters, saloons, fly-by-night markets,
burned, rebuilt, standing, crumbling, spreading like the itch –
the new Hiroshima,
head shiny with hair oil,
barefaced in its resurgence;
already visible all over the place,
in growing numbers, billboards in English;
one of these: 'Historic A-Bomb Site.'

Enclosed by a painted fence
on a corner of the bank steps,
stained onto the grain of the dark red stone:
a quiet pattern.

That morning
a flash tens of thousands of degrees hot
burned it all of a sudden onto the thick slab of granite:
someone's trunk.

Burned onto the step, cracked and watery red,
the mark of the blood that flowed as intestines melted to mush:
a shadow.

Ah! If you are from Hiroshima
and on that morning,
amid indescribable flash and heat and smoke,
were buffeted in the whirlpool of the glare of the flames, the shadow
    of the cloud,
crawled about dragging skin that was peeling off,
so transformed that even your wife and children
would not have known you,
this shadow
is etched in tragic memory
and will never fade.

Right beside the street where the people of the city come and go,
well-meaning but utterly indifferent,
assaulted by the sun, attacked by the rain, covered over by dust,
growing fainter year by year: this shadow.

The bank with the 'Historic Site' sign at the foot of its steps
dumped out into the street pieces of stone and glass, burned gritty,
completed a major reconstruction,
and set the whole enormous building sparkling in the evening sun.
In the vacant lot diagonally across,
drawing a crowd: a quack in the garb of a mountain ascetic.

Indifferent, the authorities say: 'If we don't protect it with glass or
    something,
it will fade away,' but do nothing.
Today, too,
foreign sailors amble up in their white leggings,
come to a stop with a click of their heels,
and, each having taken a snapshot, go off;
the shoeshine boy who followed them here
peers over the fence, wonders why all the fuss,
and goes on his way.

Translated from the Japanese by Richard H. Minear.

D. J. Enright

Apocalypse

'After the New Apocalypse, very few members were still in possession of their instruments. Hardly a musician could call a decent suit his own. Yet, by the early summer of 1945, strains of sweet music floated on the air again. While the town still reeked of smoke, charred buildings and the stench of corpses, the Philharmonic Orchestra bestowed the everlasting and imperishable joy which music never fails to give.'

> – from *The Muses on the Banks of the Spree*,
> a Berlin tourist brochure

It soothes the savage doubts.
One Bach outweighs ten Belsens. If 200,000 people
Were remaindered at Hiroshima, the sales of So-and-So's
New novel reached a higher figure in as short a time.
So, imperishable paintings reappeared:
Texts were reprinted:
Public buildings reconstructed:
Human beings reproduced.

After the Newer Apocalypse, very few members
Were still in possession of their instruments
(Very few were still in possession of their members),
And their suits were chiefly indecent.
Yet, while the town still reeked of smoke etc.,
The Philharmonic Trio bestowed, etc.

A civilization vindicated,
A race with three legs still to stand on!
True, the violin was shortly silenced by leukaemia,
And the pianoforte crumbled softly into dust.
But the flute was left. And one is enough.
All, in a sense, goes on. All is in order.

And the ten-tongued mammoth larks,
The forty-foot crickets and the elephantine frogs
Decided that the little chap was harmless,
At least he made no noise, on the banks of whatever river it used to
    be.

One day, a reed-warbler stepped on him by accident.
However, all, in a sense, goes on. Still the everlasting and
    imperishable joy
Which music never fails to give is being given.

Edwin Muir

The Horses

Barely a twelvemonth after
The seven days war that put the world to sleep,
Late in the evening the strange horses came.
By then we had made our covenant with silence,
But in the first few days it was so still
We listened to our breathing and were afraid.
On the second day
The radios failed; we turned the knobs; no answer.
On the third day a warship passed us, heading north,
Dead bodies piled on the deck. On the sixth day
A plane plunged over us into the sea. Thereafter
Nothing. The radios dumb;
And still they stand in corners of our kitchens,
And stand, perhaps, turned on, in a million rooms
All over the world. But now if they should speak,
If on a sudden they should speak again,
If on the stroke of noon a voice should speak,
We would not listen, we would not let it bring
That old bad world that swallowed its children quick
At one great gulp. We would not have it again.

Sometimes we think of the nations lying asleep,
Curled blindly in impenetrable sorrow,
And then the thought confounds us with its strangeness.
The tractors lie about our fields; at evening
They look like dank sea-monsters couched and waiting.
We leave them where they are and let them rust:
'They'll moulder away and be like other loam'.
We make our oxen drag our rusty ploughs,
Long laid aside. We have gone back
Far past our fathers' land.
                                                And then, that evening
Late in the summer the strange horses came.
We heard a distant tapping on the road,
A deepening drumming; it stopped, went on again
And at the corner changed to hollow thunder.
We saw the heads
Like a wild wave charging and were afraid.
We had sold our horses in our fathers' time
To buy new tractors. Now they were strange to us
As fabulous steeds set on an ancient shield
Or illustrations in a book of knights.
We did not dare go near them. Yet they waited,
Stubborn and shy, as if they had been sent
By an old command to find our whereabouts
And that long-lost archaic companionship.
In the first moment we had never a thought
That they were creatures to be owned and used.
Among them were some half-a-dozen colts
Dropped in some wilderness of the broken world,
Yet new as if they had come from their own Eden.
Since then they have pulled our ploughs and borne our loads,
But that free servitude still can pierce our hearts.
Our life is changed; their coming our beginning.

FROM NEUTRAL TONE TO ANGRY:
THE FIFTIES

The Fifties was a transitional period, with the first half making good the destruction of the War and generally attempting to return to pre-war modes. Post 1956, rising prosperity, the arrival of television, rock 'n' roll, and jet air travel, brought a new era of consumerism and rapid artistic development. The poetry of the early period tended towards a clipped restraint, in Britain going under the label, The Movement. But from 1955 on, some of the potential of the Modernism at the beginning of the century began to be realized by the Beat poets. High culture was infiltrated by popular culture and a new note of insouciance and vivacity, so long suppressed by world events, began to be heard.

Peter Bland

Lament for a Lost Generation

Between V-J Day and 1951
we wore our first grey longs.
Drab, insular, short of vitamin C,
much given to fags and the fumbled grope

we became – like prefabs
or the last steam train –
something slightly embarrassing
that goes on and on: fodder for talks like

The Ration-Book Age or
The Wartime Growth of the Working Mum.
We were few; conceived in the slump;
brought up in shelters and under the stairs;

eleven-plus boys; post-war conscripts
who lowered the flag on better days.
What we lacked was a style!
We were make-do-and-menders,

utility-grey men, the last of a line.
You can tell us a mile off, even now;
there's a touch of austerity
under the eyes; a hint of carbolic

in our after-shave; a lasting doubt
about the next good time.

Sean O'Brien

Interior

The fields and 'the wooded escarpments'
Inherit the shades of old furniture –
The dun and could-be-blood and lacks-conviction green
Of sofas jammed up rear passageways
In under-advertised hotels whose afterlife is spent
Not being read about in waiting-rooms.
The date is Nineteen Fifty-X. The residents
Have died but not been told. They jostle bonily
To hog the yellow *Telegraph* through days
In steep decline from gin-and-it
To after-dinner coma. Why detain them further?
As if there were choices, as if on the nod
You could crate them all up in the mind of God.
Deep in the retarded shires whose very
Names have been abolished, they persist,
Clandestinely, immortally defunct.
Now if we took that other turning
We should find them, arrayed in rank order

Across the parterre, stripped now
Of rivers and jungles, all rheumily glaring
As though the prow of our canoe displayed
A threatening pronouncement
They could very nearly read.
Though we go by a different route
We can smell the old country – a pillow
On a yellow face, the endless nagging corridors
Where damp and dust and gas contend.
It lingers in the senile tearooms
And in the crusty carpets of emporia
Where what's for sale is sentimental horror,
The used-to-be, the bad idea.
We hear the silence in the churches wait
For regiments disbanded on the Somme
To swim back through the mud and give
Due thanks, the ploughmen and the gentry
With their proper limbs restored.
Two Ridings later we come to the sea.
On this neglected coast it rolls
Indifferently ashore, a grey-white swell
Unburdening itself, then sliding back
Across the rotted boulder-clay
And muttering *history, history*, as if
That should explain these haunted roads,
Ancestral nowheres, *proper drains and class distinction.*

proper drains and class distinction: an allusion to Betjeman's poem 'In Westminster Abbey'. 'Think of what our Nation stands for,/. . . class distinction,/Democracy and proper drains.'

Adrian Mitchell

Remember Suez?

England, unlike junior nations,
Wears officers' long combinations.
So no embarrassment was felt
By the Church, the Government or the Crown.
But I saw the Thames like a grubby old belt
And England's trousers falling down.

When the Egyptian leader Gamal Abdul Nasser nationalized the Suez Canal in 1956, Britain, France and Israel undertook a joint operation to wrest it from Egyptian control. The operation was halted after threats from both Russia and America. The episode marked the end of British independent action in the world.

Peter Porter

John Marston Advises Anger

All the boys are howling to take the girls to bed.
Our betters say it's a seedy world. The critics say
Think of them as an Elizabethan Chelsea set.
Then they've never listened to our lot – no talk
Could be less like – but the bodies are the same:
Those jeans and bums and sweaters of the King's Road
Would fit Marston's stage. What's in a name,
If Cheapside and the Marshalsea mean Eng. Lit.
And the Fantasie, Sa Tortuga, Grisbi, Bongi-Bo
Mean life? A cliché? What hurts dies on paper,
Fades to classic pain. Love goes as the MG goes.
The colonel's daughter in black stockings, hair
Like sash cords, face iced white, studies art,
Goes home once a month. She won't marry the men
She sleeps with, she'll revert to type – it's part
Of the side-show: Mummy and Daddy in the wings,
The bongos fading on the road to Haslemere
Where the inheritors are inheriting still.

Marston's Malheureux found his whore too dear;
Today some Jazz Club girl on the social make
Would put him through his paces, the aphrodisiac cruel.
His friends would be the smoothies of our Elizabethan age –
The Rally Men, Grantchester Breakfast Men, Public School
Personal Assistants and the fragrant PROs,
Cavalry-twilled tame publishers praising Logue,
Classics Honours Men promoting Jazzetry,
Market Researchers married into Vogue.
It's a Condé Nast world and so Marston's was.
His had a real gibbet – our death's out of sight.
The same thin richness of these worlds remains –
The flesh-packed jeans, the car-stung appetite
Volley on his stage, the cage of discontent.

John Updike

The Newlyweds

After a one-day honeymoon, the Fishers rushed off to a soft drink
bottlers' convention, then on to a ball game, a TV rehearsal and
a movie preview.   – *Life*

'We're married,' said Eddie.
Said Debbie, 'Incredi-

ble! When is our honey-
moon?' 'Over and done,' he

replied. 'Feeling logy?
Drink Coke.' 'Look at Yogi

go!' Debbie cried. 'Groovy!'
'Rehearsal?' 'The movie.'

'Some weddie,' said Debbie.
Said Eddie, 'Yeah, mebbe.'

the Fishers: film stars Debbie Reynolds and Eddie Fisher.

Thom Gunn

Elvis Presley

Two minutes long it pitches through some bar:
Unreeling from a corner box, the sigh
Of this one, in his gangling finery
And crawling sideburns, wielding a guitar.

The limitations where he found success
Are ground on which he, panting, stretches out
In turn, promiscuously, by every note.
Our idiosyncrasy and our likeness.

We keep ourselves in touch with a mere dime:
Distorting hackneyed words in hackneyed songs
He turns revolt into a style, prolongs
The impulse to a habit of the time.

Whether he poses or is real, no cat
Bothers to say: the pose held is a stance,
Which, generation of the very chance
It wars on, may be posture for combat.

Lawrence Ferlinghetti

Sometime during eternity . . .

Sometime during eternity
                                        some guys show up
and one of them
                    who shows up real late
                                        is a kind of carpenter
        from some square-type place
                        like Galilee

and he starts wailing
          and claiming he is hip
   to who made heaven
          and earth
               and that the cat
    who really laid it on us
          is his Dad

And moreover
   he adds
      It's all writ down
          on some scroll-type parchments
   which some henchmen
        leave lying around the Dead Sea somewheres
   a long time ago
        and which you won't even find
for a coupla thousand years or so
            or at least for
nineteen hundred and fortyseven
         of them
     to be exact
        and even then
nobody really believes them
        or me
          for that matter

You're hot
    they tell him

And they cool him

They stretch him on the Tree to cool

And everybody after that
          is always making models
   of this Tree
      with Him hung up
and always crooning His name
        and calling Him to come down

and sit in
              on their combo
     as if he is *the* king cat
                      who's got to blow
     or they can't quite make it

     Only he don't come down
                      from His Tree

Him just hang there
              on His Tree
                      looking real Petered out
              and real cool
                      and also
     according to a roundup
                      of late world news
     from the usual unreliable sources
                      real dead

Allen Ginsberg

America

America I've given you all and now I'm nothing.
America two dollars and twentyseven cents January 17, 1956.
I can't stand my own mind.
America when will we end the human war?
Go fuck yourself with your atom bomb.
I don't feel good don't bother me.
I won't write my poem till I'm in my right mind.
America when will you be angelic?
When will you take off your clothes?
When will you look at yourself through the grave?
When will you be worthy of your million Trotskyites?
America why are your libraries full of tears?
America when will you send your eggs to India?

I'm sick of your insane demands.
When can I go into the supermarket and buy what I need with my
    good looks?
America after all it is you and I who are perfect not the next world.
Your machinery is too much for me.
You made me want to be a saint.
There must be some other way to settle this argument.
Burroughs is in Tangiers I don't think he'll come back it's sinister.
Are you being sinister or is this some form of practical joke?
I'm trying to come to the point.
I refuse to give up my obsession.
America stop pushing I know what I'm doing.
America the plum blossoms are falling.
I haven't read the newspapers for months, everyday somebody goes
    on trial for murder.
America I feel sentimental about the Wobblies.
America I used to be a communist when I was a kid I'm not sorry.
I smoke marijuana every chance I get.
I sit in my house for days on end and stare at the roses in the closet.
When I go to Chinatown I get drunk and never get laid.
My mind is made up there's going to be trouble.
You should have seen me reading Marx.
My psychoanalyst thinks I'm perfectly right.
I won't say the Lord's Prayer.
I have mystical visions and cosmic vibrations.
America I still haven't told you what you did to Uncle Max after he
    came over from Russia.

I'm addressing you.
Are you going to let your emotional life be run by Time Magazine?
I'm obsessed by Time Magazine.
I read it every week.
Its cover stares at me every time I slink past the corner candystore.
I read it in the basement of the Berkeley Public Library.
It's always telling me about responsibility. Businessmen are serious.
    Movie producers are serious. Everybody's serious but me.
It occurs to me that I am America.
I am talking to myself again.

Asia is rising against me.

I haven't got a chinaman's chance.

I'd better consider my national resources.

My national resources consist of two joints of marijuana millions of genitals an unpublishable private literature that jet-planes 1400 miles an hour and twentyfive-thousand mental institutions.

I say nothing about my prisons nor the millions of underprivileged who live in my flowerpots under the light of five hundred suns.

I have abolished the whorehouses of France, Tangiers is the next to go.

My ambition is to be President despite the fact that I'm a Catholic.

America how can I write a holy litany in your silly mood?

I will continue like Henry Ford my strophes are as individual as his automobiles more so they're all different sexes.

America I will sell you strophes $2500 apiece $500 down on your old strophe

America free Tom Mooney

America save the Spanish Loyalists

America Sacco & Vanzetti must not die

America I am the Scottsboro boys.

America when I was seven momma took me to Communist Cell meetings they sold us garbanzos a handful per ticket a ticket costs a nickel and the speeches were free everybody was angelic and sentimental about the workers it was all so sincere you have no idea what a good thing the party was in 1935 Scott Nearing was a grand old man a real mensch Mother Bloor the Silk-strikers' Ewig-Weibliche made me cry I once saw the Yiddish orator Israel Amter plain. Everybody must have been a spy.

America you don't really want to go to war.

America it's them bad Russians.

Them Russians them Russians and them Chinamen. And them Russians.

The Russia wants to eat us alive. The Russia's power mad. She wants to take our cars from out our garages.

Her wants to grab Chicago. Her needs a Red *Reader's Digest*. Her wants our auto plants in Siberia. Him big bureaucracy running our fillingstations.

That no good. Ugh. Him make Indians learn read. Him need big

black niggers. Hah. Her make us all work sixteen hours a day.
    Help.
America this is quite serious.
America this is the impression I get from looking in the television set.
America is this correct?
I'd better get right down to the job.
It's true I don't want to join the Army or turn lathes in precision
    parts factories, I'm nearsighted and psychopathic anyway.
America I'm putting my queer shoulder to the wheel.

Wobblies: the Industrial Workers of the World, a revolutionary syndicalist trade union founded in Chicago in 1905. The origin of the name is disputed.
Tom Mooney: socialist agitator and union activist, imprisoned for a bomb outrage in San Francisco which killed ten people in 1916. He was pardoned by the Governor of California in 1939.
Sacco & Vanzetti: Italian immigrants to the USA executed in 1927 for allegedly murdering a postmaster. They were widely believed to have been convicted because they were anarchists and immigrants, the USA being in one of its periodic Red Scares when they were first arrested in 1920.
the Scottsboro boys: a *cause célèbre* of Civil Rights in the Thirties. Nine black youths were accused of raping two white girls on a freight train. After many trials four were released in 1937, the last not till 1950.
Scott Nearing: a radical agitator tried and acquited in 1919 for his anti-war pamphlet *The Great Madness* (1917).

Yevgeny Yevtushenko

The Angries

Great twentieth century: sputnik century:
what an angst is in you, what wide perplexity!
You are a good century and a century of the pit,
cannibal-century to the ideas you beget,
century of the angry young men's target.

Young men get very angry indeed.
Their eyes flash scorn for this period.
They scorn government and they scorn party,
they scorn the church and provisions of philosophy,
they scorn women – and sleep with them,

they scorn the world, its banks and tills,
they scorn, with a painful insight, the ills
that their own miserable scorn leaves them.
The twentieth century is only their stepfather.
The depth of their hate for it, O the depth of it!
The virulently seething teenage fervour
beats dark and thick along the Hudson River;
by Tiber, Seine, and Thames the same teenagers
gather like black dogs come from the same manger.
The sharp, the cross, the sulky, and the weird –
no century has seen their like before.
I see what they don't want – that's clear;
but how to grasp what they are standing for?
It can't – or can it – be a young man's credo
to scold solid and be scolded, nothing more?
Well then, here I am, in the city of Moscow
speaking to them, plainly, as man to man:
what I say is, if I am angry I am
angry only within the love I've fed on,
the love of my own land; loud, but not loud
to hail a poor unbelief. And I am glad
that I can put my trust in the truth of Lenin,
in hammer and ploughshare true to human hand.
If I get angry about this or that –
the anger is within a dignity
of knowing I address friends, knowing I fight
in a front line for a fighter's integrity.
What then is wrong with you? Is it truth you frown for?
'Mass psychosis,' the medicos say with a sigh.
All over Europe the boys slouch and glower.
The boys slouch and glower through the USA.

Twentieth century: great sputnik century:
tear them out of their thunderous mixed-up scenery!
Give them – no, not a cosy lassitude,
but give them faith in what is right, what is good.
A child is not an enemy. Twentieth century, you
must help them, do you hear? – you help them through!

Translated from the Russian by Edwin Morgan.

Allen Ginsberg

From *Howl*

II

What sphinx of cement and aluminum bashed open their skulls and
    ate up their brains and imagination?
Moloch! Solitude! Filth! Ugliness! Ashcans and unobtainable dollars!
    Children screaming under the stairways! Boys sobbing in
    armies! Old men weeping in the parks!
Moloch! Moloch! Nightmare of Moloch! Moloch the loveless!
    Mental Moloch! Moloch the heavy judger of men!
Moloch the incomprehensible prison! Moloch the crossbone soulless
    jailhouse and Congress of sorrows! Moloch whose buildings
    are judgment! Moloch the vast stone of war! Moloch the
    stunned governments!
Moloch whose mind is pure machinery! Moloch whose blood is
    running money! Moloch whose fingers are ten armies!
    Moloch whose breast is a cannibal dynamo! Moloch whose
    ear is a smoking tomb!
Moloch whose eyes are a thousand blind windows! Moloch whose
    skyscrapers stand in the long streets like endless Jehovahs!
    Moloch whose factories dream and croak in the fog! Moloch
    whose smokestacks and antennae crown the cities!
Moloch whose love is endless oil and stone! Moloch whose soul is
    electricity and banks! Moloch whose poverty is the specter
    of genius! Moloch whose fate is a cloud of sexless hydrogen!
    Moloch whose name is the Mind!
Moloch in whom I sit lonely! Moloch in whom I dream Angels!
    Crazy in Moloch! Cocksucker in Moloch! Lacklove and
    manless in Moloch!
Moloch who entered my soul early! Moloch in whom I am a
    consciousness without a body! Moloch who frightened me
    out of my natural ecstasy! Moloch whom I abandon! Wake
    up in Moloch! Light streaming out of the sky!

Moloch! Moloch! Robot apartments! invisible suburbs! skeleton
     treasuries! blind capitals! demonic industries! spectral
     nations! invincible madhouses! granite cocks! monstrous
     bombs!
They broke their backs lifting Moloch to Heaven! Pavements, trees,
     radios, tons! lifting the city to Heaven which exists and is
     everywhere about us!
Visions! omens! hallucinations! miracles! ecstasies! gone down the
     American river!
Dreams! adorations! illuminations! religions! the whole boatload of
     sensitive bullshit!
Breakthroughs! over the river! flips and crucifixions! gone down the
     flood! Highs! Epiphanies! Despairs! Ten years' animal
     screams and suicides! Minds! New loves! Mad generation!
     down on the rocks of Time!
Real holy laughter in the river! They saw it all! the wild eyes! the
     holy yells! They bade farewell! They jumped off the roof! to
     solitude! waving! carrying flowers! Down to the river! into
     the street!

Moloch: Old Testament deity to whom parents sacrificed their children.

BEHIND THE CURTAIN: COMMUNISM 1945–1989

Eastern European countries pursued enforced separate development after World War II as satellites of Soviet Russia. These societies were more uniform than Western societies, many forms of expression being banned or limited. Revolts in Hungary in 1956 and Czechoslovakia in 1968 were suppressed. This era produced some remarkable poetry which became widely known in English translation. Whether writing directly from a position of exile, or from the inside in veiled allegory, the background of tyranny and uniformity gave the poets' utterances a significance they possessed nowhere else. The technique of allegory, as a means of evading the censor, flourished as never before. In Czesław Miłosz, Miroslav Holub and Zbigniew Herbert the period produced some of the greatest poets of the century.

Zbigniew Herbert

Damastes (Also Known As Procrustes) Speaks

My movable empire between Athens and Megara
I ruled alone over forests ravines precipices
without the advice of old men foolish insignia with a simple club
dressed only in the shadow of a wolf
and terror caused by the sound of the word Damastes

I lacked subjects that is I had them briefly
they didn't live as long as dawn however it is slander
to say I was a bandit as the falsifiers of history claim

in reality I was a scholar and social reformer
my real passion was anthropometry

I invented a bed with the measurements of a perfect man
I compared the travellers I caught with this bed
it was hard to avoid – I admit – stretching limbs cutting legs
the patients died but the more there were who perished
the more I was certain my research was right
the goal was noble progress demands victims

I longed to abolish the difference between the high and the low
I wanted to give a single form to disgustingly varied humanity
I never stopped in my efforts to make people equal

my life was taken by Theseus the murderer of the innocent Minotaur
the one who went through the labyrinth with a woman's ball of yarn
an impostor full of tricks without principles or a vision of the future

I have the well-grounded hope others will continue my labour
and bring the task so boldly begun to its end

Translated from the Polish by
John Carpenter and Bogdana Carpenter.

Procrustes: an Ancient Greek brigand notorious for his bed to which victims had to fit,
either by being stretched or by having their limbs chopped off.

Yuz Aleshkovsky

Comrade Stalin

A Song of Political Prisoners from Stalin's Camps

Comrade Stalin, you are a great scholar
Well known in the ways of tongues,
While I am a simple Soviet prisoner
And my comrade is the gray Briansk wolf.
While I am a simple Soviet prisoner
And my comrade is the gray Briansk wolf.

Why am I doing time, I honestly don't know,
But the prosecutors are usually right,
And so I am a prisoner in Turuchan
Where you too were exiled in tsarist times.
And so I am a prisoner in Turuchan
Where you too were exiled in tsarist times . . .

And so in Turuchan I serve time
Where the guards are strict and cruel,
I, of course, can understand all of this
As the intensified class struggle rule.
I, of course, can understand all of this
As the intensified class struggle rule.

We immediately confessed to others' sins,
In a convoy we went to meet that fate.
We trusted you so, Comrade Stalin,
Perhaps even more than we trusted ourselves.
We trusted you so, Comrade Stalin,
Perhaps even more than we trusted ourselves.

There were gnats, snow, and rain,
In the taiga day in and day out.
Here from a spark you incited a blaze,
Thanks a bunch, I am warm by the fire.
Here from a spark you incited a blaze,
Thanks a bunch, I am warm by the fire.

Comrade Stalin, you don't sleep nights
Listening for the slightest rustle of rain,
While we sleep on bunks heaped in piles
And the insomnia of our leaders seems strange.
While we sleep on bunks heaped in piles
And the insomnia of our leaders seems strange.

Translated from the Russian by Sarah W. Bliumis.

Well known in the ways of tongues: literally 'well known in the field of linguistics'. In 1950 an article by Stalin in *Pravda* critically devastated the dubious linguistic theories of the Soviet philologist Nikolai Marr. Major Soviet professors of linguistics immediately associated themselves with Stalin's critique and hailed him as a great scholar of linguistics. A second mocking implication of the line is that Stalin was a master at obtaining confessions.

taiga: coniferous forest typical of Siberia.

spark: *Iskra* (*The Spark*) was the illegal Marxist Social-Democratic party newspaper published in the West (beginning in 1900) and widely distributed in tsarist Russia. It was the spark that was to incite the blaze of Revolution. – Translator's note.

Tom Paulin

Where Art is a Midwife

In the third decade of March,
A Tuesday in the town of Z –

The censors are on day-release.
They must learn about literature.

There are things called ironies,
Also symbols, which carry meaning.

The types of ambiguity
Are as numerous as the enemies

Of the state. Formal and bourgeois,
Sonnets sing of the old order,

Its lost gardens where white ladies
Are served wine in the subtle shade.

This poem about a bear
Is not a poem about a bear.

It might be termed a satire
On a loyal friend. Do I need

To spell it out? Is it possible
That none of you can understand?

Marin Sorescu

The Glass Wall

To make the one world in which we live
more comfortable,
with a glass wall we have divided it
into two zones.

Every advance, of course,
has its drawbacks.
If, for instance, one feels
like having a good bath,
one now has to cross over
into the other world
to get the soap.

All the same,
each one of us can boast
of a two-world apartment
(furnished in different styles,
it goes without saying)
with a communal sun, for the moment,
and separate access
to earth.

> *Translated from the Romanian by*
> *Michael Hamburger.*

György Petri

On the 24th Anniversary of the Little October Revolution

Uncle Imre, Uncle Pista and Co
corrected the world's course just a tiny bit.
They were hanged or locked up.

(Uncles Mátyás and Ernö buggered off
to Moscow. And the rest of them shall be nameless.)
Then came the land of Prester John:
'We'll never die!'
The total number of corpses –
and that includes both residents and intruders –
is estimated at somewhere between three thousand
and thirty thousand.
The figure is hard to verify so long
after the event. Many vanished.
Many were made to vanish.
Some people are put on the rack
of forgetlessness.
Some people were put on the rack.
Reality always reckons without herself.
Would she get her sums wrong? Settle her accounts?
A unified and indivisible entity
she failed her eleven-plus
has never properly learnt to count.
I say just two numbers:
56
68.
You can add them, subtract them,
divide or multiply.
Your innumerable doctrines, baseness is their basis,
have failed, are bankrupt.

Translated from the Hungarian by
Clive Wilmer and George Gömöri.

Imre: Imre Nagy was a reformist Prime Minister of Hungary, 1953–5, who came back
to power in October 1956. In November 1956 his regime was brutally suppressed by
Soviet Russia with many thousands killed, including Nagy, who was executed.
Pista: István Bibó, one of the key reformers with Nagy.
Mátyás: Mátyás Rákosi, Stalinist leader of Hungary from 1947 to 1956.
Ernö: Ernö Gerö, Hungarian Communist Party chief who called for Russia to intervene
in the Hungarian crisis.

Dmitry Bobyshev

Upon the Launching of a Sputnik

What a rotten life this is!
And the whole damn world's like that.
The five o'clock robots mob the newsstands;
in the post office the workers' hands are calloused,
sorting out letters;
and we municipal garbage collectors
puke in the backyards.
There's no free food yet,
and no free clothes.

O universal emptiness
and empty universes,
we are zooming another Sputnik
into another planet,
probably to a hard landing.
So that's man!
For a short hitch he eats and makes love,
but even the young kids
launch from their mother's breast
with a cosmological finger.

Hey, tell me, where the hell
should a garbage collector live?
Should I double my back to gather calluses?
And where are my food and clothes?
Don't I pick up the filth of the whole bloody town,
eh? So that's man?
Free, once in a while, for an hour
in all his sickly fears?

O you magnificent failures,
poking around in your heavy uniforms
in dark and smelly hallways,

why don't you ever repair the goddamn place
and help clean the kitchens
and their filthy cans?

At least I'm a true collector of garbage,
and I, too, have a rage to live.

Translated from the Russian by
Joseph Langland, Tomas Axzel and Laszlo Tikos.

Sputnik: the first earth-orbital satellite, Sputnik I, was launched on 4 October 1957,
apparently giving Russia a technological lead over the USA.

Bogdan Czaykowski

Threnos

I

Fingers grasp the flame
and before he's set alight
he hesitates, alone,
then saves the flame from thought,
it catches and in the square
he blazes like a torch.

II

You wish to know how a man burns?
A poem will not explain.
Put your hands in the flames
hold them for the blink
of a lash-singed eyelid.

Put your hands in the fire
if you're a man.

III

Then you'll understand
that before he fetched the fuel-can
he clasped his head in his hands
and thus he burned, alone
like a man.

IV

Then you'll understand that Jan
before he came to the square
tested the match
soaked his clothes
shook the proffered hands
quietened someone's cry
and tightly wrapped in his coat
entered the dark not blinking an eye.

V

Put your hands in the flame
if you're a man.

19 January 1969

*Translated from the Polish by
Adam Czerniawski.*

Jan: Jan Palách, a Czech student who, on 16 January 1969, five months after the Soviet invasion of Czechoslovakia that put an end to the Prague Spring, set fire to himself in Wenceslas Square, Prague, as a 'protest against the current political situation'. He died three days later.

Ernest Bryll

In a Fever

I dreamed that in a light-industry mill
Where tired women choke and cough up dust
One worn-out woman failed her masters' trust.
She couldn't stick it out to closing time –

It's rough but then the pay's not bad, and still
When the night shift's done you can stand in line,
Then get the kids to school with what they need –
Instead she broke down, and began to bleed.
Her white twill shirt turned red. Her piercing scream
Burst the factory gates, and in my dream
A horde of women poured into the street.

It overflowed, and no one dared to meet
Them face to face, though Warsaw phone calls warned
That this must stop . . .
      The local party hacks
Sank clutching their receivers, drowned
In human seas. One of them yelled: 'Hand out some meat,
And then remind these gals to watch their step,
Families can get hurt, better turn back
Now.' Others whispered to the guards who kept
Watch over Them, the nation's true elite:
'Don't sweat, boys. It's just women. Running scared.
They're old and ugly, too. We couldn't care
Less . . .'
   It was true. Their hair was gray with grime,
Their faces worn and wrinkled, and their weary
Bodies had paid the price of working overtime.

When they finally came in range, then you could see
That those who yelled at you, yelled toothlessly . . .

No, better wake up. Now. Before a terse
Voice gives the order no one can reverse.

6 April 1986

Translated from the Polish by
Stanisław Barańczak and Clare Cavanagh.

Stanisław Barańczak

These Men, So Powerful

These men, so powerful, always shown
a little from below by crouching cameramen, lifting
a heavy foot to crush me, no, to
mount the aircraft steps, lifting their hands
at me, no, in order to greet crowds
obediently waving flags, those signing
my death warrant, no, only a trade
agreement dried immediately with an obliging
blotter,

those so brave, with such uplifted brows
standing in open cars, so
manfully inspecting the front of harvest work, as though
when stepping into a furrow they entered a trench,
those with a hard fist, capable of thumping lecterns
and patting shoulders
of men bent in salute, just pinned
with medals to black suits,

always
you feared them so,
you were so tiny
compared to them, always standing above
you, on stairs, rostrums, tribunes,
but surely it's enough to stop being
afraid for at least one moment, let's say:
start being afraid a little less
so that you realise
it is they who are most afraid

Translated from the Polish by Adam Czerniawski.

END OF EMPIRE:
DECOLONIZATION 1947–

Although many colonial possessions remained until the Sixties, the Second World War had sounded the death-knell of the European empires. As the Caribbean poet Louise Bennett wittily points out, the result has been a process of 'colonization in reverse', with large populations emigrating from former colonies. This has added a new dimension to the increasing plurality and mobility of societies everywhere. The situation has thrown up many cultural ironies but there is no doubt that poetry in English has been refreshed by work from former colonies. As Joseph Brodsky said: 'Because civilizations are finite, in the life of each of them comes a moment when centres cease to hold ... The job of holding at such times is done by the men from the provinces, from the outskirts.'

W. H. Auden

Partition

Unbiassed at least he was when he arrived on his mission,
Having never set eyes on this land he was called to partition
Between two peoples fanatically at odds,
With their different diets and incompatible gods.
'Time,' they had briefed him in London, 'is short. It's too late
For mutual reconciliation or rational debate:
The only solution now lies in separation.
The Viceroy thinks, as you will see from his letter,
That the less you are seen in his company the better,
So we've arranged to provide you with other accommodation.
We can give you four judges, two Moslem and two Hindu,
To consult with, but the final decision must rest with you.'

Shut up in a lonely mansion, with police night and day
Patrolling the gardens to keep assassins away,
He got down to work, to the task of settling the fate
Of millions. The maps at his disposal were out of date
And the Census Returns almost certainly incorrect,
But there was no time to check them, no time to inspect
Contested areas. The weather was frightfully hot,
And a bout of dysentery kept him constantly on the trot,
But in seven weeks it was done, the frontiers decided,
A continent for better or worse divided.

The next day he sailed for England, where he quickly forgot
The case, as a good lawyer must. Return he would not,
Afraid, as he told his Club, that he might get shot.

Partition: The lawyer Sir Cyril Radcliffe, later Lord Radcliffe (1899–1977), chaired the
boundary commissions that fixed the borders between India and Pakistan in the disputed
areas of the Punjab and Bengal in August 1947.

Derek Walcott

A Far Cry from Africa

A wind is ruffling the tawny pelt
Of Africa. Kikuyu, quick as flies,
Batten upon the bloodstreams of the veldt.
Corpses are scattered through a paradise.
Only the worm, colonel of carrion, cries:
'Waste no compassion on these separate dead!'
Statistics justify and scholars seize
The salients of colonial policy.
What is that to the white child hacked in bed?
To savages, expendable as Jews?

Threshed out by beaters, the long rushes break
In a white dust of ibises whose cries

Have wheeled since civilization's dawn
From the parched river or beast-teeming plain.
The violence of beast on beast is read
As natural law, but upright man
Seeks his divinity by inflicting pain.
Delirious as these worried beasts, his wars
Dance to the tightened carcass of a drum,
While he calls courage still that native dread
Of the white peace contracted by the dead.

Again brutish necessity wipes its hands
Upon the napkin of a dirty cause, again
A waste of our compassion, as with Spain,
The gorilla wrestles with the superman.
I who am poisoned with the blood of both,
Where shall I turn, divided to the vein?
I who have cursed
The drunken officer of British rule, how choose
Between this Africa and the English tongue I love?
Betray them both, or give back what they give?
How can I face such slaughter and be cool?
How can I turn from Africa and live?

Louise Bennett

Colonization in Reverse

Wat a joyful news, Miss Mattie,
I feel like me heart gwine burs
Jamaica people colonizin
Englan in reverse.

By de hundred, by de tousan
From country and from town,
By de ship-load, by de plane-load
Jamaica is Englan boun.

Dem a pour out a Jamaica,
Everybody future plan
Is fe get a big-time job
An settle in de mother lan.

What a islan! What a people!
Man an woman, old an young
Jus a pack dem bag an baggage
An tun history upside dung!

Some people doan like travel,
But fe show dem loyalty
Dem all a open up cheap-fare-
To-Englan agency.

An week by week dem shippin off
Dem countryman like fire,
Fe immigrate an populate
De seat a de Empire.

Oonoo see how life is funny,
Oonoo see de tunabout?
Jamaica live fe box bread
Out a English people mout'.

For wen dem ketch a Englan,
An start play dem different role,
Some will settle down to work
An some will settle fe de dole.

Jane say de dole is not too bad
Because dey payin she
Two pounds a week fe seek a job
Dat suit her dignity.

Me say Jane will never fine work
At de rate how she dah look,
For all day she stay pon Aunt Fan couch
An read love-story book.

Wat a devilment a Englan!
Dem face war an brave de worse,
But me wonderin how dem gwine stan
Colonizin in reverse.

James Berry

From Lucy: Englan' Lady

You ask me 'bout the lady. Me dear,
old centre here still shine
with Queen. She affec' the place
like the sun: not comin' out oft'n
an' when it happ'n everybody's out
smilin', as she wave a han'
like a seagull flyin' slow slow.

An' you know she come from
dust free rooms an' velvet
an' diamond. She make you feel
this on-an'-on town, London,
where long long time deeper than mind.
An' han's after han's die away,
makin' streets, putt'n' up bricks,
a piece of brass, a piece of wood
an' plantin' trees: an' it give
a car a halfday job gett'n' through.

An' Leela, darlin', no, I never
meet the Queen in flesh. Yet
sometimes, deep deep, I sorry for her.

Everybody expec' a show
from her, like she a space touris'
on earth. An' darlin', unless
you can go home an' scratch up
you' husban', it mus' be hard

strain keepin' good graces for
all hypocrite faces.

Anyhow, me dear, you know what
ole time people say,
'Bird sing sweet for its nest.'

Keki N. Daruwalla

Collage I

Rock'n'rollers around Ravi Shankar
mods around Maharishi Mahesh
and Beatles around both
and we are thrilled.
They have a lot to learn
from the ragas still, these bums!
It is that same sentiment
that Tagore-euphoria
after the Nobel prize.

At times we do well
in dog-shows.

Since Oppenheimer quoted Bhagavad Gita
after the first A-bomb.
Since Allen Ginsberg and the psychedelics
wore dhotis, and with clanging cymbals
chanted cow and Krishna
I stand bowled by Indian culture
and Indian hemp.

Who says we have done nothing?
We have abolished zamindari
and liquor and English
and driven out the whores from the G.B. Road.

What have we forbidden
veils in front of eyes
or eyes behind veils?

We have inaugurated crematoriums
with an unclaimed corpse.
A VIP has opened
the sluice-gates of a drain
and given it an epithet
'the drain of hope'.

Some day, here
the sun will refuse
to light the path for lepers.
In India
the left hand is outcaste
because it cleans the ass.

Discussing personal destiny
and collective destiny
you turn bitter.
My horoscope is only a half-truth.
Where are inflation and taxes
floor-crossing and black gold
written on it?

If we had plague
Camus-style
and doctors searched for the virus
there would be black-market in rats.

zamindari: the zamindars were Indian rural landlords in a system devised by the British.
Zamindari was abolished in a major Act of 1950.

Fred D'Aguiar

El Dorado Update

Riddle me, riddle me, riddle.
One people, one nation, one destiny?
   Let's take a walk
   not to stay, just to see.

You pass a man at Customs,
returning from an island;
he wears several tin chains,
tin rings on every finger,
and tin bracelets that jingle
as his arms swing.

Customs ensure
what he declares
tallies with their list made
when he departed
with identical amounts
of gold.

You know his jaunt by heart:
   The stricter the government,
   the wiser the population.

Riddle me, riddle me, riddle.
In an overloaded taxi, you are warned
not to lean against the door
that is not a door; you spend your journey
keeping your feet out of gaps in the floor;
you share a begging bowl with children and ministers;
what coins you earn are only good for wells.

To pass the betting shop you must cross the road;
people congregate from opening time to close;
they place the day's meal from pawned things

on a favourite or outsider and pray it will multiply;
they throw hands in a partner:

> They are you and I
> forced to take the reflection
> in the puddle for sky.

> *Riddle me, riddle me, riddle.*
Big business has pulled out overnight:
houses left to servants, shops to cockroaches.
You separate the twin-ply of toilet rolls,
pinch grammes off every measurement
and spread your goods on the floor
for the morning's trade
in a sheet you can fold quick.

Broken bones cannot be set;
simple wounds go septic.
It's back to losing toe-nails
on stony roads.

> *Back to back, belly to belly,*
> *we don't give a damn,*
> *we done dead already.*

You think it's easy?
You walk down the middle
of the road with your head
in the air.

Crowd on the left-hand side shout,
'Stop for something to eat, no?
Wheat-flour scarce,
rice-flour is eye-pass,
we got cassava bread,
mauby and class.'

Crowd on the right side
play a different tune,
they point smoking guns,

they say, 'All eat rice,
that is revolutionary food,
don't bother with wheat import,
imperialist food;
we're the proprietor of this country,
not the administrator.'

   Riddle me, riddle me, riddle.
You get choke-and-rob,
call the police;
you don't know in the dark
you can't tell Jack from Jill;
you say 'I'm Indian,
the deed was done by an African';
they show you an identity parade
full of Indians;
they're going to charge you
for wasting precious time,
if you don't leave their station.

You think it's easy?
Police don't have radio, nor hook;
they can't catch crook by telepathy,
much less get from A to B.
Their ink-well run dry
so they can't take your statement;
plus they're busy, bad bad bad,
capturing smuggler,
possessor of garlic, onion,
wheat-flour, and trade union sympathiser.

It's true; it's cheaper to get convicted
for possession of marijuana than bread;
they spot-check schoolchildren's packed lunches
for bake; they raid weddings and seize
roti and cake.

Lord, what to do in this fowl-coop
republic, risk my neck on a demo
or in a food queue?

Let's take a walk
  not to say, just to see.
What people, what nation, what destiny?
  Riddle me, riddle me, riddle.

Linton Kwesi Johnson

Inglan Is a Bitch

w'en mi jus' come to Landan toun
mi use to work pan di andahgroun
but workin' pan di andahgroun
y'u don't get fi know your way aroun'

Inglan is a bitch
dere's no escapin' it
Inglan is a bitch
dere's no runnin' whey fram it

mi get a lickle jab in a big 'otell
an' awftah a while, mi woz doin' quite well
dem staat mi aaf as a dish-washah
but w'en mi tek a stack, mi noh tun clack-watchah!

Inglan is a bitch
dere's no escapin' it
Inglan is a bitch
noh baddah try fi hide fram it

w'en dem gi' yu di lickle wage packit
fus dem rab it wid dem big tax racket
y'u haffi struggle fi mek en's meet
an' w'en y'u goh a y'u bed y'u jus' cant sleep

Inglan is a bitch
dere's no escapin' it
Inglan is a bitch fi true
a noh lie mi a tell, a true

mi use to work dig ditch w'en it cowl noh bitch
mi did strang like a mule, but, bwoy, mi did fool
den awftah a while mi jus' stap dhu ovahtime
den awftah a while mi jus' phu dung mi tool

Inglan is a bitch
dere's no escapin' it
Inglan is a bitch
y'u haffi know how fi suvvive in it

well mi dhu day wok an' mi dhu nite wok
mi dhu clean wok an' mi dhu dutty wok
dem seh dat black man is very lazy
but if y'u si how mi wok y'u woulda seh mi crazy

Inglan is a bitch
dere's no escapin' it
Inglan is a bitch
y'u bettah face up to it

dem have a lickle facktri up inna Brackly
inna disya facktri all dem dhu is pack crackry
fi di laas fifteen years dem get mi laybah
now awftah fifteen years mi fall out a fayvah

Inglan is a bitch
dere's no escapin' it
Inglan is a bitch
dere's no runnin' whey fram it

mi know dem have work, work in abundant
yet still, dem mek mi redundant
now, at fifty-five mi gettin' quite ol'
yet still, dem sen' mi fi goh draw dole

Inglan is a bitch
dere's no escapin' it
Ingland is a bitch fi true
is whey wi a goh dhu 'bout it?

THE DIFFICULT LAND: RURAL LIFE

Although the century has seen an inexorable move towards city life and secular technological consumerism, large parts of the world have never entered the twentieth-century hypermarket of realizable dreams. Until the 1980s, poetry, being a traditional art, was probably always biased towards the rural. In some countries, Ireland, for example, it still is. Poets have always been drawn towards elegizing supposedly vanishing traditions and declining ways of life. D. J. Enright's 'A Polished Performance' encapsulates the essential irony of the urban/rural interface.

Patrick Kavanagh

Epic

I have lived in important places, times
When great events were decided, who owned
That half a rood of rock, a no-man's land
Surrounded by our pitchfork-armed claims.
I heard the Duffys shouting 'Damn your soul'
And old McCabe stripped to the waist, seen
Step the plot defying blue cast-steel! –
'Here is the march along these iron stones'
That was the year of the Munich bother. Which
Was more important? I inclined
To lose my faith in Ballyrush and Gortin
Till Homer's ghost came whispering to my mind
He said: I made the Iliad from such
A local row. Gods make their own importance.

R. S. Thomas

A Peasant

Iago Prytherch his name, though, be it allowed,
Just an ordinary man of the bald Welsh hills,
Who pens a few sheep in a gap of cloud.
Docking mangels, chipping the green skin
From the yellow bones with a half-witted grin
Of satisfaction, or churning the crude earth
To a stiff sea of clods that glint in the wind –
So are his days spent, his spittled mirth
Rarer than the sun that cracks the cheeks
Of the gaunt sky perhaps once in a week.
And then at night see him fixed in his chair
Motionless, except when he leans to gob in the fire.
There is something frightening in the vacancy of his mind.
His clothes, sour with years of sweat
And animal contact, shock the refined,
But affected, sense with their stark naturalness.
Yet this is your prototype, who, season by season
Against siege of rain and the wind's attrition,
Preserves his stock, an impregnable fortress
Not to be stormed even in death's confusion.
Remember him, then, for he, too, is a winner of wars,
Enduring like a tree under the curious stars.

Sujata Bhatt

Muliebrity

I have thought so much about the girl
who gathered cow-dung in a wide, round basket
along the main road passing by our house
and the Radhavallabh temple in Maninagar.

I have thought so much about the way she
moved her hands and her waist
and the smell of cow-dung and road-dust and wet canna lilies,
the smell of monkey breath and freshly washed clothes
and the dust from crows' wings which smells different –
and again the smell of cow-dung as the girl scoops
it up, all these smells surrounding me separately
and simultaneously – I have thought so much
but have been unwilling to use her for a metaphor,
for a nice image – but most of all unwilling
to forget her or to explain to anyone the greatness
and the power glistening through her cheekbones
each time she found a particularly promising
mound of dung –

Amrita Pritam

Daily Wages

In a corner of blue sky
The mill of night whistles,
A white thick smoke
Pours from the moon-chimney.

In dream's many furnaces
Labourer love
Is stoking all the fires

I earn our meeting
Holding you for a while,
My day's wages.

I buy my soul's food
Cook and eat it
And set the empty pot in the corner.

I warm my hands at the dying fire
And lying down to rest
Give God thanks.

The mill of night whistles
And from the moon-chimney
Smoke rises, sign of hope.

I eat what I earn,
Not yesterday's left-overs,
And leave no grain for tomorrow.

*Translated from the Punjabi
by Charles Brasch with
Amrita Pritam.*

D. J. Enright

A Polished Performance

Citizens of the polished capital
  Sigh for the towns up country,
And their innocent simplicity.

People in the towns up country
  Applaud the unpolished innocence
Of the distant villages.

Dwellers in the distant villages
  Speak of a simple unspoilt girl,
Living alone, deep in the bush.

Deep in the bush we found her,
  Large and innocent of eye,
Among gentle gibbons and mountain ferns.

Perfect for the part, perfect,
    Except for the dropsy
Which comes from polished rice.

In the capital our film is much admired,
    Its gentle gibbons and mountain ferns,
Unspoilt, unpolished, large and innocent of eye.

Ciaran Carson

Céilí

If there was a house with three girls in it,
It only took three boys to make a dance.
You'd see a glimmer where McKeown's once was
And follow it till it became a house.
But maybe they'd have gone on, up the hill
To Loughran's, or made across the grazing,
Somewhere else. All those twistings and turnings,
Crossroads and dirt roads and skittery lanes:
You'd be glad to get in from the dark.

And when you did get in, there'd be a power
Of poteen. A big tin creamery churn,
A ladle, those mugs with blue and white bars.
Oh, good and clear like the best of water.
The music would start up. This one ould boy
Would sit by the fire and rosin away,
Sawing and sawing till it fell like snow.
That poteen was quare stuff. At the end of
The night you might be fiddling with no bow.

When everyone was ready, out would come
The tin of Tate and Lyle's *Golden Syrup*,
A spoon or a knife, a big farl of bread.
Some of those same boys wouldn't bother with
The way you were supposed to screw it up.

There might be courting going on outside,
Whisperings and cacklings in the barnyard;
A spider thread of gold-thin syrup
Trailed out across the glowing kitchen tiles
Into the night of promises, or broken promises.

Céilí: an informal social gathering with folk music and dancing.

Philip Gross

A Breton Dance

A stone grey town with a name like a bell:
Tinténiac. Was this the place? The time?
The square was empty, blinkered for the night.
On, out beyond a hoarding *ZONE INDUSTRIELLE*

we drove between vacant Euro-factories,
beached white whales. And this was it:
a lorry-park like a floodlit airstrip,
and the dancers. Then the bark and wheeze

of the *bombarde* cut the hubbub, keen
as bad cider. The shock of it flowed
among them, losing young and old
in a pattern of spirals, yet a single line.

A hundred heel-and-toes became one long
slow shudder, like a snake down all its scales.
We backed away. It flexed its coils.
The pipe throbbed round and round and on

into the night, needling, defying rhyme,
reason, development or cure: the sweet ache
of dreaming yourself a nation. When you wake
the place is always wrong. That, or the time.

bombarde: a raucous, tuba-like instrument.

THE COLD WAR: 1945–1989

From 1945 to 1989 the fear of nuclear war was a persistent ground bass beneath the life of the period, waxing and waning with recurrent crises in relations between the two superpowers, the USA and the Soviet Union. The phrase 'Bomb Culture' became current in the Sixties after the time of maximum tension, the Cuban Missile Crisis in October 1962. In retrospect, it can be seen that, damaging (particularly in the Third World) and potentially catastrophic though it was, the Cold War was a stable world arrangement that everyone understood and which gave a pattern to people's lives on both sides of the Iron Curtain. Dick Allen's 'Ode to the Cold War' reminds us of some of the contours of this vanished world. Ten years of nuclear quiescence and limited disarmament followed the end of the Cold War, but a new, ominous age seemed to begin with the Indian and Pakistani nuclear tests in May 1998.

Eugène Guillevic

Another War

While catacombs beneath the torn earth
Still cry out
And flesh still quits the bones of skeletons,

While the children
Of those who go to rot in factories
Have knees as bare
As screws,

While the mutilated sigh
For artificial limbs,

While the Jews
Are still the Jews,
And negroes negroes, their songs
The tears of negroes,

You are preparing for another war.

. . .

You are not hungry
There is little left
For you to envy;
All you need
Is still more power
To endure.

. . .

Disturb the skeleton's repose
To do your will

And see your power
In a world made absolute
Of sand and servitors.

. . .

You know that flowers, everywhere,
Exist for those that work.

You know that space,
The colours of the sky and fields
Are theirs alone.

This you know: it is for these
The frequent day appears.

You know that nothing more
Is yours on earth.

Yet what you want is that
Which trickles through your fingers.

And it's war
You want

Against those who work
Contentedly on earth
To make this world
A festival of toil.

. . .

Bauxite, wolfram, tungsten
For the war.

Planes, lorries, tanks, conscription
For the war.

Convert the factories
For the war.

Enlist the scientists and engineers
For the war.

Foreign buying, national production
For the war.

Hoards of fine materials
For the war.

Supersonic speed
For the war.

Use the stratosphere
For the war.

Operate in polar regions
For the war.

Directed missiles
For the war.

Atomic force
For the war.

Recurrent fever
For the war.

Psittacosis, lead-poisoning, bubonic plague
For the war.

Printing presses, radiodiffusion
For the war.

Women's thighs
For the war.

Basilisks
For the war.

. . .

There's nothing more for you to know
You near the gulf and think you can
Escape, but from this place will grow
For you alone a full-blown rose
While for the rest the hurricane
That blows will sweep them on –
White corpses.

. . .

You stagger.

You are reeling before the gaze of crowds who come
From new-discovered happiness.

The sun is theirs
They have the right to see.

Translated from the French by William Alwyn.

Peter Porter

Your Attention Please

The Polar DEW has just warned that
A nuclear rocket strike of
At least one thousand megatons
Has been launched by the enemy
Directly at our major cities.
This announcement will take
Two and a quarter minutes to make,
You therefore have a further
Eight and a quarter minutes
To comply with the shelter
Requirements published in the Civil
Defence Code – section Atomic Attack.
A specially shortened Mass
Will be broadcast at the end
Of this announcement –
Protestant and Jewish services
Will begin simultaneously –
Select your wavelength immediately
According to instructions
In the Defence Code. Do not
Take well-loved pets (including birds)
Into your shelter – they will consume
Fresh air. Leave the old and bed-
ridden, you can do nothing for them.
Remember to press the sealing
Switch when everyone is in
The shelter. Set the radiation
Aerial, turn on the geiger barometer.
Turn off your television now.
Turn off your radio immediately
The Services end. At the same time
Secure explosion plugs in the ears

Of each member of your family. Take
Down your plasma flasks. Give your children
The pills marked one and two
In the CD green container, then put
Them to bed. Do not break
The inside airlock seals until
The radiation All Clear shows
(Watch for the cuckoo in your
perspex panel), or your District
Touring Doctor rings your bell.
If before this, your air becomes
Exhausted or if any of your family
Is critically injured, administer
The capsules marked 'Valley Forge'
(Red pocket in No. 1 Survival Kit)
For painless death. (Catholics
Will have been instructed by their priests
What to do in this eventuality.)
This announcement is ending. Our President
Has already given orders for
Massive retaliation – it will be
Decisive. Some of us may die.
Remember, statistically
It is not likely to be you.
All flags are flying fully dressed
On Government buildings – the sun is shining.
Death is the least we have to fear.
We are all in the hands of God,
Whatever happens happens by His Will.
Now go quickly to your shelters.

DEW: Distant Early Warning, the radar tracking system for intercontinental ballistic missiles.

Paul Muldoon

Cuba

My eldest sister arrived home that morning
In her white muslin evening dress.
'Who the hell do you think you are,
Running out to dances in next to nothing?
As though we hadn't enough bother
With the world at war, if not at an end.'
My father was pounding the breakfast-table.

'Those Yankees were touch and go as it was –
If you'd heard Patton in Armagh –
But this Kennedy's nearly an Irishman
So he's not much better than ourselves.
And him with only to say the word.
If you've got anything on your mind
Maybe you should make your peace with God.'

I could hear May from beyond the curtain.
'Bless me, Father, for I have sinned.
I told a lie once, I was disobedient once.
And, Father, a boy touched me once.'
'Tell me, child. Was this touch immodest?
Did he touch your breast, for example?'
'He brushed against me, Father. Very gently.'

In October 1962 American reconnaissance showed that Russia was installing offensive missiles in Cuba, within easy reach of America. The resulting confrontation created widespread fear of nuclear war until the Russians agreed to remove the missiles.

Carol Ann Duffy

The B Movie

At a preview of That Hagen Girl *in 1947, when actor Ronald Reagan became the first person on screen to say 'I love you, will you marry me?' to the nineteen-year-old Shirley Temple, there was such a cry of 'Oh, no!' from the invited audience that the scene was cut out when the film was released.*

Lap dissolve. You make a man speak crap dialogue,
one day he'll make you eat your words. OK?
Let's go for a take. Where's the rest of me? '*Oh, no!*'

Things are different now. He's got star billing,
star wars, applause. Takes her in his arms.
I'm talking about a *real* weepie. Freeze frame. '*Oh, no!*'

On his say-so, the train wipes out the heroine
and there ain't no final reel. How do you like that?
My fellow Americans, we got five minutes. '*Oh, no!*'

Classic. He holds the onion to water such sorrow.
We need a Kleenex the size of Russia here, no kidding.
Have that kid's tail any time he wants to. *Yup*.

Adam Zagajewski

July 6, 1980

A world power, prompted by concern
for its security, occupies
the neighboring country. A million refugees,
women, children, old people among them, are camping
close to the border of their native land.

Men armed with nineteenth-century
rifles go to the mountains in order to fight
the invader who longs for security.
The president of another world power
smiles sadly. For three weeks,
Europeans feverishly discuss
the development of events. Young
German leftists protest against
armaments and in case of war they plan
the formation of small, mobile
self-defense units armed with those nineteenth-century
rifles. An American conductor urges us
to listen to Beethoven's music in the last
few days before the end of the world. A retired
bank employee presents on television
tapes with the recorded voices
of the dead. The dead don't have much
to say, they tell their names,
weep, or greet us with birdlike
screeches, short as sighing.
You and I sit in front of the open window,
we look at the dark green leaves of a maple tree,
it's Sunday, it's raining, we laugh at
the omniscience of journalists, at the vanity
of politicians, we're unprotected
and calm; it appears to us we understand
more than the others.

Translated from the Polish by
Renata Gorzynski.

In December 1979 the Soviet Union invaded Afghanistan, intervening in a civil war. In an echo of Vietnam, the Russians were outgunned by guerrillas (with substantial arms supplied by America) and forced to leave in February 1989.

John Levett

SDI

Ten miles above the tits at St Tropez
A satellite's remote, panoptic eye
Is tracking us and quietly waiting for
The gesture that could culminate in war;
You scratch your nose, I finish my ice-cream
And screw the silver paper in the sand.
Your milky skin is tanning like a dream.
That ultra-violet shadow is my hand.
The camera rolls on, its frozen lens
Picks out the agriculture of the Fens
Then swaps the filters for the infra-red
Cupolas of beleaguered Leningrad.

You shift and turn, you shoulder-blade could be
The smooth lid on some high-tech armoury
And fear stirs in the craters that begin
To open on my weakly bearded chin.
White clouds wind like a turban round the peaks
That top the Himalayas, and the sun,
Its compost of alchemical techniques,
Transmutes the globe and lets us focus on
Calcutta pullulating with its poor,
The psychopaths that bleed El Salvador
The human tides of Tokyo and then
The terrifying silence of Phnom Penh.

The earth speeds up, its shrunken polar caps
Like parachutes tumescently collapse,
The tilting coasts of snow give way to ice
Then bergs of light on Asian belts of rice.
At eight you plan to have the hotel fix
Your hair and come to meet me in the town,

Its chill and its salinity that pricks
And tightens up a skin that's nicely brown:
Those stars we hope to drink beneath tonight
Are pledged to North America, their light
An Ice Age brilliance turning even now
The obsolescent hardware of the Plough.

SDI: the Strategic Defense Initiative, better known as Star Wars, an extremely expensive American military programme of dubious promise, launched by President Reagan in 1983, which was intended to intercept incoming ballistic missiles before they re-entered the earth's atmosphere. As the Soviet Union became less of a threat under Gorbachev from 1985 on, the scheme became unnecessary.

Dick Allen

Ode to the Cold War

I

A faint light blinking in the Bering Strait,
The dead face of a Russian boy, the spy
Never returned from Berlin – these were yours;
And body bags, Chinese horns, the pounding shoe,
    A riderless horse in Washington,
Turning radar screens beneath an arctic sky,
Yours, yours. In you, the State triumphant,
        Rambo, Big Brother,
        MacArthur, Eisenhower,
        Stalin, the Politburo,
French bodies hanging on the wires at Dien Bien Phu,
        Space, Time, Chaos, satellites,
        Kindergarten children
        Hiding under desks, Castro,
A thousand missiles rising from their buried silos.

II

In you, *The Gulag Archipelago*
Took its windswept shape; Neil Armstrong
Stepped upon the moon. As your governments
Raged over him, the peasant in the field
Could hope for freedom or equality, not both,
        But either choice
Better than the hopelessness he felt
Landless, penniless, voiceless, while the rich
        Danced in mansions filled
        With songs he could have sung,
        Rose arbors that he could have leaned upon,
Tasting the wine, talking of the truth,
        The voting booth,
Were he not poor, uneducated, sprung
From serfs and slaves and brutal legacies.
Your fingers reaching from the cold, you promised him
If he would die for you, that history
Would lift his children to a street of gold.

III

Thing of walls, thing of barriers, thing of parallels,
Of caves and steppes and slums and jungles,
        Thing of withering away,
        Of straying aircraft, tracer fire,
Mushroom clouds and cancer wards,
Airlifts, Disneyland, ill-shaved McCarthy,
Blacklists and defections, KGB,
        CIA, SANE,
        MIGs, Phantoms,
Tanks turning back towards Hungary,
Thing of suspicion, hatred, body snatchers,
        Shortwave radios,
Interrogation, Orwell, streams of refugees,
        Doctor Zhivago,
Crete, Chernobyl, and the great economies
Bound to you. Thing of waking up in Leningrad,
Chicago, New York, London, Paris, Budapest,

Moscow . . . or in a tiny shed
Deep in the Urals or Louisiana bayous,
And you there, you always in your place
With your equivalent of twenty tons
        Of TNT
For every human on the planet's face:
First strike, second strike, and then
            Oblivion . . .

                        IV

You organized our lives. You made our sacrifices
    Possible. With you, we could forgive
The empty shelves, the shoddy stores,
    Learn to ignore
The homeless pushing shopping carts, the poor
    Slouched in Grand Central,
Shrug our shoulders at the Trumps and Brodskys,
    Museums, dachas,
    Crack, cocaine,
    Savings & Loan,
    TV Guide, People.
Umbrellas of defense would rise above us,
Star Wars would protect us,
And Reagan would shine on through history.
    The poor deserve their misery,
    Praise heavy industry,
May Day parades, the Fourth of July,
    The Internationale,
Jack London, Yevtushenko, Voznesensky,
    Steinbeck, Abram Tertz
('What is to be done?' wrote Tolstoi),
Bourgeois, proletariat, and democrat,
    Republican Capitalist pigs,
        Communist dogs.
You helped us as we pulled the fallen logs
        Across Siberia,
You laid out in the Harlem slums,
In crime-mugged streets, in Selma, Alabama.

You had come
From Hobbes and Locke and Marx and Engels
Against dictatorships,
To kiss our fervent lips
And save us from confronting what was real.

V

Among the cemetery tombs of Leningrad,
A souvenir seller lays his cap aside
And openly prays: *Comrade, comrade,*
Do not regret the cause for which you died.
All of us die for causes, large and small,
Silly and noble. History gloves our hands,
Clothes us in its uniforms and clouds our minds,
Leads us to or leaves us where we fall.
The great snows come. The cold war ends,
Warm bloody fingers crack the window blinds.

VI

And this your epitaph:
For fifty years you froze us in your path.
And now no more
Lake Placid miracles, Nadia's theme,
Whittaker Chambers, Alger Hiss,
The Rosenbergs,
Smuggled manuscripts, the Marshall Plan,
'Ich bin ein Berliner,'
Profumo scandal,
Wiretapping Hoover,
James Bond, Samantha Fox –
All jumbled, all confused: John Glenn,
Yuri Gagarin.
The Bay of Pigs, sold orphan children,
Chile overthrown, Che Guevara killed,
The iron curtain,
Cement and Hemingway,
The Bolshoi Ballet,

Tribes, religions, nationalities
Held together for the greater cause;
The advertisers' and the lawyers' paradise
   Of twisted laws,
Leaving in their wake our shattered
    Ships of state
    Ice-bound no more,
The reign of selfishness supreme.
       How you entertained us,
      How you toyed with us,
    How you betrayed us,
How you left us empty in your empty husk.
   'Ask not
What your country can do for you,
But what you can do for your country.'
   'Workers of the world unite,
   You have nothing to lose but your chains' –
Cacophony, faded cacophony,
   Cast votes,
   Flute notes,
I sing the Song of Myself.

Dien Bien Phu: the crucial battle of the French–Indo-Chinese war took place from March to May 1954. France's defeat led to America's involvement in South East Asia.
The Gulag Archipelago: Solzhenitsyn's book about the Soviet prison camp system (Gulag).
SANE: Society for the Abolition of Nuclear Explosions.
Abram Tertz: the pseudonym of the dissident writer Andrei Sinyavsky, tried, with Yuli Daniel, for anti-Soviet activities in February 1966.
Alger Hiss: in 1948, Alger Hiss, a former State Department official was accused by a *Time* magazine editor, Whittaker Chambers, of being a communist (Chambers himself certainly had been a communist). The case was taken by Richard Nixon before the House of Representatives Un-American Activities Commission and Hiss was eventually jailed for almost four years.
The Rosenbergs: Ethel and Julius Rosenberg were executed as Russian spies on 19 June 1953.
the Marshall Plan: on 5 June 1947 US Secretary of State George Marshall unveiled a plan for European Economic Recovery. From 1948 to 1951 $12,500 million were disbursed to sixteen countries. Aid was offered to the countries of Eastern Europe, but they were forbidden by Stalin to accept it.

YOUNGER THAN THAT NOW:
THE SIXTIES

In the Sixties insouciance became a way of life in the West – the long pall of hardship and privation that had dominated life for millions through two world wars, the Slump and post-war austerity finally gave way to a new hedonism and cultural inventiveness. Life became, in Larkin's words (used ruefully and ironically) 'a brilliant breaking of the bank'. The rise of rock music and its associated drug culture reached a peak in 1967; the 'Summer of Love', and some of the best poetry of the period can be found in song lyrics. A witty and irreverent popular poetry emerged in Liverpool, influenced by the Beats, pop music and earlier populist poets such as Jacques Prévert. The other main strand of the Sixties was the political activism that reached a peak in the student uprisings of 1968, represented here in an ironic view by the Russian poet Naum Korzhavin. Both the hedonism and the activism had burned themselves out on cue by the end of the decade.

Roy Fuller

From a Foreign Land

On the death of John F. Kennedy

Sceptical of the cult, suspicious of the nation,
Nevertheless we had to grant the amelioration
Of the one by the other; and certainly the alternative
Had seemed of depressing threat.

Given this tepid and grudging view, why do we yet
Flinch from the murdered consul's images, remember
(In the far February following the November)
That the spouse still has to live?

It's not that by their taste for intellect disarmed
We were unconsciously adherents all the time,
Nor that strong vulnerable youth unfairly charmed,
But that the senseless crime

Is what for us he had the power to postpone
Who now approach within the assassin's range alone.

Edwin Morgan

The Death of Marilyn Monroe

What innocence? Whose guilt? What eyes? Whose breast?
Crumpled orphan, nembutal bed,
white hearse, Los Angeles,
DiMaggio! Los Angeles! Miller! Los Angeles! America!
That Death should seem the only protector –
That all arms should have faded, and the great cameras and lights
    become an inquisition and a torment –
That the many acquaintances, the autograph-hunters, the inflexible
    directors, the drive-in admirers should become a blur of
    incomprehension and pain –
That lonely Uncertainty should limp up, grinning, with bewildering
    barbiturates, and watch her undress and lie down and in her
    anguish
call for him! call for him to strengthen her with what could only
    dissolve her! A method
of dying, we are shaken, we see it. Strasberg!
Los Angeles! Olivier! Los Angeles! Others die
and yet by this death we are a little shaken, we feel it,
America.
Let no one say communication is a cantword.
They had to lift her hand from the bedside telephone.
But what she had not been able to say
perhaps she had said: 'All I had was my life.

I have no regrets, because if I made
any mistakes, I was responsible.
There is now – and there is the future.
What has happened is behind. So
it follows you around? So what?' – This
to a friend, ten days before.
And so she was responsible.
And if she was not responsible, not wholly responsible, Los Angeles?
    Los Angeles? Will it follow you around? Will the slow white
    hearse of the child of America follow you around?

Peter Porter

A Consumer's Report

The name of the product I tested is *Life*,
I have completed the form you sent me
and understand that my answers are confidential.

I had it as a gift,
I didn't feel much while using it,
in fact I think I'd have liked to be more excited.
It seemed gentle on the hands
but left an embarrassing deposit behind.
It was not economical
and I have used much more than I thought
(I suppose I have about half left
but it's difficult to tell) –
although the instructions are fairly large
there are so many of them
I don't know which to follow, especially
as they seem to contradict each other.
I'm not sure such a thing
should be put in the way of children –
It's difficult to think of a purpose

for it. One of my friends says
it's just to keep its maker in a job.
Also the price is much too high.
Things are piling up so fast,
after all, the world got by
for a thousand million years
without this, do we need it now?
(Incidentally, please ask your man
to stop calling me 'the respondent',
I don't like the sound of it.)
There seems to be a lot of different labels,
sizes and colours should be uniform,
the shape is awkward, it's waterproof
but not heat resistant, it doesn't keep
yet it's very difficult to get rid of:
whenever they make it cheaper they seem
to put less in – if you say you don't
want it, then it's delivered anyway.
I'd agree it's a popular product,
it's got into the language; people
even say they're on the side of it.
Personally I think it's overdone,
a small thing people are ready
to behave badly about. I think
we should take it for granted. If its
experts are called philosophers or market
researchers or historians, we shouldn't
care. We are the consumers and the last
law makers. So finally, I'd buy it.
But the question of a 'best buy'
I'd like to leave until I get
the competitive product you said you'd send.

Douglas Dunn

The Clothes Pit

The young women are obsessed with beauty.
Their old-fashioned sewing machines rattle in Terry Street.
They must keep up, they must keep up.

They wear teasing skirts and latest shoes,
Lush, impermanent coats, American cosmetics.
But they lack intellectual grooming.

In the culture of clothes and little philosophies,
They only have clothes. They do not need to be seen
Carrying a copy of *International Times*.

Or the Liverpool Poets, the wish to justify their looks
With things beyond themselves. They mix up colours,
And somehow they are often fat and unlovely.

They don't get high on pot, but get sick on cheap
Spanish Burgundy, or beer in rampant pubs,
And come home supported and kissed and bad-tempered.

But they have clothes, bright enough to show they dream
Of places other than this, an inarticulate paradise,
Eating exotic fowl in sunshine with courteous boys.

Three girls go down the street with the summer wind.
The litter of pop rhetoric blows down Terry Street,
Bounces past their feet, into their lives.

International Times: the paper of the LSD/hippie culture in the mid-Sixties.

Bob Dylan

My Back Pages

Crimson flames tied through my ears
Rollin' high and mighty traps
Pounced with fire on flaming roads
Using ideas as my maps
'We'll meet on edges, soon,' said I
Proud 'neath heated brow.
Ah, but I was so much older then,
I'm younger than that now.

Half-racked prejudice leaped forth
'Rip down all hate,' I screamed
Lies that life is black and white
Spoke from my skull. I dreamed
Romantic facts of musketeers
Foundationed deep, somehow.
Ah, but I was so much older then,
I'm younger than that now.

Girls' faces formed the forward path
From phony jealousy
To memorizing politics
Of ancient history
Flung down by corpse evangelists
Unthought of, though, somehow.
Ah, but I was so much older then,
I'm younger than that now.

A self-ordained professor's tongue
Too serious to fool
Spouted out that liberty
Is just equality in school
'Equality,' I spoke the word
As if a wedding vow.

Ah, but I was so much older then,
I'm younger than that now.

In a soldier's stance, I aimed my hand
At the mongrel dogs who teach
Fearing not that I'd become my enemy
In the instant that I preach
My pathway led by confusion boats
Mutiny from stern to bow.
Ah, but I was so much older then,
I'm younger than that now.

Yes, my guard stood hard when abstract threats
Too noble to neglect
Deceived me into thinking
I had something to protect
Good and bad, I define these terms
Quite clear, no doubt, somehow.
Ah, but I was so much older then,
I'm younger than that now.

Adrian Henri

Mrs Albion, You've Got a Lovely Daughter

For Allen Ginsberg

Albion's most lovely daughter sat on the banks of the Mersey
   dangling her landing stage in the water.

The daughters of Albion
   arriving by underground at Central Station
   eating hot ecclescakes at the Pierhead
   writing 'Billy Blake is fab' on a wall in Mathew St

   taking off their navyblue schooldrawers and
   putting on nylon panties ready for the night

The daughters of Albion
  see the moonlight beating down on them in Bebington
  throw away their chewinggum ready for the goodnight kiss
sleep in the dinnertime sunlight with old men
  looking up their skirts in St Johns Gardens
comb their darkblonde hair in suburban bedrooms
powder their delicate little nipples/wondering if tonight will
  be the night
their bodies pressed into dresses or sweaters
lavender at The Cavern or pink at The Sink

The daughters of Albion wondering how to explain why they
  didn't go home

The daughters of Albion
  taking the dawn ferry to tomorrow
  worrying about what happened
  worrying about what hasn't happened
  lacing up blue sneakers over brown ankles
  fastening up brown stockings to blue suspenderbelts

  Beautiful boys with bright red guitars
  in the spaces between the stars

  Reelin' an' a-rockin'
  Wishin' an' a-hopin'
  Kissin' an' a-prayin'
  Lovin' an' a-layin'

Mrs Albion, you've got a lovely daughter.

Joni Mitchell

Woodstock

I came upon a child of God
He was walking along the road
And I asked him, where are you going
And this he told me
I'm going on down to Yasgur's farm
I'm going to join in a rock 'n' roll band
I'm going to camp out on the land
And try an' get my soul free
We are stardust
We are golden
And we've got to get ourselves
Back to the garden

Then can I walk beside you
I have come here to lose the smog
And I feel to be a cog in something turning
Well maybe it is just the time of year
Or maybe it's the time of man
I don't know who I am
But life is for learning
We are stardust
We are golden
And we've got to get ourselves
Back to the garden

By the time we got to Woodstock
We were half a million strong
And everywhere there was song and celebration
And I dreamed I saw the bombers
Riding shotgun in the sky
And they were turning into butterflies
Above our nation
We are stardust
We are golden

And we've got to get ourselves
Back to the garden

Yasgur's farm: the huge open-air concert held on the farm of Max and Miriam Yasgur
at Woodstock, Upstate New York, from 15 to 17 August 1969 was a great focal point
of the rock counter-culture.

Naum Korzhavin

Imitation of Monsieur Béranger

An uproar in Leuven, insurrection in the Sorbonne.
Who's doing it? Intellectuals alone!
Like a lover waiting for the moment of rendezvous,
They are thirsting for revolution.

And in our country in the past this was amusement.
Time to repent, clear out, and curse.
Only I wouldn't like to leave.
Let Soviet power come to them.

Let it come to them – to meet their passion,
So that their dreams will be realized in the open,
Give them everything they need for happiness.
Without it – I will survive.

You laugh, but I don't feel like laughing.
And though I see a gaping maw,
I don't want to go to them from Russia,
Let Soviet power come to them.

They only need a special kind
Of freedom . . . So be it! . . . And I'd be fully
Satisfied with a banal sort of freedom:
Everything else is with me and in me.

Only not it – that is what's amusing.
And there won't be – any such occurrence.

Anyway I don't want to go to them –
Let Soviet power come to them.

Let it come to them – to the champions of the Goal.
Let them rejoice on the brink of misery
And entrust Comrade Angela Davis
With the reins of government.

And she'll win success
And cause them to fall on their knees.
No, there are reasons why I don't want to go to them,
Let Soviet power come to them.

Let it come to them – the devil himself doesn't scare them,
If freedom is not nice at all.
Very sorry – but they drag prison shitpots
Back and forth for such things.

I don't laugh – this is not funny at all:
Is it joyful that the world will fail?
No, my friends – I don't want to go to them.
Let Soviet power come to them.

Let it lead hungry years to them.
Let lies corrode them, like smoke.
Let it happen! . . . Under the protection of banal freedom
I'll honestly feel sorry for them.

I myself passed through those successes,
Suffered myself and was tormented to my heart's content . . .
No, I don't see any sense in going to them.
Let Soviet power come to them.

Translated from the Russian by Albert C. Todd.

In May 1968 student unrest spread throughout Western Europe. It was most extreme in France, where, for a while, it seemed as if De Gaulle's government would fall. *Monsieur Béranger*: Jean Pierre de Béranger (1780–1857), a French poet who articulated the voice of the people. *Angela Davis*: a prominent black American activist in the late 1960s.

John Lennon and Paul McCartney

A Day in the Life

I read the news today, oh boy,
About a lucky man who made the grade
And though the news was rather sad
Well I just had to laugh
I saw the photograph.
He blew his mind out in a car
He didn't notice that the lights had changed
A crowd of people stood and stared
They'd seen his face before
Nobody was really sure
If he was from the House of Lords.

I saw a film today, oh boy,
The English army had just won the war
A crowd of people turned away
But I just had to look
Having read the book.
I'd love to turn you on.

Woke up, fell out of bed,
Dragged a comb across my head
Found my way downstairs and drank a cup,
And looking up I noticed I was late.
Found my coat and grabbed my hat
Made the bus in seconds flat
Found my way upstairs and had a smoke,
Somebody spoke and I went into a dream.

I read the news today, oh boy,
Four thousand holes in Blackburn,
Lancashire
And though the holes were rather small
They had to count them all
Now they know how many holes it takes to fill the Albert Hall
I'd love to turn you on.

STRANGE FRUIT: CIVIL RIGHTS
1930S–1968

In the aftermath of the American Civil War the emancipation of black people seemed set on a firm course. Many black soldiers had distinguished themselves in battle; Frederick Douglas, an ex-slave, was an eloquent spokesman. But although two black senators were elected from Mississippi in the 1870s, not another was elected until 1966. In the first half of the century political progress was minimal and there was a new outbreak of lynching in the South in the Twenties. The Second World War and a return to full employment stirred a new demand for change. Matters came to a head in the mid-Fifties with the attempt to end the segregation which had applied to most aspects of Southern life. During the Sixties, black culture, particularly the Blues, became influential in Western societies and black American poets, drawing on the Blues, jazz and the tradition of Baptist revivalist rhetoric, began to be influential in America.

Lewis Allen

'Strange Fruit'

Southern trees bear strange fruit
Blood on the leaves and blood at the root
Black body swinging in the Southern breeze
Strange fruit hanging from the poplar trees

Pastoral scene of the gallant South
The bulging eyes and the twisted mouth
Scent of magnolia sweet and fresh
Then the sudden smell of burning flesh

Here is a fruit for the crows to pluck
For the rain to gather, for the wind to suck
For the sun to rot, for the tree to drop
Here is a strange and bitter crop

Gwendolyn Brooks

The Chicago Defender Sends a Man to Little Rock

Fall, 1957

In Little Rock the people bear
Babes, and comb and part their hair
And watch the ads, put repair
To roof and latch. While wheat toast burns
A woman waters multiferns.

Time upholds or overturns
The many, tight, and small concerns.

In Little Rock the people sing
Sunday hymns like anything,
Through Sunday pomp and polishing.

And after testament and tunes,
Some soften Sunday afternoons
With lemon tea and Lorna Doones.

I forecast
And I believe
Come Christmas Little Rock will cleave
To Christmas tree and trifle, weave,
From laugh and tinsel, texture fast.

In Little Rock is baseball; Barcarolle.
That hotness in July . . . the uniformed figures raw and implacable
And not intellectual,
Batting the hotness or clawing the suffering dust.
The Open Air Concert, on the special twilight green . . .
When Beethoven is brutal or whispers to lady-like air.
Blanket-sitters are solemn, as Johann troubles to lean
To tell them what to mean . . .

There is love, too, in Little Rock. Soft women softly
Opening themselves in kindness,
Or, pitying one's blindness,
Awaiting one's pleasure
In azure
Glory with anguished rose at the root . . .
To wash away old semi-discomfitures.
They re-teach purple and unsullen blue.
The wispy soils go. And uncertain
Half-havings have they clarified to sures.

In Little Rock they know
Not answering the telephone is a way of rejecting life,
That it is our business to be bothered, is our business
To cherish bores or boredom, be polite
To lies and love and many-faceted fuzziness.

I scratch my head, massage the hate-I-had.
I blink across my prim and pencilled pad.
The saga I was sent for is not down.
Because there is a puzzle in this town.
The biggest News I do not dare
Telegraph to the Editor's chair:
'They are like people everywhere.'

The angry Editor would reply
In hundred harryings of Why.

And true, they are hurling spittle, rock,
Garbage and fruit in Little Rock.

And I saw coiling storm a-writhe
On bright madonnas. And a scythe
Of men harassing brownish girls.
(The bows and barrettes in the curls
And braids declined away from joy.)

I saw a bleeding brownish boy . . .

The lariat lynch-wish I deplored.

The loveliest lynchee was our Lord.

Little Rock: in this town in Arkansas, in 1957, Governor Orval Faubus defied an attempt by the local schools (with Federal assistance) to end segregated schooling.

Bob Dylan

The Lonesome Death of Hattie Carroll

William Zanzinger killed poor Hattie Carroll
With a cane that he twirled around his diamond ring finger
At a Baltimore hotel society gath'rin'.
And the cops were called in and his weapon took from him
As they rode him in custody down to the station
And booked William Zanzinger for first-degree murder.
But you who philosophize disgrace and criticize all fears,
Take the rag away from your face.
Now ain't the time for your tears.

William Zanzinger, who at twenty-four years
Owns a tobacco farm of six hundred acres
With rich wealthy parents who provide and protect him
And high office relations in the politics of Maryland,
Reacted to his deed with a shrug of his shoulders
And swear words and sneering, and his tongue it was snarling,
In a matter of minutes on bail was out walking.

But you who philosophize disgrace and criticize all fears,
Take the rag away from your face.
Now ain't the time for your tears.

Hattie Carroll was a maid of the kitchen.
She was fifty-one years old and gave birth to ten children
Who carried the dishes and took out the garbage
And never sat once at the head of the table
And didn't even talk to the people at the table
Who just cleaned up all the food from the table
And emptied the ashtrays on a whole other level,
Got killed by a blow, lay slain by a cane
That sailed through the air and came down through the room,
Doomed and determined to destroy all the gentle.
And she never done nothing to William Zanzinger.
But you who philosophize disgrace and criticize all fears,
Take the rag away from your face.
Now ain't the time for your tears.

In the courtroom of honor, the judge pounded his gavel
To show that all's equal and that the courts are on the level
And that the strings in the books ain't pulled and persuaded
And that even the nobles get properly handled
Once that the cops have chased after and caught 'em
And that the ladder of law has no top and no bottom,
Stared at the person who killed for no reason
Who just happened to be feelin' that way without warnin'.
And he spoke through his cloak, most deep and distinguished,
And handed out strongly, for penalty and repentance,
William Zanzinger with a six-month sentence.
Oh, but you who philosophize disgrace and criticize all fears,
Bury the rag deep in your face
For now's the time for your tears.

Brother Will Hairston

Alabama Bus

Stop that Alabama bus	I don't wanna ride
Stop that Alabama bus	I don't wanna ride
Stop that Alabama bus	I don't wanna ride
Lord an Alabama boy	'cause I don't wanna ride

Stop that Alabama bus	I don't wanna ride
Stop that Alabama bus	I don't wanna ride
Stop that Alabama bus	I don't wanna ride
Lord an Alabama boy	'cause I don't wanna ride

Lord, there come a bus don't have no load
You know, they tell me that a human being stepped on board
You know, they tell me that the man stepped on the bus
You know, they tell me that the driver began to fuss
He said, Lookit here, man, you from the Negro race
And don't you know you sitting in the wrong place?
The driver told the man, I know you paid your dime
But if you don't move you gonna pay a fine
The man told the driver, My feets are hurting
The driver told the man to move behind the curtain

Stop that Alabama bus	I don't wanna ride
Stop that Alabama bus	I don't wanna ride
Stop that Alabama bus	I don't wanna ride
Lord an Alabama boy	'cause I don't wanna ride

I wanna tell you 'bout the Reverend Martin Luther King
You know, they tell me that the people began to sing
You know, the man God sent out in the world
You know, they tell me that the man had a mighty nerve
You know, the poor man didn't have a bus to rent
You know, they tell me, Great God, he had *a mighty spent*

And he reminded me of Moses in Israel land
He said, A man ain't nothing but a man
He said, Lookit here, Alabama, don't you see
He says, A all of my people gonna follow me
You know, they tell me Reverend King was very hurt
He says, A all of my people gonna walk to work
They said, Lookit here, boy, you hadn't took a thought
So, don't you know you broke the anti-boycott law
They tell me Reverend King said, Treat us right
You know, in the Second World War my father lost his sight
You know, they tell me Abraham signed the pledge one night
He said that all of these men should have their equal rights
You know, they had the trial and Clayton Powell was there
You know, they tell me Clayton Powell asked the world for prayer
You know, they sent down there to go his bail
You know, they PUT REVEREND KING IN A ALABAMA JAIL

Stop that Alabama bus   I don't wanna ride
Stop that Alabama bus   I don't wanna ride
Stop that Alabama bus   I don't wanna ride
Lord an Alabama boy   'cause I don't wanna ride

Stop that Alabama bus   I don't wanna ride
Stop that Alabama bus   I don't wanna ride
Stop that Alabama bus   I don't wanna ride
Lord an Alabama boy   'cause I don't wanna ride

You know, they tell me Reverend King was *a violence 'bide*
A when all the buses passed, and no body will ride
You know, they tell me that the Negroes was ready to go
They had a walked along the streets until their feets was sore
You know, they tell me Reverend King had spreaded the word
'Bout an Alabama bus ride, so I heard
You know, they spent a lot of money since King go on
You know, in nineteen and twenty-nine that man was born
You know, the five hundred dollars aren't very heavy
You know, the poor man was born the fifteenth of January

Stop that Alabama bus	I don't wanna ride
Stop that Alabama bus	I don't wanna ride
Stop that Alabama bus	I don't wanna ride
Lord an Alabama boy	'cause I don't wanna ride

From December 1955 to December 1956, the Black community in Montgomery, Alabama, led by Revd. Martin Luther King, boycotted the buses in an attempt to end the segregation of public transport. In November 1956 the Supreme Court ruled that segregation was unlawful. On 21 December 1956 King boarded a bus and sat where he liked.

Maya Angelou

Riot: 60's

Our
YOUR FRIEND CHARLIE pawnshop
was a glorious blaze
I heard the flames lick
then eat the trays
of zircons
mounted in red gold alloys

Easter clothes and stolen furs
burned in the attic
radios and teevees
crackled with static
plugged in
only to a racial outlet

Some
thought the FRIENDLY FINANCE FURNITURE CO.
burned higher
When a leopard-print sofa with gold legs
(which makes into a bed)
caught fire
an admiring groan from the waiting horde
'Absentee landlord
you got that shit'

Lighting: a hundred Watts
Detroit, Newark and New York
Screeching nerves, exploding minds
lives tied to
a policeman's whistle
a welfare worker's doorbell
finger

Hospitality, southern-style
corn pone grits and you-all smile
whole blocks novae
brand-new stars
policemen caught in their
brand-new cars
Chugga chugga chigga
git me one nigga
lootin' n burnin'
he won't git far

Watermelons, summer ripe
grey neckbones and boiling tripe
supermarket roastin' like the
noonday sun
national guard nervous with his shiny gun
goose the motor quicker
here's my nigga picka
shoot him in the belly
shoot him while he run

RIDING SHOTGUN IN THE SKY:
VIETNAM 1964–1973

For American poets, Vietnam was a cause like that of the Spanish Civil War in the Thirties. The American establishment had developed an obsessive belief in the necessity of drawing a line against communism in South East Asia. The justification for this was the Domino Theory, in which successive Asian countries were expected to succumb to communism, leaving America alone to face them, unless the pass could be held at South Vietnam. The war coincided, in America, with the most widespread prosperity and cultural buoyancy the world has ever seen. The result was to accelerate the emergence of a counter-culture, with the Beats as founding fathers. Poets have never been so engaged again since.

Robert Duncan

Up Rising

Now Johnson would go up to join the simulacra of men,
    Hitler and Stalin, to work his fame
    with planes roaring out from Guam over Asia,
all America become a sea of toiling men
    stirrd at his will, which would be a bloated thing,
    drawing from the underbelly of the nation
    such blood and dreams as swell the idiot psyche
    out of its courses into an elemental thing
    until his name stinks with burning meat and heapt honors

And men wake to see that they are used like things
    spent in a great potlatch, this Texas barbecue
        of Asia, Africa, and all the Americas,
And the professional military behind him, thinking
    to use him as they thought to use Hitler
    without losing control of their business of war,

But the mania, the ravening eagle of America
    as Lawrence saw him 'bird of men that are masters,
    lifting the rabbit-blood of the myriads up into . . .'
    into something terrible, gone beyond bounds, or
As Blake saw America in figures of fire and blood raging,
    . . . in what image? the ominous roar in the air,
the omnipotent wings, the all-American boy in the cockpit
    loosing his flow of napalm, below in the jungles
    'any life at all or sign of life' his target, drawing now
        not with crayons in his secret room
the burning of homes and the torture of mothers and fathers and
        children,
    their hair a-flame, screaming in agony, but
in the line of duty, for the might and enduring fame
    of Johnson, for the victory of American will over its victims,
    releasing his story of destruction over the enemy,
in terror and hatred of all communal things, of communion,
    of communism
has raised from the private rooms of small-town bosses and
        businessmen,
from the council chambers of the gangs that run the great cities,
    swollen with the votes of millions,
from the fearful hearts of good people in the suburbs turning the
    savoury meat over the charcoal burners and heaping their barbecue
    plates with more than they can eat,
from the closed meeting-rooms of regents of universities and sessions
    of profiteers

– back of the scene: the atomic stockpile; the vials of synthesized
    diseases eager biologists have develop over half a century dreaming
    of the bodies of mothers and fathers and children and hated rivals
    swollen with new plagues, measles grown enormous, influenzas
    perfected; and the gasses of despair, confusion of the senses, mania,
    inducing terror of the universe, coma, existential wounds, that
    chemists we have met at cocktail parties, passt daily with a
    happy 'Good Day' on the way to classes or work, have workt to
    make war too terrible for men to wage –

raised this secret entity of America's hatred of Europe, of Africa, of Asia,
the deep hatred for the old world that had driven generations of

America out of itself,
and for the alien world, the new world about him, that might have
    been Paradise
but was before his eyes already cleard back in a holocaust of burning
    Indians, trees and grasslands,
reduced to his real estate, his projects of exploitation and profitable
        wastes,

this specter that in the beginning Adams and Jefferson feard and knew
would corrupt the very body of the nation
    and all our sense of our common humanity,
this black bile of old evils arisen anew,
takes over the vanity of Johnson;
and the very glint of Satan's eyes from the pit of the hell of America's
    unacknowledged, unrepented crimes that I saw in Goldwater's eyes
now shines from the eyes of the President
    in the swollen head of the nation.

Denise Levertov

Overheard over SE Asia

'White phosphorus, white phosphorus,
mechanical snow,
where are you falling?'

'I am falling impartially on roads and roofs,
on bamboo thickets, on people.
My name recalls rich seas on rainy nights,
each drop that hits the surface eliciting
luminous response from a million algae.
My name is a whisper of sequins. Ha!
Each of them is a disk of fire,
I am the snow that burns.
            I fall

wherever men send me to fall –
but I prefer flesh, so smooth, so dense:
I decorate it in black, and seek
the bone.'

Adrian Mitchell

To Whom It May Concern
(Tell Me Lies about Vietnam)

I was run over by the truth one day.
Ever since the accident I've walked this way
    So stick my legs in plaster
    Tell me lies about Vietnam.

Heard the alarm clock screaming with pain,
Couldn't find myself so I went back to sleep again
    So fill my ears with silver
    Stick my legs in plaster
    Tell me lies about Vietnam.

Every time I shut my eyes all I see is flames.
Made a marble phone book and I carved all the names
    So coat my eyes with butter
    Fill my ears with silver
    Stick my legs in plaster
    Tell me lies about Vietnam.

I smell something burning, hope it's just my brains.
They're only dropping peppermints and daisy-chains
    So stuff my nose with garlic
    Coat my eyes with butter
    Fill my ears with silver
    Stick my legs in plaster
    Tell me lies about Vietnam.

Where were you at the time of the crime?
Down by the Cenotaph drinking slime

So chain my tongue with whisky
Stuff my nose with garlic
Coat my eyes with butter
Fill my ears with silver
Stick my legs in plaster
Tell me lies about Vietnam.

You put your bombers in, you put your conscience out,
You take the human being and you twist it all about
So scrub my skin with women
Chain my tongue with whisky
Stuff my nose with garlic
Coat my eyes with butter
Fill my ears with silver
Stick my legs in plaster
Tell me lies about Vietnam.

James Fenton

In a Notebook

There was a river overhung with trees
With wooden houses built along its shallows
From which the morning sun drew up a haze
And the gyrations of the early swallows
Paid no attention to the gentle breeze
Which spoke discreetly from the weeping willows.
There was a jetty by the forest clearing
Where a small boat was tugging at its mooring.

And night still lingered underneath the eaves.
In the dark houseboats families were stirring
And Chinese soup was cooked on charcoal stoves.
Then one by one there came into the clearing
Mothers and daughters bowed beneath their sheaves.
The silent children gathered round me staring
And the shy soldiers setting out for battle
Asked for a cigarette and laughed a little.

From low canoes old men laid out their nets
While on the bank young boys with lines were fishing.
The wicker traps were drawn up by their floats.
The girls stood waist-deep in the river washing
Or tossed the day's rice on enamel plates
And I sat drinking bitter coffee wishing
The tide would turn to bring me to my senses
After the pleasant war and the evasive answers.

There was a river overhung with trees.
The girls stood waist-deep in the river washing,
And night still lingered underneath the eaves
While on the bank young boys with lines were fishing.
Mothers and daughters bowed beneath their sheaves
While I sat drinking bitter coffee wishing –
And the tide turned and brought me to my senses.
The pleasant war brought the unpleasant answers.

The villages are burnt, the cities void;
The morning light has left the river view;
The distant followers have been dismayed;
And I'm afraid, reading this passage now,
That everything I knew has been destroyed
By those whom I admired but never knew;
The laughing soldiers fought to their defeat
And I'm afraid most of my friends are dead.

Dick Allen

A Short History of the Vietnam War Years

Nothing was said until the house grew dark
And a fishnet of stars was cast upon its windows.
In the tall bedroom mirror, the door to Watergate
Opened again. A helicopter tiny as a moth
Flew across the lovers' flanks, its slow pinwheel blades
Making the sound of grief and churning rivers.

Placards lifted, the marchers of the Sixties
Stood in green meadows. Then folk songs began
Rising from their lips like blue leaves in summer
And time was a slipstream where a Phantom jet
Rolled in the sun. The lovers ran their hands
Over the rice fields and the panting oxen.

Deep in itself, the bedside clock unwound
By the edge of a pool, casting its minutes out
To a shoal of Destroyers. *Be still*, the lovers whispered.
In the room above the hall a mud-stained jeep
Backed up to a wooden brothel in Saigon,
An orange-robed monk knelt down in billowed flame.

The lovers grew sad. A soft rainy wind from Ohio
Brushed gunfire bursts and tear gas over them.
We will never love money, they said, clinging to each other,
Or dress like television, work like IBM.
We will grow flowers to slide into rifle barrels,
And we will dance barefoot on Wall Street's glass chin.

That was when hope was a temple bell, a bleeding eye,
A circle of books around the lovers' bed
As the soldiers looked on. Mai Lai fell half-asleep
Under the full thrust moon. On bruised hands and knees,
Tet advanced along the shadowed railroad ties
And the deltas awoke and flooded Washington.

We will drift to Cambodia, the lovers said,
Dance in People's Park, burn incense tapers
At Buddhist shrines. The house wrapped its black armband
Over the lovers as they lay entwined.
And if you listened, you could hear the mortar fire
Walking up the valleys like an old blind man.

Mai Lai: on 16 May 1968 a platoon of American soldiers, under Lieutenant William
Calley Jr, massacred hundreds of innocent Vietnamese civilians at Mai Lai. Calley was
sentenced to life imprisonment for twenty-two murders.
Tet: the Vietnamese New Year, beginning on 31 January. On that date in 1968 the
Vietcong began a huge offensive. Although all the attacks were eventually beaten off
by the Americans, Tet is regarded as the turning point of the war.

LOST TRIBES:
THE MIDDLE EAST 1948–

The foundation of the state of Israel produced, at least at first, a quasi-European country in the Middle East. Yehuda Amichai, Israel's best-known living poet, is a typical figure in the new state: born in Wurzburg, Germany, in 1924, he went to Palestine with his parents in 1936 and fought in the Second World War, the Israeli War of Independence (1948) and the Israeli–Arab wars of 1956 and 1973. The fate of Arab poets has been parlous. The experiences of the great Palestinian poet Mahmoud Darwish are fairly representative. Born in Galilee in 1942, he and his family fled to Lebanon in 1948, but soon returned to Haifa, without papers. Darwish was thus stateless and was imprisoned several times in the Sixties. He left for Egypt in 1971 and was in Beirut from 1973, where he worked as a radical journalist. The Israeli attack on Beirut in 1982 drove him into exile in Paris.

Yehuda Amichai

From *Travels of the Last Benjamin Tudela*

Tanks from America, fighter planes from France, Russian
jet-doves, armored chariots from England, Sisera's regiments
who dried the swamps with their corpses, a flying Massada,
Beitar slowly sinking, Yodfat on wheels, the Antonia,
    ground-to-ground
ground, ground-to-air air, ground-to-sky sky. Massada won't fall
    again, won't fall again,
won't fall again, Massada, won't. Multiple automatic
prayer beads and also in single shots. Muezzins armed with
three-stage missiles, paper-rips and battle-cries
of holy wars in all seven kinds,
shtreimls like mines in the road and in the air, deep philosophical

depth charges, a heart lit up with a green light inside
the engine of a red-hot bomber, Elijah's ejection-seat leaping up
at a time of danger, hurling circumcision knives, thundering
dynamite fuses from heart to heart, a Byzantine tank
with a decorated window in which an icon appears
lit up in purity and softness, *mezuzahs* filled with
explosives, don't kiss them or they'll blow up, dervishes
with powdered rococo curls, the Joint Chiefs of Staff
consisting of Job, his friends, Satan, and God, around a sand-table.
A pricking with bannered pins in the live flesh
of hills and valleys made of naked
humans lying in front of them,
underwater synagogues, periscope rabbis,
cantors out of the depths, jeeps armed with women's hair
and with wild girls' fingernails, ripping their
clothes in rage and mourning. Supersonic angels
with wings of women's fat thighs,
letters of a Torah scroll in ammunition straps, machine guns,
flowers in the pattern of a fortified bunker,
fingers of dynamite, prosthetic legs of dynamite
eight empty bullet-shells for a *Hanukkah menorah*,
explosives of eternal flame, the cross of a crossfire,
a submachine gun carried in phylactery straps,
camouflage nets of thin lacy material
from girlfriends' panties, used women's dresses
and ripped diapers to clean the cannon mouth,
offensive hand-grenades in the shape of bells,
defensive hand-grenades in the shape of a spice box
for the close of the Sabbath, sea mines
like the prickly apples used as smelling-salts on Yom Kippur
in case of fainting, half my childhood in
a whole armored truck, a grandmother clock
for starting a time-egg filled with
clipped fingernails of bad boys
with a smell of cinnamon, Dürer's
praying hands sticking up
like a vertical land mine, arms with an attachment
for a bayonet, a good-night fortified with sand bags,

the twelve little minor prophets
in a night ambush with warm breath,
cannon barrels climbing like ivy, shooting
cuckoo shells every fifteen minutes: cuckoo,
boom-boom. Barbed-wire testicles,
eye-mines bulging and hurting,
aerial bombs with the heads of
beautiful women like the ones that used to be carved
on ships' prows, the mouth of a cannon
open like flower petals,
MIRV, SWAT, ICBM, IBM,
POW, RIP, AWOL,
SNAFU, INRI, JDL, LBJ,
ESP, IRS, DNA, GOD.
Sit down. Today is the day of judgment. Today there was war.

Translated from the Hebrew by
Chana Bloch and Stephen Mitchell.

Benjamin [of] Tudela: the greatest medieval Jewish traveller. The name has been adopted by other figures, historical and fictional. Amichai was living on Tudela Street when he wrote the poem.
Sisera: an enemy of the Jews in biblical times.
Massada, Yodfat, the Antonia: ancient fortresses in Israel involved in the war against the Romans.
Beitar: a youth movement from the time of the establishment of the state of Israel.
shtreimls: round, fur-trimmed hats worn by ultra-Orthodox Jews on the Sabbath.
Elijah: the prophet who was thought to have been whirled up to heaven in a chariot on great winds of fire.
mezuzahs: small carved wooden objects containing a portion of a holy scroll, hung on the door of a Jewish house.
Hanukkah menorah: the candelabrum used to celebrate the Jewish Festival of light in mid-winter.
phylactery: case containing biblical texts on parchment, bound by straps to the arm.

James Fenton

Jerusalem

I

Stone cries to stone,
Heart to heart, heart to stone,
And the interrogation will not die
For there is no eternal city
And there is no pity
And there is nothing underneath the sky
No rainbow and no guarantee
There is no covenant between your God and me.

II

It is superb in the air.
Suffering is everywhere
And each man wears his suffering like a skin.
My history is proud.
Mine is not allowed.
This is the cistern where all wars begin,
The laughter from the armoured car.
This is the man who won't believe you're what you are.

III

This is your fault.
This is a crusader vault.
The Brook of Kidron flows from Mea She'arim.
I will pray for you.
I will tell you what to do.
I'll stone you. I shall break your every limb.
Oh I am not afraid of you
But maybe I should fear the things you make me do.

IV

This is not Golgotha.
This is the Holy Sepulchre,
The Emperor Hadrian's temple to a love
Which he did not much share.
Golgotha could be anywhere.
Jerusalem itself is on the move.
It leaps and leaps from hill to hill
And as it makes its way it also makes its will.

V

The city was sacked.
Jordan was driven back.
The pious Christians burned the Jews alive.
This is a minaret.
I'm not finished yet.
We're waiting for reinforcements to arrive.
What was your mother's real name?
Would it be safe today to go to Bethlehem?

VI

This is the Garden Tomb.
No, *this* is the Garden Tomb.
I'm an Armenian. I am a Copt.
This is Utopia.
I came here from Ethiopia.
This hole is where the flying carpet dropped
The Prophet off to pray one night
And from here one hour later he resumed his flight.

VII

Who packed your bag?
I packed my bag.
Where was your uncle's mother's sister born?
Have you ever met an Arab?
Yes I am a scarab.
I am a worm. I am a thing of scorn.
I cry Impure from street to street
And see my degradation in the eyes I meet.

VIII

I am your enemy.
This is Gethsemane.
The broken graves look to the Temple Mount.
Tell me now, tell me when
When shall we all rise again?
Shall I be first in that great body count?
When shall the tribes be gathered in?
When, tell me, when shall the Last Things begin?

IX

You are in error.
This is terror.
This is your banishment. This land is mine.
This is what you earn.
This is the Law of No Return.
This is the sour dough, this the sweet wine.
This is my history, this my race
And this unhappy man threw acid in my face.

X

Stone cries to stone,
Heart to heart, heart to stone.
These are the warrior archaeologists.
This is us and that is them.
This is Jerusalem.
These are the dying men with tattooed wrists.
Do this and I'll destroy your home.
I have destroyed your home. You have destroyed my home.

December 1988

Jon Silkin

Jews without Arabs

Did we make them leave, did they turn the wheel
of dispersion? We flee
through desert prairie, those grasses
that never flower, though the cold at night
is the thought of the day's herbage
glimpsed in heat. Where are they, and the grasses?
They left, as if
we were boys to be shunned, without our sex,
miniature unicorns, but flatteringly;
like guano, like the bats' cave.
Their absence is our loneliness.
A fan full circle. If we stepped
into our shadow, we'd have no breath.

Here is a provision of bread the sun bakes,
a space in rock hiding Moses
God seeks to kill. We're Jewish Pharoahs
flicking water, whipping it. Canute's deathless stick
that parts the sea – fringed with Sinai's bog-cotton,
its flags of small dissension. All soldiers,
weapons, manuals, sweethearts
in kodak, sink, with the claws of a tank's tread
and the howling metal roar.
Ezekiel has bitter signs: in the lilac sky
his wheel turns
its inner circle in reverse. I free a soldier

like a fly, into desert meadows
of pebble, pale and fine as sugar. 'Unacceptable,'
in delicate abandon
in fine shunning wings, the mayfly cries.
She, the humming-bird's constant intrepid companion.
Theirs the mixed family of creation.

Our enemy's absence, which is the spear of loneliness,
an undying son we each have,
the unimaginable, unsought-for child
with us by a sandy spring, where we substantiate
our constant debarment – it mutely hammers
the dreaming part of our lives: a bruise, an inescapable
panic of inseparable pain.
The milk in our mouths is burnt for ever.
Friends, friends, what may we change to?

Mahmoud Darwish

From *Beirut*

Beirut
Witness of the heart
I leave her streets and leave myself
Clutched by an endless poem.
My fire won't die down,
The doves are on the rooftops
Peace upon the remnants of the rooftops.
I fold the city as I fold my papers
And carry it away, a sack of clouds.
I wake and look in my body's clothing
For myself.
We laugh and say that we are still alive.
I open up the narrow street for wind
For footsteps
For the crafty seller of hot bread.
Grace of Beirut as she stands in fog,
Gratitude to Beirut as she stands in ruin.
The conquerors have led me to the poem
I carry language docile as a cloud
Above the pavement
Of reading and of writing
This sea has left its eyes with us
And gone back towards sea.

From a stone they built their ghetto nation
From a stone we'll build a lover's country
From a stone
I voice my slow farewell
The city drowns in repetitious phrases
The wound grows on the sword
And both come near to cut me.

I descend the stairs
That do not end in cellars of festivity
I descend the stairs
That do not end in poems.
For longing's sake I head towards Damascus
Perhaps I'll have a vision
Perhaps the ringing bells will echo
Till they make me shy.
Words were consequential
When they changed the one who spoke them.
Farewell to all that's yet to come
To dawn about to break and break us
To cities returning us to other cities
To curved swords and palm.
Our journey lengthens with our wound.

Translated from the Arabic by
Rana Kabbani.

Beirut: in the summer of 1982 Israel invaded Lebanon and besieged Beirut, with the aim of driving the Palestine Liberation Organization (PLO) out of the country. The PLO left, under international supervision, between 21 August and 1 September 1982.

TO BE THE POWERS: POLITICS

Many poets in the twentieth century have been forced to become political by circumstances. A few, like Brecht, Wole Soyinka, Erich Fried and Tony Harrison, are political to their bone marrow. 'Poetry makes nothing happen,' said Auden, but in repressive regimes, poets who utter forbidden truths can be lightning conductors for opposition. A high proportion of the poems in this book address the great public themes; the poems in this section are concerned with the political process itself, its rituals and recurrent patterns. Poetry has never perhaps been as politically effective as fiction and journalism (the connection between clear language and good politics and vice versa was most vividly expressed by George Orwell), but a poem like Gottfried Benn's 'Foreign Minister', in its offhand ironies, captures the slipperiness of politics perfectly and seems as true of the contemporary circus of international negotiations as it was of the early twentieth-century political and diplomatic rituals it mocks.

Robinson Jeffers

Skunks

The corruptions of war and peace, the public and wholesale crimes
    that make war, the greed and lies of the peace
And victor's vengeance: how at a distance
They soften into romance – blue mountains and blossomed marshes
    in the long landscape of history – Caligula
Becomes an amusing clown, and Genghiz
A mere genius, a great author of tragedies. Our own time's chiefs of
    massacre – Stalin died yesterday –
Watch how soon blood will bleach, and gross horror
Become words in a book.

We have little animals here, slow-stepping
cousins of stoat and weasel,
Striped skunks, that can spit from under their tails
An odor so vile and stifling that neither wolf nor wildcat dares to
come near them; they walk in confidence,
Solely armed with this loathsome poison-gas.
But smelled far off – have you noticed? – it is surprisingly pleasant.
It is like the breath of ferns and wet earth
Deep in a wooded glen in the evening,
Cool water glides quietly over the moss-grown stones, quick trout
dimple the pool. – Distance makes clean.

John Fuller

From *Europe*

XIX

To be the powers! To sit with microphones
At tables gently circular as the
Great globe itself, speaking aloud from thrones
Disguised as sofas, turning photography
Into an hourly ikon of their trust,
Their rage and their responsibility!
The powers are never threatened. If they must,
They will react to power. And agree.

But hearts are fragile to enforce a bond.
Not a blade's fineness but its fore-edge weight
Counts most, they say, in the cutting of the knife.
Only at length, and wearily, they respond
To the pert brandished arguments of state,
Never to something broken like a life.

Gottfried Benn

Foreign Minister

Taken all in all
peoples are worth a Mass,
but in particular: let the trumpet speak to the kettle drum,
now the King is toasting Hamlet –
a splendid turn-out and show,
but the sword-tip is poisoned.

'Iswolski laughed.'
Quotations pat, quips in the kitbag,
now cool, now *chaleureux*, peace and goodwill,
better a flute too many at times,
Witte's handshakes in Portsmouth (1905)
were a record, but the peace terms improved.

In parliament – not at all humbug by any means,
but methodic like Sanskrit or nuclear physics,
vast laboratory: official advisors, press releases, empiricism,
character too must be felt to be at work,
seriously: character they do have, those come to the top,
not because of possible law suits
but it's their moral sex appeal –
true, what is the State?
'One existing thing among many others,'
Plato said long ago.

'Discrepancy between public
and real opinion' (Keynes), Opalize!
One lives between *les hauts* and *les bas*,
President of the Council first, then minor post in the Balkans,
finally virtual Prime Minister,
then a new re-shuffle,
and one retires to one's estate.

Easy to say: misguided policies.
When misguided? Today? After ten years? After a century?

Misalliances, betrayal, intrigues,
one is blamed for them all,
one must put on the oilskin
before embarking,
observe whether the eagles are flying on the right or the left,
the sacred hens are refusing their feed.
When Hannibal crossed the Simplon with his elephants
everything was in order,
when Carthage fell later
Salammbo wept.

Socialism – capitalism – if the grapevine grows
and national industry processes the juice
thanks to extraordinary inventions and manipulations
into sparkling wine – then, presumably one must drink it too?
Or should one condemn the Celts
for carrying the Massilian stock
into Gaul for barter –
that would be to damn every historic process
and the whole dissemination of culture.

In a two-hour conference the foreign ministers
arrived at a provisional agreement
(questions of oil and pipelines),
three of them were wearing morning coats,
one a *burnouse*.

Translated from the German by Michael Hamburger.

Iswolski: Alexander Iswolski was the Russian Foreign Minister who took part in the Peace Talks at Portsmouth, New Hampshire, USA, in 1905, following the Russo-Japanese War.
Witte: Sergei Witte was the Russian Finance Minister at the same talks.
Massilian: from Marseilles.
burnouse: Arabic garment consisting of a long cloak with hood attached.

Vicki Raymond

The People, No

You never hear 'the People' now:
that thundering, slightly frightening sea
has been oiled flat.
But 'people' you hear everywhere,
a baby chirrup sensuously drawn out.

The People used to be a little
too fond of crowds for their own good.
Like movie extras, they
were sent from place to place, kept standing
long hours in the sun and, finally,
given their fortnight's pay.

People, on the other hand,
were sensitive, and cared;
and they agreed they needed
to keep their weight down, running
around the park each morning.
No wonder that they superseded

that poor old dinosaur, the People,
who smoked, and never understood
that to survive you have to be quite small,
and sometimes seem not to be there at all.

Let's hear it, then, for people,
their sensitivity and taste,
their sets of values
like sets of willow pattern,
so delicate, so easily replaced.

Nissim Ezekiel

The Patriot

I am standing for peace and non-violence.
Why world is fighting fighting
Why all people of world
Are not following Mahatma Gandhi,
I am simply not understanding.
Ancient Indian Wisdom is 100% correct.
I should say even 200% correct.
But Modern generation is neglecting –
Too much going for fashion and foreign thing.

Other day I'm reading in newspaper
(Every day I'm reading Times of India
To improve my English Language)
How one goonda fellow
Throw stone at Indirabehn.
Must be student unrest fellow, I am thinking.
Friends, Romans, Countrymen, I am saying (to myself)
Lend me the ears.
Everything is coming –
Regeneration, Remuneration, Contraception.
Be patiently, brothers and sisters.

You want one glass lassi?
Very good for digestion.
With little salt lovely drink,
Better than wine;
Not that I am ever tasting the wine.
I'm the total teetotaller, completely total.
But I say
Wine is for the drunkards only.

What you think of prospects of world peace?
Pakistan behaving like this,
China behaving like that,
It is making me very sad, I am telling you.
Really, most harassing me.
All men are brothers, no?
In India also
Gujaraties, Maharashtrians, Hindiwallahs
All brothers –
Though some are having funny habits.
Still, you tolerate me,
I tolerate you,
One day Ram Rajya is surely coming.

You are going?
But you will visit again
Any time, any day,
I am not believing in ceremony.
Always I am enjoying your company.

Erich Fried

Weaker

They are getting stronger again
Who is?
They are

Why should they be?
They should not be
they just are

Stronger than who?
Than you
soon perhaps than many

What do they want?
First of all
to get stronger again

Why do you say all this?
Because I can still
say it

Can't this get you into trouble?
Yes
for they are getting stronger

What makes you so sure?
Your own words
that I can get into trouble

*Translated from the German
by Stuart Hood.*

William Stafford

A Documentary from America

When the Presidential candidate came to our town
he had used up his voice, but he delivered a speech
written by a committee, through a friend of his
running on the same ticket. The candidate smiled.
We cheered his courage, and a cynic hissed:
'Fools, you are on TV and have just helped elect that man!'

Later at a motel in Nanton, Alberta
(a town on the plains with a special surprise –
a pipe that gushes a drink like a flash by the road),
we tuned in a show with a variety of plots
to stalk viewers with (whereas Westerns had only
to open up with one, say a .44) there in the twilight.

In the midst of a commercial we had democratically
elected and now found delivered forever on the screen,
we were interrupted to learn we had just won a war,
certified by experts to be correct. We felt at ease,
conscience a subliminal bonus, delivered
by flags and that eerie music when the enemy appeared.

Then there was our candidate smiling at our crowd,
just as an interviewer invaded our motel to ask what program
we were watching. 'Oh God,' we said, 'we were watching
us, watching us.' And in a terrible voice he roared,
'Quick, be smiling; you are on the air again!' and –
a terrible thing – we said just as he said, 'How do you do.'

AFTERMATH: THE SEVENTIES

The Seventies has always seemed a depressed and aimless decade, a pale hangover from the Sixties. It was dominated by oil crises, terrorism (especially in the Middle East and Ireland), Watergate and the resignation of President Nixon, the ending of the war in Vietnam, and the massacre of perhaps 3 million Cambodians by Pol Pot's Khmer Rouge. In the affluent Western economies, it was the decade of stagflation, the appropriately ugly coinage for the phenomenon of a simultaneous rise in unemployment and inflation, previously thought to be opposing tendencies. After the excitements of Sixties pop poetry, it was generally a conservative time in poetry. The one strong positive tendency of the decade was the rise of the Women's Movement, and many women poets were caught up in this.

Carol Rumens

Disco on the 'Queen of Denmark'

The North Sea drags our keel from noon to noon,
And, when she kicks, we who have trawled the moon,
And pinned those dead, glass oceans to our maps,
Tumble below to flay with Scotch and Schnapps
The old god, Fear. An oil-rig, dressed to kill
In lights, our messianic money-mill,
Stands starboard, crying 'Blessed is the Pound!'
And in the flickering Disco, to the sound-
Track from *Jaws*, elaborately we prey.
Our streamered hair glows pink, as surf makes way
For civilisation with its fizzing measure
Of music, sex and hope, its will to pleasure
Edged like a stylus, bravely swinging north
Between the winter stars, the berg's white tooth.

Michael Hofmann

On Fanø

Acid rain from the Ruhr strips one pine in three . . .
To supplement their living, the neutral Danes
let out their houses during the summer months –
exposure, convexity, clouds and the shadows of clouds.
Wild grass grows on the manure of their thatch.

There are concrete bunkers among the sand dunes –
bomb shelters, or part of Heligoland and the V2s . . . ?
German hippies have taken them over, painted them
with their acid peace dreams; a cave art of
giant people, jungles, a plague of dragonflies.

Maxine Kumin

The Summer of the Watergate Hearings

I wake in New Hampshire.
The sun is still withheld.
For six days Amanda has stood
through drizzles and downpours.

This morning she steams.
Little pyramids of her droppings
surround her. Dead worms
shine in them like forgotten

spaghetti, proof she has eaten
the sugar-coated cure.
Four dozen ascarids, ten strongyles –
I count them to make sure.

And all the while in Washington
worms fall out of the government
pale as the parasites that drain
from the scoured gut of my mare.

They blink open on the television screen.
Night after night on the rerun.
I count them to make sure.

Watergate: on two occasions in May and June 1972 a special unit, known as the Plumbers, broke into the Democratic Party's headquarters in the Watergate building in Washington. On the second occasion they were arrested and the subsequent cover-up of responsibility for the crime led to the resignation of President Richard Nixon on 7 August 1974.

Allen Curnow

An Urban Guerrilla

*The real stress came from life in the group . . . we were caught up
in a game that to the present day I still don't fully see through.*
    – Michael Baumann, 'most sought-after' German terrorist

It was a feather of paint
in a corner of the window,
a thread hanging from the hem
of the curtain, it was
the transistor standing on the corner
of the fridge, the switches
on the transistor, the way they were placed
in a dead design, it was where
the table stood, it was the label
Grappa Julia on the bottle
not quite half empty,

the faces that came and went,
the seven of us comrades
like the days of the week repeating

themselves, themselves,
it was cleaning your gun ten times
a day, taking time
washing your cock, no love
lost, aimlessly fondling
the things that think faster than fingers,
trigger friggers, gunsuckers.
People said Andreas Baader

'had an almost sexual relationship
with pistols', his favourite fuck
was a Heckler & Koch. Not that sex
wasn't free for all and in all
possible styles, but not all of us
or any of us all of the time –
while agreeing, in principle,
that any combination of abcdefg
encoded orgasm, X being any
given number – got our sums right.

Dust thickened on the mirror,
the once gay playmate,
on the dildo in the drawer,
dust on the file of newspapers;
silence as dusty as death
on the radio, nobody can hear
the police dragging their feet;
sometimes we squabbled, once
could have shot one another
in the dusty time, we had to be
terrible news, or die.

Michael Baumann and *Andreas Baader* were part of the wave of terrorism that swept Germany in the Seventies. The Baader–Meinhof gang, also known as the Red Army Faction (RAF), led by Baader with Ulrike Meinhof, were the best known. Beginning in 1970 they carried out bomb outrages, bank robberies and kidnappings. They were arrested in June 1972 and tried in 1975. Michael Baumann was a member of the terrorist group Second June.

Ernesto Cardenal

A Museum in Kampuchea

We went into a museum that used to be a high school
but under Pol Pot the high school became
                    the biggest prison in Cambodia.
The classrooms divided into little cells.
Here one only came to die.
More than 20,000 prisoners passed through here
                    of whom only 17 survived,
the ones who hadn't yet been killed when the liberating
                                    troops arrived.
                This was Pol Pot's 'Democratic Kampuchea'.
Here are the photos taken of them on entering.
                        They took photos of them all.
Some with their hands tied, others wearing chains
                            and iron collars.
    The worst thing to see was the horror in their faces.
You could see they weren't looking at the camera, but at death
                and the torture before death.
But even more shocking was a smiling face:
a girl, or teenage boy, someone innocent, unaware
evidently of what was going to happen to them.
            And photos of mothers with babies.
Some crude device for pulling out fingernails.
Tongs for tearing off nipples.
        A great many different kinds of tools . . .
The tank where they were held underwater.
The posts where they were hanged.
The cell where Pol Pot's Minister of Information was also held
                before being killed.
More than 100 mass graves where they buried them
                                have been found.
The infants buried with their milk bottles and pacifiers.
And the skulls, large piles of skulls
                that nobody wants to see.

They killed 3 of the 8 million inhabitants.
They destroyed the factories, the schools, the medicines.
They'd jail someone for wearing glasses.
                    The towns remained deserted.
The whole world knew about this.
How can it be that now, since Kampuchea was liberated,
the North American press doesn't speak badly of Pol Pot?
Finally we went outside.
                            There were flowers outside.
In a clean puddle a white duck fluttered
            bathing itself in the water and sun.
The young women who passed by on the street
looked like pagodas.

Translated from the Spanish by Jonathan Cohen.

In April 1975, Pol Pot's Khmer Rouge, a fanatical communist faction, triumphed in the Cambodian (Kampuchean) civil war which had begun when America invaded in 1970 in an escalation of the Vietnam War. In Phnom Penh, the capital, they tortured and massacred a large part of the population and drove the rest into the countryside where many more died.

Carol Rumens

The Freedom Won by War for Women

From hassock, cradle-side and streaming walls
– The fogs of faith and wash-day – thin lives beaten
Blank and hung to weep, the fair are gone.
Raw-fingered saints who've tipped their pedestals

And dried their hands at Father Empire's yell,
They chivvy cautious husbands, rebel sons
With bloodiest white. But they'll take the same poison,
Hands deft among his axle-trees and shells.

True warriors, they were furnace-forged when bombs
Jumped roof-high. From tongue to lung the taste
Of lead rolled death. Massed engines pumped their Somme.

It was a flowering and a laying waste
– Man's skills found shining at the heart of woman,
His vengeance, too, expediently unlaced.

Adrienne Rich

After Twenty Years

For A. P. C.

Two women sit at a table by a window. Light breaks
unevenly on both of them.
Their talk is a striking of sparks
which passers-by in the street observe
as a glitter in the glass of that window.
Two women in the prime of life.
Their babies are old enough to have babies.
Loneliness has been part of their story for twenty years,
the dark edge of the clever tongue,
the obscure underside of the imagination.
It is snow and thunder in the street.
While they speak the lightning flashes purple.
It is strange to be so many women,
eating and drinking at the same table,
those who bathed their children in the same basin
who kept their secrets from each other
walked the floors of their lives in separate rooms
and flow into history now as the woman of their time
living in the prime of life
as in a city where nothing is forbidden
and nothing permanent.

Margaret Atwood

A Women's Issue

The woman in the spiked device
that locks around the waist and between
the legs, with holes in it like a tea strainer
is Exhibit A.

The woman in black with a net window
to see through and a four-inch
wooden peg jammed up
between her legs so she can't be raped
is Exhibit B.

Exhibit C is the young girl
dragged into the bush by the midwives
and made to sing while they scrape the flesh
from between her legs, then tie her thighs
till she scabs over and is called healed.
Now she can be married.
For each childbirth they'll cut her
open, then sew her up.
Men like tight women.
The ones that die are carefully buried.

The next exhibit lies flat on her back
while eighty men a night
move through her, ten an hour.
She looks at the ceiling, listens
to the door open and close.
A bell keeps ringing.
Nobody knows how she got here.

You'll notice that what they have in common
is between the legs. Is this
why wars are fought?

Enemy territory, no man's
land, to be entered furtively,
fenced, owned but never surely,
scene of these desperate forays
at midnight, captures
and sticky murders, doctors' rubber gloves
greasy with blood, flesh made inert, the surge
of your own uneasy power.

This is no museum.
Who invented the word *love*?

A STUMBLING BLOCK: IRELAND

One of the three or four greatest poets writing in English in the early twentieth century was Irish; the exemplary poet of the mid-century was an Ulsterman. Yeats and MacNeice remind us that in poetry Ireland has an importance out of all proportion to its size. But the poetry has generally been overshadowed by tragic politics. The rise of Northern Irish poetry and the Catholic Civil Rights movement in the late Sixties, and the subsequent Troubles, were linked. In the Sixties, the first generation of university-educated Catholics, which included Seamus Heaney, graduated and began to articulate the voice of a previously oppressed population. Louis MacNeice, a notably cosmopolitan and unsectarian figure, was an inspiration for many poets. By common consent, the dominant poetry written in English during the Seventies – by poets such as Seamus Heaney, Paul Muldoon, Derek Mahon and Tom Paulin – came from Northern Ireland.

W. B. Yeats

From *Easter 1916*

I have met them at close of day
Coming with vivid faces
From counter or desk among grey
Eighteenth-century houses.
I have passed with a nod of the head
Or polite meaningless words,
Or have lingered awhile and said
Polite meaningless words,

And thought before I had done
Of a mocking tale or a gibe
To please a companion
Around the fire at the club,
Being certain that they and I
But lived where motley is worn:
All changed, changed utterly:
A terrible beauty is born.

That woman's days were spent
In ignorant good-will,
Her nights in argument
Until her voice grew shrill.
What voice more sweet than hers
When, young and beautiful,
She rode to harriers?
This man had kept a school
And rode our wingèd horse;
This other his helper and friend
Was coming into his force;
He might have won fame in the end,
So sensitive his nature seemed,
So daring and sweet his thought.
This other man I had dreamed
A drunken, vainglorious lout.
He had done most bitter wrong
To some who are near my heart,
Yet I number him in the song;
He, too, has resigned his part
In the casual comedy;
He, too, has been changed in his turn,
Transformed utterly:
A terrible beauty is born.

The Irish Easter Rising in 1916 was one of many disturbances that accompanied the
First World War. Republicans seized the Post Office in Dublin. The revolt was quelled
by the British and fifteen of the leaders executed, but the formation of the Irish Free
State followed in 1922.

Louis MacNeice

From *Autumn Journal*

XVI

Nightmare leaves fatigue:
  We envy men of action
Who sleep and wake, murder and intrigue
  Without being doubtful, without being haunted.
And I envy the intransigence of my own
  Countrymen who shoot to kill and never
See the victim's face become their own
  Or find his motive sabotage their motives.
So reading the memoirs of Maud Gonne,
  Daughter of an English mother and a soldier father,
I note how a single purpose can be founded on
  A jumble of opposites:
Dublin Castle, the vice-regal ball,
  The embassies of Europe,
Hatred scribbled on a wall,
  Gaols and revolvers.
And I remember, when I was little, the fear
  Bandied among the servants
That Casement would land at the pier
  With a sword and a horde of rebels;
And how we used to expect, at a later date,
  When the wind blew from the west, the noise of shooting
Starting in the evening at eight
  In Belfast in the York Street district;
And the voodoo of the Orange bands
  Drawing an iron net through darkest Ulster,
Flailing the limbo lands –
  The linen mills, the long wet grass, the ragged hawthorn.
And one read black where the other read white, his hope
  The other man's damnation:
Up the Rebels, To Hell with the Pope,
  And God Save – as you prefer – the King or Ireland.

The land of scholars and saints:
　　Scholars and saints my eye, the land of ambush,
Purblind manifestoes, never-ending complaints,
　　The born martyr and the gallant ninny;
The grocer drunk with the drum,
　　The land-owner shot in his bed, the angry voices
Piercing the broken fanlight in the slum,
　　The shawled woman weeping at the garish altar.

Casement: Sir Roger Casement was an Irish Nationalist leader during the First World War, knighted by the British government for earlier services rendered. In 1916 he went to Germany to recruit Irish prisoners of war to fight for independence. He landed near Tralee with two comrades but was soon arrested. He was executed at Pentonville on 3 August 1916.

Seamus Heaney

Punishment

I can feel the tug
of the halter at the nape
of her neck, the wind
on her naked front.

It blows her nipples
to amber beads,
it shakes the frail rigging
of her ribs.

I can see her drowned
body in the bog,
the weighing stone,
the floating rods and boughs.

Under which at first
she was a barked sapling
that is dug up
oak-bone, brain-firkin:

her shaved head
like a stubble of black corn,
her blindfold a soiled bandage,
her noose a ring

to store
the memories of love.
Little adulteress,
before they punished you

you were flaxen-haired,
undernourished, and your
tar-black face was beautiful.
My poor scapegoat,

I almost love you
but would have cast, I know,
the stones of silence.
I am the artful voyeur

of your brain's exposed
and darkened combs,
your muscles' webbing
and all your numbered bones:

I who have stood dumb
when your betraying sisters,
cauled in tar,
wept by the railings,

who would connive
in civilized outrage
yet understand the exact
and tribal, intimate revenge.

Derek Mahon

Ecclesiastes

God, you could grow to love it, God-fearing, God-
    chosen purist little puritan that,
for all your wiles and smiles, you are (the
    dank churches, the empty streets,
the shipyard silence, the tied-up swings) and
    shelter your cold heart from the heat
of the world, from woman-inquisition, from the
    bright eyes of children. Yes you could
wear black, drink water, nourish a fierce zeal
    with locusts and wild honey, and not
feel called upon to understand and forgive
    but only to speak with a bleak
afflatus, and love the January rains when they
    darken the dark doors and sink hard
into the Antrim hills, the bog-meadows, the heaped
    graves of your fathers. Bury that red
bandana and stick, that banjo, this is your
    country, close one eye and be king.
Your people await you, their heavy washing
    flaps for you in the housing estates –
a credulous people. God, you could do it, God
    help you, stand on a corner stiff
with rhetoric, promising nothing under the sun.

Paul Durcan

In Memory: The Miami Showband –
Massacred 31 July 1975

Beautiful are the feet of them that preach the gospel of peace,
Of them that bring glad tidings of good things.

In a public house, darkly lit, a patriotic (sic)
Versifier whines into my face: 'You must take one side
Or the other, or you're but a fucking romantic.'
His eyes glitter hate and vanity, porter and whiskey,
And I realise that he is blind to the braille connection
Between a music and a music-maker.
'You must take one side or the other
Or you're but a fucking romantic:'
The whine is icy
And his eyes hang loose like sheets from poles
On a bare wet hillside in winter
And his mouth gapes like a cave in ice;
It is a whine in the crotch of whose fear
Is fondled a dream gun blood-smeared;
It is in war – not poetry or music –
That men find their niche, their glory hole;
Like most of his fellows
He will abide no contradiction in the mind.
He whines: 'If there is birth, there cannot be death'
And – jabbing a hysterical forefinger into my nose and eyes –
'If there is death, there cannot be birth.'
Peace to the souls of those who unlike my fellow poet
Were true to their trade
Despite death-dealing blackmail by racists:
You made music, and that was all: You were realists
And beautiful were your feet.

John Hewitt

The Anglo-Irish Accord

These days the air is thick with bitter cries,
as baffled thousands dream they are betrayed,
stripped of the comfort of safe loyalties,
their ancient friends considered enemies,
alone among the nations and afraid.

And those who now most loudly mouth their fears
are webbed in spirals of rash verbiage
which, coarse with coloured epithets, appears
a rhetoric of cudgels, torches, spears,
loaded with vivid enmity and rage.

This land we stand on holds a history
so complicated, gashed with violence,
split by belief, by blatant pageantry,
that none can safely stir and still feel free
to voice his hope with any confidence.

Slave to and victim of this mirror hate,
surely there must be somewhere we could reach
a solid track across our quagmire state,
and on a neutral sod renew the old debate
which all may join without intemperate speech.

The Anglo-Irish Accord: an agreement reached between the British and Irish governments
on 15 November 1985, recognizing their mutual interest in a peaceful settlement in
Northern Ireland.

MOTHER NATURE ON THE RUN:
THE ENVIRONMENT

For so long a constant wellspring of poetry, nature in the twentieth century has become problematical. Reduced to a mechanical food factory for the cities, the countryside is no longer a reach-me-down metaphor for fruition and ease. Scientific knowledge of nature and an awareness of ecology now inform nature poetry, and have led to a poetry which stresses nature's awesome power rather than its beauty. But poetry itself is a kind of climate: the four seasons' poems here, by James Tate, Louis MacNeice, Vernon Scannell and Ted Hughes, effectively map the weather of the twentieth-century soul. Gardens and allotments represent, like poems, temporary stays against confusion but the overriding truth about nature this century is embodied in the wind blowing from Chernobyl, and the desert, in Primo Levi's poem, eating into the rain-forest and our hearts alike.

Dylan Thomas

The Force That Through the Green
Fuse Drives the Flower

The force that through the green fuse drives the flower
Drives my green age; that blasts the roots of trees
Is my destroyer.
And I am dumb to tell the crooked rose
My youth is bent by the same wintry fever.

The force that drives the water through the rocks
Drives my red blood; that dries the mouthing streams
Turns mine to wax.
And I am dumb to mouth unto my veins
How at the mountain spring the same mouth sucks.

The hand that whirls the water in the pool
Stirs the quicksand; that ropes the blowing wind
Hauls my shroud sail.
And I am dumb to tell the hanging man
How of my clay is made the hangman's lime.

The lips of time leech to the fountain head;
Love drips and gathers, but the fallen blood
Shall calm her sores.
And I am dumb to tell a weather's wind
How time has ticked a heaven round the stars.

And I am dumb to tell the lover's tomb
How at my sheet goes the same crooked worm.

W. H. Auden

From *Letter to Lord Byron. III*

The mountain-snob is a Wordsworthian fruit;
        He tears his clothes and doesn't shave his chin,
He wears a very pretty little boot,
        He chooses the least comfortable inn;
        A mountain railway is a deadly sin;
His strength, of course, is as the strength of ten men,
He calls all those who live in cities wen-men.

I'm not a spoil-sport, I would never wish
        To interfere with anybody's pleasures;
By all means climb, or hunt, or even fish,
        All human hearts have ugly little treasures;
        But think it time to take repressive measures
When someone says, adopting the 'I know' line,
The Good Life is confined above the snow-line.

Besides, I'm very fond of mountains, too;
          I like to travel through them in a car;
I like a house that's got a sweeping view;
          I like to walk, but not to walk too far.
          I also like green plains where cattle are,
And trees and rivers, and shall always quarrel
With those who think that rivers are immoral.

Not that my private quarrel gives quietus to
          The interesting question that it raises;
Impartial thought will give a proper status to
          This interest in waterfalls and daisies,
          Excessive love for the non-human faces,
That lives in hearts from Golders Green to Teddington;
It's all bound up with Einstein, Jeans, and Eddington.

It is a commonplace that's hardly worth
          A poet's while to make profound or terse,
That now the sun does not go round the earth,
          That man's no centre of the universe;
          And working in an office makes it worse.
The humblest is acquiring with facility
A Universal-Complex sensibility.

For now we've learnt we mustn't be so bumptious
          We find the stars are one big family,
And send out invitations for a scrumptious
          Simple, old-fashioned, jolly romp with tea
          To any natural objects we can see.
We can't, of course, invite a Jew or Red
But birds and nebulae will do instead.

The Higher Mind's outgrowing the Barbarian,
          It's hardly thought hygienic now to kiss;
The world is surely turning vegetarian;
          And as it grows too sensitive for this,
          It won't be long before we find there is
A Society of Everybody's Aunts
For the Prevention of Cruelty to Plants.

James Tate

Spring Was Begging to Be Born

After a winter of seclusion
I curtsy farewell to my pagoda:
Friend, tinfoil gangster, deviant silo,
I leave you to your own stale resources
to wander this spring in my disguises,
in my new naked zigzagging across
the pulsating battlefields of my own kind.

*

Murmur of cherry blossoms, I winced, glassy-eyed:
Had not I dreamed their color in my fairy tale?
Then hush; homeless now, I am arriving
at my one true home, the barricades melting.
The further I delved into these murderous zones
the more crisscrossed and woven became
the life within my fussy warehouse and that
beside this celebrated outer cherry.

*

Your wish is my command, I said to no one special.
Feeling festive now, and somewhat fraudulent,
I waited for the zodiac to sneak a glance
at my horoscope. Was this to be, spluttering,
with the plumes of raspberry light
erasing my hearsay and stifling my double?
I picked a thread from the zillion squiggles
and followed it around the corner to where
an orchestra was looking askance and
asking for complete silence.

*

Men sat outside their factories playing dominoes.
Their bodies were swollen, as after a hurricane.
I had dreamed of this hour; and yet, standing there,
my dream seemed suddenly, monotonously, attenuated,
as though a tugboat were the wiser to ignore
this sinking ship. I moved on, sobbing, giggling,
and looked back more than once to no hands waving.

Spring was truly begging to be born
like a cipher that aspires to the number one.
Hush. It is all hearsay, irresistible hearsay.

Louis MacNeice

The Cyclist

Freewheeling down the escarpment past the unpassing horse
Blazoned in chalk the wind he causes in passing
Cools the sweat of his neck, making him one with the sky,
In the heat of the handlebars he grasps the summer
Being a boy and to-day a parenthesis
Between the horizon's brackets; the main sentence
Waits to be picked up later but these five minutes
Are all to-day and summer. The dragonfly
Rises without take-off, horizontal,
Underlining itself in a sliver of peacock light.

And glaring, glaring white
The horse on the down moves within his brackets,
The grass boils with grasshoppers, a pebble
Scutters from under the wheel and all this country
Is spattered white with boys riding their heat-wave,
Feet on a narrow plank and hair thrown back

And a surf of dust beneath them. Summer, summer –
They chase it with butterfly nets or strike it into the deep
In a little red ball or gulp it lathered with cream
Or drink it through closed eyelids; until the bell
Left-right-left gives his forgotten sentence
And reaching the valley the boy must pedal again
Left-right-left but meanwhile
For ten seconds more can move as the horse in the chalk
Moves unbeginningly calmly
Calmly regardless of tenses and final clauses
Calmly unendingly moves.

Vernon Scannell

Autumn

It is the football season once more
And the back pages of the Sunday papers
Again show the blurred anguish of goalkeepers.

In Maida Vale, Golders Green and Hampstead
Lamps ripen early in the surprising dusk;
They are furred like stale rinds with a fuzz of mist.

The pavements of Kensington are greasy;
The wind smells of burnt porridge in Bayswater,
And the leaves are mushed to silence in the gutter.

The big hotel like an anchored liner
Rides near the park; lit windows hammer the sky.
Like the slow swish of surf the tyres of taxis sigh.

On Ealing Broadway the cinema glows
Warm behind glass while mellow the church clock chimes
As the waiting girls stir in their delicate chains.

Their eyes are polished by the wind,
But the gleam is dumb, empty of joy or anger.
Though the lovers are long in coming the girls still linger.

We are nearing the end of the year.
Under the sombre sleeve the blood ticks faster
And in the dark ear of Autumn quick voices whisper.

It is a time of year that's to my taste,
Full of spiced rumours, sharp and velutinous flavours,
Dim with the mist that softens the cruel surfaces,
Makes mirrors vague. It is the mist that I most favour.

Ted Hughes

Tractor

The tractor stands frozen – an agony
To think of. All night
Snow packed its open entrails. Now a head-pincering gale,
A spill of molten ice, smoking snow,
Pours into its steel.
At white heat of numbness it stands
In the aimed hosing of ground-level fieriness.

It defies flesh and won't start.
Hands are like wounds already
Inside armour gloves, and feet are unbelievable
As if the toe-nails were all just torn off.
I stare at it in hatred. Beyond it
The copse hisses – capitulates miserably
In the fleeing, failing light. Starlings,
A dirtier sleetier snow, blow smokily, unendingly, over
Towards plantations eastward.
All the time the tractor is sinking
Through the degrees, deepening
Into its hell of ice.

The starter lever
Cracks its action, like a snapping knuckle.
The battery is alive – but like a lamb
Trying to nudge its solid-frozen mother –
While the seat claims my buttock-bones, bites
With the space-cold of earth, which it has joined
In one solid lump.

I squirt commercial sure-fire
Down the black throat – it just coughs.
It ridicules me – a trap of iron stupidity

I've stepped into. I drive the battery
As if I were hammering and hammering
The frozen arrangement to pieces with a hammer
And it jabbers laughing pain-crying mockingly
Into happy life.

And stands
Shuddering itself full of heat, seeming to enlarge slowly
Like a demon demonstrating
A more-than-usually-complete materialization –
Suddenly it jerks from its solidarity
With the concrete, the lurches towards a stanchion
Bursting with superhuman well-being and abandon
Shouting Where Where?

Worse iron is waiting. Power-lift kneels,
Levers awake imprisoned deadweight,
Shackle-pins bedded in cast-iron cow-shit.
The blind and vibrating condemned obedience
Of iron to the cruelty of iron,
Wheels screeched out of their night-locks –

Fingers
Among the tormented
Tonnage and burning of iron

Eyes
Weeping in the wind of chloroform

And the tractor, streaming with sweat,
Raging and trembling and rejoicing.

Jonathan Holden

Tumbleweed

Arms with hands grasping seek to clutch at the prows. Bodies
thrown recklessly in the way are cut aside.
                                    – William Carlos Williams

This morning the March wind is huge, and there are many of them
struggling across the fields, but they travel singly.
They do not know each other. Sometimes one, like a chicken
just beheaded, shudders in a spasm across the road,
gets caught on a bumper, and the car wears it for awhile
like a badge, though it stands for nothing, a poor man's jewelry,
a burr. A fat one, like the architecture
of a small cumulus cloud, hesitates in the right-hand lane,
makes its move. 'Hit it!' my son urges. Wind buffets us.
We catch it flush, feel its shriveled limbs clutch
the bumper and, clinging, travel with us, its weightless anatomy
continuing in a new direction, perpendicular
to the rest of their southern migration
as we forge westward through it, casting guilty glances
north where more of them are bouncing in the distance, bouncing
in place, and we notice, closer, the barbed-wire hedge,
how they are plastered to it, stuck, clawing like insects
begging, determined to climb it and to cross
the highway. *Why did the chicken cross the road?* Tourists,
we stare out the window at fields, a roaring tundra
spread-eagled under the force of the sky, at the tumbleweed
endlessly bobbing toward us as if eager for something,
and feel a kind of pity for the dead, who are truly homeless,
at the way the body, when it's shed its soul
is physically driven on, regardless, a bristle of matter. Wind
leans on the car, and we wonder if we, ourselves, aren't
being buffetted across some frigid field as randomly
as these mops of tumbleweed snagged on the barbed-wire
perimeter, shivering there in a row, miles of prisoners
facing the moat they have to get across
as the gods sail by all day, at sixty miles an hour, free.

Carol Ann Duffy

The Legend

Some say it was seven tons of meat in a thick black hide
you could build a boat from, stayed close to the river
on the flipside of the sun where the giant forests were.

Had shy, old eyes. You'd need both those hands for *one*.
Maybe. Walked in placid herds under a jungly, sweating roof
just breathing; a dry electric wind you could hear a mile off.

Huge feet. Some say if it rained you could fish in a footprint,
fruit fell when it passed. It moved, food happened, simple.
You think of a warm, inky cave and you got its mouth all right.

You dream up a yard of sandpaper, damp, you're talking tongue.
Eat? Its own weight in a week. And water. Some say
the sweat steamed from its back in small grey clouds.

But *big*. Enormous. Spine like the mast on a galleon.
Ears like sails gasping for a wind. You picture
a rope you could hang a man from, you're seeing its tail.

Tusks like bannisters. I almost believe myself. Can you
drum up a roar as wide as a continent, a deep hot note
that bellowed out and belonged to the melting air? You got it.

But people have always lied! You know some say it had a trunk
like a soft telescope, that it looked up along it at the sky
and balanced a bright, gone star on the end, and it died.

Bernard Spencer

Allotments: April

Cobbled with rough stone which rings my tread
The path twists through the squared allotments.
Blinking to glimpse the lark in the warming sun,
In what sense am I joining in
Such a hallooing, rousing April day,
Now that the hedges are so gracious and
Stick out at me moist buds, small hands, their opening scrolls and fans?

Lost to some of us the festival joy
At the bursting of the tomb, the seasonal mystery,
God walking again who lay all winter
As if in those long barrows built in the fields
To keep the root-crops warm. On squires' lawns
The booted dancers twirl. But what I hear
A spade slice in pebbled earth, swinging the nigger-coloured loam.

And the love-songs, the mediaeval grace,
The fluting lyrics, 'The only pretty ring-time,'
These have stopped singing. For love detonates like sap
Up into the limbs of men and bears all the seasons
And the starving and the cutting and hunts terribly through lives
To find its peace. But April comes as
Beast-smell flung from the fields, the hammers, the loud-speaking weir.

The rough voices of boys playing by the hedge
As manly as possible, their laughter, the big veins
Sprawled over the beet-leaf, light-red fires
Of flower pots heaped by the huts; they make a pause in
The wireless voice repeating pacts, persecutions,
And imprisonments and deaths and heaped violent deaths,
Impersonal now as figures in the city news.

Behind me, the town curves. Its parapeted edge,
With its burnt look, guards towards the river.
The worry about money, the eyeless work
Of those who do not believe, real poverty,

The sour doorways of the poor; April which
Delights the trees and fills the roads to the South,
Does not deny or conceal. Rather it adds

What more I am; excites the deep glands
And warms my animal bones as I go walking
Past the allotments and the singing water-meadows
Where hooves of cattle have plodded and cratered, and
Watch today go up like a single breath
Holding in its applause at masts of height
Two elms and their balanced attitude like dancers, their arms like
    dancers.

Christopher Reid

The Gardeners

I love these gardens, all their show
of antiquated art nouveau:
the buxom ironwork, candle-drips
and blobby leafage.
                    It is as if
someone had stumbled by surprise
on Alaodin's paradise.

It rains all evening – knives and forks.
The meteors drop by like corks.
Perpetuum mobile, a wind
hums in its box, as gardeners spend
endless, hermetic, twilight hours,
stooping above their hungry flowers.

This is the world's arcanest grove.
The borborygmus of a dove
calls from the belly of its bush.
How carefully the gardeners push
between the clumps of guzzling shrubs,
that line the way in wooden tubs.

With mashing faces, curled-up claws,
most of these blooms are carnivores.
Anyone sees, who wanders here,
a ruby clinging to an ear,
fat fingers, an outlandish wig . . .
The flowers grow slovenly and big,

as gardeners in white linen coats
rotate about their captious throats.
They have a god here, stern and jealous,
wearing four hats and five umbrellas,
who contemplates them, as they strive
to keep strange appetites alive.

Alaodin's paradise: the garden of Sheikh Alaodin, as described in Marco Polo, *The Travels*.
borborygmus: literally, the rumbling of intestinal gases.

Michael Hofmann

47° *Latitude*

I was lying out on the caesium lawn,
on the ribs and ligatures of a split deckchair,
under the Roman purple of a copper beech,
a misgrown fasces, all rods and no axe.

It was the double-zero summer, where the birds
stunned themselves on the picture windows
with no red bird cardboard cut-out doubles to warn them,
where the puffball dandelion grew twice as high,

where it was better not to eat parsley.
Every Friday, the newspapers gave fresh readings,
and put Turkish hazelnuts on the index.
A becquerel might be a fish or a type of mushroom.

In Munich, cylindrical missile balloons
bounced table-high, head-high, caber-high, house-high.

The crowds on the Leopoldstrasse were thick as pebbles
on the beach. I lay out on the caesium lawn.

The fallout from the explosion at Chernobyl nuclear power station in the Ukraine on
26 April 1986 caused many local deaths and casualties, and spread across every country
in Western Europe.
caesium: a fall-out element of nuclear fission.   *becquerel*: a unit of radiation.

Primo Levi

Almanac

The indifferent rivers
Will keep on flowing to the sea
Or ruinously overflowing dikes,
Ancient handiwork of determined men.
The glaciers will continue to grate,
Smoothing what's under them
Or suddenly fall headlong,
Cutting short fir trees' lives.
The sea, captive between
Two continents, will go on struggling,
Always miserly with its riches.
Sun stars planets and comets
Will continue on their course.
Earth too will fear the immutable
Laws of the universe.
Not us. We, rebellious progeny
With great brainpower, little sense,
Will destroy, defile
Always more feverishly.
Very soon we'll extend the desert
Into the Amazon forests,
Into the living heart of our cities,
Into our very hearts.

2 January 1987

Translated from the Italian by
Ruth Feldman.

TRAINS AND BOATS AND PLANES:
TRAVEL

By the end of the century, tourism had become the world's largest industry in terms of income and employment (about one in fourteen of the working population). Rapid development of the technological means to travel has either met or induced an insatiable wanderlust. The rootless condition of the traveller is a close metaphor for the poet, who 'visits' the territory of each poem for a limited period, sometimes researching quite deeply and sometimes physically travelling in pursuit of the poem, and then goes home. Despite Amis's and Larkin's well-directed jibes against poets who are too eager to show you the labels on their suitcase, many poets have drawn great inspiration from places they've known only temporarily. And the infrastructure of travel has its own appeal for writers.

C. Day Lewis

The Tourists

Arriving was their passion.
Into the new place out of the blue
Flying, sailing, driving –
How well these veteran tourists knew
Each fashion of arriving.

Leaving a place behind them,
There was no sense of loss: they fed
Upon the act of leaving –
So hot their hearts for the land ahead –
As a kind of pre-conceiving.

Arrival has stern laws, though,
Condemning men to lose their eyes
If they have treated travel
As a brief necessary disease,
A pause before arrival.

And merciless the fate is
Of him who leaves nothing behind,
No hostage, no reversion:
He travels on, not only blind
But a stateless person.

Fleeing from love and hate,
Pursuing change, consumed by motion,
Such arrivistes, unseeing,
Forfeit through endless self-evasion
The estate of simple being.

Bernard Spencer

Boat Poem

I wish there were a touch of these boats about my life;
so to speak, a tarring,
the touch of inspired disorder and something more than that,
something more too
than the mobility of sails or a primitive bumpy engine,
under that tiny hot-house window,
which eats up oil and benzine perhaps
but will go on beating in spite of the many strains
not needing with luck to be repaired too often,
with luck lasting years piled on years.

There must be a kind of envy which brings me peering
and nosing at the boats along the island quay
either in the hot morning
with the lace-light shaking up against their hulls from the water,

or when their mast-tops
keep on drawing lines between stars.
(I do not speak here of the private yachts from the clubs
which stalk across the harbour like magnificent white cats
but sheer off and keep mostly to themselves.)

Look for example at the Bartolomé; a deck-full
of mineral water and bottles of beer in cases
and great booming barrels of wine from the mainland,
endearing trade;
and lengths of timber and iron rods for building
and, curiously a pig with flying ears
ramming a wet snout into whatever it explores.

Or the Virgen del Pilar, mantled and weavy with drooping nets
PM/708/3A
with starfish and pieces of cod drying on the wheel-house roof
some wine, the remains of supper on an enamel plate
and trousers and singlets 'passim';
both of these boats stinky and forgivable like some great men –
both needing paint,
but both, one observes, armoured far better than us against jolts
by a belt of old motor-tyres lobbed round their sides for buffers.

And having in their swerving planks and in the point of their bows
the never-enough-to-be-praised
authority of a great tradition, the sea-shape
simple and true like a vase,
Something that stays too in the carved head of an eagle
or that white-eyed wooden hound crying up beneath the bowsprit.

Qualities clearly admirable. So is their response to occasion,
how they celebrate such times
and suddenly fountain with bunting and stand like ocean maypoles
on a Saint's Day when a gun bangs from the fortifications,
and an echo-gun throws a bang back
and all the old kitchen bells start hammering from the churches.

Admirable again
how one of them, perhaps tomorrow, will have gone with no hooting
    or fuss,
simply absent from its place among the others,
occupied, without self-importance, in the thousands-of-
millions-of-sea.

Raymond Queneau

Crossing the Channel in 1922

How can so many people be seasick at once
was the question I found myself forced to enquire
by the sight of an acridly vomiting choir
steaming over to England and leaving fair France
far from Cap d'Antifer though there's quite a good chance
that I've got it all wrong and the quays at Dieppe
saw my monoglot self climb on board to perfect
its English along with the good old one-step
Yes just outside Dieppe the big breakers rose higher
and the seasick grew sicker till seascapes were wrecked
Through the beauty of night wafts the stench from below
bringing engine-oil galley-grease ill winds that blow
from those souls with dyspepsia much overwrought
their distress made me smug their ills I'd never catch
having natural sea-legs and stomach to match
Boastful vanity: whether with seasickness fraught
or immune one way led to the anglican port
all I knew how to say then was yes sometimes no
indiscriminately and there wasn't an ounce
of good sense I could make from attempts to pronounce
by the King's customs-men my name Raymond Queneau
and when I went home one month later or two
hardly adding a word to my minuscule score
those customs-men still lacked the foggiest clue
and were quite in the dark like our ship with its crew

and its chorus on deck being seasick once more
Boastful vanity: leaving old England's grey shore
with my marvellous sea-legs there wasn't a doubt
I knew Shakespeare's tongue no more than when I'd set out

Translated from the French by Edward Lucie-Smith.

Elizabeth Bishop

Filling Station

Oh, but it is dirty!
– this little filling station,
oil-soaked, oil-permeated
to a disturbing, over-all
black translucency.
Be careful with that match!

Father wears a dirty,
oil-soaked monkey suit
that cuts him under the arms,
and several quick and saucy
and greasy sons assist him
(it's a family filling station),
all quite thoroughly dirty.

Do they live in the station?
It has a cement porch
behind the pumps, and on it
a set of crushed and grease-
impregnated wickerwork;
on the wicker sofa
a dirty dog, quite comfy.

Some comic books provide
the only note of color –
of certain color. They lie
upon a big dim doily
draping a taboret
(part of the set), beside
a big hirsute begonia.

Why the extraneous plant?
Why the taboret?
Why, oh why, the doily?
(Embroidered in daisy stitch
with marguerites, I think,
and heavy with gray crochet.)

Somebody embroidered the doily.
Somebody waters the plant,
or oils it, maybe. Somebody
arranges the rows of cans
so that they softly say:
ESSO – SO – SO – SO
to high-strung automobiles.
Somebody loves us all.

Karl Shapiro

Auto Wreck

Its quick soft silver bell beating, beating,
And down the dark one ruby flare
Pulsing out red light like an artery,
The ambulance at top speed floating down
Past beacons and illuminated clocks
Wings in a heavy curve, dips down,
And brakes speed, entering the crowd.
The doors leap open, emptying light;

Stretchers are laid out, the mangled lifted
And stowed into the little hospital.
Then the bell, breaking the hush, tolls once,
And the ambulance with its terrible cargo
Rocking, slightly rocking, moves away,
As the doors, an afterthought, are closed.

We are deranged, walking among the cops
Who sweep glass and are large and composed.
One is still making notes under the light.
One with a bucket douches ponds of blood
Into the street and gutter.
One hangs lanterns on the wrecks that cling,
Empty husks of locusts, to iron poles.

Our throats were tight as tourniquets,
Our feet were bound with splints, but now,
Like convalescents intimate and gauche,
We speak through sickly smiles and warn
With the stubborn saw of common sense,
The grim joke and the banal resolution.
The traffic moves around with care,
But we remain, touching a wound
That opens to our richest horror.
Already old, the question Who shall die?
Becomes unspoken Who is innocent?
For death in war is done by hands;
Suicide has cause and stillbirth, logic;
And cancer, simple as a flower, blooms.

But this invites the occult mind,
Cancels our physics with a sneer,
And spatters all we knew of denouement
Across the expedient and wicked stones.

Evgeny Vinokurov

Siberian Restaurant-Cars

Siberian restaurant-cars designed for passenger
Comfort over thousands and thousands of miles! . . .
Here, over a carafe, people sing and quarrel
And wounded hearts are torn and torn again.
The sailor hurrying back from leave, the beetle-browed
Actor about to go on tour: for miles
And miles these friends against their will sit there,
Touch foreheads, and they stare into each other's
Eyes. And all the pain of half a lifetime,
And all that they have hidden deep within them,
They dare confide to one another's hearts
Among the passengers as if in private.
Your whole life, espousals, separations,
Sad mistakes of former days, the need of
Human nature for confession – stronger
Than diffidence. How many novels, stories,
Poems here, if you dug about enough.
How remember them and not go crazy!
The friends are mumbling: light, darkness, and light,
Darkness once more, break across their faces.
If only they could forget about all this
How simple their heavy lot would be.

Through the window, unpeopled Siberia
And midnight forests stretch for a thousand miles.

Translated from the Russian by
Anthony Rudolf and Daniel Weissbort.

Harry Clifton

Taking the Waters

There are taps that flow, all day and all night,
From the depths of Europe,
Inexhaustibles taken for granted,

Slaking our casual thirsts
At a railway station
Heading south, or here in the Abruzzo

Bursting cold from an iron standpipe
While our blind mouths
Suck at essentials, straight from the water table.

Our health is too good, we are not pilgrims,
And the nineteenth century
Led to disaster. Aix and Baden Baden –

Where are they now, those ladies with the vapours
Sipping at glasses of hydrogen sulphide
Every morning, while the pumphouse piano played

And Russian radicals steamed and stewed
For hours in their sulphur tubs
Plugged in to the cathodes of Revolution?

Real cures, for imaginary ailments
Diocletian's, or Vespasian's.
History passes, only the waters remain,

Bubbling up, through their carbon sheets,
To the other side of catastrophe
Where we drink, at a forgotten source,

Through the old crust of Europe
Centuries deep, restored by a local merchant
Of poultry and greens, inscribing his name in Latin.

James Applewhite

Iron Age Flying

I

What's the red light? Oh Boarding Boarding.
I'm walking down a ramp into a tunnel.
Jesus, it's raining. Top of the plane
Seems a wet slick whale's back.
Jonah to England, with my sins
All upon me.
Why does it feel so like dying?
Riding the river in the speedboat with father,
I didn't feel fearful.
I wasn't so personal.
A kid's just anyone,
One drop of light into the sun's bright water.

Inside it's a cave.
Maybe find a seat by a window.
Important personalities are Cadillacs.
Black shams, limousines
Appropriate for funerals. The child soul inside.
How do you believe in this idiotic century?
I wasn't inventing the things I remembered.
Father as if mowing the evening,
The light in particles of dust
But they were shining.
Seatbelt. Good, we're moving.

Faster and faster. Like rising
Toward heaven. Is this how it will be?
Regret and desire. Memories.
The red fire jumping as if speaking in tongues.
He drove away the tanker for our lives, through
The gasoline sea of her fear.

*

My neck feels cramped. What time
Could it be? Must have been asleep.
Move the pillow from the window.
And *where* could we be?
With lights down below.
A city. A galaxy.
Beautiful with distance and darkness.
Perhaps my life,
If seen from that remove –
With irregular beads, it becomes a necklace
Stringing a peninsula –
Are there rocks by the lights and black-foil water?
It's a bay within the land's last arms.

II

We are going and we have been:
To climb along the Somerset headlands
Resurrected from an underground England.
We'll scramble clay holes through
Iron age forts – no stones of Camelot –
Considering the blades from Saxon barrows.

Iron age, hand
In a rusty glove handle
My throat, my thoughts,
Gently.

I began with a boy, whose sight
Was marked by a snake.
Though his brown time drains
With the Pamlico River,
Everything seen in his life
Flows in an underground stream
Where a new sun burns.

Over our horizon to the east, the constant
Night of Earth's own shadow
Cones standing still
So that children, animals, weeds, and jewels

Spin through it, where a vision
Lies buried
Like treasure: one gleaming
Bearing the world revolves on,
Earth-lidded eyeball, wink of the Cyclops.

Underground sun, give us prospect
On our landscape's mud, our poor map of paths
Which spin, recombine, in the head,
Like threads dyed red
From sheepfolds,
To stitch incorrigible imagination's pastoral.

Iron age flying, over
The planet's body where dawn still hides,
Telescope fields: the contours
Planted with a garden not realized.
Egg of earth holds the sun inside.

Rolf Dieter Brinkmann

Hymn to an Italian Piazza

O Piazza Bologna in Rome! Banca Nazionale Del
Lavoro and Banco Di Santo Spirito, Pizza Mozzarella
Barbiere, Gomma Sport! Gipsi Boutique and Willi,
Tavola Calda, Esso Servizio, Fiat, Ginnastica,

Estetica, Yoga, Sauna! O Bar Tabacchi and Gelati,
wide bums in Levi's jeans, breasts or tits,
all firm, tightly squeezed, Pasticcieria, Macelleria!
O little table lamps, Vini, Oli, Per Via Aerea,

Eldorado Steak, Tecnotica Caruso! O Profumeria
Estivi, Chiuso per Ferie Agosto, O Lidia di Firenze,
Lady Wool! Cinestop! Green Bus! O lines 62 and 6, the
small change! O green Avanti! O where? P. T. and Tee Freddo.

Visita Da Medico Ocultista, Lenti A Contatto!
O Auto Famose! Ritz Cracker, Nuota Con Noi, O Grazie!
Tutte Nude! O Domenica, scraps, plastic horns, pink!
Vacanze Carissime, O Nautica! skin, back, thighs

tanned, O oil stain, Ragazzi, autovox, gravel! And Oxford,
Neon, Il Gatto Di Brooklyn Aspirante Detective, Melone!
Walls! Mortar! Garlic! Grated Parmesan! O dark
Minimarket Di Frutta, Istituto Pirandello, Englese

pubs, shutters! O golden brown dog! Around the corner
Banca Commerciale Italia, flea market, air pressure brakes, BP
coupons, Zoom! O Eva Moderna, Medaglioni, Tramezzini,
Bollati! Aperto! Locali Provvisori! Balcone, O patch

of oil, leaves, Trasferita, O Ente Communale Di
Consumo, to the wall! O iron-grilled Bar Ferranzi!
O street calm! Guerlain, dog turds, Germain Montail!
O Bar Fascista Riservata Permanente, Piano! O soldiers,

Operetta, gun on the hips, O Super Pensione!
O animal image. O Farmacia Bologna, ruined house corner,
Senso Unico! O Scusi! O Casa Bella! O Ultimo Tango
Pomodoro! O Sciopero! O Lire! O shit!

Translated from the German by Peter Forbes and P. D. Royce.

THE MISERY OF MANILLA FOLDERS:
WORK

Primo Levi said of work: 'This boundless region, the region of *le boulot*, the job, *il rusco* – of daily work, in other words – is less known than the Antarctic,' which conjures up a dazzling prospect of work as a *terra incognita* for writers, in which oil refineries glitter like palaces, executives strut through the roadhouses of southern England like minor Sheikhs, and the humble book-keeper draws the bottom line under life, the universe and everything. There are poems here on all these themes. The oppressions of work, its tedium, intimidations and unfairnesses are also a goad to poets. Patterns of work changed more rapidly during the century than ever before, with successive waves of technological innovation. Elegies for once awe-inspiringly powerful industries have become commonplace. But despite periods of mass unemployment, and recurrent predictions of an age of leisure at hand notwithstanding, the twentieth century has been a great age for work and the creation of new niches in the economy, including, towards the end of the century, such jobs as Resident Poet with a law firm and Official Poet of the Barnsley Football Club.

Roger McGough

cosy biscuit

What I wouldn't give for a nine to five.
Biscuits in the right hand drawer,
teabreaks, and typists to mentally undress.

The same faces. Somewhere to hang
your hat and shake your umbrella.
Cosy.   Everything in its place.

Upgraded every few years. Hobbies.
Glass of beer at lunchtime
Pension to look forward to.

Two kids.   Homeloving wife.
Bit on the side when the occasion arises
H.P.   Nothing fancy.   Neat semi.

* * *

What I wouldn't give for a nine to five.
Glass of beer in the right hand drawer
H.P. on everything at lunchtime.

The same 2 kids. Somewhere to hang
your wife and shake your bit on the side.
Teabreaks and a pension to mentally undress.

The same semifaces upgraded.
Hobbies every few years, neat typists
in wet macs when the umbrella arises.

What I wouldn't give for a cosy biscuit.

John Betjeman

Executive

I am a young executive. No cuffs than mine are cleaner;
I have a Slimline brief-case and I use the firm's Cortina.
In every roadside hostelry from here to Burgess Hill
The *maîtres d'hôtel* all know me well and let me sign the bill.

You ask me what it is I do. Well actually, you know,
I'm partly a liaison man and partly PRO.
Essentially I integrate the current export drive
And basically I'm viable from ten o'clock till five.

For vital off-the-record work – that's talking transport-wise –
I've a scarlet Aston-Martin – and does she go? She flies!
Pedestrians and dogs and cats – we mark them down for slaughter.
I also own a speed-boat which has never touched the water.

She's built of fibre-glass, of course. I call her 'Mandy Jane'
After a bird I used to know – No soda, please, just plain –
And how did I acquire her? Well to tell you about that
And to put you in the picture I must wear my other hat.

I do some mild developing. The sort of place I need
Is a quiet country market town that's rather run to seed.
A luncheon and a drink or two, a little *savoir faire* –
I fix the Planning Officer, the Town Clerk and the Mayor.

And if some preservationist attempts to interfere
A 'dangerous structure' notice from the Borough Engineer
Will settle any buildings that are standing in our way –
The modern style, sir, with respect, has really come to stay.

Theodore Roethke

Dolor

I have known the inexorable sadness of pencils,
Neat in their boxes, dolor of pad and paper-weight,
All the misery of manilla folders and mucilage,
Desolation in immaculate public places,
Lonely reception room, lavatory, switchboard,
The unalterable pathos of basin and pitcher,
Ritual of multigraph, paper-clip, comma,
Endless duplication of lives and objects.
And I have seen dust from the walls of institutions,
Finer than flour, alive, more dangerous than silica,
Silt, almost invisible, through long afternoons of tedium,
Dropping a fine film on nails and delicate eyebrows,
Glazing the pale hair, the duplicate grey standard faces.

Craig Raine

Insurance, Real Estate &
Powders Pharmaceutical

In the panelled, sound-proofed Penthouse Suite,
the Big Cheese contemplates the creases in his pants,
practises putts and (depressive) swallows down his stimulants.

Outside his doubledoors, a sunray (dusty) from the street
projects a movie on the parquet floor. Willie the Seam
(10 stitches) (with a hernia from humping the adding machine)
gingerly crosses his legs in the beam –
a double-cross performed on screen.

Hank (with hepatitis) checks his eyeballs (topaz) in a spoon,
eases down a (saffron) inch of milky cuff,
and dreams (*Take a TRAIN – Vacation SOON!*)

(O that lush Miami scene!) Life is tough
at Insurance, Real Estate & Powders Pharmaceutical
(Protection, Pitch & Dope): whole days are spent
easing back a cuticle,
buffing shoes, receiving rent.

One night, round six or so,
(quite likely) wearing shades, a janitor
from Lethe Co.
(the wrong side of the tracks)
will slam (impossible) the sliding door
and make them die of income tax.

Hans Magnus Enzensberger

The Ironmonger's Shop

Two elderly orphans
who inherited it
when they were nineteen,
nineteen years ago.

Nuns in washed-out aprons,
walled in by leaden chests
of drawers,
tacks and adjusting screws
between their lips.

Their rosy devotion,
their greying eagerness
under the naked light bulb,
the grey smell of grease,
of rubber, metal and putty.

Enormous wrenches, breast drills
in unloved hands.
The moist tongue
longing for another mouth
while the bill is made out.

Is this what you dreamt of,
Primal Soup? *Weltgeist*,
did you have your wits about you?
Was that all you had in mind,
Divine Providence?

Two elderly sisters
imprisoned for life
in an ironmonger's shop?

Their rosy eagerness,
their grey devotion
to the emery-paper?

Translated from the German by
the author.

Wendy Cope

Engineers' Corner

Why isn't there an Engineers' Corner in Westminster Abbey? In
Britain we've always made more fuss of a ballad than a blueprint
. . . How many schoolchildren dream of becoming great engineers?
– Advertisement placed in The Times by the Engineering Council

We make more fuss of ballads than of blueprints –
That's why so many poets end up rich.
While engineers scrape by in cheerless garrets
Who needs a bridge or dam? Who needs a ditch?

Whereas the person who can write a sonnet
Has got it made. It's always been the way,
For everybody knows that we need poems
And everybody reads them every day.

Yes, life is hard if you choose engineering –
You're sure to need another job as well;
You'll have to plan your projects in the evenings
Instead of going out. It must be hell.

While well-heeled poets ride around in Daimlers.
You'll burn the midnight oil to earn a crust.
With no hope of a statue in the Abbey,
With no hope, even, of a modest bust.

No wonder small boys dream of writing couplets
And spurn the bike, the lorry and the train.
There's far too much encouragement for poets –
That's why this country's going down the drain.

Alan Gould

South Coast Mechanic

We watch with two eyes, I reckon, outer and inner.
So I eat lunch slowly, one eye on the apprentices
where sheet-sunlight through the roll-a-door,
catches them in their huddle. They're guzzling soft drinks,
raucously outdoing each other in their scorn
for the latest model. *Yah, couldn' scrape*
the skin from off rice puddn', says the one
too young for his licence who they call Fucknuckle.

But speed is too like bolting your food – time
retaliates with indigestion or a curve's
slippy camber. Machinery's the same;
a job rushed is like marital discord;
the good mechanic is a lifelong bridegroom,
watchful, tender, deliberate. That's why
it's the slow watchful fellow from that lot who,
once he's done his time, I'll put on full wages here.

He's got good ears. It's ears let you see an engine
in X-ray, tappet squeak, a carby's ill-music.
But my other eye is on my fingernails, reflective-like.
There's grit under there goes back to Airforce days,
Trobriand nights of torsos gleaming to get
a Beaufighter's engines changed by dawn –
we did that – which would have been a week's work
for a peacetime crew. But that was efficiency,

not speed, the brain and hand in sync, in trance.
With machinery, I guess, it's the thought of sync,
those greased parts dancing behind their cowls,
which makes me fall in love over and over,
and me, the listening angel with a spanner,
repairing, refining. That thought cost me a wife.
She cleared out with the boy, benzine stench
and carburettor bits all over the white laminex

got to her, she said. Had a point.
Once I could improvise from a box of junk,
but now it's all kit-form; *Three days, lady,*
depending on the supplier. You should've bought
a paperback, eh! I've had honeymooners
find each other in my car yard, their campervans
waiting on a clutchplate; romance conked
beside a ditch for sump-oil, and that lover's moon

high above the cyclone fence; an image
for our times, you reckon? Domestic bliss;
my idea is a bed and fridge at the less
decorated end of a vast workshop, but
through habit I've kept the marriage weatherboards
with their empty rooms. As for the Cosmos,
sure, I've seen it, wheeling there above
the wire when I lock up of a winter's night.

The Grand Machine in sync, greased on air,
it's nice engineering, though wearing out, I'm told,
and spare parts, yeah, well, problems, foreign supplier.

Now which of my eyes was looking at that?

Robert Pinsky

The Refinery

'. . . *our language, forged in the dark by centuries of violent pressure,*
underground, out of the stuff of dead life.'

Thirsty and languorous after their long black sleep
The old gods crooned and shuffled and shook their heads
Dry, dry. By railroad they set out
Across the desert of stars to drink the world
Our mouths had soaked
In the strange sentences we made
While they were asleep: a pollen-tinted
Slurry of passion and lapsed
Intention, whose imagined
Taste made the savage deities hiss and snort.

In the lightless carriages, a smell of snake
And coarse fur, glands of lymphless breath
And ichor, the avid stenches of
Immortal bodies.

Their long train clicked and sighed
Through the gulfs of night between the planets
And came down through the evening fog
Of redwood canyons. From the train
At sunset, fiery warehouse windows
Along a wharf. Then dusk, a gash of neon:
Bar. Black pinewoods, a junction crossing, glimpses
Of sluggish surf among the rocks, a moan
Of dreamy forgotten divinity calling and fading
Against the windows of a town. Inside
The train, a flash
Of dragonfly wings, an antlered brow.

Black night again, and then
After the bridge, a palace on the water:

The great Refinery – impossible city of lights.
A million bulbs tracing its turreted
Boulevards and mazes. The castle of a person
Pronounced alive, the Corporation: a fictional
Lord real in law.

Barbicans and torches
Along the siding where the engine slows
At the central tanks, a ward
Of steel palisades, valved and chandeliered.

The muttering gods
Greedily penetrate those bright pavilions –
Libation of Benzene, Naphthalene, Asphalt,
Gasoline, Tar: syllables
Fractioned and cracked from unarticulated

Crude, the smeared keep of life that fed
On itself in pitchy darkness when the gods
Were new – inedible, volatile
And sublimated afresh to sting
Our tongues who use it, refined from oil of stone.

The gods batten on the vats, and drink up
Lovecries and memorized Chaucer, lines from movies
And songs hoarded in mortmain: exiles' charms,
The basal or desperate distillates of breath
Steeped, brewed and spent
As though we were their aphids, or their bees,
That monstered up sweetness for them while they dozed.

Muriel Rukeyser

Alloy

This is the most audacious landscape. The gangster's
stance with his gun smoking and out is not so
vicious as this commercial field, its hill of glass.

Sloping as gracefully as thighs, the foothills
narrow to this, clouds over every town
finally indicate the stored destruction.

Crystalline hill: a blinded field of white
murdering snow, seamed by convergent tracks;
the travelling cranes reach for the silica.

And down the track, the overhead conveyor
slides on its cable to the feet of chimneys.
Smoke rises, not white enough, not so barbaric.

Here the severe flame speaks from the brick throat,
electric furnaces produce this precious, this clean,
annealing the crystals, fusing at last alloys.

Hottest for silicon, blast furnaces raise flames,
spill fire, spill steel, quench the new shape to freeze,
tempering it to perfected metal.

Forced through this crucible, a million men.
Above this pasture, the highway passes those
who curse the air, breathing their fear again.

The roaring flowers of the chimney-stacks
less poison, at their lips in fire, than this
dust that is blown from off the field of glass;

blows and will blow, rising over the mills,
crystallized and beyond the fierce corrosion
disintegrated angel on these hills.

Norman Nicholson

On the Closing of Millom Ironworks

September 1968

Wandering by the heave of the town park, wondering
Which way the day will drift,
On the spur of a habit I turn to the feathered
Weathercock of the furnace chimneys.
                                    But no grey smoke-tail
Pointers the mood of the wind. The hum
And blare that for a hundred years
Drummed at the town's deaf ears
Now fills the air with the roar of its silence.
They'll need no more to swill the slag-dust off the windows;
The curtains will be cleaner
And the grass plots greener
Round the Old Folk's council flats. The tanged autumnal mist
Is filtered free of soot and sulphur,
And the wind blows in untainted.
It's beautiful to breathe the sharp night air.
But, morning after morning, there
They stand, by the churchyard gate,
Hands in pockets, shoulders to the slag,
The men whose fathers stood there back in '28,
When their sons were at school with me.
                                    The town
Rolls round the century's bleak orbit.
                                    Down
On the ebb-tide sands, the five-funnelled
Battleship of the furnace lies beached and rusting;
Run aground, not foundered;
Not a crack in her hull;
Lacking but a loan to float her off.
                                    The Market
Square is busy as the men file by
To sign on at the 'Brew'. But not a face
Tilts upward, no one enquires of the sky.

The smoke prognosticates no how
Or why of any practical tomorrow.
For what does it matter if it rains all day?
And what's the good of knowing
Which way the wind is blowing
When whichever way it blows it's a cold wind now.

Brew: the local term used for 'Bureau' – i.e. Labour Exchange – widely used in the Thirties. – Author's note.

Simon Armitage

Eighties, Nineties

Firstly, we worked in laughable conditions.
The photocopier
defied definition,
the windows were sealed with a decade of paintwork,
the thought of a cigarette triggered the sprinklers
and the security door
was open to question.
Any excuse got me out of the office.

I found the letter in the 'pending' folder,
a handwritten thing
signed T. Ruth O'Reilly
on a perfumed leaf of watermarked vellum.
It requested recognition, or maintenance even
from a putative father,
one William Creamstick
who was keeping shtum in the Scottish Borders.

At midnight I took the decision to risk it.
I darned the elbows
of my corduroy jacket,
threw a few things in an old army surplus
and thumbed it to Ringway for a stand-by ticket.

At dawn I was still
going round in circles
in a five mile stack over Edinburgh airspace.

I accepted a lift to Princes Street Gardens
from an aftershave rep
who slipped me some samples.
It was Marie Celeste-ville in the shopping centre
so I borrowed a pinta from the library doorstep
and a packet of rusks
from the all-night chemist
then kipped for an hour in the cashpoint lobby.

Creamstick's house was just as I'd pictured:
pigs in the garden,
geese in the kitchen.
He was toasting his feet on the coal fired Aga
as I rapped the window with my umbrella handle
and he beckoned me in,
thinking I'd come
to spay the bitches in his sheep-dog's litter.

He listened, nodding, as though I were recounting
the agreeable facts
from another man's story.
Then producing a bread knife the size of a cutlass
he suggested, in short, that I vacate his premises
and keep my proboscis
out of his business
or he'd reacquaint me with this morning's breakfast.

In a private wood on the way to the trunk-road
I stumbled on a fish farm
and beyond its embankment
was a fish that had jumped too far from the water.
Two more minutes of this world would have killed it.
I carried it, drowned it,
backstroked its gills
till it came to its senses; disappeared downwards.

Back at Head Office they were all going apeshit.
Hadn't I heard of
timesheets, or clearance,
or codes of conduct, or agency agreements?
As I typed out my notice and handed my keys in
I left them with this
old tandem to ride on:
if you only pay peanuts, you're working with monkeys.

Jonathan Holden

From *The Crash*

October 1987, Wall Street

II. 10/19/87, BLACK MONDAY

Noon. The bus comes swinging in, doors
wheeze open. He enters blindly. The weather's
pretty, yet (he can't quite put
his finger on it) false.
Ever since that Wednesday, October 7,
when the Fed jacked up the prime
a full half point, sending the Dow stumbling
ninety points downstairs,
to close at 2516,
the market's been subject to odd moods.
Down 34 that Friday, even further down
last Friday – down 57 points –
and it's headed down today. He needs
something to relax him.
She strips efficiently, he fumbles with his belt.
He checks his watch. She notices
how compulsively he checks his watch.
He doesn't take it off. No one could possibly
know his whereabouts right now, yet he acts
as if at any second the telephone is going to ring
for him. 'Are you okay?' she asks. 'Sure.'

She draws the curtains closed.
But, flopped on the waterbed, one arm flung
limply over her flank, he finds himself unable
to make the usual 'poem'. He's imagining
instead his telephone ringing
three quarters of a mile away and ringing,
and ringing. Money, like a screaming
infant, requires attention immediately, *this
instant*, while he lies here, helpless, pitying
his poor, distracted penis. It's like the market.
Neither will go up.
Outside the midday sun is shining uninterrupted
in a major key. The sky is blue, without a blemish.
The world seems not the least aware
of this other weather, an exotic weather only he
can see, The Market – told only in the barometer.
That she is real – her tongue and teeth real
as raw oysters on the half shell –
should reassure him. And that she is here
while billions of dollars are ceasing to exist.
They're not going up in smoke or steam. They're
not going anywhere. There is no 'where' for money.
No 'here'. Or 'there'. *Honey,
are you okay?* He cannot answer her,
because he's neither here nor there.

Alison Brackenbury

Bookkeeping

These are not (you understand) the figures
which send cold judgement into the backbone
which leave us, workless, shrunk at home
staring in a sky grown black with leaves.

These are like the ticking of a clock,
the daily sums, a van's new brakes,
three drums of trichloroethylene on the back
of a thrumming lorry; yet they take
a day to make: thin bars of figures. While
I try to balance them, light scurries round
like a glad squirrel. Radio music stales –
until shut off.

                    What's left when it is done,
the green book closed? There is no sea to swim
no mouth to kiss. Even the light is gone.
Bookkeepers drink over-sugared tea
lie in dark rooms; are always hunched and tired.

Where I stretch up the low bulb burns and whirls.
And in it, I see him. The dusky gold wing folds
across his face. The feathers' sharp tips smudge
his margins.

Sunk, in his own shadows, deep
in scattered ledgers of our petty sins:
he, the tireless angel:
Unaccountably, he sleeps.

THE GREAT INDOORS: HOME

The century of travel, emigration and enforced exile has also been for many the century, at least in the second half, of Do-It-Yourself, of nest-making. Poets in the twentieth century have been more inclined to see the fantastic in the ordinary than to domesticate the wild places. It is striking how many poems see the house as a mirror of the soul, its integrity or lack of it an index of the health of the occupants. Even stripping walls and old dressers can thus come to seem like acts of spiritual renewal. In André Frénaud's poem 'House for Sale' the fateful feeling that in buying a house you are buying a life, complete with ghosts, has never been better expressed.

André Frénaud

House for Sale

So many people have lived here, who loved
love, waking up and kicking up the dust.
The well is bottomless and has no moon,
the last lot have gone and taken nothing with them.
The ivy fattens under yesterday's sun,
the soot and their coffee grounds remain.
I hitch myself to frayed dreams.
I love the dross of other people's souls,
mixed with these slivers of garnet,
the sweat of failed endeavours.
Caretaker! I'll buy it, I'll buy the shack.
If it poisons me, I'll go to blazes.
We'll open the windows . . . Replace the sign.
A man enters, sniffs around, starts again.

Translated from the French by Peter Forbes.

Brian Jones

Stripping Walls

I have been practical as paint today, wholesome as bread –
I have stripped walls. I rose early and felt clean-limbed
And steady-eyed and said 'Today I will strip those walls.'
I have not been chewing my nails and gazing through windows
And grovelling for a subject or happiness. There was the subject,
Simple and tall. And when the baker called he was civil
And looking at me with some respect he said
'I see you're stripping walls' – I could see he liked me.
And when I opened the door to the greengrocer, I glinted my eyes
And leaned nonchalantly and poked some tomatoes and said as an
    aside
'I'm stripping walls today.' 'Are you?' he asked, interested, and I said
'Yes, just stripping those walls.' I could feel my forearms thicken,
    grow
Hairy, and when the laundry arrived I met it with rolled sleeves.
'Stripping walls?' he asked. 'Yeah,' I said, as if it were unimportant,
'Stripping walls. You know.' He nodded and smiled as if he knew.
And with a step like a spring before the meal I strode
Down to the pub and leaned and sipped ale and heard them talk
How one had cleared land that morning, another chopped wood.
When an eye caught mine I winked and flipped my head. 'I've been
Stripping walls,' I said. 'Have you?' 'Yeah, you know, just stripping.'
They nodded. 'Can be tricky,' one mumbled. I nodded. 'It can be
    that.'
'Plaster,' another said. 'Holes,' I said. 'Workmanship,' said another
And shook his head. 'Yeah, have a drink,' I said.
And I whistled through the afternoon, and stood once or twice
At the door-jamb, the stripper dangling from my fingers.
'Stripping?' asked passing neighbours. I nodded and they went on
    happy –
They were happy that I was stripping walls. It meant a lot.

When it grew dark, I went out for the freshness. 'Hey!' I called up,
'I've been stripping walls!' 'Just fancy that!' answered the moon with
A long pale face like Hopkins. 'Hey, fellers!' he called to the stars,
'This little hairy runt has been stripping walls!' 'Bully for him,'
      chimed
The Pole star, remote and cool as Vergil, 'He's a good, good lad.'
I crept to the kitchen, pursued by celestial laughter.
'You've done well today,' she said. 'Shall we paint tomorrow?'
'Ah, shut up!' I said, and started hacking my nails.

Blake Morrison

Pine

Growing up under the weight of wardrobes,
we have awarded ourselves pine. The old veneers
have been stripped away. A Swedish wife welcomes us
with her frank stare and enlightened ideas.

White wood, bright wood, your blonde shavings
fall away like the curls of a pampered child.
My fingers drift across the grainy fingerprints,
the dusty contours, the tumuli and cliffs.

Only these knots hold me, like some feud
from the past – the bad migraines
mother used to get, or a trough of low pressure
swishing its cloudbursts on the childhood fête.

But we will chamfer all that. When you called
this morning I was clearing our old dresser
of its tea-rings and nicks, the yellow sawdust
heaping up like salt-sift in a glass.

It's a walk through sand-dunes down to the sea,
the space where honesty might begin,
if we knew how, no corners to hide in,
the coming clean of our loyalties, and lies.

Miroslav Holub

At Home

At home we register the existence of a pernicious rampant growth, of lethal mutations or self-destructive diseases in the body of the world without uneasiness or vertigo. Home is a place of immunity provided that everyone has changed into slippers in the hall and that the gravy contains the customary amount of cornflour.

Home is a state in which the photograph album is a source of immortality and the image in the mirror persists without limit, like a butterfly in a beam of light.

Home is a semi-lethal mutation of the world with the emphasis on the prefix semi-.

Translated from the Czech by Ewald Osers.

Craig Raine

An Enquiry into Two Inches of Ivory

We live in the great indoors:
the vacuum cleaner grazes
over the carpet, lowing,
its udder a swollen wobble . . .

At night, the switches stare
from every wall like flat-faced
barn-owls, and light ripens
the electric pear.

Esse is percipi – Berkeley knew
the gentle irony of objects, how
they told amusing lies and drew laughter,
if only we believed our eyes.

Daily things. Objects
in the museum of ordinary art.
Two armless Lilliputian queens
preside, watching a giant bathe.
He catches the slippery cubist fish
with perfumed eggs. Another
is a yogi on the scrubbing brush.
Water painlessly breaks his bent
Picasso legs.

Clothes queue up in the wardrobe,
an echo to the eye, or a jangle of Euclid.
The wall-phone wears a pince-nez
even in the dark – the flex
is Jewish orthodox.

Day begins.
The milkman delivers
penguins with their chinking atonal fuss.
Cups commemorate the War
of Jenkins' Ear.
Without thinking, the giant
puts a kettle on the octopus.

Esse is percipi: being is perceiving.

Peter Redgrove

Old House

I lay in an agony of imagination as the wind
Limped up the stairs and puffed on the landings,
Snuffled through floorboards from the foundations,
Tottered, withdrew into flaws, and shook the house.
Peppery dust swarmed through all cracks,
The boiling air blew a dry spume from other mouths,
From other hides and function:
Scale of dead people fountained to the ceiling –
What sort of a house is this to bring children to,

Burn it down, build with new-fired brick;
How many times has this place been wound up
Around the offensive memories of a dead person,
Or a palette of sick colours dry on the body,
Or bare arms through a dank trapdoor to shut off water,
Or windows filmed over the white faces of children:
'This is no place to bring children to'

I cried in a nightmare of more
Creatures shelled in bone-white,
Or dead eyes fronting soft ermine faces,
Or mantled in carnation, dying kings of creation,
Or crimson mouth-skirts flashing as they pass:
What a world to bring new lives into,

Flat on my back in a warm bed as the house around me
Lived in the wind more than the people that built it;
It was bought with all our earned money,
With all the dust I was nearly flying from my body
That whipped in the wind in this normal November,
And outstretched beside her in my silly agony
She turned in her sleep and called for me,
Then taught me what children were to make a home for.

Delmore Schwartz

Tired and Unhappy, You Think of Houses

Tired and unhappy, you think of houses
Soft-carpeted and warm in the December evening,
While snow's white pieces fall past the window,
And the orange firelight leaps.
                                        A young girl sings
That song of Gluck where Orpheus pleads with Death;
Her elders watch, nodding their happiness
To see time fresh again in her self-conscious eyes:
The servants bring the coffee, the children retire,
Elder and younger yawn and go to bed,
The coals fade and glow, rose and ashen,
It is time to shake yourself! and break this
Banal dream, and turn your head
Where the underground is charged, where the weight
Of the lean buildings is seen,
Where close in the subway rush, anonymous
In the audience, well-dressed or mean,
So many surround you, ringing your fate,
Caught in an anger exact as a machine!

TIME WAS AWAY: LOVE & SEX

The poet Glyn Maxwell has said that love poetry in the twentieth century is no different to that of any other era – 'What else can you do with it?' But the sexual revolution is one of the century's chief characteristics and even before it (usually dated from Larkin's 'Sexual intercourse began in nineteen sixty-three'), poets were writing in a very different mode to that of the nineteenth-century love lyric: more likely to notice the books behind the loved one's head, more likely to contextualize and ironize the disparity between the islanded world of passion and the indifferent churning of the machine beyond the window (a trait also found in the Metaphysical poets of the seventeenth century but not in the two centuries in between). But *no* previous century's poetry has managed the whimsical sexiness of E. E. Cummings' 'may i feel said he' or the cool, unhysterical look of Fleur Adcock's 'Against Coupling'. In a century of great dislocation it is not surprising that failed relationships should have produced so many good poems. Especially noteworthy is Hans Magnus Enzensberger's forensic analysis of one of the century's scourges, divorce. Another great theme of the last quarter of the century was a greater tolerance of homosexuality and lesbianism, with the development of a burgeoning gay subculture – progress marred, since the early Eighties, by the emergence of Acquired Immune Deficiency Syndrome (AIDS), predominantly, in the Western world, in homosexual men.

Louis MacNeice

Meeting Point

Time was away and somewhere else,
There were two glasses and two chairs
And two people with the one pulse
(Somebody stopped the moving stairs):
Time was away and somewhere else.

And they were neither up nor down;
The stream's music did not stop
Flowing through heather, limpid brown,
Although they sat in a coffee shop
And they were neither up nor down.

The bell was silent in the air
Holding its inverted poise –
Between a clang and clang a flower,
A brazen calyx of no noise:
The bell was silent in the air.

The camels crossed the miles of sand
That stretched around the cups and plates;
The desert was their own, they planned
To portion out the stars and dates:
The camels crossed the miles of sand.

Time was away and somewhere else.
The waiter did not come, the clock
Forgot them and the radio waltz
Came out like water from a rock:
Time was away and somewhere else.

Her fingers flicked away the ash
That bloomed again in tropic trees:
Not caring if the markets crash
When they had forests such as these,
Her fingers flicked away the ash.

God or whatever means the Good
Be praised that time can stop like this,
That what the heart has understood
Can verify in the body's peace
God or whatever means the Good.

Time was away and she was here
And life no longer what it was,
The bell was silent in the air
And all the room one glow because
Time was away and she was here.

Boris Pasternak

Marburg

I quivered. I flared up, and then was extinguished.
I shook. I had made a proposal – but late,
Too late. I was scared, and she had refused me.
I pity her tears, am more blessed than a saint.

I stepped into the square. I could be counted
Among the twice-born. Every leaf on the lime,
Every brick was alive, caring nothing for me,
And reared up to take leave for the last time.

The paving-stones glowed and the street's brow was swarthy.
From under their lids the cobbles looked grim,
Scowled up at the sky, and the wind like a boatman
Was rowing through limes. And each was an emblem.

Be that as it may, I avoided their glances,
Averted my gaze from their greeting or scowling.
I wanted no news of their getting and spending.
I had to get out, so as not to start howling.

The tiles were afloat, and an unblinking noon
Regarded the rooftops. And someone, somewhere
In Marburg, was whistling, at work on a crossbow,
And someone else dressing for the Trinity fair.

Devouring the clouds, the sand showed yellow,
A storm wind was rocking the bushes to and fro,
And the sky had congealed where it touched a sprig
Of woundwort that staunched its flow.

Like any rep Romeo hugging his tragedy,
I reeled through the city rehearsing you.
I carried you all that day, knew you by heart
From the comb in your hair to the foot in your shoe.

And when in your room I fell to my knees,
Embracing this mist, this perfection of frost
(How lovely you are!), this smothering turbulence,
What were you thinking? 'Be sensible!' Lost!

Here lived Martin Luther. The Brothers Grimm, there.
And all things remember and reach out to them:
The sharp-taloned roofs. The gravestones. The trees.
And each is alive. And each is an emblem.

I shall not go tomorrow. Refusal –
More final than parting. We're quits. All is clear.
And if I abandon the streetlamps, the banks –
Old pavingstones, what will become of me here?

The mist on all sides will unpack its bags,
In both windows will hang up a moon.
And melancholy will slide over the books
And settle with one on the ottoman.

Then why am I scared? Insomnia I know
Like grammar, by heart. I have grown used to that.
In line with the four square panes of my window
Dawn will lay out her diaphanous mat.

The nights now sit down to play chess with me
Where ivory moonlight chequers the floor.
It smells of acacia, the windows are open,
And passion, a grey witness, stands by the door.

The poplar is king. I play with insomnia.
The queen is a nightingale I can hear calling.
I reach for the nightingale. And the night wins.
The pieces make way for the white face of morning.

Translated from the Russian by
Jon Stallworthy and Peter France.

John Berryman

From *The Dream Songs*

IV

Filling her compact & delicious body
with chicken páprika, she glanced at me
twice.
Fainting with interest, I hungered back
and only the fact of her husband & four other people
kept me from springing on her

or falling at her little feet and crying
'You are the hottest one for years of night
Henry's dazed eyes
have enjoyed, Brilliance.' I advanced upon
(despairing) my spumoni. – Sir Bones: is stuffed,
de world, wif feeding girls.

– Black hair, complexion Latin, jewelled eyes
downcast . . . The slob beside her feasts . . . What wonders is
she sitting on, over there?
The restaurant buzzes. She might as well be on Mars.
Where did it all go wrong? There ought to be a law against Henry.
– Mr Bones: there is.

Michèle Roberts

Magnificat

For Sian, after thirteen years

oh this man
what a meal he made of me
how he chewed and gobbled and sucked
in the end he spat me all out

you arrived on the dot, in the nick
of time, with your red curls flying
I was about to slip down the sink like grease
I nearly collapsed, I almost
wiped myself out like a stain
I called for you, and you came, you voyaged
fierce as a small archangel with swords and breasts
you declared the birth of a new life
in my kitchen there was an annunciation
and I was still, awed by your hair's glory

you commanded me to sing of my redemption

oh my friend, how
you were mother for me, and how
I could let myself lean on you
comfortable as an old cloth
familiar as enamel saucepans
I was a child again, pyjama'ed
in winceyette, my hair plaited, and you

listened, you soothed me like cake and milk
you listened to me for three days, and I poured
it out, I flowed all over you like wine, like oil
you touched the place where it hurt
at night, we slept together in my big bed
your shoulder eased me towards dreams

when we met, I tell you
it was a birthday party, a funeral
it was a holy communion
between women, a Visitation
it was two old she-goats butting
and nuzzling each other in the smelly fold

Adrienne Rich

Living in Sin

She had thought the studio would keep itself;
no dust upon the furniture of love.
Half heresy, to wish the taps less vocal,
the panes relieved of grime. A plate of pears,
a piano with a Persian shawl, a cat
stalking the picturesque amusing mouse
had risen at his urging.
Not that at five each separate stair would writhe
under the milkman's tramp; that morning light
so coldly would delineate the scraps
of last night's cheese and three sepulchral bottles;
that on the kitchen shelf among the saucers
a pair of beetle-eyes would fix her own –
envoy from some village in the moldings . . .
Meanwhile, he, with a yawn,
sounded a dozen notes upon the keyboard,
declared it out of tune, shrugged at the mirror,
rubbed at his beard, went out for cigarettes;
while she, jeered by the minor demons,
pulled back the sheets and made the bed and found
a towel to dust the table-top,
and let the coffee-pot boil over on the stove.
By evening she was back in love again,
though not so wholly but throughout the night
she woke sometimes to feel the daylight coming
like a relentless milkman up the stairs.

Gregory Corso

Marriage

Should I get married? Should I be good?
Astound the girl next door with my velvet suit and faustus hood?
Don't take her to movies but to cemeteries
tell all about werewolf bathtubs and forked clarinets
then desire her and kiss her and all the preliminaries
and she going just so far and I understanding why
not getting angry saying You must feel! It's beautiful to feel!
Instead take her in my arms lean against an old crooked tombstone
and woo her the entire night the constellations in the sky –

When she introduces me to her parents
back straightened, hair finally combed, strangled by a tie,
should I sit knees together on their 3rd degree sofa
and not ask Where's the bathroom?
How else to feel other than I am,
often thinking Flash Gordon soap –
O how terrible it must be for a young man
seated before a family and the family thinking
We never saw him before! He wants our Mary Lou!
After tea and homemade cookies they ask What do you do for a
    living?

Should I tell them? Would they like me then?
Say All right get married, we're losing a daughter
but we're gaining a son –
And should I then ask Where's the bathroom?

O God, and the wedding! All her family and her friends
and only a handful of mine all scroungy and bearded
just wait to get at the drinks and food –
And the priest! he looking at me as if I masturbated
asking me Do you take this woman for your lawful wedded wife?
And I trembling what to say say Pie Glue!
I kiss the bride all those corny men slapping me on the back

She's all yours, boy! Ha-ha-ha!
And in their eyes you could see some obscene honeymoon going on –

Then all that absurd rice and clanky cans and shoes
Niagara Falls! Hordes of us! Husbands! Wives! Flowers! Chocolates!

All streaming into cozy hotels
All going to do the same thing tonight
The indifferent clerk he knowing what was going to happen
The lobby zombies they knowing what
The whistling elevator man he knowing
The winking bellboy knowing
Everybody knowing! I'd be almost inclined not to do anything!
Stay up all night! Stare that hotel clerk in the eye!
Screaming: I deny honeymoon! I deny honeymoon!
running rampant into those almost climactic suites
yelling Radio belly! Cat shovel!
O I'd live in Niagara forever! in a dark cave beneath the Falls
I'd sit there the Mad Honeymooner
devising ways to break marriages, a scourge of bigamy
a saint of divorce –

But I should get married I should be good
How nice it'd be to come home to her
and sit by the fireplace and she in the kitchen
aproned young and lovely wanting my baby
and so happy about me she burns the roast beef
and comes crying to me and I get up from my big papa chair
saying Christmas teeth! Radiant brains! Apple deaf!
God what a husband I'd make! Yes, I should get married!
So much to do! like sneaking into Mr Jones' house late at night
and cover his golf clubs with 1920 Norwegian books
Like hanging a picture of Rimbaud on the lawnmower
like pasting Tannu Tuva postage stamps all over the picket fence
like when Mrs Kindhead comes to collect for the Community Chest
grab her and tell her There are unfavourable omens in the sky!
And when the mayor comes to get my vote tell him
When are you going to stop people killing whales!

And when the milkman comes leave him a note in the bottle
Penguin dust, bring me penguin dust, I want penguin dust —

Yet if I should get married and it's Connecticut and snow
and she gives birth to a child and I am sleepless, worn,
up for nights, head bowed against a quiet window, the past behind
    me,
finding myself in the most common of situations a trembling man
knowledged with responsibility not twig-smear nor Roman coin
    soup —
O what would that be like!
Surely I'd give it for a nipple a rubber Tacitus
For a rattle a bag of broken Bach records
Tack Della Francesca all over its crib
Sew the Greek alphabet on its bib
And build for its playpen a roofless Parthenon

No, I doubt I'd be that kind of father
not rural not snow no quiet window
but hot smelly tight New York City
seven flights up roaches and rats in the walls
a fat Reichian wife screeching over potatoes Get a job!
And five nose running brats in love with Batman
And the neighbors all toothless and dry haired
like those hag masses of the 18th century
all wanting to come in and watch TV
The landlord wants his rent
Grocery store Blue Cross Gas & Electric Knights of Columbus
Impossible to lie back and dream Telephone snow, ghost parking —
No! I should not get married I should never get married!
But — imagine if I were married to a beautiful sophisticated woman
tall and pale wearing an elegant black dress and long black gloves
holding a cigarette holder in one hand and a highball in the other
and we lived high up in a penthouse with a huge window
from which we could see all of New York and ever farther on clearer
    days
No, can't imagine myself married to that pleasant prison dream —

O but what about love? I forget love
not that I am incapable of love
it's just that I see love as odd as wearing shoes –
I never wanted to marry a girl who was like my mother
And Ingrid Bergman was always impossible
And there's maybe a girl now but she's already married
And I don't like men and –
but there's got to be somebody!
Because what if I'm 60 years old and not married,
all alone in a furnished room with pee stains on my underwear
and everybody else is married! All the universe married but me!

Ah, yet well I know that were a woman possible as I am possible
then marriage would be possible –
Like SHE in her lonely alien gaud waiting her Egyptian lover
so I wait – bereft of 2,000 years and the bath of life.

Philip Larkin

Annus Mirabilis

Sexual intercourse began
In nineteen sixty-three
(Which was rather late for me) –
Between the end of the *Chatterley* ban
And the Beatles' first LP.

Up till then there'd only been
A sort of bargaining,
A wrangle for a ring,
A shame that started at sixteen
And spread to everything.

Then all at once the quarrel sank:
Everyone felt the same,
And every life became
A brilliant breaking of the bank,
A quite unlosable game.

So life was never better than
In nineteen sixty-three
(Though just too late for me) –
Between the end of the *Chatterley* ban
And the Beatles' first LP.

E. E. Cummings

may i feel said he . . .

may i feel said he
(i'll squeal said she
just once said he)
it's fun said she

(may i touch said he
how much said she
a lot said he)
why not said she

(let's go said he
not too far said she
what's too far said he
where you are said she)

may i stay said he
(which way said she
like this said he
if you kiss said she

may i move said he
is it love said she)
if you're willing said he
but you're killing said she

but it's life said he
but your wife said she

now said he
ow said she

tiptop said he
don't stop said she
oh no said he
go slow said she

(cccome?said he
ummm said she)
you're divine!said he
(you are Mine said she)

Fleur Adcock

Against Coupling

I write in praise of the solitary act:
of not feeling a trespassing tongue
forced into one's mouth, one's breath
smothered, nipples crushed against the
ribcage, and that metallic tingling
in the chin set off by a certain odd nerve:

unpleasure. Just to avoid those eyes would help –
such eyes as a young girl draws life from,
listening to the vegetal
rustle within her, as his gaze
stirs polypal fronds in the obscure
sea-bed of her body, and her own eyes blur.

There is much to be said for abandoning
this no longer novel exercise –
for not 'participating in
a total experience' – when
one feels like the lady in Leeds who
had seen *The Sound of Music* eighty-six times;

or more, perhaps, like the school drama mistress
producing *A Midsummer Night's Dream*
for the seventh year running, with
yet another cast from 5B.
Pyramus and Thisbe are dead, but
the hole in the wall can still be troublesome.

I advise you, then, to embrace it without
encumbrance. No need to set the scene,
dress up (or undress), make speeches.
Five minutes of solitude are
enough – in the bath, or to fill
that gap between the Sunday papers and lunch.

John Whitworth

From *Careless Love*

XV

The real problem is the fence posts. Most of them
Are rotted right through, close to the ground, and so
Quite useless as fence posts, beating to and fro
In the worst September gales since God-knows-when.
He considers the situation. Sound wood from the bum supports
Could be bolted together. Then take
Two of the old beams stored in the garage. Yes. Such make
Do and mend is a delight to his soul. It's the sort

Of problem he knows he's good at. The boy,
Five-year-old Dominic, is also pleased, and renders
Assistance, tugging old nails out with his own hammer,
Which Mummy does not approve of. But she's away
At her intermediate Italian, off with the Volvo,
And that's all right. Her husband whistles a phrase
Inaccurately from his Albinoni record, and lays
Clean timber carefully along the patio,

As the cat rubs its back on the remains of the fence
And evening ambles down the gardens to Mrs
Thing next door taking in washing. Suddenly this is
Too much like an advertisement for life insurance,
Shimmering and sinister. There are things which
Are obviously wrong with the life of this chap.
His job's a washout. He can't get it up.
The boy's neurotic and the wife's a bitch

Screwing around with his best friend. Here's his best friend
Vaulting over the back gate in a posh
Red and white tracksuit. He's come to play squash –
You can tell by the very good squash-racket in his hand.
Grinning like a grand piano he chats up Dominic.
Even the cat begins to purr.
The wronged husband goes to the refrigerator,
Proffers ice-cold lager and grins back.

This is the real problem, more knotty.
Does he push the adulterer's pleasant face out through
The back of his suntanned neck? This is the man who
Is, after all, his best friend. It'd be a pity
Not to play squash on a Saturday morning,
Not to sit in the public with his old mate,
Swapping stories and pints, chewing the fat
About nothing in particular. In the kitchen

They discuss the first problem of the fence posts
As they wait for Mummy to return with the Volvo.
There is a kind of concrete spur, does he know?
Something made specifically for rotten fence posts.
They get fairly involved in this. Dominic discovers
A new game with the cat and his yo-yo.
Door chimes means Mummy has mislaid her key.
She stands apologetically on the step, lovelier than ever,

Which is another problem.

Hans Magnus Enzensberger

The Divorce

At first it was only an imperceptible quivering of the skin –
'As you wish' – where the flesh is darkest.
'What's wrong with you?' – Nothing. Milky dreams
of embraces; next morning, though,
the other looks different, strangely bony.
Razor-sharp misunderstandings. 'That time, in Rome –'
I never said that. A pause. And furious palpitations,
a sort of hatred, strange. 'That's not the point.'
Repetitions. Radiantly clear, this certainty:
From now on all is wrong. Odourless and sharp,
like a passport photo, this unknown person
with a glass of tea at table, with staring eyes.
It's no good, no good, no good:
litany in the head, a slight nausea.
End of reproaches. Slowly the whole room
Fills with guilt right up to the ceiling.
This complaining voice is strange, only not
the shoes that drop with a bang, not the shoes.
Next time, in an empty restaurant,
slow motion, bread crumbs, money is discussed,
laughing – The dessert tastes of metal.
Two untouchables. Shrill reasonableness.
'Not so bad really.' But at night
the thoughts of vengeance, the silent fight, anonymous
like two bony barristers, two large crabs
in water. Then the exhaustion. Slowly
the scab peels off. A new tobacconist,
a new address. Pariahs, horribly relieved.
Shades growing paler. These are the documents.
This is the bunch of keys. This is the scar.

Translated from the German by Michael Hamburger.

John Fuller

Her Morning Dreams

I trail in my sculpted sheets to the misty window
And rub a patch there like a liquid bruise.
Yes. Stooping in blue. Propped bicycle.

But absence is your only sort of news.
Over the toast and the slit boring letters
The damp end flares in ribbons like a fuse.

What do I think? Do I think it matters?
Do I think what matters? Do I think?
Oh yes, I think. Don't worry, you wouldn't notice.

The unmade bed. Finger on my pink.
Dead as he groaned upon a linen ocean,
Who would have thought he had such little ink?

Dreams for you. The head is cut in walking.
Sour puff balls. Silence. Clouds of dust.
It's a bad day for any sort of singing.

I thought that you were someone I could trust.
I can begin. Well, I can try beginning
If only somebody will say I must.

Are you my pal? Are you Ardent Ardvaark?
At first I took you for the kind who while
He sobs sinks fangs, while he sings does murder

In blue clothes, greets with insinuating smile
Across the gravel with his hands extended
In preacher or in nightclub singer style

Under a pained yet cheerful load of welcome.
Now you are someone in my morning dreams.
I was so bored that summer. Can you imagine

Life shrunk and wrinkled to its seams,
Its hopes on threads, its memories in pockets,
The sluggish mouth disowning all its streams?

Can you imagine the clean shock of naming,
And love acknowledging its paradigm?
With you misery had as little meaning

As backfriends to fingers galloping in time
With the Catalan pupil of the Neapolitan master,
Each note as true as an expected rhyme.

Perhaps you never meant that sort of magic,
Perhaps the fault was mine, grateful allure
Scoring a million in the cheated darkness,

Pretending the experience was pure.
God help us, darling, aren't we only human?
Kiss me again and let's be really sure.

I believe all disasters now, believe all pain.
As for your life, however much you hate it,
However bad it smells upon your bed,

You simply cannot go back and create it:
Something will tell you that you have to cry,
Something will tell you this was always fated.

So I have tried beginning. Or is it ending?
Things I remember cover me with shame,
They linger obstinately every morning.

Stupid. But every day it is the same.
And nothing felt like that is ever final.
Not you. Not me. Nobody is to blame.

Dreams. You walking down a dusty pavement.
Your head is always strangely turned away,
Carried as though bandaged, with little movement.

Now is the time to say it: nothing to say.
You came and went with carefully rolled forearms.
You held life in their empty space that day.

I pad from bed to stove to fill a pan.
Sometimes a step is just a step too far:
No time to think what it has got you into.

Even the job of knowing where you are
Becomes a full-time dangerous occupation.
It's honey at the bottom of the jar

But no one can be sure until it's eaten.
Not everything is right. What's possible?
I pull the whole drawer of my mind down on

My foot. Hell. The cat's beneath the bedspread
Like a blister, showing that you have gone.
I walk from room to room, trying the answer:

One from two is wrong, and one from one
Is neater. Morning dreams are calmer weeping.
All my indignities spill from the sun.

Listen to it now. All night like wedded chaos
The creeper's down, the storm makes such a fuss.
Trying to count the blows of rain is useless.

I shall sit it out, here by the misty glass,
Till I can face the morning's empty graces,
The window sill become an abacus.

Anne Sexton

For My Lover, Returning to His Wife

She is all there.
She was melted carefully down for you
and cast up from your childhood,
cast up from your one hundred favorite aggies.

She has always been there, my darling.
She is, in fact, exquisite.
Fireworks in the dull middle of February
and as real as a cast-iron pot.

Let's face it, I have been momentary.
A luxury. A bright red sloop in the harbor.
My hair rising like smoke from the car window.
Littleneck clams out of season.
She is more than that. She is your have to have,
has grown you your practical your tropical growth.
This is not an experiment. She is all harmony.
She sees to oars and oarlocks for the dinghy,

has placed wild flowers at the window at breakfast,
sat by the potter's wheel at midday,
set forth three children under the moon,
three cherubs drawn by Michelangelo,

done this with her legs spread out
in the terrible months in the chapel.
If you glance up, the children are there
like delicate balloons resting on the ceiling.

She has also carried each one down the hall
after supper, their heads privately bent,
two legs protesting, person to person,
her face flushed with a song and their little sleep.

I give you back your heart.
I give you permission –
for the fuse inside her, throbbing
angrily in the dirt, for the bitch in her
and the burying of her wound –
for the burying of her small red wound alive –

for the pale flickering flare under her ribs,
for the drunken sailor who waits in her left pulse,
for the mother's knee, for the stockings,
for the garter belt, for the call –

the curious call
when you will burrow in arms and breasts
and tug at the orange ribbon in her hair
and answer the call, the curious call.

She is so naked and singular.
She is the sum of yourself and your dream.
Climb her like a monument, step after step.
She is solid.

As for me, I am a watercolor.
I wash off.

Marina Tsvetaeva

An Attempt at Jealousy

How is your life with the other one,
    simpler, isn't it? One   stroke of the oar
then a long coastline, and soon
    even the memory of me

will be a floating island
    (in the sky, not on the waters):
spirits, spirits, you will be
    sisters, and never lovers.

How is your life with an ordinary
   woman?   without godhead?
Now that your sovereign has
   been deposed (and you have stepped down).

How is your life? Are you fussing?
   flinching? How   do you get up?
The tax of deathless vulgarity
   can you cope with it, poor man?

'Scenes and hysterics   I've had
   enough! I'll rent my own house.'
How is your life with the other one
   now, you that I chose for my own?

More to your taste, more delicious
   is it, your food? Don't moan if you sicken.
How is your life with an *image*
   you, who walked on Sinai?

How is your life with a stranger
   from this world? Can you (be frank)
love her? Or do you   feel shame
   like Zeus' reins on your forehead?

How is your life? Are you
   healthy? How do you   sing?
How do you deal with the pain
   of an undying conscience, poor man?

How is your life with a piece of market
   stuff, at a steep price.
After Carrara marble,
   how is your life with the dust of

plaster now? (God was hewn from
   stone, but he is smashed to bits.)
How do you live with one of a
   thousand women   after Lilith?

Sated with newness, are you?
    Now you are grown cold to magic,
how is your life with an
    earthly woman, without a sixth

sense? Tell me: are you happy?
    Not? In a shallow pit? How is
your life, my love? Is it as
    hard as mine with another man?

Translated from the Russian by
Elaine Feinstein.

Thom Gunn

The Missing

Now as I watch the progress of the plague,
The friends surrounding me fall sick, grow thin,
And drop away. Bared, is my shape less vague
– Sharply exposed and with a sculpted skin?

I do not like the statue's chill contour,
Not nowadays. The warmth investing me
Led outward through mind, limb, feeling, and more
In an involved increasing family.

Contact of friend led to another friend,
Supple entwinement through the living mass
Which for all that I knew might have no end,
Image of an unlimited embrace.

I did not just feel ease, though comfortable:
Aggressive as in some ideal of sport,
With ceaseless movement thrilling through the whole,
Their push kept me as firm as their support.

But death – Their deaths have left me less defined:
It was their pulsing presence made me clear.
I borrowed from it, I was unconfined,
Who tonight balance unsupported here,

Eyes glaring from raw marble, in a pose
Languorously part-buried in the block,
Shins perfect and no calves, as if I froze
Between potential and a finished work.

– Abandoned incomplete, shape of a shape,
In which exact detail shows the more strange,
Trapped in unwholeness, I find no escape
Back to the play of constant give and change.

August 1987

THE SPIRIT IS TOO BLUNT AN
INSTRUMENT: CHILDREN & FAMILY

The repeated invocation of 'family values' by politicians towards its end suggests that the century was not a good one for the family. And Philip Larkin's 'This Be The Verse' ('They fuck you up, your mum and dad . . .') is presumably one of the most often quoted poems of the last quarter century for some reason. Whatever the strains, poets have been eloquent dissectors of disaster and, in one area at least, a note of celebration has been possible. The fierce pride of Sharon Olds' 'The Language of the Brag' and the detachment of Sylvia Plath's 'Morning Song' and Anne Stevenson's 'The Spirit is too Blunt an Instrument' have replaced nineteenth-century silence over that great rite of passage, child-bearing. Andreas Okopenko's sardonic 'The End of Teenagers' marks one of the century's innovations: a new staging-post in the ages of men and women – the teenager.

Sharon Olds

The Language of the Brag

I have wanted excellence in the knife-throw,
I have wanted to use my exceptionally strong and accurate arms
and my straight posture and quick electric muscles
to achieve something at the centre of a crowd,
the blade piercing the bark deep,
the haft slowly and heavily vibrating like the cock.

I have wanted some epic use for my excellent body,
some heroism, some American achievement
beyond the ordinary for my extraordinary self,
magnetic and tensile, I have stood by the sandlot
and watched the boys play.

I have wanted courage, I have thought about fire
and the crossing of waterfalls, I have dragged around

my belly big with cowardice and safety,
my stool black with iron pills,
my huge breasts oozing mucus,
my legs swelling, my hands swelling,
my face swelling and darkening, my hair
falling out, my inner sex
stabbed again and again with terrible pain like a knife.
I have lain down.

I have lain down and sweated and shaken
and passed blood and faeces and water and
slowly alone in the centre of a circle I have
passed the new person out
and they have lifted the new person free of the act
and wiped the new person free of that
language of blood like praise all over the body.

I have done what you wanted to do, Walt Whitman,
Allen Ginsberg, I have done this thing,
I and the other women this exceptional
act with the exceptional heroic body,
this giving birth, this glistening verb,
and I am putting my proud American boast
right here with the others.

Sylvia Plath

Morning Song

Love set you going like a fat gold watch.
The midwife slapped your footsoles, and your bald cry
Took its place among the elements.

Our voices echo, magnifying your arrival. New statue.
In a drafty museum, your nakedness
Shadows our safety. We stand round blankly as walls.

I'm no more your mother
Than the cloud that distills a mirror to reflect its own slow
Effacement at the wind's hand.

All night your moth-breath
Flickers among the flat pink roses. I wake to listen:
A far sea moves in my ear.

One cry, and I stumble from bed, cow-heavy and floral
In my Victorian nightgown.
Your mouth opens clean as a cat's. The window square

Whitens and swallows its dull stars. And now you try
Your handful of notes;
The clear vowels rise like balloons.

Anne Stevenson

The Spirit is too Blunt an Instrument

The spirit is too blunt an instrument
to have made this baby.
Nothing so unskilful as human passions
could have managed the intricate
exacting particulars: the tiny
blind bones with their manipulating tendons,
the knee and the knucklebones, the resilient
fine meshings of ganglia and vertebrae,
the chain of the difficult spine.

Observe the distinct eyelashes and sharp crescent
fingernails, the shell-like complexity
of the ear, with its firm involutions

concentric in miniature to minute
ossicles. Imagine the
infinitesimal capillaries, the flawless connections
of the lungs, the invisible neural filaments
through which the completed body
already answers to the brain.

Then name any passion or sentiment
possessed of the simplest accuracy.
No, no desire or affection could have done
with practice what habit
has done perfectly, indifferently,
through the body's ignorant precision.
It is left to the vagaries of the mind to invent
love and despair and anxiety
and their pain.

Philip Larkin

This Be The Verse

They fuck you up, your mum and dad.
   They may not mean to, but they do.
They fill you with the faults they had
   And add some extra, just for you.

But they were fucked up in their turn
   By fools in old-style hats and coats,
Who half the time were soppy-stern
   And half at one another's throats.

Man hands on misery to man.
   It deepens like a coastal shelf.
Get out as early as you can,
   And don't have any kids yourself.

D. H. Lawrence

Piano

Softly, in the dusk, a woman is singing to me;
Taking me back down the vista of years, till I see
A child sitting under the piano, in the boom of the tingling strings
And pressing the small, poised feet of a mother who smiles as she
     sings.

In spite of myself, the insidious mastery of song
Betrays me back, till the heart of me weeps to belong
To the old Sunday evenings at home, with winter outside
And hymns in the cosy parlour, the tinkling piano our guide.

So now it is vain for the singer to burst into clamour
With the great black piano appassionato. The glamour
Of childish days is upon me, my manhood is cast
Down in the flood of remembrance, I weep like a child for the past.

Brian Jones

The Children of Separation

While waiting for you to come, I imagine you sitting
in a stopped train between stations, feeling
at peace in no-man's-land, where there is no need
to say 'we' or 'our' or 'home', or other impossible words,

where the poppies among the corn
recall distant universal pain
cushioned in history and innocence.
How unusual it must be for you now to enjoy silence,

with no-one to crave your assurance, no-one to grasp
your hands, stare into your face, and guiltily ask
'Are you all right? Are you unhappy? Will you say?'
No-one you must gratify

with tears, or the absence of tears.
Suddenly, you are among the ranks of those
who once seemed as unlikely, as remote,
as the handicapped, the poor, the mad –

the children of separation, those who are given
two Christmases to halve the pain
and find it doubled, those who are more prey
to nostalgia than old men, who have been betrayed

by language and now handle it like bombs,
for whom affection is a thicket of spies, and surnames
amputations with the ache of wholeness.
Every book taken down is inscribed by loving parents,

and albums of photographs refuse to be otherwise.
What can be done with memories?
What remains of the self if everything that was
is now framed in the inverted commas of 'seemed'?

I imagine the brakes sighing to the inevitable,
and the train resuming the purpose of the rails.
Soon you will step out into my story
whose pages for too long I kept closed to you.

We will walk through fields I am still making mine,
and when the time comes for someone to say 'Let's go home'
no-one will say it. On the platform, we will wait to be parted,
your hand clutching a ticket to somewhere rejected.

Andreas Okopenko

The End of Teenagers

I had not cursed them: they were quite attractive
I'd often longed to put my gob in their hair
the mauvely tinted like candyfloss
into their gobstopper gobs or under their miniskirts

I had not cursed them: somebody else must have done it
so that iron fell from the sky, and red-hot at that
after all I'm no grumpy man-eating founder
flinging the stuff about without rhyme or reason

Admittedly, I never discovered among them
Sonia who converted Raskolnikov to Siberia
Elizabeth out of 'Immensee' who'd let me make up for something
Madame de Staël who dared to be clever

Nonetheless I regret that now in Nevada
where the worldquake wind has blown me for a season
I can walk whole days and not find one teenager
only the girl-eyed desert jerboa-mouse

Translated from the German by Michael Hamburger.

Tony Harrison

From *Long Distance*

II

Though my mother was already two years dead
Dad kept her slippers warming by the gas,
put hot water bottles her side of the bed
and still went to renew her transport pass.

You couldn't just drop in. You had to phone.
He'd put you off an hour to give him time
to clear away her things and look alone
as though his still raw love were such a crime.

He couldn't risk my blight of disbelief
though sure that very soon he'd hear her key
scrape in the rusted lock and end his grief.
He *knew* she'd just popped out to get the tea.

I believe life ends with death, and that is all.
You haven't both gone shopping; just the same,
in my new black leather phone book there's your name
and the disconnected number I still call.

ALL THE LONELY PEOPLE:
THE INDIVIDUAL

The century of mass consumption, mass killing and social upheaval has also been the century of the individual – often alienated, lonely and confused. Poetry has always been a medium for the still small voice and in the twentieth century the range of expression of stubborn or disturbed individuality is greater than ever. The loss of certainties and the comforts of traditional belief has made us all existentialists now. The poems here are not only concerned with alienation and torment – there are poems of resolution and defiance, such as Jenny Joseph's 'Warning' and Roger McGough's 'Let Me Die a Youngman's Death'.

Robert Frost

Acquainted with the Night

I have been one acquainted with the night.
I have walked out in rain – and back in rain.
I have outwalked the furthest city light.

I have looked down the saddest city lane.
I have passed by the watchman on his beat
And dropped my eyes, unwilling to explain.

I have stood still and stopped the sound of feet
When far away an interrupted cry
Came over houses from another street,

But not to call me back or say good-bye;
And further still at an unearthly height
One luminary clock against the sky

Proclaimed the time was neither wrong nor right.
I have been one acquainted with the night.

Fran Landesman

The Ballad of the Sad Young Men

All the sad young men
Sitting in the bars
Knowing neon lights
Missing all the stars

All the sad young men
Drifting through the town
Drinking up the night
Trying not to drown

Sing a song of sad young men
Glasses full of rye
All the news is bad again
Kiss your dreams goodbye

All the sad young men
Seek a certain smile
Someone they can hold
For a little while

Tired little girl
Does the best she can
Trying to be gay
For a sad young man

Autumn turns the leaves to gold
Slowly dies the heart
Sad young men are growing old
That's the cruellest part

While a grimy moon
Watches from above
All the sad young men
Play at making love

Misbegotten moon
Shine for sad young men
Let your gentle light
Guide them home again
All the sad young men

John Fuller

Retreat

I should like to live in a sunny town like this
Where every afternoon is half-day closing
And I would wait at the terminal for the one train
Of the day, pacing the platform, and no one arriving.

At the far end of the platform is a tunnel, and the train
Slows out of it like a tear from a single eye.
You couldn't get further than this, the doors all opened
And the porter with rolled sleeves wielding a mop.

Even if one restless traveller were to arrive
With leather grip, racquets under the arm,
A belted raincoat folded over the shoulder,
A fishing hat, and a pipe stuck in his mouth,

There would be nowhere for him to move on to
And he would settle down to tea in the lounge
Of the Goat Hotel, doing yesterday's crossword,
And would emerge later, after a nap, for a drink.

You meet them in the bar, glassy-eyed, all the time.
They never quite unpack, and expect letters
From one particular friend who doesn't write.
If you buy them a drink they will tell you their life history:

'I should have liked to live in a sunny town like this,
Strolling down to the harbour in the early evening,
Looking at the catch. Nothing happens here.
You could forget the ill-luck dogging you.

'I could join the Fancy Rat Society and train
Sweet peas over the trellised porch
Of my little slice of stuccoed terrace. I could
Be in time for the morning service at Tesco's.

'I expect death's like this, letters never arriving
And the last remembered failure at once abandoned
And insistent, like a card on a mantelpiece.
What might it be? You can take your choice.

' "I shook her by the shoulders in a rage of frustration."
"I smiled, and left the room without saying a word."
"I was afraid to touch her, and never explained."
"I touched her once, and that was my greatest mistake." '

You meet them before dinner. You meet them after dinner,
The unbelieved, the uncaressed, the terrified.
Their conversation is perfectly decent but usually
It slows to a halt and they start to stare into space.

You would like it here. Life is quite ordinary
And the self-pity oozes into the glass like bitters.
What's your poison? Do you have a desire to drown?
We're all in the same boat. Join us. Feel free.

And when the bar closes we can say goodbye
And make our way to the terminal where the last
(Or is it the first?) train of the day is clean and waiting
To take us slowly back to where we came from.

But will we ever return? Who needs us now?
It's the town that requires us, though the streets are empty.
It's become a habit and a retreat. Or a form of justice.
Living in a sunny town like this.

Pablo Neruda

Walking Around

It happens that I am tired of being a man.
It happens that I go into the tailor's shops and the movies
all shrivelled up, impenetrable, like a felt swan
navigating on a water of origin and ash.

The smell of barber shops makes me sob out loud.
I want nothing but the repose either of stones or of wool,
I want to see no more establishments, no more gardens,
nor merchandise, nor glasses, nor elevators.

It happens that I am tired of my feet and my nails
and my hair and my shadow.
It happens that I am tired of being a man.

Just the same it would be delicious
to scare a notary with a cut lily
or knock a nun stone dead with one blow of an ear.
It would be beautiful
to go through the streets with a green knife
shouting until I died of cold.

I do not want to go on being a root in the dark,
hesitating, stretched out, shivering with dreams,
downwards, in the wet tripe of the earth,
soaking it up and thinking, eating every day.

I do not want to be the inheritor of so many misfortunes.
I do not want to continue as a root and as a tomb,
as a solitary tunnel, as a cellar full of corpses,
stiff with cold, dying with pain.

For this reason Monday burns like oil
at the sight of me arriving with my jail-face,
and it howls in passing like a wounded wheel,
and its footsteps towards nightfall are filled with hot blood.

HANS MAGNUS ENZENSBERGER   327

And it shoves me along to certain corners, to certain damp houses,
to hospitals where the bones come out of the windows,
to certain cobblers' shops smelling of vinegar,
to streets horrendous as crevices.

There are birds the colour of sulphur, and horrible intestines
hanging from the doors of the houses which I hate,
there are forgotten sets of teeth in a coffee-pot,
there are mirrors
which should have wept with shame and horror,
there are umbrellas all over the place, and poisons, and navels.

I stride along with calm, with eyes, with shoes,
with fury, with forgetfulness,
I pass, I cross offices and stores full of orthopaedic appliances,
and courtyards hung with clothes on wires,
underpants, towels and shirts which weep
slow dirty tears.

Translated from the Spanish by W. S. Merwin.

Hans Magnus Enzensberger

At Thirty-Three

It was all so different from what she'd expected.
Always those rusting Volkswagens.
At one time she'd almost married a baker.
First she read Hesse, then Handke.
Now often she does crosswords in bed.
With her, men take no liberties.
For years she was a Trotskyist, but in her own way.
She's never handled a ration card.
When she thinks of Kampuchea she feels quite sick.
Her last lover, the professor, always wanted her to beat him.
Greenish batik dresses, always too wide for her.
Greenflies on her *Sparmannia*.

Really she wanted to paint, or emigrate.
Her thesis, *Class Struggles in Ulm 1500*
to 1512 and References to them in Folksong:
Grants, beginnings and a suitcase full of notes.
Sometimes her grandmother sends her money.
Tentative dances in her bathroom, little grimaces,
cucumber juice for hours in front of the mirror.
She says, whatever happens I shan't starve.
When she weeps she looks like nineteen.

Translated from the German by
Michael Hamburger.

Weldon Kees

Aspects of Robinson

Robinson at cards at the Algonquin; a thin
Blue light comes down once more outside the blinds.
Gray men in overcoats are ghosts blown past the door.
The taxis streak the avenues with yellow, orange, and red.
This is Grand Central, Mr Robinson.

Robinson on a roof above the Heights; the boats
Mourn like the lost. Water is slate, far down.
Through sounds of ice cubes dropped in glass, an osteopath,
Dressed for the links, describes an old Intourist tour.
– Here's where old Gibbons jumped from, Robinson.

Robinson walking in the Park, admiring the elephant.
Robinson buying the *Tribune*, Robinson buying the *Times*.
Robinson Saying, 'Hello. Yes, this is Robinson. Sunday
At five? I'd love to. Pretty well. And you?'
Robinson alone at Longchamps, staring at the wall.

Robinson afraid, drunk, sobbing Robinson
In bed with a Mrs Morse. Robinson at home;
Decisions: Toynbee or luminol? Where the sun
Shines, Robinson in flowered trunks, eyes toward
The breakers. Where the night ends, Robinson in East Side bars.

Robinson in Glen plaid jacket, Scotch-grain shoes,
Black four-in-hand and oxford button-down,
The jeweled and silent watch that winds itself, the brief-
Case, covert topcoat, clothes for spring, all covering
His sad and usual heart, dry as a winter leaf.

Stevie Smith

Not Waving but Drowning

Nobody heard him, the dead man,
But still he lay moaning:
I was much further out than you thought
And not waving but drowning.

Poor chap, he always loved larking
And now he's dead
It must have been too cold for him his heart gave way,
They said.

Oh, no no no, it was too cold always
(Still the dead one lay moaning)
I was much too far out all my life
And not waving but drowning.

Roy Fuller

Freud's Case Histories

Not the real people in my life
But the Rat Man and Little Hans
And other text book creatures have
Supplied me with romance.

In these the repetitive motives of
The family were convolved,
Though I myself from duty, hate
And affection seem absolved.

From these my forgotten infancy
I saw was not forgotten
But steamed behind the ordered man,
Rich-smelling, live and rotten.

I realised that in his dreams,
His illnesses and love,
The human makes for all below
great symbols from above;

And that the poet, lonely in
A cold society,
Is the true archetype of man,
Loneliest when most free.

To see your father as a horse,
The penis as what devours,
Is art without the stigma of
The artist's ivory towers.

And though the hand that wrote them down,
To understand and heal,
Was not entirely guiltless, these
Strange histories are real.

Yes, real the pince-nez blinkers, real
The rats that gnaw the heart –
Emblems of human longing to
Approximate to art.

the Rat Man: Freud's patient Ernst Lanzer was an obsessive neurotic who could not ward off fantasies of rats gnawing at the bodies of those he loved, in particular his father and a woman friend.
Little Hans: Freud's patient Little Hans (Herbert Graf) had a fear of being bitten by a horse, which Freud believed resulted from suppressed hostility towards his father.

Mark Halliday

Reality USA

I feel I should go to Norfolk Virginia and drink
gin with sailors on leave from the *Alabama*, talking
baseball and Polaris missiles and Steve Martin movies,
another gin with lime juice, then Balto, Balto,
hitch-hike in and out of Baltimore for days
back and forth for days in a row discussing the jobs
of whoever gives me rides, salesmen, shippers,
small-time dispatchers of the much that can be
dispatched. For the ACTUALITY of it!

Books dominate my head. I read in them, I read at them,
I'm well into my thirties. What about real life?
The woman in the light-blue skirt
on the cigarette billboard has such big thighs!
What is it about thighs? Smooth and weighty,
weighty and smooth: you can tell there's really
something *there*. And to think that
the woman must really exist, it's a photo after all
not a painting, she is somewhere in America –
and to think that some guy gets to lie down
on her and her thighs . . . She's a model,
she probably lives in New York, New York baffles me,
I know I could never find her there – but

listen, her sister lives in Baltimore,
hanging out sheets to dry from the balcony
of a light-blue house, lifting her arms –
reality. Along with

her dimly dangerous ex-husband, her speed pills,
his clumsy minor embezzlement of funds from
Pabst Auto Supply, and what else?
The boxing matches he goes to, and the stock-car races
and – maybe I should go to Indianapolis?
But I feel sure I'd be bored in Indianapolis
despite the smoky reality of Indianapolis.
But it's this idea of American experience, how I don't
have it, how I ought to know the way things are really
and not just from Hemingway or Dreiser, John O'Hara or
James T. Farrell
or, say, Raymond Carver or Bruce Springsteen
but directly: first-hand: hands-on learning.
What if I were to take a Greyhound to Memphis,
quit shaving, learn to drink whiskey straight,
lift some weights (maybe I should do the weights before I go)
and get a tattoo on one bicep saying KISS OFF
and meet a guy named Eddie who chain-smokes
and rob a record store with Eddie! Yes,
we smash the glass at 3 a.m. on Davis Avenue in Memphis
and grab 300 albums and 600 compact discs,
pile them into Eddie's red pickup and bingo, we're gone
in five minutes. Next day we paint the pickup yellow
and change the plates, no sweat. Eddie knows,
he knows stuff, he knows how to fence the loot
and he says next we hit a certain TV store,
he slugs my shoulder laughing, I get my piece of cash
but really it's not the cash I care about,
it's the being *involved*.
                              Eddie thinks that's weird,
he says 'You're weird, man'
and starts to act mistrustful so I leave town.
Kansas City here I come.

No, skip Kansas City, I want to save Kansas City.
Just in case.
– In case what? What am I talking about?
How many lives does a person get,
one, right? And me,
                              I love my life with books! –
Of course it's not *just* books, I've got bills
and friends and milkshakes, the supermarket, laundromat
oh shit but still I keep feeling this thing about
reality –

the world is so loaded: a green beer bottle is chucked
half-full from a speeding Ford Mercury and that beer sloshes
exactly like this loaded world – what?
Forget the world, just take America,
sure there's the same hamburgers everywhere
and gasoline fumes but among the fumes and burgers
there's *de*tail, tons of it, you can smell it.
There are variations . . . All the stuff
Whitman claimed he saw, there's the really *seeing* that stuff!
There's –
I don't know – there's a waitress in an Arby's Roast Beef
and her name is either Donna or Nadine,
you buy the Special on the right day and you get
a free Batman 10-ounce glass, she makes a joke about it,
you say 'What time do you get off work' (only this time
it's really happening) and that night Donna
or Nadine does for you what you thought they only did
in fiction . . . That's right. Next morning
her bottom in the light from the window looks so pearly
it's like home, just glad to be home.
It's April, all cool and sunny,
and across the street from Arby's there is
a ten-year-old black boy wearing red hightops
and we talk about the Braves (this is in Georgia, now,
and the asphalt glistens) and the kid says
something beautiful that I'll never forget.
Good. So then, the kid's uncle sells me some cocaine
or teaches me how to aim a pistol

or takes me for a ride in his helicopter –
there must be a few black men who own helicopters?
Up we go roaring over Georgia!
The roofs and poles and roofs,
the components,
the components!
Ohhh . . . Already they've worn me out.

Primo Levi

Memorandum Book

In such a night as this,
Of north wind and rain mixed with snow,
There is someone who drowses in front of a TV,
Someone who resolves to rob a bank.
In such a night as this,
Distant as it takes light to travel in five days,
There is a comet that plummets onto us
From the black womb without height or depth.
The same one Giotto painted,
It will bring neither luck nor disasters,
But ancient ice and a reply, perhaps.
In such a night as this
There is a half-mad old man,
Fine metalworker in his day,
But his day was not our day,
And now he sleeps at Porta Nuova, drinks.
In such a night as this
Someone stretches out next to a woman
And feels he no longer has weight,
His tomorrows no longer have weight.
It's today that counts and not tomorrow,
And the flow of time pauses briefly.
In such a night as this
Witches used to choose hemlock and hellebore
To pick by the light of the moon

And cook in their kitchens.
        In such a night as this
There's a transvestite on Corso Matteotti
Who would give a kidney and a lung
To grow hollow and become a woman.
        In such a night as this
There are seven young men in white lab coats,
Four of them smoking pipes.
They are designing a very long channel
In which to unite a bundle of protons
Almost as swift as light.
If they succeed, the world will blow up.
        In such a night as this,
A poet strains his bow, searching for a word
That can contain the typhoon's force,
The secrets of blood and seed.

                    Translated from the Italian by
                    Ruth Feldman and Brian Swann.

Jenny Joseph

Warning

When I am an old woman I shall wear purple
With a red hat which doesn't go, and doesn't suit me.
And I shall spend my pension on brandy and summer gloves
And satin sandals, and say we've no money for butter.
I shall sit down on the pavement when I'm tired
And gobble up samples in shops and press alarm bells
And run my stick along the public railings
And make up for the sobriety of my youth.
I shall go out in my slippers in the rain
And pick the flowers in other people's gardens
And learn to spit.

You can wear terrible shirts and grow more fat
And eat three pounds of sausages at a go
Or only bread and pickle for a week
And hoard pens and pencils and beermats and things in boxes.

But now we must have clothes that keep us dry
And pay our rent and not swear in the street
And set a good example for the children.
We must have friends to dinner and read the papers.

But maybe I ought to practise a little now?
So people who know me are not too shocked and surprised
When suddenly I am old, and start to wear purple.

P. J. Kavanagh

On the Way to the Depot

It's a pleasant night. So tonight I'll talk on the way
Of the images I seem to think in every day
Five strange years after:
Of how my life appears to me.
I don't speak of it, the thing itself, not that,
But of how I seem to see our lives in the light of it.
It's as though you live in big rooms filled with laughing;
I see little tables, and shining black pianos,
And you very busy. And me outside in the street
(Don't laugh) sweeping it.
The place I suppose is my idea of heaven.
I haven't described it (who could?)
But I've put in some writing desks and black pianos
Because that's, if I'm honest, the best my poor brain can rise to
Without inventing. Spirits, like flames, that meet
Melting into each other – yes, that makes sense to me often
But not (and you know this) every day.
Anyway, here I am
Out on the pavement. And every night

I wheel my day's collection to the depot
Where it's assessed. But
(And here's the odd part)
I don't know who does the assessing
Or what it's best to bring. One just leaves it all there
And goes to bed; every day.
The streets and dreams and faces that I've seen now
Without you. Or with you? . . .
It's late.
Time to turn in my collection.
Heaven knows how I'm doing!
When I sleep
Visit me then, reassure me. Don't share my puzzle.
And let me hear you laugh at my dustman's hat . . .

Roger McGough

Let Me Die a Youngman's Death

Let me die a youngman's death
not a clean and inbetween
the sheets holywater death
not a famous-last-words
peaceful out of breath death

When I'm 73
and in constant good tumour
may I be mown down at dawn
by a bright red sports car
on my way home
from an allnight party

Or when I'm 91
with silver hair
and sitting in a barber's chair
may rival gangsters
with hamfisted tommyguns burst in
and give me a short back and insides

Or when I'm 104
and banned from the Cavern
may my mistress
catching me in bed with her daughter
and fearing for her son
cut me up into little pieces
and throw away every piece but one

Let me die a youngman's death
not a free from sin tiptoe in
candle wax and waning death
not a curtains drawn by angels borne
'what a nice way to go' death

W. H. Auden

Funeral Blues

Stop all the clocks, cut off the telephone,
Prevent the dog from barking with a juicy bone,
Silence the pianos and with muffled drum
Bring out the coffin, let the mourners come.

Let aeroplanes circle moaning overhead
Scribbling on the sky the message He Is Dead,
Put crêpe bows round the white necks of the public doves,
Let the traffic policemen wear black cotton gloves.

He was my North, my South, my East and West,
My working week and my Sunday rest,
My noon, my midnight, my talk, my song;
I thought that love would last for ever: I was wrong.

The stars are not wanted now; put out every one,
Pack up the moon and dismantle the sun,
Pour away the ocean and sweep up the wood;
For nothing now can ever come to any good.

POWERLESS, WITH A GUITAR:
OPPRESSION & EXILE

Despite the increasing freedom and independence of great masses of people during its second half, the twentieth century brought persecution to a gruesome new peak. As early as 1919 Anna Akhmatova was asking 'Why is our century worse than any other?' – perhaps because the growth of populations, communications between them, and modern weaponry have increased the means and opportunity for oppression whilst nothing has been learned to defuse tribal hostilities. On the contrary, one of the century's innovations has been in techniques for whipping up mass hysteria and hatred, as perfected by the Nazis. The consequence of oppression, when it isn't death, is exile, a condition all too widely evident in the century's poetry.

W. H. Auden

The Shield of Achilles

She looked over his shoulder
   For vines and olive trees,
Marble well-governed cities
   And ships upon untamed seas,
But there on the shining metal
   His hands had put instead
An artificial wilderness
   And a sky like lead.

A plain without a feature, bare and brown,
   No blade of grass, no sign of neighborhood,
Nothing to eat and nowhere to sit down,
   Yet, congregated on its blankness, stood
   An unintelligible multitude,
A million eyes, a million boots in line,
Without expression, waiting for a sign.

Out of the air a voice without a face
    Proved by statistics that some cause was just
In tones as dry and level as the place:
    No one was cheered and nothing was discussed;
    Column by column in a cloud of dust
They marched away enduring a belief
Whose logic brought them, somewhere else, to grief.

    She looked over his shoulder
        For ritual pieties,
    White flower-garlanded heifers,
        Libation and sacrifice,
    But there on the shining metal
        Where the altar should have been,
    She saw by his flickering forge-light
        Quite another scene.

Barbed wire enclosed an arbitrary spot
    Where bored officials lounged (one cracked a joke)
And sentries sweated for the day was hot:
    A crowd of ordinary decent folk
    Watched from without and neither moved nor spoke
As three pale figures were led forth and bound
To three posts driven upright in the ground.

The mass and majesty of this world, all
    That carries weight and always weighs the same
Lay in the hands of others; they were small
    And could not hope for help and no help came:
    What their foes liked to do was done, their shame
Was all the worst could wish; they lost their pride
And died as men before their bodies died.

    She looked over his shoulder
        For athletes at their games,
    Men and women in a dance
        Moving their sweet limbs
    Quick, quick, to music,
        But there on the shining shield

His hands had set no dancing-floor
   But a weed-choked field.

A ragged urchin, aimless and alone,
   Loitered about that vacancy; a bird
Flew up to safety from his well-aimed stone:
   That girls are raped, that two boys knife a third,
   Were axioms to him, who'd never heard
Of any world where promises were kept,
Or one could weep because another wept.

   The thin-lipped armorer,
      Hephaestos, hobbled away,
   Thetis of the shining breasts
      Cried out in dismay
   At what the god had wrought
      To please her son, the strong
   Iron-hearted man-slaying Achilles
      Who would not live long.

In the *Iliad*, Book XVIII, Homer describes the making of a new shield for Achilles, the Greeks' greatest warrior, by Hephaestos, god of fire and master-smith. The goddess Thetis was Achilles' mother.

Salvatore Quasimodo

Man of My Time

You are still the one with the stone and the sling,
man of my time. You were there in the cockpit
winged with hatred, dials set for death
– I saw you – in the armoured car, at the gallows,
at the torturer's wheel. I saw it! – it was you,
devoting your exact science to destruction,
without love, without Christ. You kill today
as always, as your fathers killed, as the beasts
that saw you for the first time also killed.

And this blood smells as rank as in the day
one brother said to another brother: 'Let us
go to the fields'. And that cold, stubborn echo
has penetrated now to you, to the bones of your life.
Blot from your memory, O sons, the clouds of blood
that mount and mount from the earth, forget your fathers:
their tombs are sinking into the ashes, the wind
and the dark birds cover over their hearts.

Translated from the Italian by Edwin Morgan.

Edwin Brock

Five Ways to Kill a Man

There are many cumbersome ways to kill a man:
you can make him carry a plank of wood
to the top of a hill and nail him to it. To do this
properly you require a crowd of people
wearing sandals, a cock that crows, a cloak
to dissect, a sponge, some vinegar and one
man to hammer the nails home.

Or you can take a length of steel,
shaped and chased in a traditional way,
and attempt to pierce the metal cage he wears.
But for this you need white horses,
English trees, men with bows and arrows,
at least two flags, a prince and a
castle to hold your banquet in.

Dispensing with nobility, you may, if the wind
allows, blow gas at him. But then you need
a mile of mud sliced through with ditches,
not to mention black boots, bomb craters,
more mud, and a plague of rats, a dozen songs
and some round hats made of steel.

In an age of aeroplanes, you may fly
miles above your victim and dispose of him by
pressing one small switch. All you then
require is an ocean to separate you, two
systems of government, a nation's scientists,
several factories, and a psychopath and
land that no one needs for several years.

These are, as I began, cumbersome ways
to kill a man. Simpler, direct, and much more neat
is to see that he is living somewhere in the middle
of the twentieth century, and leave him there.

Peter Porter

Mort aux Chats

There will be no more cats.
Cats spread infection,
cats pollute the air,
cats consume seven times
their own weight in food a week,
cats were worshipped in
decadent societies (Egypt
and Ancient Rome), the Greeks
had no use for cats. Cats
sit down to pee (our scientists
have proved it). The copulation
of cats is harrowing; they
are unbearably fond of the moon.
Perhaps they are all right in
their own country but their
traditions are alien to ours.
Cats smell, they can't help it,
you notice it going upstairs.
Cats watch too much television,
they can sleep through storms,
they stabbed us in the back

last time. There have never been
any great artists who were cats.
They don't deserve a capital C
except at the beginning of a sentence.
I blame my headache and my
plants dying on to cats.
Our district is full of them,
property values are falling.
When I dream of God I see
a Massacre of Cats. Why
should they insist on their own
language and religion, who
needs to purr to make his point?
Death to all cats! The Rule
of Dogs shall last a thousand years!

Yehuda Amichai

Of Three or Four in a Room

Of three or four in a room
there is always one who stands beside the window.
He must see the evil among thorns
and the fires on the hill.
And how people who went out of their houses whole
are given back in the evening like small change.
Of three or four in a room
there is always one who stands beside the window,
his dark hair above his thoughts.
Behind him, words.
And in front of him, voices wandering without a knapsack,
hearts without provisions, prophecies without water,
large stones that have been returned
and stay sealed, like letters that have no
address and no one to receive them.

Translated from the Hebrew by
Chana Bloch and Stephen Mitchell.

Erica Marx

No Need for Nuremberg

From a man to his torturer

You will never forget the look on my face
    While you live. As you die
You will see the blue stare of one buried eye
    And the spread of my mouth –
No longer a speaking slit in its place
But a buckled distortion, gaping from north to south.

You will never forget: remember the words I can't spill –
    You will never forget
How the need of your joy-sick lips for violet
    Was deprived of its grin
As your whip came down white in its will
To colour a man undyeable for lack of sinew and skin.

You will never forget what has never been said:
    How your torture-bent touch
Found nothing to prey with in a man's crutch –
    How your planetless face
Absorbed jellies of blood that obscured a man's head –
Unknowing of reason and language and meaning and Grace.

You will never forget: my mutilate visage will rear
A living and dying reflection of hell and of fear.
It is you by your act who are murdered in light of good sun:
You are cloven, divided, dispersed – you can never be one.

In 1945–6 Nazi war criminals were prosecuted by a specially convened War Crimes
Tribunal at Nuremberg.

Edwin Muir

From *The Good Town*

Look at it well. This was the good town once,
Known everywhere, with streets of friendly neighbours,
Street friend to street and house to house. In summer
All day the doors stood open; lock and key
Were quaint antiquities fit for museums
With gyves and rusty chains. The ivy grew
From post to post across the prison door.
The yard behind was sweet with grass and flowers,
A place where grave philosophers loved to walk.
Old Time that promises and keeps his promise
Was our sole lord, indulgent and severe,
Who gave and took away with gradual hand
That never hurried, never tarried, still
Adding, subtracting. These our houses had
Long fallen into decay but that we knew
Kindness and courage can repair time's faults,
And serving him breeds patience and courtesy
In us, light sojourners and passing subjects.
There is a virtue in tranquillity
That makes all fitting, childhood and youth and age,
Each in its place.

         Look well. These mounds of rubble,
And shattered piers, half-windows, broken arches
And groping arms were once inwoven in walls
Covered with saints and angels, bore the roof,
Shot up the towering spire. These gaping bridges
Once spanned the quiet river which you see
Beyond that patch of raw and angry earth
Where the new concrete houses sit and stare.
Walk with me by the river. See, the poplars
Still gather quiet gazing on the stream.
The white road winds across the small green hill
And then is lost. These few things still remain.

Some of our houses too, though not what once
Lived there and drew a strength from memory.
Our people have been scattered, or have come
As strangers back to mingle with the strangers
Who occupy our rooms where none can find
The place he knew but settles where he can.
No family now sits at the evening table;
Father and son, mother and child are *out*,
A quaint and obsolete fashion. In our houses
Invaders speak their foreign tongues, informers
Appear and disappear, chance whores, officials
Humble or high, frightened, obsequious,
Sit carefully in corners. My old friends
(Friends ere these great disasters) are dispersed
In parties, armies, camps, conspiracies.
We avoid each other. If you see a man
Who smiles good-day or waves a lordly greeting
Be sure he's a policeman or a spy.
We know them by their free and candid air.

Keki N. Daruwalla

Routine

The putties were left behind by the Raj,
a strip of fire round the legs in June.
Within the burning crash-helmet
the brain is a fire-pulp. The asphalt
gives way beneath our boots and sticks.
The edges of the crowd give way;
a ring of abuse re-forms behind us.
We hardly hear them for we are used to it.
Their gamut ranges from 'mother-' to 'sister-seducer'.
Karam Singh marching in the same rank as I
curses under his breath,
'I have children older than them,
these kids whose pubes have hardly sprouted!'

We march to the street-crossing where young blood
fulfils itself by burning tramcars.
Beneath our khaki we are a roasted brown
but unconvinced, they wish to burn our khaki skins.
We are a platoon against a thousand.
It's all well rehearsed; a few words of warning –
a chill formality lost in fiery slogans!
'Load!' I put a piece of death up the spout.
It is well rehearsed: I alone point
my barrel into them as I squeeze the trigger.
The rest aim into the sun!

They have gone. The Salvage Squad comes
and takes the body to the autopsy room
and tows the tramcar away.
Tension oozes out as armpits run with sweat.
Depressed and weary we march back to the Lines.
A leader says over the evening wireless,
'We are marching forward.'

Pablo Neruda

The United Fruit Co.

When the trumpet sounded, it was
all prepared on the earth,
the Jehovah parcelled out the earth
to Coca Cola, Inc., Anaconda,
Ford Motors, and other entities:
The Fruit Company, Inc.
reserved for itself the most succulent,
the central coast of my own land,
the delicate waist of America.
It rechristened its territories
as the 'Banana Republics'
and over the sleeping dead,
over the restless heroes

who brought about the greatness,
the liberty and the flags,
it established the comic opera:
abolished the independencies,
presented crowns of Caesar,
unsheathed envy, attracted
the dictatorship of the flies,
Trujillo flies, Tacho flies,
Carias flies, Martines flies,
Ubico flies, damp flies
of modest blood and marmalade,
drunken flies who zoom
over the ordinary graves,
circus flies, wise flies
well trained in tyranny.

Among the blood-thirsty flies
the Fruit Company lands its ships,
taking off the coffee and the fruit;
the treasure of our submerged
territories flow as though
on plates into the ships.

Meanwhile Indians are falling
into the sugared chasms
of the harbours, wrapped
for burial in the mist of the dawn:
a body rolls, a thing
that has no name, a fallen cipher,
a cluster of dead fruit
thrown down on the dump.

Translated from the Spanish by
James Wright and Robert Bly.

Trujillo, Tacho, Carias, Martines and *Ubico*: South American dictators.

Rita Dove

Parsley

I   The Cane Fields

There is a parrot imitating spring
in the palace, its feathers parsley green.
Out of the swamp the cane appears

to haunt us, and we cut it down. El General
searches for a word; he is all the world
there is. Like a parrot imitating spring,

we lie down screaming as rain punches through
and we come up green. We cannot speak an R –
out of the swamp, the cane appears

and then the mountain we call in whispers *Katalina*.
The children gnaw their teeth to arrowheads.
There is a parrot imitating spring.

El General has found his word: *perejil*.
Who says it, lives. He laughs, teeth shining
out of the swamp. The cane appears

in our dreams, lashed by wind and streaming.
And we lie down. For every drop of blood
there is a parrot imitating spring.
Out of the swamp the cane appears.

II   The Palace

The word the general's chosen is parsley.
It is fall, when thoughts turn
to love and death; the general thinks
of his mother, how she died in the fall
and he planted her walking cane at the grave
and it flowered, each spring stolidly forming
four-star blossoms. The general

pulls on his boots, he stomps to
her room in the palace, the one without
curtains, the one with a parrot
in a brass ring. As he paces he wonders
Who can I kill today. And for a moment
the little knot of screams
is still. The parrot, who has traveled

all the way from Australia in an ivory
cage, is, coy as a widow, practising
spring. Ever since the morning
his mother collapsed in the kitchen
while baking skull-shaped candies
for the Day of the Dead, the general
has hated sweets. He orders pastries
brought up for the bird; they arrive

dusted with sugar on a bed of lace.
The knot in his throat starts to twitch;
he sees his boots the first day in battle
splashed with mud and urine
as a soldier falls at his feet amazed –
how stupid he looked! – at the sound
of artillery. *I never thought it would sing*
the soldier said, and died. Now

the general sees the fields of sugar
cane, lashed by rain and streaming.
He sees his mother's smile, the teeth
gnawed to arrowheads. He hears
the Haitians sing without R's
as they swing the great machetes:
Katalina, they sing, *Katalina*,

mi madle, mi amol en muelte. God knows
his mother was no stupid woman; she
could roll an R like a queen. Even
a parrot can roll an R! In the bare room

the bright feathers arch in a parody
of greenery, as the last pale crumbs
disappear under the blackened tongue. Someone

calls out his name in a voice
so like his mother's, a startled tear
splashes the tip of his right boot.
My mother, my love in death.
The general remembers the tiny green sprigs
men of his village wore in their capes
to honor the birth of a son. He will
order many, this time, to be killed

for a single, beautiful word.

On 2 October 1937, Rafael Trujillo (1891–1961), dictator of the Dominican Republic, ordered 20,000 blacks killed because they could not pronounce the letter 'r' in *perejil*, the Spanish word for parsley. – Author's note.

Rafael Alberti

Millares, 1965

In Rome or in Paris,
New York, Buenos Aires, Madrid, Calcutta, Cairo . . .
in so many places right now there are
gunny sacks in shreds,
pieces of shoe stuck to the bone,
amputated stumps, stiff human leftovers,
trash reduced to ashes,
yawning holes, dried up
worlds of rusty things that have been overlooked,
of coagulated blood,
human skin gnawed through like dead lava,
tragic shriveled skin, signs that accuse, cry out
even when they have no mouth,

choked back howls that are just as painful
as the silence.
Where did all this start, these wrecks,
these maimed human ruins,
these holes that are being ripped even wider,
slow rags of twisted silk with slashed threads,
caked lumps of something like dough, flying clouds of chalky clay,
sealing-wax reds, where?
What will come flying out of all this, what will happen,
what will break loose from these desperate scarecrows,
what will pull down this blind, seedy bundle of pelts
when it bursts its fibers, when it makes its open seams
suddenly start biting, when it lets the light in on its black colors,
its iron ochers, its stark whites with their sweeping glare
that can breathe life into a new kind of loveliness?
But, ah, in the meantime
a HANDS OFF. DANGER OF DEATH is lying unseen
under all this patched-up reality with its frayed strings.
Keep, keep your hands off,
don't even stick out one finger, you with your polished nails.
Rats, don't try to come into these sewers.
Back, back! You are sallow-faced from usury,
white-faced with emptiness, don't come a step closer,
don't even risk a footprint or a signal with your eye.
An electric charge runs through here that can blast you to kingdom
       come,
and a light also, a light, a hidden light
kneading the faces of these sad human ruins.

Translated from the Spanish by Hardie St Martin.

Kit Wright

I Found South African Breweries Most Hospitable

Meat smell of blood in locked rooms I cannot smell it,
Screams of the brave in torture loges I never heard nor heard of
Apartheid I wouldn't know how to spell it,
None of these things am I paid to believe a word of
For I am a stranger to cant and contumely.
I am a professional cricketer.
My only consideration is my family.

I get my head down nothing to me or mine
Blood is geysering now from ear, from mouth, from eye,
How they take a fresh guard after breaking the spine,
I must play wherever I like or die
So spare me your news your views spare me your homily.
I am a professional cricketer.
My only consideration is my family.

Electrodes wired to their brains they should have had helmets,
Balls wired up they should have been wearing a box,
The danger was the game would turn into a stalemate,
Skin of their feet burnt off I like thick woollen socks
With buckskin boots that accommodate them roomily
For I am a professional cricketer.
My only consideration is my family.

They keep falling out of the window they must be clumsy
And unprofessional not that anyone told me,
Spare me your wittering spare me your whimsy,
Sixty thousand pounds is what they sold me
And I have no brain. I am an anomaly.
I am a professional cricketer.
My only consideration is my family.

In March 1982 a rebel English cricket team, sponsored by South African Breweries,
toured South Africa, which was barred from international sport at the time.

Wole Soyinka

Your Logic Frightens Me, Mandela

Your logic frightens me, Mandela
Your logic frightens me. Those years
Of dreams, of time accelerated in
Visionary hopes, of savoring the task anew,
The call, the tempo primed
To burst in supernovae round a 'brave new world'!
Then stillness. Silence. The world closes round
Your sole reality; the rest is . . . dreams?

Your logic frightens me.
How coldly you disdain legerdemains!
'Open Sesame' and – two decades' rust on hinges
Peels at the touch of a conjurer's wand?
White magic, ivory-topped black magic wand,
One moment wand, one moment riot club
Electric cattle prod and whip or *sjambok*
Tearing flesh and spilling blood and brain?

This bag of tricks, whose silk streamers
Turn knotted cords to crush dark temples?
A rabbit punch sneaked beneath the rabbit?
Doves metamorphosed in milk-white talons?
Not for you the olive branch that sprouts
Gun muzzles, barbed-wire garlands, tangled thorns
To wreathe the brows of black, unwilling Christs.

Your patience grows inhuman, Mandela.
Do you grow food? Do you make friends
Of mice and lizards? Measure the growth of grass
For time's unhurried pace?
Are you now the crossword puzzle expert?
Chess? Ah, no! Subversion lurks among
Chess pieces. Structured clash of black and white,
Equal ranged and paced? An equal board? No!
Not on Robben Island. Checkers? Bad to worse.

That game has no respect for class or king-serf
Ordered universe. So, scrabble?

Monopoly? Now, that . . . ! You know
The game's modalities, so do they.
Come collection time, the cards read 'White Only'
In the Community Chest. Like a gambler's coin
Both sides heads or tails, the 'Chance' cards read:
Go to jail. Go straight to jail. Do not pass 'GO'.
Do not collect a hundredth rand. Fishes feast,
I think, on those who sought to by-pass 'GO'
On Robben Island.

Your logic frightens me, Mandela, your logic
Humbles me. Do you tame geckos?
Do grasshoppers break your silences?
Bats' radar pips pinpoint your statuesque
Gaze transcending distances at will?
Do moths break wing
Against a light bulb's fitful glow
That brings no searing illumination?
Your sight shifts from moth to bulb,
Rests on its pulse-glow fluctuations –
Are kin feelings roused by a broken arc
Of tungsten trapped in vacuum?

Your pulse, I know, has slowed with earth's
Phlegmatic turns. I know your blood
Sagely warms and cools with seasons,
Responds to the lightest breeze
Yet scorns to race with winds (or hurricanes)
That threaten change on tortoise pads.

Is our world light-years away, Mandela?
Lost in visions of that dare supreme
Against a dire supremacy of race,
What brings you back to earth? The night guard's
Inhuman tramp? A sodden eye transgressing through
The Judas hole? Tell me Mandela,
That guard, is he *your* prisoner?

Your bounty threatens me, Mandela, that taut
Drumskin of your heart on which our millions
Dance. I fear we latch, fat leeches
On your veins. Our daily imprecisions
Dull keen edges of your will.
Compromises deplete your act's repletion –
Feeding will-voided stomachs of a continent,
What will be left of you, Mandela?

Nelson Mandela was released on 11 February 1990 after 28 years in prison.

James Fenton

Tiananmen

Tiananmen
Is broad and clean
And you can't tell
Where the dead have been
And you can't tell
What happened then
And you can't speak
Of Tiananmen.

You must not speak.
You must not think.
You must not dip
Your brush in ink.
You must not say
What happened then,
What happened there
In Tiananmen.

The cruel men
Are old and deaf
Ready to kill
But short of breath

And they will die
Like other men
And they'll lie in state
In Tiananmen.

They lie in state.
They lie in style.
Another lie's
Thrown on the pile,
Thrown on the pile
By the cruel men
To cleanse the blood
From Tiananmen.

Truth is a secret.
Keep it dark.
Keep it dark
In your heart of hearts.
Keep it dark
Till you know when
Truth may return
To Tiananmen.

Tiananmen
Is broad and clean
And you can't tell
Where the dead have been
And you can't tell
When they'll come again.
They'll come again
To Tiananmen.

Hong Kong,
15 June 1989

In June 1989 huge pro-democracy demonstrations in Beijing's Tiananmen Square were brutally suppressed, putting an end to hopes that China would move towards democracy in a similar manner to that of the East European countries.

Mahmoud Darwish

We Travel Like Other People

We travel like other people, but we return to nowhere. As if
    travelling
Is the way of the clouds. We have buried our loved ones in the
    darkness of the clouds, between the roots of the trees.
And we said to our wives: go on giving birth to people like us for
    hundreds of years so we can complete this journey
To the hour of a country, to a metre of the impossible.
We travel in the carriages of the psalms, sleep in the tent of the
    prophets and come out of the speech of the gypsies.
We measure space with a hoopoe's beak or sing to while away the
    distance and cleanse the light of the moon.
Your path is long so dream of seven women to bear this long path
On your shoulders. Shake for them palm trees so as to know their
    names and who'll be the mother of the boy of Galilee.
We have a country of words. Speak speak so I can put my road on
    the stone of a stone.
We have a country of words. Speak Speak so we may know the end
    of this travel.

Translated from the Arabic by Abdulah al-Udhari.

Nazim Hikmet

Prague Dawn

In Prague it's growing light
and snowing –
            sleety,
                leaden.
In Prague the baroque slowly lights up:
                        uneasy, distant,
            its gilt grief-blackened.

The statues on Charles Bridge
    look like birds descended from a dead star.

In Prague the first trolley has left the garage,
its windows glow yellow and warm.
But I know
        it's ice-cold inside:
no passenger's breath has warmed it.
In Prague Pepik drinks his coffee and milk,
the wood table spotless in the white kitchen.
In Prague it's growing light
and snowing –
        sleety,
           leaden.

In Prague a cart –
      a one-horse wagon –
passes the Old Jewish Cemetery.
The cart is full of longing for another city,
             I am the driver.
In Prague the baroque slowly lights up:
          uneasy, distant,
      its gilt grief blackened.
In Prague's Jewish Cemetery, death is breathless, stone-still.

Ah my rose, ah my rose,
exile is worse than death.

20 December 1956

Translated from the Turkish by
Randy Blasing and Mutlu Konuk.

Dan Pagis

The Souvenir

The town where I was born, Radautz, in the county of Bukovina, threw me out when I was ten. On that day she forgot me, as if I had died, and I forgot her too. We were both satisfied with that.

Forty years later, all at once, she sent me a souvenir. Like an unpleasant aunt whom you're supposed to love just because she is a blood relative. It was a new photograph, her latest winter portrait. A canopied wagon is waiting in the courtyard. The horse, turning its head, gazes affectionately at an elderly man who is busy closing some kind of gate. Ah, it's a funeral. There are just two members left in the Burial Society: the gravedigger and the horse.

But it's a splendid funeral; all around, in the strong wind, thousands of snowflakes are crowding, each one a crystal star with its own particular design. So there is still the same impulse to be special, still the same illusions. Since all snow-stars have just one pattern: six points, a Star of David in fact. In a minute they will all start melting and turn into a mass of plain snow. In their midst my elderly town has prepared a grave for me too.

Translated from the Hebrew by Stephen Mitchell.

Radautz: a town in the Bukovina, a region of northern Romania which had a large German-speaking Jewish population before the war. Paul Celan also came from the area.

THE DARK SIDE:
CRIME, VICE & LOW LIFE

Crime is officially regarded as an aberration whose decline is both earnestly desired and probably imminent. But crime is institutionalized: it is part of the human condition. Poets rarely write about terrible crimes (Blake Morrison's 'Ballad of the Yorkshire Ripper' is an exception), but the more picaresque aspects have a perennial appeal. And vices. The century has seen a gradual tightening up of official attitudes to drink and drugs whilst at the same time indulgence has increased. Wherever consumerism has flourished, puritanism has been in retreat. Amongst other things, poetry itself is a minor vice: there are always more important things to do than to write a poem. But what the hell.

Artyemy Mikhailov

Song about Crooks

Hey, look!
How great to be a crook.
They are always so smartly clad,
and just think of the girls they have had.
And in addition, and this is really a smash,
they've also got the cash.
Just in case you never happened to sup with them,
let me tell you that things are changing so fast
　　　nowadays that only a crook can keep up with them;
one day we are praising corn on the cob, and the next
　　　it's apt to be squash;
therefore, neither can be had in the market unless
　　　you just happen to be flush.
Indeed, whether you do or don't go by the book,
it's so great to be a crook.

You talk about counterfeiters? They're so innocent
        it isn't even funny;
they forge only money.
But what about those others who forge our highest ideals,
as though patriotism and humanism and truth and
        democracy and poetry and history and even bread
        and love were merely idle panaceas!
Oh, a crook is an easygoing fellow;
some of them are downright mellow.
Like dandelions obeying the prevailing wind,
they go where it goes and, therefore, have never even sinned.
And should that wind suddenly blow from the opposite direction
they are the first to change, since this is their only intention.
Even among tailcoats and silk,
they skim the cream off milk.
And since they have nothing to overestimate
they are successful and gay.
Indeed, wherever you look,
they are loved by hook and by crook.

> *Translated from the Russian by*
> *Joseph Langland, Tomas Axzel and Laszlo Tikos.*

Robert Greacen

Captain Fox on J. Edgar Hoover

G-Man extraordinary, super-cop, crime-buster
With the pug face and four bullet-proof Cadillacs;
Snooper on public figures in private suites,
Flailer of deviates, sacker of G-Men
Who failed to observe the regulation haircut,
He never married but lived with Mom
Till she died when he was in his forties.
England should remember how he loved dogs.
Top Good Guy who licked the Baddies,
He was society's spiked fist.

Let's call his register of enemies:
George 'Machine Gun' Kelly, Ma and Pa Barker,
'Baby Face' Nelson, Alvin Karpis,
Frederick Duquesne, Julius and Ethel Rosenberg,
Harry Gold, Colonel Abel, the Brinks gang,
Hauptmann and Joe Valachi,
Dillinger and 'Pretty Boy' Floyd.

His life was lived for Bad Guys:
Kidnappers, robbers, extortionists, traitors,
Jostling for their name in history
Like any President or poet or Attorney General.
The spur's a footnote in some mammoth book,
Nothing so vulgar as a hundred grand.

Said Lyndon Baines Johnson:
'I'd rather have him inside the tent peeing out
Than outside peeing in.'

Said Richard Nixon to the ageing G-Man:
'I want to discuss retirement.'
And Mr America replied:
'Ridiculous. You're still a young man.'

This is the picture then, within whose frame
You see the Good Guys and the Bad.

The trick is knowing which is which.

Hoover: J. Edgar Hoover was Director of the Federal Bureau of Investigation from 1924 to 1972.
G-Man: FBI detectives were known as G-Men.

Blake Morrison

From *The Ballad of the Yorkshire Ripper*

Everyweer in Yorkshire
were a creepin fear an thrill.
At Elland Road fans chanted
'Ripper 12 Police Nil.'

Lasses took up karate,
judo an self-defence,
an jeered at lads in porn shops,
an scrawled stuff in pub Gents,

like: 'Ripper's not a psychopath
but every man in pants.
All you blokes would kill like him
given half a chance.

'Listen to your beer-talk –
"hammer", "poke" and "screw",
"bang" and "score" and "lay" us:
That's what the Ripper does too.'

Aye, e did it again one last time,
to a student, Jacqueline Hill,
in a busy road, wi streetlights,
in a way more twisted still,

blammin er wi is Phillips –
but rest o that ah'll leave,
out o respect to t'family
an cos it meks me eave.

Now cops stepped up on pressure.
George, e got is cards.
Files were took from is ands
an put in Scotland Yard's.

They talked to blokes on lorries
an called at Pete's ouse twice,
but Sonia allus elped im out
wi rock-ard alibis.

It were fluke what finally nabbed im.
E'd parked is car in t'gates
of a private drive in Sheffield
wi ripped off numberplates.

Lass oo e'd got wi im
were known to work this patch.
Cops took em both to t'station
but adn't twigged yet, natch.

Ad e meant to kill er?
E'd brought an ammer an knife
but maundered on alf evenin
ow e cunt stand sight o t'wife.

Then lass passed im a rubber
an come on all coquettish.
But still e didn't touch er.
It were like a sort o death-wish.

E managed to ide is tackle
sayin e wanted a pee.
But later on is ammer
were found by a young PC.

So cops they lobbed im questions
through breakfast, dinner, tea,
till e said: 'All right, you've cracked it.
Ripper, aye, it's me.

'Ah did them thirteen killins.
Them girls live in mi brain,
mindin me o mi evil.
But ah'd do it all again.

'Streets are runnin sewers.
Streets are open sores.
Ah went there wi mi armoury
to wipe away all t'oors.

'Ah were carryin out God's mission.
Ah were followin is commands.
E pumped me like a primus.
Ah were putty in is ands.'

Peter Sutcliffe, the Yorkshire Ripper, was convicted in May 1981 on thirteen charges
of murder. He claimed to have had a divine mission to eliminate prostitutes.

Elizabeth Bartlett

Deviant

I know you. I saw you once following me
along the tow path by the canal. A bicycle
reared rusty handle-bars from the grey water,
and your grubby mac flapped round your knees.
I only waited for the first button to be undone,
and ran instinctively, scraping my knuckles
on walls and wire, back to the milling people
and the fancy hat shops and the staring windows
of arcades which sold no such clothes as the ones
you wore.

I know you. I saw you again at the back
of the bandstand where the paint had hardly dried
from the summer season, creeping past the piles
of municipal deck chairs, stencilled on the backs,
brown canvas piles, folded and unfolded each day,
a screen for your ambush; a knot of string
round your old army coat this time and a hat

from nowhere, palpable and shapeless, mildewed
with age and rain. I went round to the front,
seeing your strange gaze.

I know you, because I was your victim, going
for solitary walks at odd times of the day,
carrying my books and my brown bag of scraps
for stray cats, avoiding the holiday crowds.
You are a victim also, in your own curious way,
loitering in lonely places, patiently waiting
like a bird-man in a shuffling shabby hide,
with your sudden quick and sad revelation
of unattainable memory, picking your girls
with a practised eye.

Padraig Rooney

Pool

*'There's always a pool parlor wherever one goes (think I'll use this
line in a poem) if one gets bored.'*   – Elizabeth Bishop, *Letters*

There's always a pool parlour wherever one goes.
I travel light, with a two-bit screw-together cue
in this customised case, my monogram worked
into the Italian leather. I looked like a hit-man,
or -woman, in the old days, stepping off the trains
into a scuzzy underworld where I'd play pool,

professionally, for money – in those station pool
parlours cum barbershops where the Mafia goes.
I'd chat up hoods in the smokers of the trains –
faggot amateur, they'd think, fingering my screwy cue,
but time and again they fell for it to a man.
My smooth-faced con trick always worked.

In these Med towns the men are over-worked
or on the dole. Either way they're game for pool.
I loved the crack of the break, the man-to-man
lickety-split of the shoeshine boy as he goes
about his blowjob in the john, the tick of the cue
in smoke-blue parlours underneath the trains.

Ah, those runaway cross-dressers riding the trains
with stiletto hearts and false eyelashes. They'd worked
nights since they were boys and could come right on cue!
On bank holiday weekends we'd celebrate and pool
our stakes, live it up in Naples or in Rome. Money goes
quickly with low-life Romeos. I took it like a woman,

but where it mattered I potted them like a man,
one by one under the arriving and departing trains,
the reds, the yellows, the blues. Luck comes and goes
but with me it's skill in adversity that's always worked,
the hormone rush that comes with beating men at pool
I've had since I was twelve, and chalked my first cue.

My Scrabble dictionary says it's a variation of *queue*.
You wouldn't care to play to pass the time, young man?
I'm a dab hand at Scrabble, but nothing like I am at pool,
and we've hours to kill before we board our trains.
Truth is, my con-man tricks haven't really worked
in these *termini* for years. Youth too comes and goes,

like a cue-ball potting back and forth in sixteen goes.
I'm worked to death these days picking up a man,
and a spot of pool might do the trick until our trains.

Elton Glaser

Smoking

I like the cool and heft of it, dull metal on the palm,
And the click, the hiss, the spark fuming into flame,
Boldface of fire, the rage and sway of it, raw blue at the base
And a slope of gold, a touch to the packed tobacco, the tip
Turned red as a warning light, blown brighter by the breath,
The pull and the pump of it, and the paper's white
Smoothed now to ash as the smoke draws back, drawn down
To the black crust of lungs, tar and poisons in the pink,
And the blood sorting it out, veins tight and the heart slow,
The push and wheeze of it, a sweep of plumes in the air
Like a shako of horses dragging a hearse through the late
    centennium,
London, at the end of December, in the dark and fog.

Louis MacNeice

Alcohol

On golden seas of drink, so the Greek poet said,
Rich and poor are alike. Looking around in war
We watch the many who have returned to the dead
Ordering time-and-again the same-as-before:

Those Haves who cannot bear making a choice,
Those Have-nots who are bored with having nothing to choose,
Call for their drinks in the same tone of voice,
Find a factitious popular front in booze.

Another drink: Bacchylides was right
And self-deception golden – Serve him quick,
The siphon stutters in the archaic night,
The flesh is willing and the soul is sick.

Another drink: Adam is back in the Garden.
Another drink: the snake is back on the tree.
Let your brain go soft, your arteries will harden;
If God's a peeping tom he'll see what he shall see.

Another drink: Cain has slain his brother.
Another drink: Cain, they say, is cursed.
Another and another and another –
The beautiful ideologies have burst.

A bottle swings on a string. The matt-grey iron ship,
Which ought to have been the Future, sidles by
And with due auspices descends the slip
Into an ocean where no auspices apply.

Take away your slogans; give us something to swallow,
Give us beer or brandy or schnapps or gin;
This is the only road for the self-betrayed to follow –
The last way out that leads not out but in.

Bacchylides: classical Greek lyric poet who wrote between 452 and 485 BC.

Simon Armitage

The Stuff

We'd heard all the warnings; knew its nicknames.
It arrived in our town by word of mouth
and crackled like wildfire through the grapevine
of gab and gossip. It came from the south

        so we shunned it, naturally;
        sent it to Coventry

and wouldn't have touched it with a barge pole
if it hadn't been at the club one night.

Well, peer group pressure and all that twaddle
so we fussed around it like flies round shite

    and watched,
    and waited

till one kid risked it, stepped up and licked it
and came from every pore in his body.
That clinched it. It snowballed; whirlpooled. Listen,
no one was more surprised than me to be

    cutting it, mixing it,
    snorting and sniffing it

or bulking it up with scouring powder
or chalk, or snuff, or sodium chloride
and selling it under the flyover.
At first we were laughing. It was all right

    to be drinking it, eating it,
    living and breathing it

but things got seedy; people went missing.
One punter surfaced in the ship-canal
having shed a pair of concrete slippers.
Others were bundled in the back of vans

    and were quizzed, thumped,
    finished off and dumped

or vanished completely like Weldon Kees:
their cars left idle under the rail bridge
with its cryptic hoarding which stumped the police:
'Oldham – Home of the tubular bandage.'

    Others were strangled.
    Not that it stopped us.

Someone bubbled us. CID sussed us
and found some on us. It was cut and dried.
They dusted, booked us, cuffed us and pushed us
down to the station and read us our rights.

Possession and supplying:
we had it, we'd had it.

In Court I ambled up and took the oath
and spoke the addict's side of the story.
I said grapevine, barge pole, whirlpool, chloride,
concrete, bandage, station, story. Honest.

Zsuzsa Rakovszky

Pornographic Magazine

They're all of them so lean and pink
these men and women, and which
face sits on whose/what kind of neck
doesn't matter much;

their bodies in every possible pose –
hygienic, cheerful – connect:
as if on the beach or at keep-fit class,
the flesh is almost abstract.

Indeed it *is* so, for, if the know-how
possessed were put in use,
a momentary epileptic fit
might be induced . . .

But if so, why, to what end does anyone
take as their sole good
just one, the only one, the unique
sweet body, the soul's food,

that body, that face which leads you to
    the deep no mortal visits –
obsession, torment, bondage, fever,
    the erotic-as-metaphysics,

a detour which leads you to the world
    by leading from it . . .
and if part of the other, just a tiny part,
    were different, you wouldn't want it?

The replaceable is meek and mild,
    it is all in the same class.
But whatever occurs no more than once,
    that, demons possess.

Translated from the Hungarian by
Clive Wilmer and George Gömöri.

WORKOUT IN REALITY GYM:
THE EIGHTIES & NINETIES

The decade when the gap between rich and poor widened also showed a convergence of behaviour between the extremes. The lager louts in Eleanor Brown's poem 'The Lads' might be City dealers on £100K bonuses or unemployed skinheads. In Britain in the 1980s a mood of brash triumphalism came in with the Falklands War and sleaze seemed to infect high and low life equally, a mood brilliantly caught by Carol Ann Duffy's tout in 'Translating the English, 1989'. The emblematic activity of the period seems to be the workout – a physical regime for lives no longer compelled to be physical, symptom of a late stage of capitalism in which artificiality has overtaken necessity. The sections which follow elaborate on aspects of this new reality.

Tony Harrison

From *v*.

Jobless though they are how can these kids,
even though their team's lost one more game,
believe that the 'Pakis', 'Niggers', even 'Yids'
sprayed on the tombstones here should bear the blame?

What is it that these crude words are revealing?
What is it that this aggro act implies?
Giving the dead their xenophobic feeling
or just a *cri-de-coeur* because man dies?

So what's a cri-de-coeur, *cunt? Can't you speak*
the language that yer mam spoke. Think of 'er!
Can yer only get yer tongue round fucking Greek?
Go and fuck yerself with cri-de-coeur!

'She didn't talk like you do for a start!'
I shouted, turning where I thought the voice had been.
She didn't understand yer fucking 'art'!
She thought yer fucking poetry obscene!

I wish on this skin's word deep aspirations,
first the prayer for my parents I can't make
then a call to Britain and to all the nations
made in the name of love for peace's sake.

Aspirations, cunt! Folk on t'fucking dole
'ave got about as much scope to aspire
above the shit they're dumped in, cunt, as coal
aspires to be chucked on t'fucking fire.

OK, forget the aspirations. Look, I know
United's losing gets you fans incensed
and how far the HARP inside you makes you go
but *all* these Vs: against! against! against!

Ah'll tell yer then what really riles a bloke.
It's reading on their graves the jobs they did —
butcher, publican and baker. Me, I'll croak
doing t'same nowt ah do now as a kid.

'ard birth ah wor, mi mam says, almost killed 'er.
Death after life on t'dole won't seem as 'ard!
Look at this cunt, Wordsworth, organ builder,
this fucking 'aberdasher Appleyard!

If mi mam's up there, don't want to meet 'er
listening to me list mi dirty deeds,
and 'ave to pipe up to St fucking Peter
ah've been on t'dole all mi life in fucking Leeds!

Then t' Alleluias stick in t' angels' gobs.
When dole-wallahs fuck off to the void
what'll t'mason carve up for their jobs?
The cunts who lieth 'ere wor unemployed?

This lot worked at one job all life through.
Byron, 'Tanner', 'Lieth 'ere interred'.
They'll chisel fucking poet when they do you
and that, yer cunt, 's a crude four-letter word.

'Listen, cunt!' *I* said, 'before you start your jeering
the reason why I want this in a book
's to give ungrateful cunts like you a hearing!'
A book, yer stupid cunt, 's not worth a fuck!

'The only reason why I write this poem at all
on yobs like you who do the dirt on death
's to give some higher meaning to your scrawl.'
Don't fucking bother, cunt! Don't waste your breath!

'You piss-artist skinhead cunt, you wouldn't know
and it doesn't fucking matter if you do,
the skin and poet united fucking Rimbaud
but the *autre* that *je est* is fucking you.'

Ah've told yer, no more Greek . . . That's yer last warning!
Ah'll boot yer fucking balls to Kingdom Come.
They'll find yer cold on t'grave tomorrer morning.
So don't speak Greek. Don't treat me like I'm dumb.

'I've done my bits of mindless aggro too
not half a mile from where we're standing now.'
Yeah, ah bet yer wrote a poem, yer wanker you!
'No, shut yer gob a while. Ah'll tell yer 'ow . . .

'Herman Darewski's band played operetta
with a wobbly soprano warbling. Just why
I made my mind up that I'd got to get her
with the fire hose I can't say, but I'll try.

It wasn't just the singing angered me.
At the same time half a crowd was jeering
as the smooth Hugh Gaitskell, our MP,
made promises the other half were cheering.

What I hated in those high soprano ranges
was uplift beyond all reason and control
and in a world where you say nothing changes
it seemed a sort of prick-tease of the soul.

I tell you when I heard high notes that rose
above Hugh Gaitskell's cool electioneering
straight from the warbling throat right up my nose
I had all your aggro in *my* jeering.

And I hit the fire extinguisher ON knob
and covered orchestra and audience with spray.
I could run as fast as you then. A good job!
They yelled "damned vandal" after me that day . . .'

And then yer saw the light and gave up 'eavy!
And knew a man's not how much he can sup . . .
Yer reward for growing up's this super-bevvy,
a meths and champagne punch in t' FA Cup.

Ah've 'eard all that from old farts past their prime,
'ow now yer live wi' all yer once detested . . .
Old farts with not much left 'll give me time.
Fuckers like that get folks like me arrested.

Covet not thy neighbour's wife, thy neighbour's riches.
Vicar and cop who say, to save our souls,
Get thee behind me, Satan, drop their breeches
and get the Devil's dick right up their 'oles!

It was more a working marriage that I'd meant,
a blend of masculine and feminine.
Ignoring me, he started looking, bent
on some more aerosolling, for his tin.

'It was more a working marriage that I mean!'
Fuck, and save mi soul, eh? That suits me.
Then as if I'd egged him on to be obscene
he added a middle slit to one daubed V.

Don't talk to me of fucking representing
the class yer were born into any more.
Yer going to get 'urt and start resenting
it's not poetry we need in this class war.

Yer've given yerself toffee, cunt. Who needs
yer fucking poufy words. Ah write mi own.
Ah've got mi work on show all over Leeds
like this UNITED 'ere on some sod's stone.

'OK!' (thinking I had him trapped) 'OK!'
'If you're so proud of it then sign your name
when next you're full of HARP and armed with spray,
next time you take this short cut from the game.'

He took the can, contemptuous, unhurried
and cleared the nozzle and prepared to sign
the UNITED sprayed where mam and dad were buried.
He aerosolled his name. And it was mine.

Michael Hofmann

Albion Market

Warm air and no sun – the sky was like cardboard,
the same depthless no-colour as the pavements and buildings.
It was May, and pink cherry blossoms lay and shoaled
in the gutter, bleeding as after some wedding . . .

Broken glass, corrugated tin and spraygunned plywood saying
Arsenal rules the world. Twenty floors up Chantry Point,
the grey diamond panels over two arsoned windows
were scorched like a couple of raised eyebrows.

Tireless and sick, women hunted for bargains.
Gold and silver were half-price. Clothes shops
started up, enjoyed a certain vogue, then
went into a tailspin of permanent sales,

cutting their throats. A window waved *Goodbye, Kilburn,*
and *Everything Must Go.* The *Last Day* was weeks ago –
it didn't. The tailor's became *Rock Bottom.*
On the pavement, men were selling shoelaces.

A few streets away, in the renovated precinct,
girls' names and numbers stood on every lamp-post,
phone-booth, parking meter and tree. Felt tip on sticky labels,
'rubber', and 'correction' for the incorrigible.

At night, the taxis crawled through Bayswater,
where women dangled their 'most things considered' from the kerb.
A man came down the street with the meth-pink eyes
of a white rat, his gait a mortal shuffle.

A British bulldog bowler hat clung to his melting skull.
. . . Game spirits, tat and service industries,
an economy stripped to the skin trade. Sex and security,
Arsenal boot boys, white slaves and the SAS.

Gavin Ewart

The Falklands, 1982

This must have been more like the Boer War
than anything seen in our lifetime,
with the troopships and the cheering,
the happy homecoming, the sweetheart-and-wifetime,
everything looking over and solved,
and no civilians involved –

except a few stewardesses, Chinese in the galleys
almost by accident taken
willy-nilly on The Great Adventure,
where the Argentine fusing of the shells was often mistaken –
lucky for each floating sitting duck.
Oh yes, we had luck!

Luck that the slaughtered World War I soldiers
who died on the Somme and at Arras
would have welcomed, in their dismal trenches –
though that's not to belittle the victory of the Paras,
who lost, all in all, very few dead,
good men, well led.

At home, indeed, it was terribly like the World Cup,
though far less bright, commentated, stagey,
security making the war news nil, mostly,
but good value when they finally stopped being cagey.
Was the *General Belgrano* really offside?
A few hundred died.

And the outstanding achievements of the great Press,
particularly that section called 'yellow',
that wrote 'Up yours!' on missiles, went berserk
and shouted 'GOTCHA!' in a giant coward's bellow –
and circulation rises, like *The Sun*.
But was it well done?

Kipling's 'Recessional' told us to beware of Hubris,
and not give way to flag-waving
(they don't in the Lebanon, or Northern Ireland) –
if men's lives are worth giving, they're also worth saving.
Who let them start the bloody thing?
That's the question, there's the sting.

Argentina invaded the Falklands Islands with its approximately 2,000 British subjects
in April 1982. A Task Force from Britain had regained the islands by the end of June.

Sean O'Brien

Summertime

For Richard Richardson, Kent NUM

The news is old. A picket line
Is charged and clubbed by mounted police.
Regrettable. Necessity.
You have to take a balanced view.
That kind of thing can't happen here
And when it does it isn't true.

Adore yourself and in the body's
Shrivelled province bask and breed.
Indulge your fudged affairs and lust
For what your terror says you need.
It's hot. Lie down and vegetate.
There are no politics, no state.

At noon on Brighton beach it's clear
Why heatwaves make the English glad.
Beneath that burnt imperative
In oiled, obedient ranks they lie,
To forge a beachhead close to home
And found the final colony.

You have to take a balanced view.
That kind of thing can't happen here,
And when it does it isn't true.

NUM: in April 1984 the National Union of Mineworkers (NUM) in Britain went on strike over a drastic programme of pit closures. The Metropolitan Police were deployed in baton charges against provincial mass pickets. The strike lasted one year and failed.

Hans Magnus Enzensberger

Short History of the Bourgeoisie

That was the moment when, without
noticing it, for five minutes
we were vastly rich, magnificent
and electric, air-conditioned in July,
or, in case it was November,
the flown-in Finnish wood blazed
in Tudor fireplaces. Funny,
it was all there, just flew in
by itself, as it were. Elegant
we were, no one could bear us.
We threw solo concerts around,
chips, orchids in cellophane. Clouds
that said, I. Unique!

Flights everywhere. Even our sighs
went on credit cards. Like sailors
we bandied curses. Each one
had his own misfortune under the seat,
ready to grab at it. A waste, really.
It was so practical. Water
flowed out of taps just like that.
Remember? Simply stunned
by our tiny emotions,
we ate little. If only we'd guessed
that all this would pass
in five minutes, the roast beef Wellington
would have tasted different, quite different.

Translated from the German by
Michael Hamburger.

Mark Halliday

Population

Isn't it nice that everyone has a grocery list
except the very poor you hear about occasionally
we all have a grocery list on the refrigerator door;
at any given time there are thirty million lists in America
that say BREAD. Isn't it nice
not to be alone in this. Sometimes
you visit someone's house for the first time
and you spot the list taped up on a kitchen cabinet
and you think Yes, we're all in this together.
TOILET PAPER. No getting around it.
Nice to think of us all
unwrapping the new rolls at once,
forty thousand of us at any given moment.

Orgasm, of course, being the most vivid example: imagine
an electrified map wired to every American bed:
those little lights popping
on both sides of the Great Divide,
popping to beat the band. But
we never beat the band: within an hour or day
we're horny again, or hungry, or burdened with waste.
But isn't it nice not to be alone in
any of it; nice to be not noticeably responsible,
acquitted eternally in the rituals of the tribe:
it's only human! It's only human and that's not much.

So, aren't you glad we have such advanced farm machinery,
futuristic fertilizers, half a billion chickens
almost ready to die. Here comes the loaves of bread for us
thup thup thup thup for all of us thup thup thup
except maybe the very poor
thup thup
and man all the cattle we can fatten up man,

there's no stopping our steaks. And that's why
we can make babies galore, baby:
let's get on with it. Climb aboard.
Let's be affirmative here, let's be pro-life for God's sake
how can life be wrong?
People *need* people and the happiest people are
surrounded with friendly flesh.
If you have ten kids they'll be so sweet –
ten really sweet kids! Have twelve!
What if there were 48 pro baseball teams,
you could see a damn lot more games!
And in this fashion we get away
from tragedy. Because tragedy comes when someone
gets too special. Whereas,

if forty thousand kitchen counters
on any given Sunday night
have notes on them that say
I CAN'T TAKE IT ANYMORE
I'M GONE, DON'T TRY TO FIND ME
you can feel how *your* note is
no big thing in America,
so, no *horrible* heartbreak,
it's more like a TV episode,
you've seen this whole plot lots of times
and everybody gets by –
you feel better already –
everybody gets by
and it's nice. It's a people thing.
You've got to admit it's nice.

James Lasdun

Buying a Dress

Thirty a day and enough gin to float
A goldfish, Guinness sluicing down her throat,
The barman's spaniel, one damp eye a-cock,
Wiggling his nose like a toe in a sock
As he watched her mechanic's hands tip back
And twist the beaker till the rim's last black
Oil-heavy droplet splashed her scarlet lipstick
(Even a tampon was like a dipstick
In those hands). She had myths for everything;
I was the last of the line, the inbred king,
Witless, chinless, myopic, coughing up gold,
Herself the gene-rich gutter-urchin, bold
As ersatz brass and hungrier than a till,
Her mouth wide open, sieving the world for its krill
Of creature comforts – 'would you like that?' 'Yes.'
I'm thinking of the day we bought a dress,
Trying on most of London's stock for size –
From Columbine to Pantaloon my eyes
Were washed in primal splashes, polka dots,
In patterned mascots of the male world – yachts,
Hot-air balloons, and motorbikes that traced
A knee-high Capricorn, Equator waist;
My little Earth, each louvered stall a night
She'd break from, like a planet into light,
Massed colours, samite, lace, merino wool,
And where she stood, each mirror's pool seemed full
To bursting, like a swollen waterdrop's
Bulging convexity . . .
                              Outside the shops,
Where summer riots were simmering in the heat
And shoals of gauzy dresses swam the street,
Fate, in a painter's shape, began to dip
His brush in wet vermilion, letting drip
Every minute or so one beady gout

Onto the street below . . .
                              Meanwhile a shout
Of triumph told me that the job was done –
Each wished-for detail gathered into one
Wrapped-round expanse of yellow silk, held tight
About her waist – a fluted fall of light,
Half-light and shadow, billowing at the sleeves –
Picture a ship's bell melting, harvest sheaves,
Their brilliance hatching with the crack of dawn,
Gold cobbled light on streams – I could go on,
But what I most remember is the way
She wore it; buckled turbulence, the spray
Of water on zinc, a beehive's boiling throng,
The way a budded peony breasts the strong
Rotunda of its sheath; improbable
Compression, not of flesh, but of the soul,
As if she'd torn through every veil, but found
Matter itself in Purdah, nature bound
And yashmak'd in some chemical Sharia
She'd never overthrow. Her heart's desire
Rippled in the mirror, and she turned
Quickly; the knowledge framed inside it burned
Too violently . . .
                       She wore it from the shop
And step by step we zeroed on the drop –
Slick globule that prefigured my one spurt
Of infidelity (I blabbed, the hurt
Exploded in her body like a gun)
Oh Exegetes, behold her now, the sun
Falling upon her in gambades and curls
Of gold, the whipped-cream, thixotropic swirls
Of virgin silk notating on the air
The way a body registers despair;
I see it in slow motion: the surprise,
The torso's whiplash twist, neck arched, the eyes
Widening as the tugged silk slides around,
And with it, like a perfect bullet wound,
One molten ruby. Silence. *No harm done;*
Nothing we can't put right (much later on

The same words met the same astonished look);
Endings are swift – we taxied home, she took
The dress off, checked the damage, nodded, gripped
A bunch of fabric in each fist, and ripped.

Elizabeth Garrett

Moules à la Marinière

We scoured the secret places of the creek,
Parting blistered fronds of bladder-wrack
To find the concupiscent clusters, rocked
In their granite crêche. Jack-knives prised
The molluscs out. Slick blue-blacks bruised
Slowly dull; and the sea expunged our tracks.

Bouquet of Muscadet, bouquet garni recall
The tuck and chuckle of mussels in a bucket
Behind the door. Damp and aromatic,
Steam insinuates itself into all
The kitchen clefts, and clings in briny beads
Above the flame where mussels chirp and wheeze.

I pour on wine; it seems they beg for more,
The beaked shells yearning wide as if in song –
Yet dumb – and lewdly lolling parrot-tongues.
Cream licks the back of a spoon and drawls a slur
Of unctuous benediction for this feast.
We smooth our cassocks; bow our heads; and eat.

It rained all night as though to wash away
A brininess that tanged the atmosphere:
Dreams – of forbidden fruit, of *fruits de mer*
Wrenched from their secret beds, of tastes that lay
Like sea's after-sting on the tongue. Still lingers
A trace of guilt. I wash my salty fingers.

Peter Reading

From *Going On*

These are the days of the horrible headlines,
Bomb Blast Atrocity, Leak From Reactor,
Soccer Fans Run Amok, Middle East Blood Bath,
PC Knocks Prisoner's Eye Out In Charge Room.
Outside, the newsvendors ululate. Inside,
lovers seek refuge in succulent plump flesh,
booze themselves innocent of the whole shit-works.
Why has the gentleman fallen face-forward
into his buttered asparagus, Garçon?
He and his girlfriend have already drunk two
bottles of Bollinger and they were half-tight
when they arrived at the place half-an-hour since.
Waiters man-handle the gentleman upright,
aim him (with smirks at the lady) towards his
quails (which he misses and slumps in the gravy –
baying, the while, for 'Encore du Savigny').
He is supplied with the Beaune, which he noses,
quaffs deeply, relishes . . . sinks to the gingham
where he reposes susurrantly. There is
'63 Sandeman fetched to revive him.
Chin on the Pont l'Evêque, elbow in ash-tray,
as from the *Book of the Dead*, he produces
incomprehensible hieroglyphs, bidding
Access surrender the price of his coma
unto the restaurateur, kindly and patient.
These are the days of the **National Health Cuts,**
days of the end of the innocent liver;
they have to pay for it privately, who would seek anaesthetic.

Eleanor Brown

The Lads

The lads, the lads, away the lads;
we are the Boys, who make this Noise: hoo, ha; hoo-*ha*;
a-*way*, awayawayaway, a-way, away;
ere we go, ere we go, ere we go;
we are the Boys, who make this Noise:
hoo *ha*.

Away the lads. I love your poetry.
It strips the artform down to nakedness,
distilling it to spirituous drops
of utter purity.
I like the way you shout it all so loud,
revelling in the shamelessness
of its repetitiousness; the way it never stops
delighting
you. You've every right to be proud
of your few, brief, oral formulae –
any of which will do, for *Match of the Day*,
or Friday night, Lads' Night Out,
lagered up and fighting –
you are the lads. You've every right to shout.

Your poetry belligerently asserts
what nobody would trouble to deny:
that you are the lads; that there you go;
that yours will never be to reason why.
My unsingable songs cannot do more for me
than rid me of my epicene disgust,
after I've served you all ten pints and watched
you flushing up with random rage and lust.
You'll smack each other's heads tonight
and shag each other's birds;
you are the Boys, who make this Noise.
What need have you for words?

We will not argue, therefore, you and I.
Your poetry serves your purpose; mine serves mine.
You only tell me what I don't deny,
and I don't tell you anything. That's fine.

Away, the lads. Your deathless chants will be
heard in these bars and streets long after we
are dead (for lads are mortal too); your sons
will never feel the need for different ones.

Carol Ann Duffy

Translating the English, 1989

'. . . and much of the poetry, alas, is lost in translation . . .'

Welcome to my country! We have here Edwina Currie
and The Sun newspaper. Much excitement.
Also the weather has been most improving
even in February. Daffodils. (Wordsworth. Up North.) If you like
Shakespeare or even Opera we have too the Black Market.
For two hundred quids we are talking Les Miserables,
nods being as good as winks. Don't eat the eggs.
Wheel-clamp. Dogs. Vagrants. A tour of our wonderful
capital city is not to be missed. The Fergie,
The Princess Di and the football hooligan, truly you will
like it here, Squire. Also we can be talking crack, smack
and Carling Black Label if we are so inclined. Don't
drink the H₂O. All very proud we now have
a green Prime Minister. What colour yours? Binbags.
You will be knowing of Charles Dickens and Terry Wogan
and Scotland. All this can be arranged for cash no questions.
Ireland not on. Fish and chips and the Official Secrets Act
second to none. Here we go. We are liking
a smashing good time like estate agents and Neighbours,
also Brookside for we are allowed four Channels.
How many you have? Last night of Proms. Andrew
Lloyd-Webber. Jeffrey Archer. Plenty culture you will be agreeing.

Also history and buildings. The Houses of Lords. Docklands.
Many thrills and high interest rates for own good. Muggers.
Much lead in petrol. Filth. Rule Britannia and child abuse.
Electronic tagging, Boss, ten pints and plenty rape. Queen Mum.
Channel Tunnel. You get here fast no problem to my country
my country my country welcome welcome welcome.

Liz Lochhead

Bagpipe Muzak, Glasgow 1990

When A. and R. men hit the street
To sign up every second band they meet
Then marketing men will spill out spiel
About how us Glesca folk are really *real*
(Where once they used to fear and pity
These days they glamorize and patronize our city –
Accentwise once they could hear bugger all
That was not low, glottal or guttural,
Now we've 'kudos' incident'ly
And the Patter's street-smart, strictly state-of-the-art,
And our oaths are user-friendly).

It's all go the sandblaster, it's all go Tutti Frutti,
All we want is a wally close with Rennie Mackintosh putti.

Malkie Machismo invented a gismo for making whisky oot o' girders
He tasted it, came back for mair, and soon he was on to his thirders.
Rabbie Burns turned in his grave and dunted Hugh MacDiarmid,
Said: It's oor National Thorn, John Barleycorn, but I doot we'll ever
    learn it . . .

It's all go the Rotary Club, it's all go 'The Toast Tae The Lassies',
It's all go Holy Willie's Prayer and plunging your dirk in the haggis.

Robbie Coltrane flew Caledonian MacBrayne
To Lewis . . . on a Sunday!
Protesting Wee Frees fed him antifreeze
(Why God knows) till he was comatose
And didnae wake up till the Monday.

Aye it's Retro Time for Northern Soul and the whoop and the skirl
    o' the saxes.
All they'll score's more groundglass heroin and venison filofaxes.
The rent-boys preen on Buchanan Street, their boas are made of
    vulture,
It's all go the January sales in the Metropolis of Culture.

It's all go the PR campaign and a radical change of image –
Write Saatchi and Saatchi a blank cheque to pay them for the
    damage.

Tam o'Shanter fell asleep
To the sound of fairy laughter
Woke up on the cold-heather hillside
To find it was ten years after
And it's all go (again) the Devolution Debate and pro . . . pro . . .
    proportional representation.
Over pasta and pesto in a Byres Road bistro, Scotland declares
    hersel' a nation.

Margo McDonald spruced up her spouse for thon Govan By-Election
The voters they selectit him in a sideyways *left* defection,
The Labour man was awfy hurt, he'd dependit on the X-fillers
And the so-and-sos had betrayed him for thirty pieces of Sillars!

Once it was no go the SNP, they were sneered at as 'Tory' and
    tartan
And thought to be very little to do with the price of Spam in
    Dumbarton.
Now it's all go the Nationalists, the toast of the folk and the famous
– Of Billy Connolly, Muriel Gray and the Auchtermuchty
    Proclaimers.

It's all go L.A. lager, it's all go the Campaign for an Assembly,
It's all go Suas Alba and winning ten–nil at Wembley.
Are there separatist dreams in the glens and the schemes?
Well . . . it doesny take Taggart to detect it!
Or to jalouse we hate the Government
And we patently didnae elect it.
So – watch out Margaret Thatcher, and tak' tent Neil Kinnock
Or we'll tak' the United Kingdom and brekk it like a bannock.

Margo McDonald; *Jim Sillars*: politicians of the Scottish National Party (SNP).
bannock: a round, flat loaf, usually unleavened.

Durs Grünbein

Folds and Traps

People with stronger nerves than any animal,
                    More fleeting, less aware,
Became at last accustomed to the dissection
                    Of daytime. They consumed
The pizza made of hours in chunks and mostly
                    Cold and at the same time
Heard CDs while they prattled, else, blow-dried
                    The guinea-pig, wrote letters
And went a-hunting on computer screens
                    For viruses. Among
The piles of paper on the writing desk,
                    The contracts and the copies,
Was built the nest of the Origami-Bird,
                    A rustling trap. Each day
Brought, as could be reckoned up in the evening,
                    Another diagram
Of fractal calm that later in a dreamless
                    Catnap would dissolve.
If one looked closer, with that angel's patience
                    Familiar from movies,
These were colours, spread like zones of pressure
                    Across the chart of Europe,

Like cheetah fur in the encyclopaedia
                    Of mammals, like the pages
Of fingerprints on graphite dust in the records
                    Of violent criminals. Clearly
This vestige of forgetting was a whisper
                    In brains, wrinkles, faces,
Until that time the flimsiest apple skin
                    Tore on the lips.

Translated from the German by Glyn Maxwell.

John Ashbery

Definition of Blue

The rise of capitalism parallels the advance of romanticism
And the individual is dominant until the close of the nineteenth
    century.
In our own time, mass practices have sought to submerge the
    personality
By ignoring it, which has caused it instead to branch out in all
    directions
Far from the permanent tug that used to be its notion of 'home'.
These different impetuses are received from everywhere
And are as instantly snapped back, hitting through the cold
    atmosphere
In one steady, intense line.

There is no remedy for this 'packaging' which has supplanted the old
    sensations.
Formerly there would have been architectural screens at the point
    where the action became most difficult
As a path trails off into shrubbery – confusing, forgotten, yet
    continuing to exist.
But today there is no point in looking to imaginative new methods
Since all of them are in constant use. The most that can be said for
    them further

Is that erosion produces a kind of dust or exaggerated pumice
Which fills space and transforms it, becoming a medium
In which it is possible to recognize oneself.

Each new diversion adds its accurate touch to the ensemble, and so
A portrait, smooth as glass, is built up out of multiple corrections
And it has no relation to the space or time in which it was lived.
Only its existence is a part of all being, and is therefore, I suppose, to
    be prized
Beyond chasms of night that fight us
By being hidden and present.

And yet it results in a downward motion, or rather a floating one
In which the blue surroundings drift slowly up and past you
To realize themselves some day, while, you, in this nether world that
    could not be better
Waken each morning to the exact value of what you did and said,
    which remains.

Peter Wyles

Aspects of the President

President, playing the saxophone, hoping to be liked.
Hilary is hectoring the doctors, Chelsea
practices the pianola, her father's tunes.
The press are sniffing underwear in the bathroom
and Socks the cat is ripping up the platform.
– This is Washington Mr President.

President, jogging in the park, eating grease
at Arkansas Bill's Big Fat Roosters.
President, smoking dope but not inhaling,
dodging and weaving. Today the zigzag,
tomorrow the sidewalk. 'Change my mind?
Love to. Tomorrow at five? Certainly.'

President, in high heels and a garter-belt,
waggling his fat butt in Times Square,
watching the polls, sniffing the Wall St Journal,
but never inhaling, he never inhales.
President, next to his heart, a jackass,
embroidered on his boxer shorts, a weathercock.

Duncan Forbes

Downing Street Cat

I am the next Messiah and New Labour's on a roll,
We're capturing the centre at a steady Gallup poll,
My policies are pragmatist, my principles a blur:
Consensus and democracy are words that make me purr.
My record's *rasa tabula* but razor-sharp my claws,
I am a wily bureaucat who speaks without a pause.

    With permosmile and pressure chat,
    I'm grinning like the Cheshire cat,
    A cat that gets the cream.
    I practise in the mirror
    Both looking grim and trimmer,
    The winning smile, my wily guile,
    The frank, déclassé, candid style
    Which will perfect the dream.

I've never been a minister or high in public office
But there is nothing sinister in voting for a novice;
I want to catch the early worm inside the Tory bird
And redesign the kingdom before King Charles III.
My pedigree is variegate, I am a mongrel moggie,
My brain is full of northern grit, my words are southern-soggy.

    An Old Fettesian orator,
    I look like an ex-chorister
    With growing hopes of fame.

No dope-head nor draft-dodger,
I neither grope nor roger
Except one married barrister –
To name her could embarrass her
But Cherie is her name.

I promise you grand promises, I promise you no sleaze,
I am a lovely family man and desperate to appease.
I represent the Mansion House, I represent the masses
And I can play at cat and mouse with Fascists of all classes.
I brandish my bland blandishments on every telly channel
And blind with my embellishments Establishment grey flannel.

A St John's Oxford graduate,
So passionately moderate
My honorary doctorate
Could come from anywhere –
So long as the electorate,
The blessed British plebiscite,
Elects for its Protectorate
The blessèd Tony Blair.

rasa tabula: a blank sheet (usually tabula rasa).

Adrian Mitchell

My Shy Di in Newspaperland

(All the lines are quoted from the British Press on Royal Engagement
day, the only slight distortions appear in the repeats of the four-line
chorus. Written in collaboration with Alistair Mitchell.)

Who will sit where in the forest of tiaras?
She is an English rose without a thorn.
Love is in their stars, says Susie.
She has been plunged headfirst into a vast goldfish bowl.

Did she ponder as she strolled for an hour through Belgravia?
Will they, won't they? Why, yes they will.
They said so yesterday.
He said: 'Will you?'
She said: 'Yes.'
So did his mother – and so say all of us.

Who will sit where in the head of the goldfish?
She is an English forest without a tiara.
Love is in their roses, says Thorny.
She has been plunged starsfirst into a vast susie bowl.

Most of the stories in this issue were written
By James Whitaker, the *Daily Star* man
Who has always known that Diana and Prince Charles would marry.
He watched them fishing on the River Dee –
And Lady Diana was watching him too.
She was standing behind a tree using a mirror
To watch James Whitaker at his post,
James Whitaker, the man who always knew.

Who will sit where in the stars of Susie?
She is an English head without a goldfish.
Love is in their forests, says Tiara.
She has been plunged rosefirst into a vast thorn bowl.

All about Di.
Shy Di smiled and blushed.
Lady Di has her eyelashes dyed.
My shy Di.

She descends five times from Charles II –
Four times on the wrong side of the blanket
And once on the right side.

Who will sit where in the rose of thorns?
She is an English star without a susie.
Love is in their heads, says Goldfish.
She has been plunged forestfirst into a vast tiara bowl.

Flatmate Carolyn Pride was in the loo
When she heard of the engagement.
'Lady Diana told me through the door,' she said last night.
'I just burst into tears. There were floods and floods of tears.'

Who will sit where in the forest of tiaras?
She is an English rose without a thorn.
Love is in their stars, says Susie.
She has been plunged headfirst into a vast goldfish bowl.

John Ash

From *Twentieth Century*

A decadent historicism appeared in buildings, appalling to purists,
and executives of telephone companies walked daily
beneath romanesque vaults and the gilded wings of statues,

then on a clouded day no one could fix in retrospect
the body became a religion, sex a kind of makeshift sacrament,
and with nothing but this dim polestar to guide us

we must now confront the idea of continual mourning
and the necessity of pain, as a friend's handsome face
is reduced to something resembling a bruised skull.

It is a time of marvels: in midsummer a wind out of nowhere
strips the trees bare; every few minutes another Marsyas is flayed,
and the same small uncomprehending dog laps at his blood.

Twentieth century, we still have much to learn from you
concerning the refinements of cruelty and its multiplication,
banal as shopping malls on the outskirts of a town,
flourishing as the centre dies and is boarded up.

Twentieth century, you are leaving us
with resurrections of dead gods who remain dead,
twitching in their galvanised graveclothes, and this is unkind,
since we have stayed faithful to you as if you were a good mother.

We ignored your cocaine habit and your masochism –
you appearing in the Irish bar saying, when we mentioned
your face swollen like a purple cabbage: 'Oh I had a bad fall.'

What kind of staircase could do that?
Tell us whose fist it was. Twentieth century, don't lie to us.
We love you and you are leaving forever.

WE BILLION CHEERED: THE MEDIA

By the end of the century, the media had shifted from being a stenographer to reality to being the subject itself. Reality is now very often something that is created with the media in mind. Poets – whose characteristic outlet is the little magazine – have had an uneasy relationship with the media, being generally resentful of the sparse attention it has always given to poetry. Perhaps for this reason poets have observed the media sharply. Howard Nemerov's 'A Way of Life' and David Hart's 'Angelica and Bob On Line' capture the curious non-linear dislocations and conjunctions made possible by the media, tendencies that will accelerate as the Internet becomes as ubiquitous as television.

C. Day Lewis

Newsreel

Enter the dream-house, brothers and sisters, leaving
Your debts asleep, your history at the door:
This is the home for heroes, and this loving
Darkness a fur you can afford.

Fish in their tank electrically heated
Nose without envy the glass wall: for them
Clerk, spy, nurse, killer, prince, the great and the defeated,
Move in a mute day-dream.

Bathed in this common source, you gape incurious
At what your active hours have willed –
Sleep-walking on that silver wall, the furious
Sick shapes and pregnant fancies of your world.

There is the mayor opening the oyster season:
A society wedding: the autumn hats look swell:

From Little Suite for Loudspeaker — Louis Aragon

An old crocks' race, and a politician
In fishing-waders to prove that all is well.

Oh, look at the warplanes! Screaming hysteric treble
In the long power-dive, like gannets they fall steep.
But what are they to trouble –
These silver shadows to trouble your watery, womb-deep sleep?

See the big guns, rising, groping, erected
To plant death in your world's soft womb.
Fire-bud, smoke-blossom, iron seed projected –
Are these exotics? They will grow nearer home:

Grow nearer home – and out of the dream-house stumbling
One night into a strangling air and the flung
Rags of children and thunder of stone niagaras tumbling,
You'll know you slept too long.

Louis Aragon

From *Little Suite for Loudspeaker*

I

Hilversum, Kalundborg, Brno, the loud world over
Monday to Sunday, the idiot radio
Spits germs on Mozart, dedicates to you
Silence, its endlessly insulting brew

Loud Jove in love with Io, queen of cows
Has left her tethered by the waterside
She hears by radio at eventide
Cracklings of static from the hidden spouse

Like her – for this is war – hearing the Voice
Men stay in their stupidity and caress
Toulouse, PTT, Daventry, Bucharest

Their hope, the good old hope of former days
Interrogates the ether, which replies
That Carter's little liver pills are best.

Translated from the French by Rolfe Humphries.

Marina Tsvetaeva

Readers of Newspapers

It crawls, the underground snake,
Crawls, with its load of people.
And each one has his
Newspaper, his skin
Disease; a twitch of chewing:
Newspaper *caries*.
Masticator of gum,
Readers of newspaper.

And who are the readers? old men? athletes?
Soldiers? No face, no features,
No age. Skeletons – there's no
Face, only the newspaper page.
All Paris is dressed
This way from forehead to navel.
Give it up, girl, or
You'll give birth to
A reader of newspapers.

Sway – HE LIVES WITH HIS SISTER –
Swaying – HE KILLED HIS FATHER! –
They blow themselves up with vanity
As if swaying with drink.

For such gentlemen what
Is the sunset or the sunrise?
They swallow emptiness,
These readers of newspapers!

For news read: calumnies,
For news read: embezzling,
In every column slander,
Every paragraph some disgusting thing.

O with what, at the Last Judgment
Will you come before the light?
Grabbers of small moments,
Readers of newspapers,

Gone! lost! vanished!
The old maternal terror.
But mother, the Gutenberg Press
Is more terrible than Schwartz's powder.

It's better to go to a graveyard
Than into the prurient
Sick bay of scab scratchers,
These readers of newspapers.

And who is it rots our sons
Now in the prime of their life?
Those corrupters of blood
The writers of newspapers.

Look, friends – much
Stronger than in these lines! – do
I think this, when with
A manuscript in my hand

I stand before the face
– There is no emptier place –
Than before the absent
Face of an editor of news

Papers' evil filth.

Translated from the Russian by
Elaine Feinstein.

Carol Ann Duffy

Poet For Our Times

I write the headlines for a Daily Paper.
It's just a knack one's born with all-right-Squire.
You do not have to be an educator,
just bang the words down like they're screaming *Fire!*
CECIL-KEAYS ROW SHOCK TELLS EYETIE WAITER.
ENGLAND FAN CALLS WHINGEING FROG A LIAR.

Cheers. Thing is, you've got to grab attention
with just one phrase as punters rush on by.
I've made mistakes too numerous to mention,
so now we print the buggers inches high.
TOP MP PANTIE ROMP INCREASES TENSION.
RENT BOY: ROCK STAR PAID ME WELL TO LIE.

I like to think that I'm a sort of poet
for our times. My shout. Know what I mean?
I've got a special talent and I show it
in punchy haikus featuring the Queen.
DIPLOMAT IN BED WITH SERBO-CROAT.
EASTENDERS' BONKING SHOCK IS WELL-OBSCENE.

Of course, these days, there's not the sense of panic
you got a few years back. What with the box
et cet. I wish I'd been around when the Titanic
sank. To headline that, mate, would've been the tops.
SEE PAGE 3 TODAY GENTS THEY'RE GIGANTIC.
KINNOCK-BASHER MAGGIE PULLS OUT STOPS.

And, yes, I have a dream – make that a scotch, ta –
that kids will know my headlines off by heart.
IMMIGRANTS FLOOD IN CLAIMS HEATHROW WATCHER.
GREEN PARTY WOMAN IS A NIGHTCLUB TART.
The poems of the decade . . . *Stuff 'em! Gotcha!*
The instant tits and bottom line of art.

Paul Groves

Greta Garbo

A Japanese paparazzo photographer has been waiting outside her
apartment for more than three years, but has never succeeded in
getting a full-face picture.

Mostly you get the din of the Franklin D. Roosevelt Drive,
traffic plying this throughway beside
the East River. Mostly you get the sense
of being alive, of being five time zones from home,
from that family rooftree in Kawasaki, one block
from the Sojiji Temple. I have captured
kids playing pat-ball at one two-fiftieth of a second
at f4, leaves drifting to the ground on East 52nd
at proportions of that speed, but
Dame Fortune stays elusive. For thirty eight months
she has not bought zucchini. I find this remarkable.
The Americans call a swede a rutabaga;
I call this Swede the whole vocabulary,
depending on my mood: witch, goddess, foil, mantrap.
It is as if she never lived, and all I have done
for a slice of my life is kick cans,
light up another Lucky Strike, hope yet again
to strike lucky. I suppose this is an odyssey
in pursuit of elusiveness itself, a quest
for the resurrection of beauty: Odysseus
blew a decade on his errand. There's time yet.
When the wind blows, desperate, down from Maine,
and it's thirty below, I curse and stamp
and spend all day in the diner, wiping
condensation from the pane, focusing.
He brings me soup, and tuts, scratching his head.
'I thought Polacks were the limit, but
you're something else.' Life has become
a philosophical acceptance of loss, a conflation
of zilch and Zen. Something stirs,

but it is only the janitor humping garbage
onto the sidewalk for the next collection.
She made a movie called 'Joyless Street'
in 1925, the year my mother was born
high in the hills near Kawakami
where the snowflakes are huge, and the air silent.

Philip Larkin

Essential Beauty

In frames as large as rooms that face all ways
And block the ends of streets with giant loaves,
Screen graves with custard, cover slums with praise
Of motor-oil and cuts of salmon, shine
Perpetually these sharply-pictured groves
Of how life should be. High above the gutter
A silver knife sinks into golden butter,
A glass of milk stands in a meadow, and
Well-balanced families, in fine
Midsummer weather, owe their smiles, their cars,
Even their youth, to that small cube each hand
Stretches towards. These, and the deep armchairs
Aligned to cups at bedtime, radiant bars
(Gas or electric), quarter-profile cats
By slippers on warm mats,
Reflect none of the rained-on streets and squares.

They dominate outdoors. Rather, they rise
Serenely to proclaim pure crust, pure foam,
Pure coldness to our live imperfect eyes
That stare beyond this world, where nothing's made
As new or washed quite clean, seeking the home
All such inhabit. There, dark raftered pubs
Are filled with white-clothed ones from tennis-clubs,
And the boy puking his heart out in the Gents
Just missed them, as the pensioner paid
A halfpenny more for Granny Graveclothes' Tea

To taste old age, and dying smokers sense
Walking towards them through some dappled park
As if on water that unfocused she
No match lit up, nor drag ever brought near,
Who now stands newly clear,
Smiling, and recognising, and going dark.

Howard Nemerov

A Way of Life

It's been going on a long time.
For instance, these two guys, not saying much, who slog
Through sun and sand, fleeing the scene of their crime,
Till one turns, without a word, and smacks
His buddy flat with the flat of an axe,
Which cuts down on the dialogue
Some, but is viewed rather as normal than sad
By me, as I wait for the next ad.

It seems to me it's been quite a while
Since the last vision of blonde loveliness
Vanished, her shampoo and shower and general style
Replaced by this lean young lunk-
head parading along with a gun in his back to confess
How yestereve, being drunk
And in a state of existential despair,
He beat up his grandma and pawned her invalid chair.

But here at last is a pale beauty
Smoking a filter beside a mountain stream,
Brief interlude, before the conflict of love and duty
Gets moving again, as sheriff and posse expound,
Between jail and saloon, the American Dream
Where Justice, after considerable horsing around,
Turns out to be Mercy; when the villain is knocked off,
A kindly uncle offers syrup for my cough.

And now these clean-cut athletic types
In global hats are having a nervous debate
As they stand between their individual rocket ships
Which have landed, appropriately, on some rocks
Somewhere in Space, in an atmosphere of hate
Where one tells the other to pull up his socks
And get going, he doesn't say where; they fade,
And an angel food cake flutters in the void.

I used to leave now and again;
No more. A lot of violence in American life
These days, mobsters and cops all over the scene.
But there's a lot of love, too, mixed with the strife,
And kitchen-kindness, like a bedtime story
With rich food and a more kissable depilatory.
Still, I keep my weapons handy, sitting here
Smoking and shaving and drinking the dry beer.

Glyn Maxwell

We Billion Cheered

We billion cheered.
    Some threat sank in the news and disappeared.
It did because
    Currencies danced and we forgot what it was.

It rose again.
    It rose and slid towards our shore and when
It got to it,
    It laced it like a telegram. We lit

Regular fires,
    But missed it oozing along irregular wires
Towards the Smoke.
    We missed it elbowing into the harmless joke

Or dreams of our
    Loves asleep in the cots where the dolls are.
We missed it how
    You miss an o'clock passing and miss now.

We missed it where
    You miss my writing of this and I miss you there.
We missed it through
    Our eyes, lenses, screen and angle of view.

We missed it though
    It specified where it was going to go,
And when it does,
    The missing ones are ten to one to be us.

We line the shore,
    Speak of the waving dead of a waving war.
And clap a man
    For an unveiled familiar new plan.

Don't forget.
    Nothing will start that hasn't started yet.
Don't forget
    It, its friend, its foe and its opposite.

Richard Blomfield

Prélude à l'Après-Midi d'un Téléphone

That cream-coloured waiting wish-wand
Ear of a myriad nymphs and electrons
Androgynous oracle combing the cosmic fishpond,
Let us say 'The other person has now cleared . . .'
The daylight through the lattice larynx peered
To make a sheep deep in its tufted slumbers
Stir on its mattress stuffed with telephone numbers.

Who are you other person among many voices
Roller-coasting along the edge of precipices,
The peaks of Arctic ices and round the stars,
Floppy discs on which sit turbaned avatars.
Clothed in mist above a fresh green lawn
Are you the person who arose at dawn
And did you see the other other one who grieves
Over your rake's progress towards a pile of autumn leaves?

'Phone, pacific stepping-stone, dial 'a'
For aborigine, atoll and a footprint under the mimosa,
They dance minuets to the sound of Cimarosa.
The other voice said 'I'll give you a ring . . .'
But all numbers are engaged
While bees suck honey from bell and ling.

Dial Oh! and hold the line. Somewhere
The celestial goldfish smoothes its scales
Between the roses of Mayfair and the ionosphere
And where the twilight falls and fails.

David Hart

Angelica and Bob On Line

Angelica has crept out of bed and left early before getting on line.
She has missed the clip-art of a heart in the e-mail from Bob.
When Bob wakes with her gone it is from a dream of a woman
smashing through barbed wire towards the blue horizon.

Angelica in town swerves off into Uranus Precinct
and sees herself on video in the window of Dixon's.
Back at the home screen Bob frets and cries, *God only knows!*,
and for a moment this seems to be the breakthrough
he's been mousing his way through the fine folds of fields for.

The *Evening Echo*'s early edition is devoting half its front page
to a young woman covering her face caught on camera leaving
the Clearwater Centre but it isn't her. But this *is* her,
a photo from that happy summer scanned in on Bob's screen.
Enlarging it with zoom control he examines for intent
the edge of her smile. Elongating it a fraction
everything soon becomes clear. The screen doesn't lie
and he can read her lips. Her eyes, too, were somewhere else.

In her attic suite in the Delphi B & B seventy miles away
a TV News report tells Angelica the flood in the graveyard
where her mother is buried is carrying off bodies.

Back at the home screen Bob clicks open some curtains
and a woman appears with open lips, while on Angelica's screen
there's a chapel offering bliss and she moves through it
into an aureole of love dust. Bob clicks off the woman's clothes
one by one and kisses in *excelsis* her screen body: *Oh Angelica!*
Bob and the screen image groan in harmony towards ecstasy.

Angelica in her room, sipping Cola from the machine,
types **BOB** in bold caps and says in a whisper, *Bob, you bastard!*,
then sends out an e-mail to anyone who will listen
asking for pictures of chocolate. On the home screen Bob's search
continues with new vigour into the night's net
punctuated by news from Australia about the cricket.

Art has become more important as the power of traditional beliefs has waned, and the first half of the century was one of the great fertile periods in painting, music and literature. The second half of the century is more confused. The European catastrophe of World War II had a devastating effect on painting and music, but not on poetry and fiction, which may even have gained in power through adversity. The painters of the century are Picasso and Matisse, a judgement that would have been the same in 1950. The century's most characteristic art, of course, was cinema, which has been hugely influential in shaping our perception of reality. The ambiguities inherent in such a medium of virtual reality are brought out in William Scammell's poem 'The Act'.

Wallace Stevens

From *The Man With the Blue Guitar*

I

The man bent over his guitar,
A shearsman of sorts. The day was green.

They said, 'You have a blue guitar,
You do not play things as they are.'

The man replied, 'Things as they are
Are changed upon the blue guitar.'

And they said then, 'But play, you must,
A tune beyond us, yet ourselves,

A tune upon the blue guitar
Of things exactly as they are.'

II

I cannot bring a world quite round,
Although I patch it as I can.

I sing a hero's head, large eye
And bearded bronze, but not a man,

Although I patch him as I can
And reach through him almost to man.

If to serenade almost to man
Is to miss, by that, things as they are,

Say that it is the serenade
Of a man that plays a blue guitar.

III

Ah, but to play man number one,
To drive the dagger in his heart,

To lay his brain upon the board
And pick the acrid colors out,

To nail his thought across the door,
Its wings spread wide to rain and snow,

To strike his living hi and ho,
To tick it, tock it, turn it true,

To bang it from a savage blue,
Jangling the metal of the strings . . .

IV

So that's life, then: things as they are?
It picks its way on the blue guitar.

A million people on one string?
And all their manner in the thing,

And all their manner, right and wrong,
And all their manner, weak and strong?

The feelings crazily, craftily call,
Like a buzzing of flies in autumn air,

And that's life, then: things as they are,
This buzzing of the blue guitar.

'The Man With the Blue Guitar' is part of a virtuous circle of cross-referencing in modernist art. The poem comments on Picasso's painting (*The Old Guitarist*, 1903) and David Hockney later illustrated the poem in homage to both Picasso and Stevens.

Jacques Prévert

Picasso's Promenade

On a very round plate of real porcelain
an apple poses
face to face with it
a painter of reality
vainly tries to paint
the apple as it is
but
the apple won't allow it
the apple
it has its word to say about it
and several tricks in its bag of apples
the apple
and there it is turning
on its real plate
artfully on itself
blandly without budging
and like a *Duc de Guise* who disguises himself as a gas duct
because they want to draw his portrait against his will
the apple disguises itself as a beautiful fruit in disguise

and it's then
that the painter of reality
begins to realize
that all the appearances of the apple are against him
and
like the unfortunate pauper
like the poor pauper who finds himself suddenly at the
    mercy of no matter what benevolent and charitable and
    redoubtable association of benevolence charity and
    redoubtability
the unfortunate painter of reality
then suddenly finds himself the sad prey
of a numberless crowd of associations of ideas
And the apple turning evokes the apple tree
the earthly Paradise and Eve and then Adam
a watering-can a trellis Parmentier a stairway
Canadian Hesperidian Norman apples Reinette apples and
    Appian apples
the serpent of the Tennis Court and the Oath of Apple
    Juice
and original sin
and the origins of art
and Switzerland with William Tell
and even Isaac Newton
several times prizewinner at the Exhibition of Universal
    Gravitation
and the dazed painter loses sight of his model
and falls asleep
It's just then that Picasso
who's going by there as he goes by everywhere
every day as if at home
sees the apple and the plate and the painter fallen asleep
What an idea to paint an apple
says Picasso
and Picasso eats the apple
and the apple tells him Thanks
and Picasso breaks the plate
and goes off smiling

and the painter drawn from his dreams
like a tooth
finds himself all alone again before his unfinished canvas
with right in the midst of his shattered china
the terrifying pips of reality.

Translated from the French by Lawrence Ferlinghetti.

Anthony Hecht

Matisse: Blue Interior with Two Girls – 1947

*... he lived through some of the most traumatic political events
of recorded history, the worst wars, the greatest slaughters, the
most demented rivalries of ideology, without, it seems, turning a
hair ... Perhaps Matisse did suffer from fear and loathing like the
rest of us, but there is no trace of them in his work. His studio
was a world within a world: a place of equilibrium that, for
sixty continuous years, produced images of comfort, refuge, and
balanced satisfaction.*

– Robert Hughes, *The Shock of the New*

Outside is variable May, a lawn of immediate green,
    The tree as blue as its shadow.
        A shutter angles out in charitable shade.
It is a world of yearning: we yearn for it,
    Its youthful natives yearn for one another.
        Their flesh is firm as a plum, their smooth tanned waists,
Lit through the fluttered leaves above their heads,
    Are rubbed and cinctured with this morning's bangles.
        Yet each, if we but take thought, is a lean gnomon,
A bone finger with its moral point:
    The hour, the minute, the dissolving pleasure.
        (Light fails, the shadows pool themselves in hollows.)
Here, in the stifling fragrance of mock orange,
    In the casual glance, the bright lust of the eye,
        Lies the hot spring of inevitable tears.

Within is the cool blue perfect cube of thought.
   The branched spirea carefully arranged
      Is no longer random growth: it now becomes
The object of our thought, it becomes our thought.
   The room is a retreat in which the drone
      Of the electric fan is modest, unassertive,
Faithful, as with a promise of lemonade
   And other gentle solaces of summer,
      Among which, for the two serene young girls
In this cool tank of blue is an open book
   Where they behold the pure unchanging text
      Of manifold, reverberating depth,
Quiet and tearless in its permanence.
   Deep in their contemplation the two girls,
      Regarding art, have become art themselves.
Once out of nature, they have settled here
   In this blue room of thought, beyond the reach
      Of the small brief sad ambitions of the flesh.

Moniza Alvi

I Would Like to be a Dot in a Painting by Miró

I would like to be a dot in a painting by Miró.

Barely distinguishable from other dots,
it's true, but quite uniquely placed.
And from my dark centre

I'd survey the beauty of the linescape
and wonder – would it be worthwhile
to roll myself towards the lemon stripe,

Centrally poised, and push my curves
against its edge, to get myself
a little extra attention?

But it's fine where I am.
I'll never make out what's going on
around me, and that's the joy of it.

The fact that I'm not a perfect circle
makes me more interesting in this world.
People will stare forever –

Even the most unemotional get excited.
So here I am, on the edge of animation,
a dream, a dance, a fantastic construction,

A child's adventure.
And nothing in this tawny sky
can get too close, or move too far away.

Paolo Buzzi

Stravinsky

The nebulous bursts,
the semibarbarous surges
clad in the colours of Eastertide,
and he sings and dances, mystically,
and in dancing he plunders
alders, birches, larches.
All is fairtime and market and the merry-go-round,
and the barrel organ is crammed with the noisemaker
and it is raining pure vodka
and fireworks are set off
to the sparks of a pipe
and the orchestra is flaming in the wood.
A fiddle-bow Catherine-wheel, all,
and trumpets spurt skyrockets
up to the constellations
and the drums are cracking
and the tom-toms slap the stars

with terrible golden blows.
All turns to dizziness,
the moujik idiocy
vomits divine cacophonies,
the night grows sad with stars
sluggish as living chains upon the steppes.
Peace! It is Night!, O Black Earth!
But the music surges rowdily forth
from the red and inexhaustible crater.

Translated from the Italian by
Samuel Putnam.

Jackie Kay

The Red Graveyard

There are some stones that open in the night like flowers
Down in the red graveyard where Bessie haunts her lovers.
There are stones that shake and weep in the heart of night
Down in the red graveyard where Bessie haunts her lovers.

Why do I remember the blues?
I am five or six or seven in the back garden;
the window is wide open;
her voice is slow motion through the heavy summer air.
Jelly roll. Kitchen man. Sausage roll. Frying pan.

Inside the house where I used to be myself,
her voice claims the rooms. In the best room even,
something has changed the shape of my silence.
Why do I remember her voice and not my own mother's?
Why do I remember the blues?

My mother's voice. What was it like?
A flat stone for skitting. An old rock.
Long long grass. Asphalt. Wind. Hail.

Cotton. Linen. Salt. Treacle.
I think it was a peach.
I heard it down to the ribbed stone.

I am coming down the stairs in my parent's house.
I am five or six or seven. There is fat thick wallpaper
I always caress, bumping flower into flower.
She is singing. (Did they play anyone else ever?)
My father's feet tap a shiny beat on the floor.

Christ, my father says, that's some voice she's got.
I pick up the record cover. And now. This is slow motion.
My hand swoops, glides, swoops again.
I pick up the cover and my fingers are all over her face.
Her black face. Her magnificent black face.
That's some voice. His shoes dancing on the floor.

There are some stones that open in the night like flowers
Down in the red graveyard where Bessie haunts her lovers.
There are stones that shake and weep in the heart of night
Down in the red graveyard where Bessie haunts her lovers.

Bessie: Bessie Smith (1895–1937) is regarded as the greatest blues singer of all time.

Robert Wrigley

Torch Songs

I would speak of that grief
perfected by the saxophone, the slow
muted trombone, the low unforgettable cornet.
Theirs were the paths we followed
into the sexual forest, the witch's spellbound cabin,
the national anthems of longing.

Rhythm is the plod of the human heart,
that aimless walker down deserted streets
at midnight, where a tavern's neon keeps the pulse.
A horn man licks the blood
in tow, heavy and smooth,
and a song is in the veins like whiskey.

Does it matter then that men have written
the heartbreaks women make hurt?
That Holiday and Smith sang for one
but to the other? Or is everything equal
in the testimonies of power and loss?

Now your eyes are closed,
your head leaned back, and off to one side.
Living is a slow dance you know
you're dreaming, but the chill at your neck
is real, the soft, slow breathing
of someone you might always love.

Rosemary Tonks

The Sofas, Fogs and Cinemas

I have lived it, and lived it,
My nervous, luxury civilization,
My sugar-loving nerves have battered me to pieces.

. . . Their idea of literature is hopeless.
Make them drink their own poetry!
Let them eat their gross novel, full of mud.

It's quiet; just the fresh, chilly weather . . . and he
Gets up from his dead bedroom, and comes in here
And digs himself into the sofa.
He stays there up to two hours in the hole – and talks
– Straight into the large subjects, he faces up to *everything*

It's . . . . . . damnably depressing.
(That great lavatory coat . . . the cigarillo burning
In the little dish . . . And when he calls out: 'Ha!'
Madness! – you no longer possess your own furniture.)

On my bad days (and I'm being broken
At this very moment) I speak of my ambitions . . . and he
Becomes intensely gloomy, with the look of something jugged,
Morose, sour, mouldering away, with lockjaw. . . .

I grow coarser; and more modern (*I*, who am driven mad
By my ideas; who go nowhere;
Who dare not leave my frontdoor, lest an idea . . .)
All right. I admit everything, everything!

Oh yes, the opera (Ah, but the cinema)
He particularly enjoys it, enjoys it *horribly*, when someone's ill
At the last minute; and they specially fly in
A new, gigantic, Dutch soprano. He wants to help her
With her arias.   Old goat! Blasphemer!
He wants to help her with her arias!

No, I . . . go to the cinema,
I particularly like it when the fog is thick, the street
Is like a hole in an old coat, and the light is brown as laudanum.
. . . the fogs! the fogs! The cinemas
Where the criminal shadow-literature flickers over our faces,
The screen is spread out like a thundercloud – that bangs
And splashes you with acid . . . or lies derelict,
                              with lighted waters in it,
And in the silence, drips and crackles – taciturn, luxurious.
. . . The drugged and battered Philistines
Are all around you in the auditorium . . .

And he . . . is somewhere else, in his dead bedroom clothes,
He wants to make me think his thoughts
And they will be *enormous*, dull – (just the sort
To keep away from).

. . . when I see that cigarillo, when I see it . . . smoking
And he wants to face the international situation . . .
Lunatic rages! Blackness! Suffocation!

– All this sitting about in cafés to calm down
Simply wears me out. And their idea of literature!
The idiotic cut of the stanzas; the novels, full up, gross.

I have lived it, and I know too much.
My café-nerves are breaking me
With black, exhausting information.

Yevgeny Yevtushenko

To Charlie Chaplin

In parting with Chaplin –
                              there's no parting with Charlie.
He freezes, he starves –
                         he's alive, as in the beginning,
when in preposterous shoes,
                               shedding their soles,
he pounded out against Klondike frosts
                                    a tap dance of mortal sadness.
And, too eager,
               for the ludicrous,
                              for the spicy,
boring holes
          through the screen
                            with its eyes,
a world drowning in blood
                         grasped for Chaplin's cane,
                                              like a straw.
They darned the screens.
                    The generations changed.

Why
    laugh
        at tormented Charlie?
They should have
           guffawed
               murderously
at Hitler
      in time –
who might never have grown
             from a clown
                 into a führer . . .
And laughter at tragedy
          became unredeemable guilt.
So little is funny
      when the hideous
           for us is humor.
Comic sparks,
      as though real,
           flashed in millions of retinas.
And the one man not laughing at Charlie –
              was Charlie himself.
And Chaplin got an answer from Charlie,
why a never-ending callous laugh
pursued the little man?
Because he was for all that a man.
I froze and hungered.
         Both tanks and dogs
             snarled at me.
I saw fascism –
      and not the living Christ.
But if there had not been
         the sorrowful little black-haired imp, Charlie –
I would not be the same
        and the era would not be the same.
Parting with Charlie –
      is parting with a whole era,
and how good it is
      that now no one finds this funny.

Abandoning the alien movie
                    of lying sounds,
he departs for death
                    into a silent film that's his alone.
Without Chaplin people already
                         have started to be a little bored,
but Charlie remains,
                    and we will wait a little,
until for Chaplin
                Charlie clicks glasses
                              with the universe,
his empty shoe
           filled with Klondike rain.

Translated from the Russian by Albert C. Todd.

Robert Crawford

Talkies

Already there is gossip in Hollywood
About something new. Even the stars will need tests.

In the beginning was the caption,
Ringlets, a balletic flow of knees;

Crowds opened their mouths, then closed them.
Now some will never be heard of again

If between camera-loving, soundless lips
Is a foreign accent, or that timbre of voice which means

The microphone doesn't like you.
Friends swell into enormous heart-throbs:

Their voices are good. 'Retraining?
Let me get you another drink.'

At the neat wrought-iron table,
Legs crossed, she stares at the studio,

A hangar, a camp, a silo. Work
Means something else now, something other

Than what she set her heart on, black and white silk, panache.
With a longer lifespan she might become

A nostalgia executive, a Last of the, a rediscovery.
But the dates are wrong; leaving her speechless

At this technology crackling over California
Eagerly, far out of sight.

Frank O'Hara

To the Film Industry in Crisis

Not you, lean quarterlies and swarthy periodicals
with your studious incursions toward the pomposity of ants,
nor you, experimental theatre in which Emotive Fruition
is wedding Poetic Insight perpetually, nor you,
promenading Grand Opera, obvious as an ear (though you
are close to my heart), but you, Motion Picture Industry,
it's you I love!

In times of crisis, we must all decide again and again
        whom we love.
And give credit where it's due: not to my starched nurse,
        who taught me
how to be bad and not bad rather than good (and has
        lately availed
herself of this information), not to the Catholic Church
which is at best an oversolemn introduction to cosmic
        entertainment,

not to the American Legion, which hates everybody, but
    to you,
glorious Silver Screen, tragic Technicolor, amorous
    Cinemascope,
stretching Vistavision and startling Stereophonic Sound,
    with all
your heavenly dimensions and reverberations and
    iconoclasms! To
Richard Barthelmess as the 'tol'able' boy barefoot and
    in pants,
Jeanette MacDonald of the flaming hair and lips and long,
    long neck,
Sue Carroll as she sits for eternity on the damaged fender
    of a car
and smiles, Ginger Rogers with her pageboy bob like a
    sausage
on her shuffling shoulders, peach-melba-voiced Fred Astaire
    of the feet,
Eric von Stroheim, the seducer of mountain-climbers'
    gasping spouses,
the Tarzans, each and every one of you (I cannot bring
    myself to prefer
Johnny Weissmuller to Lex Barker, I cannot!), Mae West
    in a furry sled,
her bordello radiance and bland remarks, Rudolph Valentino
    of the moon,
its crushing passions, and moonlike, too, the gentle
    Norma Shearer,
Miriam Hopkins dropping her champagne glass off Joel
    McCrea's yacht
and crying into the dappled sea, Clark Gable rescuing
    Gene Tierney
from Russia and Allan Jones rescuing Kitty Carlisle from
    Harpo Marx,
Cornel Wilde coughing blood on the piano keys while
    Merle Oberon berates,
Marilyn Monroe in her little spike heels reeling through
    Niagara Falls,

Joseph Cotten puzzling and Orson Welles puzzled and
    Dolores del Rio
eating orchids for lunch and breaking mirrors, Gloria
    Swanson reclining,
and Jean Harlow reclining and wiggling, and Alice Faye
    reclining
and wiggling and singing, Myrna Loy being calm and wise,
    William Powell
in his stunning urbanity, Elizabeth Taylor blossoming, yes,
    to you

and to all you others, the great, the near-great, the
    featured, the extras
who pass quickly and return in dreams saying your one
    or two lines, my love!
Long may you illumine space with your marvellous
    appearances, delays
and enunciations, and may the money of the world
    glitteringly cover you
as you rest after a long day under the kleig lights with
    your faces
in packs for our edification, the way the clouds come often
    at night
but the heavens operate on the star system. It is a divine
    precedent
you perpetuate! Roll on, reels of celluloid, as the great
    earth rolls on!

William Scammell

The Act

Watching all those sexy Czechs
up on the wide, wide screen
with supernatural sound effects
descanting on their lightness of being

as one girl, then another, strips
down to her middle C
while the moving picture slows its steps
round pure anatomy

and Russian tanks roll into Prague
(montage, *fff* on the bass)
and girls like glossy snaps in *Vogue*
don't even think of interruptus

I wonder where the babies are,
who pays the bills, and stuff like that,
which may not rate a heavenly choir
or slow-mo-on-the-cello shot

but still the orchestra must eat
between engagements, brush its teeth
if ever they're to consummate
more than the bubble in the bath.

The act, the act! A man invades.
A woman and a country yields.
Middle Europe's torn to shreds.
The lovers kick their lovely heels

up in the sky, and squirm to die
just where the flute runs out of breath,
a nymphs-and-shepherds victory
over the stodgy march of death.

Hold on a bit. There's more to love,
invasion, exile, war and fate
than six bars of Rachmaninov
and humping in a bowler hat

and ideas, in their posy smalls,
chiaroscuro of dark nipples
cutely enamoured of themselves
and questionable parallels.

No tanks came here, yet still and all
the Iron Lady drove to town,
rumbling up against Whitehall,
shooting the consensus down.

Our chief of women, under law,
beseeching everybody's bowels,
who strips state assets from the poor
and has the hots for Samuel Smiles.

She wastes no time on levellers,
Fifth Monarchy men, the liberal wets.
Businessmen and buccaneers
are all she knows of earthly Saints.

While parliament sinks to its knees
and mumbles spells with Tony Benn
the city booms, the placemen squeeze
more blood out of the national stone.

And, like the Czechs, we take to sex
or other fiddles, impotent
as Harold in his Gannex macs
or poor Achilles in his tent.

Age of the TV anchorman,
the rock star, and the page 3 girl.
The fast buck points the way to Zion.
A swelling that you'll never feel
dispenses all the satisfaction
you ain't got, and never will.

Prague meets London; Cracow, Leeds.
Not synonyms, exactly. No!
But take a look at what succeeds
in the art house, next time you go.

The film is *The Unbearable Lightness of Being*, 1987, adapted from Milan Kundera's
novel of the same name.

THE DREAM OF WEARING SHORTS
FOREVER: SPORT & LEISURE

In the last decade of the century, sport suddenly achieved a new prominence: as surrogate warfare, as exemplary behaviour, as the engine of huge consumer industries. For many in the late twentieth century, leisure pursuits have become the real point of life and most activities have been celebrated in verse. Poets have often used sport as a metaphor for their own craft. Both William Carlos Williams' opening poem here and Lawrence Sail's snooker poem stress the inherent fleetingness and ultimate insignificance of all such activities: 'doubt dogs the game', but the dream persists.

William Carlos Williams

At the Ball Game

The crowd at the ball game
is moved uniformly

by a spirit of uselessness
which delights them –

all the exciting detail
of the chase

and the escape, the error
the flash of genius –

all to no end save beauty
the eternal –

So in detail they, the crowd,
are beautiful

for this
to be warned against

saluted and defied –
It is alive, venomous

it smiles grimly
its words cut –

The flashy female with her
mother, gets it –

The Jew gets it straight – it
is deadly, terrifying –

It is the Inquisition, the
Revolution

It is beauty itself
that lives

day by day in them
idly –

This is
the power of their faces

It is summer, it is the solstice
the crowd is

cheering, the crowd is laughing
in detail

permanently, seriously
without thought

John Whitworth

Tinned Strawberries

A Wimbledon late sky like streaky bacon
   As the last Brit dies on Centre. Out on 3
Wendy Turnbull and six-gun Riessen take on
   Old stoneface Tony Roche and Miss Bunge,
Intent and pink and fair. Roche's backhand,
   Still zonking nicely, raises clouds of dust.
A Corporation cart digests a sack and
   Roche pauses, grunts, 'They've come for me at last,'
Then flattens Wendy with a skidding bounce.
   How pretty tennis is, how instantly
Forgettable. I saw Lew Hoad once
   In ten inch quavering black and white. *Who's he?*
Riessen applauds. Roche and Miss Bunge win.
The autograph collectors amble in.

Wole Soyinka

Muhammad Ali at the Ringside, 1985

The arena is darkened. A feast of blood
Will follow duly; the spotlights have been borrowed
For a while. These ringside prances
Merely serve to whet the appetite. Gladiators,
Clad tonight in formal mufti, customized,
Milk recognition, savor the night-off, show-off
Rites. Ill fitted in this voyeur company,
The desperate arm wrap of the tiring heart
Gives place to social hugs, the slow count
One to ten to a snappy 'Give me five!'
Toothpaste grins replace the death-mask
Rubber gumshield grimaces. Promiscuous
Peck-a-cheek supplants the maestro's peek-a-boo.

The roped arena waits; an umpire tests the floor,
Tests whiplash boundaries of the rope.
The gallant's exhibition rounds possess
These foreplay moments. Gloves in silk-white sheen
Rout lint and leather. Paco Rabanne rules the air.
A tight-arsed soubriette checks her placard smile
To sign the rounds for blood and gore.

Eased from the navel of Bitch-Mother Fame
A microphone, neck-ruffed silver filigree – as one
Who would usurp the victor's garland – stabs the air
For instant prophecies. In cosy insulation, bathed
In teleglow, distant homes have built
Their own vicarious rings – the forecast claimed
Four million viewers on the cable deal alone;
Much 'bread' was loaded on the scales
At weighing hour – till scores are settled. One
Will leave the fickle womb tonight
Smeared in combat fluids, a broken fetus.
The other, toned in fire, a dogged phoenix
Oblivious of the slow countdown of inner hurts
Will thrust his leaden fists in air
Night prince of the world of dreams.

One sits still. His silence is a dying count.
At last the lens acknowledges the tested
Hulk that dominates, even in repose
The giddy rounds of furs and diamond pins.
A brief salute – the camera is kind,
Discreetly pans, and masks the doubletalk
Of medicine men – 'Has the syndrome
But not the consequence.' Promoters, handlers
It's time to throw in the towel – Parkinson's
Polysyllables have failed to tease a rhyme
From the once nimble Louisville Lips.

The camera flees, distressed. But not before
The fire of battle flashes in those eyes
Rekindled by the moment's urge to center stage.

He rules the night space even now, bestrides
The treacherous domain with thighs of bronze,
A dancing mural of delights. Oh Ali! Ale-e-e . . .

What music hurts the massive head tonight, Ali!
The drums, the tin cans, the guitars and *mbira* of Zaire?
Aa-lee! Aa-lee! Aa-lee *Bomaye! Bomaye!*
The Rumble in the Jungle? Beauty and the Beast?
Roll call of Bum-a-Month? The rope-a-dope?
The Thrilla in Manila? – Ah-lee! Ah-lee!
'The closest thing to death,' you said. Was that
The greatest, saddest prophesy of all? Oh, Ali!

Black tarantula whose antics hypnotize the foe!
Butterfly sideslipping death from rocket probes.
Bee whose sting, unsheathed, picks the teeth
Of the raging hippopotamus, then fans
The jaw's convergence with its flighty wings.
Needle that threads the snapping fangs
Of crocodiles, knots the tusks of elephants
On rampage. Cricket that claps and chirrups
Round the flailing horn of the rhinoceros,
Then shuffles, does a bugalloo, tap-dances on its tip.
Space that yields, then drowns the intruder
In showers of sparks – oh Ali! Ali!
Esu with faces turned to all four compass points
Astride a weather vane; they sought to trap him,
Slapped the wind each time. He brings a message –
All know the messenger, the neighborhood is roused –

Yet no one sees his face, he waits for no reply,
Only that combination three-four calling card,
The wasp-tail legend: I've been here and gone.
Mortar that goads the pestle: Do you call that
Pounding? The yam is not yet smooth –
Pound, dope, pound! When I have eaten the yam,
I'll chew the fiber that once called itself
A pestle! Warrior who said, 'I will not fight,'
And proved a prophet's call to arms against a war.

Cassius Marcellus, Warrior, Muhammad Prophet,
Flesh is clay, all, all too brittle mould.
The bout is over. Frayed and split and autographed,
The gloves are hung up in the Hall of Fame –
Still loaded, even from that first blaze of gold
And glory. Awed multitudes will gaze,
New questers feast on these mementos
And from their shell-shocked remnants
Reinvoke the spell. But the sorcerer is gone,
The lion withdrawn to a lair of time and space
Inaccessible as the sacred lining of a crown
When kings were kings, and lords of rhyme and pace.
The enchantment is over but the spell remains.

Glyn Maxwell

Sport Story of a Winner

For Alun and Amanda Maxwell

He was a great ambassador for the game.
                    He had a simple name.
His name was known in households other than ours.
                    But we knew other stars.
We could recall as many finalists
                    as many panellists.
But when they said this was his Waterloo,
                    we said it was ours too.

His native village claimed him as its own,
                    as did his native town,
adopted city and preferred retreat.
                    So did our own street.
When his brave back was up against the wall,
                    our televisions all
got us shouting, and that did the trick.
                    Pretty damn quick.

His colours were his secret, and his warm-up
                              raindance, and his time up
Flagfell in the Hook District, and his diet
                              of herbal ice, and his quiet
day-to-day existence, and his training,
                              and never once explaining
his secret was his secret too, and his book,
                              and what on earth he took

that meant-to-be-magic night in mid-November.
                              You must remember.
His game crumbled, he saw something somewhere.
                              He pointed over there.
The referees soothed him, had to hold things up.
                              The ribbons on the Cup
were all his colour, but the Romanoff
                              sadly tugged them off.

We saw it coming didn't we. We knew
                              something he didn't know.
It wasn't the first time a lad was shown
                              basically bone.
Another one will come, and he'll do better.
                              I see him now – he'll set a
never-to-be-beaten time that'll last forever!
                              Won't he. Trevor.

Les Murray

The Dream of Wearing Shorts Forever

To go home and wear shorts forever
in the enormous paddocks, in that warm climate,
adding a sweater when winter soaks the grass,

to camp out along the river bends
for good, wearing shorts, with a pocketknife,
a fishing line and matches,

or there where the hills are all down, below the plain,
to sit around in shorts at evening
on the plank verandah –

If the cardinal points of costume
are Robes, Tat, Rig and Scunge,
where are shorts in this compass?

They are never Robes
as other bareleg outfits have been:
the toga, the kilt, the lava-lava,
the Mahatma's cotton dhoti;

archbishops and field marshals
at their ceremonies never wear shorts.
The very word
means underpants in North America.

Shorts can be Tat,
Land-Rovering bush-environmental tat,
socio-political ripped-and-metal-stapled tat,
solidarity-with-the-Third-World tat tvam asi,

likewise track-and-field shorts worn to parties
and the further humid, modelling negligée
of the Kingdom of Flaunt,
that unchallenged aristocracy.

More plainly climatic, shorts
are farmers' rig leathery with salt and bonemeal,
are sailors' and branch bankers' rig,
the crisp golfing style
of our youngest male National Costume.

Most loosely, they are Scunge,
ancient Bengal bloomers or moth-eaten hot pants
worn with a former shirt,
feet, beach sand, hair
and a paucity of signals.

Scunge, which is real negligée
housework in a swimsuit, pyjamas worn all day,
is holiday, is freedom from ambition.
Scunge makes you invisible
to the world and yourself.

The entropy of costume,
scunge can get you conquered by more vigorous cultures
and help you to notice it less.

Satisfied ambition, defeat, true unconcern,
the wish and the knack for self-forgetfulness
all fall within the scunge ambit
wearing board shorts or similar;
it is a kind of weightlessness.

Unlike public nakedness, which in Westerners
is deeply circumstantial, relaxed as exam time,
artless and equal as the corsetry of a hussar regiment,

shorts and their plain like
are an angelic nudity,
spirituality with pockets!
A double updraft as you drop from branch to pool!

Ideal for getting served last
in shops of the temperate zone
they are also ideal for going home, into space,
into time, to farm the mind's Sabine acres
for product or subsistence.

Now that everyone who yearned to wear long pants
has essentially achieved them,
long pants, which have themselves been underwear
repeatedly, and underground more than once,
it is time perhaps to cherish the culture of shorts,

to moderate grim vigour
with the knobble of bare knees,
to cool bareknuckle feet in inland water,
slapping flies with a book on solar wind
or a patient bare hand, beneath the cadjiput trees,

to be walking meditatively
among green timber, through the grassy forest
towards a calm sea
and looking across to more of that great island
and the further topics.

Steve Ellis

Gardeners' Question Time

Well, after lagging your tubers
nest them deep in the airing-cupboard.
If you cadge your wife's old vest
it snugs 'em down lovely,
you'll get interest on your warmth in May.

Shallots, the wardrobe: my great-uncle
would entertain no other store.
In the darkness, festoon them on hangers,
you'll have to evict the wife's hats
but you'll be munching on plumpness in May.

A pair of knickers strains barrel-water
best, and I'll say something else:
if you can borrow your wife's bra
it's a smashing cradle to ripen peaches,
trembling on the washing-line in June,

scarcely reining their softness, for you.
As for mulch, there's nothing matches
blood & bone. If she's dead lately,
put your wife through the shredder,
(ask her first) and scatter it thick.

You'll be in that deckchair in August,
lungs full of lush green peace,
just you, your life, and the shed. Heaven.

Lawrence Sail

Snooker Players

They whistle the fine smoke
Of blue dust from the cue,
Suave as gunslingers, never
Twitching one muscle too few.
At ease, holstering their thumbs
In trimmest waistcoats, they await
Their opponent's slip, the easiest
of shots miscalculated.
Their sleek heads shine, spangled
With the sure knowledge of every angle.

Once at the table, they bend
In level reverence to squint
At globe after globe, each
With its window of light glinting
On cushioned greener than green,
The rounded image of reason.
One click and cosmology thrives,
All colours know their seasons
And tenderly God in white gloves
Retrieves each fallen planet with love.

Watching them, who could believe
In the world's lack of balance?
Tucked in this pocket of light
Everything seems to make sense –
Where grace is an endless break
And justice, skill repaid,
And all eclipses are merely
A heavenly snooker displayed.
Yet all around, in the framing
Darkness, doubt dogs the game.

John Updike

Ex-Basketball Player

Pearl Avenue runs past the high-school lot,
Bends with the trolley tracks, and stops, cut off
Before it has a chance to go two blocks,
At Colonel McComsky Plaza. Berth's Garage
Is on the corner facing west, and there,
Most days, you'll find Flick Webb, who helps Berth out.

Flick stands tall among the idiot pumps –
Five on a side, the old bubble-head style,
Their rubber elbows hanging loose and low.
One's nostrils are two S's, and his eyes
An E and O. And one is squat, without
A head at all – more of a football type.

Once Flick played for the high-school team, the Wizards.
He was good: in fact, the best. In '46
He bucketed three hundred ninety points,
A county record still. The ball loved Flick.
I saw him rack up thirty-eight or forty
In one home game. His hands were like wild birds.

He never learned a trade, he just sells gas,
Checks oil, and changes flats. Once in a while,
As a gag, he dribbles an inner tube,
But most of us remember anyway.
His hands are fine and nervous on the lug wrench.
It makes no difference to the lug wrench, though.

Off work, he hangs around Mae's Luncheonette.
Grease-gray and kind of coiled, he plays pinball,
Smokes those thin cigars, nurses lemon phosphates.
Flick seldom says a word to Mae, just nods
Beyond her face toward bright applauding tiers
Of Necco Wafers, Nibs, and Juju Beads.

NEW THINGS UNDER THE SUN:
SCIENCE & TECHNOLOGY

From quantum theory and Relativity at the beginning to genetic engin-
eering and the digital revolution at the end, science has been the
dominant cultural force of the century. Its enormous power, in terms
of both its leverage on the material world and its intellectual reach,
have been threatening to the claim of the arts to go deeper than superficial
entertainment. The quarrel (which reached a peak in the acrimonious
debate between C. P. Snow and F. R. Leavis in 1959) is now sinking,
with awareness of science, and its literary potential, increasing thanks
to the books of scientific popularizers such as Richard Dawkins and
Stephen Jay Gould. Specious links between poetry and science were
claimed by early Modernists – William Carlos Williams said: 'It may
seem presumptive to state that such an apparently minor activity as a
movement in verse construction could be an indication of Einstein's
discoveries in the relativity of our measurements of physical matter . . .
but such is the fact.' No such parallel can be drawn but science in its
exploration of micro-worlds and conceptual landscapes can now be
seen to provide an enlargement of poetry's subject matter.

Abba Kovner

The Scientists are Wrong

They're wrong, the scientists. The universe wasn't created
billions of years ago.
The universe is created every day.

The scientists are wrong to claim
the universe was created from one primordial
substance.
The world is created every day
from various substances with nothing in common.

Only the relative proportion of their masses,
like the elements of sorrow and hope,
make them companions
and curbstones. I'm sorry

I have to get up, in all modesty, and disagree
with what is so sure and recognized by experts:
that there's no speed faster than the speed of light,
when I and my lighted flesh
just noticed something else right here –

whose speed is even greater than the speed of light
and which also returns,
though not in a straight line, because of the curve of the universe
or because of the innocence of God.

And if we connect all this to an equation, according to the rules,
    maybe
it will make sense that I refuse to believe that her voice
and everything I always cherished
and everything so real and suddenly
lost,
is actually lost forever.

Translated from the Hebrew by Shirley Kaufman.

Boris Slutsky

Physics and Poetry

Looks like physics is in honor,
Looks like poetry is not.
It's not dry figures that matter;
Universal law, that's what.

It means that we failed in something,
Something,

which was ours to do!
It means that our cute iambics
Had weak wings and hardly flew.
Unlike Pegasus, our horses
Do not soar nor even trot . . .
That's why physics is in honor,
That's why poetry is not.

Any argument is pointless,
But even if there is one:
It is nothing so dismaying;
Rather it's amusing fun
To observe the foam-like falling
Away of our rhymes and rhythms
And to watch how greatness
                                        staidly
Retreats into logarithms.

Translated from the Russian by
Vladimir Markov and Merrill Sparks.

Wisława Szymborska

π

π deserves our full admiration
three point one four one.
All its following digits are also non-recurring,
five nine two because it never ends.
It cannot be grasped *six five three five* at a glance,
eight nine in a calculus
seven nine in imagination,
or even *three two three eight* in a conceit, that is, a comparison
four six with anything else
two six four three in the world.
The longest snake on earth breaks off after several metres.
Likewise, though at greater length, do fabled snakes.

The series comprising π
doesn't stop at the edge of the sheet,
it can stretch across the table, through the air,
through the wall, leaf, bird's nest, clouds, straight to heaven,
through all the heavens' chasms and distensions.
How short, how mouse-like, is the comet's tail!
How frail a star's ray, that it bends in any bit of space!
Meanwhile, *two three fifteen three hundred nineteen*
my telephone number the size of your shirt
the year nineteen hundred and seventy three sixth floor
the number of inhabitants sixty-five pennies
the waist measurement two fingers a charade a code,
in which *singing still dost soar, and soaring ever singest*
and *please be calm*
and also *heaven and earth shall pass away*,
but not π, no, certainly not,
she's still on with her passable *five*
above-average *eight*
the not-final *seven*
urging, yes, urging a sluggish eternity
to persevere.

Translated from the Polish by Adam Czerniawski.

Howard Nemerov

Figures of Thought

To lay the logarithmic spiral on
Sea-shell and leaf alike, and see it fit,
To watch the same idea work itself out
In the fighter pilot's steepening, tightening turn
Onto his target, setting up the kill,
And in the flight of certain wall-eyed bugs
Who cannot see to fly straight into death
But have to cast their sidelong glance at it
And come but cranking to the candle's flame —

How secret that is, and how privileged
One feels to find the same necessity
Ciphered in forms diverse and otherwise
Without kinship – that is the beautiful
In Nature as in art, not obvious,
Not inaccessible, but just between.

It may diminish some our dry delight
To wonder if everything we are and do
Lies subject to some little law like that;
Hidden in nature, but not deeply so.

Miroslav Holub

Žito the Magician

To amuse His Royal Majesty he will change water into wine.
Frogs into footmen. Beetles into bailiffs. And make a Minister
out of a rat. He bows, and daisies grow from his finger-tips.
And a talking bird sits on his shoulder.

There.

Think up something else, demands His Royal Majesty.
Think up a black star. So he thinks up a black star.
Think up dry water. So he thinks up dry water.
Think up a river bound with straw-bands. So he does.

There.

Then along comes a student and asks: Think up sine alpha
greater than one.

And Žito grows pale and sad: Terribly sorry. Sine is
between plus one and minus one. Nothing you can do about that.
And he leaves the great royal empire, quietly weaves his way
through the throng of courtiers, to his home
                                                    in a nutshell.

Translated from the Czech by George Theiner.

Sheenagh Pugh

Bumblebees and the Scientific Method

A scientist, a man of parts,
(some of which worked, in fits and starts),
by using certain apparatus
proved bees could not be aviators.
There was no doubt, declared our hero,
the fundamental laws of aero-
nautics, -dynamics and whatever
must soon convince the unbeliever
that bees were built to such a model,
they scarcely could do more than waddle.
The ratio of their body weight
to wing-span, he could demonstrate,
precluded take-off, much less flight.
Colleagues allowed his sums were right:
Professors, Fellows, Doctors, Tutors,
sweating away at their computers,
confirmed our man's results *in toto*,
and grudgingly agreed to go to
honour his triumph at a party,
(nobody really loves a smarty).
While all acclaimed his theories,
nobody thought to tell the bees,
who, never having been to college,
nor stayed abreast of modern knowledge,
kept up a stunning imitation
of wing-powered aerial navigation.

Until recently, analysis of insects in flight revealed only about one-third to one-half of
the lift necessary to support their weight. In December 1996 Charles Ellington, a
Cambridge zoologist, reported finding a spiral vortex mechanism along the leading
edge of insects' wings that could produce one and a half times the lift needed to overcome
its weight (*Nature*, Vol. 384, p. 626, 1996).

Douglas Stewart

From *Rutherford*

Mostly too busy to think – too busy thinking.
But thinking was doing; there was such satisfaction
Watching those tiny comets darting and winking
It really left no time for speculation.
Thought would go outwards, expansion; his was a shrinking,
How to get mind and hand so small, that was the problem,
That in one final thrust of concentration
They would be able to move inside an atom.

It was the most fascinating thing in the world
And out of it too, like watching some new star:
To go in there and watch the atom unfold
Its innermost secrets, right to the very core
Where star within star the racing electrons whirled
Circling that radiant centre, the white-hot nucleus,
– Held in your hands, almost, huge as you were,
Pierced by your thought like a neutron. It was miraculous

How out of steel and glass, coiled wire and lead,
The common stuff of the earth (what else could you use?),
Mere human powers could have conceived and made
These infinitely delicate instruments to pierce
Clean through matter to its end. But that was his trade;
He had it if from anyone from his father
And sometimes it seemed, alone in the universe
In the laboratory at night, they worked together,

That craftsman's hands still moving inside his own.
It was a haunted place, this tower of knowledge,
Calm with old books but wild with thoughts unknown.
All dark except for lamps like lights of courage
Where lonely scholars sought for truth in stone.
It shut the whole world out from a man and his work;
But while the white stars glittered above the college
A wheel moved somewhere far away in the dark –

And huge it was, and turned with a soft roar
Of air and water, and battered the dark and scattered
Dewdrops like stars and seemed itself the core
Of that clear atom of night whose peace it shattered
Under the mountain towering there once more!
It seemed the Rutherfords' fate to start things moving.
Yet how the white snow sparkled, the stream glittered,
How tranquilly when his mind moved into morning

That waterwheel of his father's lifted up
Water and sunlight in its wooden hands
Where the weed grew like hair, then let them drop
Back to the stream that sang on over the sands.
Once it had turned that swamp of flax to rope
Useful to man, the river was free to be river
And on its own wheel of boulders wove its strands
Of silver light through green Taranaki for ever –

Such thousands of miles from this great shadowy room
Where only, minutely exploding, the alpha particles
Flashed on the screen like sun-motes. But when he had time,
When he was quiet like this, alone among miracles,
Sometimes indeed his mind went wandering home
And, following his father's, his life seemed queer and fated.
For while, even now, dripping its light like icicles
Under the mountain, that wheel still turned as he waited,

And farmers' drays ran jolting through frost and mud
And far by emerald river and ferny hill
In long-lost Nelson wheels that his father had made,
And good wheels too, were serving the people still
– They carried the milk; they ground the flour for bread –
He too was making a wheel; but not for the water,
Not for the road or the mill, but such a wheel
He knew would carry man and all his future.

In 1917 the New Zealand physicist Ernest Rutherford, working at the Cavendish Laboratory in Cambridge, achieved the first atomic fission by bombarding nitrogen with alpha particles (helium nuclei).

Gwen Harwood

Schrödinger's Cat Preaches to the Mice

To A.D. Hope

Silk-whispering of knife on stone,
due sacrifice, and my meat came.
Caressing whispers, then my own
choice among laps by leaping flame.

What shape is space? Space will put on
the shape of any cat. Know this:
my servant Schrödinger is gone
before me to prepare a place.

So worship me, the Chosen One
in the great thought-experiment.
As in a grave I will lie down
and wait for the Divine Event.

The lid will close. I will retire
from sight, curl up and say Amen
to geiger counter, amplifier,
and a cylinder of HCN.

When will the geiger counter feel
decay, its pulse be amplified
to a current that removes the seal
from the cylinder of cyanide?

Dead or alive? The case defies
all questions. Let the lid be locked.
Truth, from your little beady eyes,
is hidden. I will not be mocked.

Quantum mechanics has no place
for what's there without observation.

Classical physics cannot trace
spontaneous disintegration.

If the box holds a living cat
no scientist on earth can tell.
But I'll be waiting, sleek and fat.
Verily, all will not be well

if, to the peril of your souls,
you think me gone. Know that this house
is mine, that kittens by mouse-holes
wait, who have never seen a mouse.

Erwin Schrödinger (1887–1961): one of the originators of quantum mechanics in 1926. His famous thought experiment, the cat paradox, hinges on the random nature of radioactive decay. A cat is sealed in a box with an ampoule of cyanide which is released when a single radioactive particle is emitted. There is an equal probability at any time that the particle will or will not have been emitted. Until we open the box the cat is considered to be both dead and alive. Opening the box makes its mind up for it.

John Updike

Cosmic Gall

Every second, hundreds of billions of these neutrinos pass through each square inch of our bodies, coming from above during the day and from below at night, when the sun is shining on the other side of the earth!
　　　　　– from 'An Explanatory Statement on Elementary Particle
　　　　　　　Physics,' by M. A. Ruderman and A. H. Rosenfeld,
　　　　　　　　　　　　　　　in *American Scientist*

Neutrinos, they are very small.
　　They have no charge and have no mass
And do not interact at all.
The earth is just a silly ball
　　To them, through which they simply pass,
Like dustmaids down a drafty hall
　　Or photons through a sheet of glass.

They snub the most exquisite gas,
Ignore the most substantial wall,
    Cold-shoulder steel and sounding brass,
Insult the stallion in his stall,
    And, scorning barriers of class,
Infiltrate you and me! Like tall
And painless guillotines, they fall
    Down through our heads into the grass.
At night, they enter at Nepal
    And pierce the lover and his lass
From underneath the bed – you call
    It wonderful; I call it crass.

Marianne Moore

Four Quartz Crystal Clocks

There are four vibrators, the world's exactest clocks;
    and these quartz time-pieces that tell
time intervals to other clocks,
    these worksless clocks work well;
independently the same, kept in
    the 41° Bell
        Laboratory time

vault. Checked by a comparator with Arlington,
    they punctualize the 'radio,
cinéma', and 'presse', – a group the
    Giraudoux truth-bureau
of hoped-for accuracy has termed
    'instruments of truth'. We know –
        as Jean Giraudoux says,

certain Arabs have not heard – that Napoleon
    is dead; that a quartz prism when
the temperature changes, feels
    the change and that the then

electrified alternate edges
    oppositely charged, threaten
        careful timing; so that

this water-clear crystal as the Greeks used to say,
    this 'clear ice' must be kept at the
same coolness. Repetition, with
    the scientist, should be
synonymous with accuracy.
    The lemur-student can see
        that an aye-aye is not

an angwan-tíbo, potto, or loris. The sea-
    side burden should not embarrass
the bell-boy with the buoy-ball
    endeavoring to pass
hotel patronesses; nor could a
    practiced ear confuse the glass
        eyes for taxidermists

with eye-glasses from the optometrist. And as
    MEridian-7 one-two
one-two gives, each fifteenth second
    in the same voice, the new
data – 'The time will be' so and so –
    you realize that 'when you
        hear the signal', you'll be

hearing Jupiter or jour pater, the day god –
    the salvaged son of Father Time –
telling the cannibal Chronos
    (eater of his proxime
newborn progeny) that punctuality
    is not a crime.

Vítězslav Nezval

From *Edison*

IV

Life is but once and then there is dark night
we are dying in the ruins of light
like day-flies, like a flash of lightning

And now the sky beyond the trees is brightening
electric wires tremble in the snow
now promenades and corsos are aglow
now our souls are viewed on the X-ray screen
like ichthyosauri from the pliocene
now the clock's hand is moving towards six
now we go off together to the flicks
now spectral shades of gamblers and of witches
are put to flight by our electric switches
and now applause and cheers ring through the house
and Thomas Edison now takes his bows

The party's over now your soul is dark
the guests have left and you are back at work
Look at those inventors and at their resources
yet the stars have not deviated from their courses
look at all those people living quietly
no this isn't work nor even energy
this is adventure as on the high seas
locking oneself in one's laboratories
look at all those people living quietly
no this isn't work it's poetry

It's intention and a bit of accident
to become one's country's president
to become a poet who's outstripped you all
to become a songbird holding you in thrall

to be always lucky at roulette
to be the discoverer of a new planet

A thousand apples have dropped in profusion
but only Newton drew the right conclusion
A thousand people have had epileptic seizures
Saint Paul alone had his converting vision
A thousand nameless deaf have sought a haven
but only one of them was Beethoven
A thousand madmen have considered ways
but only Nero could set Rome ablaze
A thousand inventions come to us each season
but only one of them was that of Edison

No sleep now all warranties must end
now burn everything that comes to hand
carbonize jute and monkey skin and kindling
dry leaves ignited by a viola string
in ancient unbelief to stray about again
around the bamboo of a Japanese fan
Woe to you sir this is a fan of love
which a masked lady gave you with a laugh
when in your youth you met her at a ball
where was it sir come do remember all
now say goodbye to her perfume on the fan
woe to you sir burn everything again
perhaps the lady was one of your Fates
wind your alarm clock now and lock your gates
back to your lab a new Columbus you
go stage another hunt for fresh bamboo
travel the country far and wide
find for your fan that magical wood
like the man searching for four golden hairs
like pearl fishers or like corsairs
like Christ on the nocturnal Appian Way
like one who seeks his happiness in drugs
like the Wandering Jew in unknown territory
like a mother blundering through a cemetery

awaiting a child's voice from beyond the grave
like a sick leper with his bell and stave
like a hermit seeking God in thirst
like gods their death when with their own cursed
like a blind poet his true face
like a pilgrim the sight of the Northern Lights
like a madman final Judgement Day
like a child a lark while kneading clay

They have all scattered to Brasilia
and to Japan land of magnolias
to Havana to die of malaria
the way white missionaries die
no doubt sir you will not deny
that you smiled under the tall bamboo
of death: already twelve replacements for you
are waiting in line ready with their gear
MacGowan spent there well over a year
then he set out for the Amazon
whose sources and end are not known
often fought adventure to the knife
on those death-bringing waters saved his life
fought ruthless gold-diggers out just for gain
came to New York and was never seen again

How should I love you roads without destination
you tropical nights in sunlit intoxication
you lights of lights you nights of misery
you lights submerged at the bottom of the sea
you all who died so cheerfully
you'll be bamboo angels presently
I'm thinking of you Who's still weeping here
now to produce new switching gear
now to engross yourself in flasks and distillate
and now to get a new propeller to rotate
look we are getting old we see time flee
search for the elements of a new alchemy
look we are getting old you're eighty now
the flags are out as for a festive show

your hands are pale and white as chalk
but no oh no this is not yet a wake

Still to see one's shadow ahead on the ground
still to analyze some corrosive compound
still to see your skin peel from pain and laughter
still to find a device for unlocking the hereafter
still to sing and never be at rest
still a compass needle for man's quest
forget everything that hurts and stifles breath
anxiety and sadness over life and death

Translated from the Czech by Ewald Osers.

Thomas Alva Edison (1847–1931) was the archetypal American inventor, with more than 1,000 inventions to his name, including the phonograph, the incandescent electric lamp and the microphone. He established the first industrial laboratory, at Menlo Park.

Adrienne Rich

Artificial Intelligence

Over the chessboard now,
Your Artificiality concludes
a final check; rests; broods –
        no – sorts and stacks a file of memories,
while I
concede the victory, bow,
and slouch among my free associations.

You never had a mother,
let's say? no digital Gertrude
whom you'd as lief have seen
Kingless? So your White Queen
was just an 'operator'.
(My Red had incandescence,
ire, aura, flare,
and trapped me several moments in her stare.)

I'm sulking, clearly, in the great tradition
of human waste. Why not
dump the whole reeking snarl
and let you solve me once for all?
(*Parameter*: a black-faced Luddite
itching for ecstasies of sabotage.)

Still, when
they make you write your poems, later on,
who'd envy you, force-fed
on all those variorum
editions of our primitive endeavors,
those frozen pemmican language-rations
they'll cram you with? denied
our luxury of nausea, you
forget nothing, have no dreams.

Robert Conquest

Guided Missiles Experimental Range

Soft sounds and odours brim up through the night
A wealth below the level of the eye;
Out of a black, an almost violet sky
Abundance flowers into points of light.

Till from the south-west, as their low scream mars
And halts this warm hypnosis of the dark,
Three black automata cut swift and stark,
Shaped clearly by the backward flow of stars.

Stronger than lives, by empty purpose blinded,
The only thought their circuits can endure is
The target-hunting rigour of their flight;

And by that loveless haste I am reminded
Of Aeschylus' description of the Furies:
'O *barren daughters of the fruitful night.*'

Dannie Abse

Tuberculosis

Not wishing to pronounce the taboo word
I used to write, 'Acid-fast organisms.'
Earlier physicians noted with a quill,
'The animalcules generate their own kind
and kill.' Some lied. Or murmured, 'Phthisis,
King's Evil, Consumption, Koch's Disease.'
But friend of student days, John Roberts, clowned,
'TB I've got. You know what TB signifies?
Totally buggered.' He laughed. His sister cried.
The music of sound is the sound of music.

And what of that other medical student,
that other John, coughing up redness on
a white sheet? 'Bring me the candle, Brown.
That is arterial blood, I cannot be deceived
in that colour. It is my death warrant.'
The cruelty of Diseases! This one, too.
For three centuries, in London, the slow, sad bell.
Helplessly, wide-eyed, one in five died of it.
Doctors prescribed, 'Horse-riding, sir, ride and ride.'
Or diets, rest, mountain air, sea-voyages.

Today, an x-ray on this oblong light
clear that was not clear. No pneumothorax,
no deforming thoracoplasty. No flaw.
The patient nods, accepts it as his right
and is right. Later, alone, I, questing for
old case-histories, open the tight desk-drawer
to smell again Schiller's rotten apples.

Tuberculosis became curable with the discovery of the antibiotic streptomycin in 1944.
Resistance to this drug appeared almost immediately and as other effective drugs
emerged, cocktails were devised to overcome the resistance problem. In the 1990s the
tuberculosis bacillus began to gain on the drugs and became a serious scourge once
more.

David Holbrook

The Maverick

In a train, between Maidenhead and Worcester,
I make a new projection of the world,
Reading a keen logical analysis of Darwin:
The Old Testament story of ruthless survival
Gives way to a world of quiet woods and rivers
Unfolding between the Thames and the Malvern Hills
Where not even a spike of moss can be explained,
And all things but display their multiplicity.

A benign mystery replaces the old savagery:
Except for the phage, the long-whip injector,
Springing his long molecules through the cell walls.
I give up the old explanations gladly,
Thumbing through an illustrated American manual
Grasping at 'what science says', and wondering
What impels the spermatozoon, furring an ovum,
Implanting their heads; or the phagocyte, stuffing
A bacterium in its jaws, engulfer of the invaders:
But then, most dreadful of all, the phage,
Congregating with its sock-tubes on the wall,
Little more than a molecule, but headed
Strangely like a man-made gas-tap, like aerial spikes,
Multiplying itself inside stuff of other creatures,
Yet with no brain, no heart, no nervous system,
No soul, no complex flux of organic life, no breath:
Simply a nut and a spring, and strings of atoms,
Searching and searching, blindly grasps and rapes.

I enjoy my sceptic, breaking the old tales.
But what do I say about this invisible tyrant?

phage: in full – bacteriophage: geometrically shaped viruses that parasitize bacteria.
They are paradoxical creatures halfway between living and non-living matter. They
can be crystallized as inert chemical substances but in the environment of a bacterium,
they fasten on to the cell wall and inject their DNA into the bacterium, causing it to
produce more phages, which accumulate until they burst the cell wall.

Carole Satyamurti

The Life and Life of Henrietta Lacks

That was me in the New Look
sassy as hell, in the days
when wicked was wicked;
not the fist on hip of a woman
who knows she's cooking
a time bomb tumour;

not a number's up smile
like a dame who figures
she'll not be getting the wear
from all those yards
of cloth she scrimped for,
who'll be dead at thirty.

Dead? For forty years
my cloned cervical cells
have had a ball in Petri dishes
gorging placenta soup,
multiplying like their crazy mother
– the first ever cell line,

flung like spider's thread
across continents I never got to visit,
the stuff of visions, profits,
reputations in Melbourne, Baltimore;
hot property, burning mindless
energy I'd have known how to use.

They never asked. Never said
How's about you live for ever,
like immortal yogurt? I'm bought,
sold like cooking salt. But I get even,
grow where I'm not supposed,
screw up experiments.

Soon, they'll have the know-how
to rebuild me from a single cell.
A rope of doubles could jitterbug
from here to Jupiter. Meantime,
I'm grabbing my piece of the action,
hungry to cry my first cry again.

Henrietta Lacks died of cancer in 1951, but her cells, now amounting to several times her original weight, were cloned and live on in laboratories around the world. – Author's note.

Ciaran Carson

A Date Called Eat Me

The American Fruit Company had genetically engineered a
    new variety of designer apple,
Nameless as yet, which explored the various Platonic ideals of
    the 'apple' synapse.

Outside the greengrocer's lighted awning it is dusky
    Hallowe'en. It is
Snowing on a box of green apples, crinkly falling on the tissue
    paper. It is

Melting on the green, unbitten, glistening apples, attracted by
    their gravity.
I yawned my teeth and bit into the dark, mnemonic cavity.

That apple-box was my first book-case. I covered it in wood-
    grain *Fablon* –
You know that Sixties stick-on plastic stuff? I thought it
    looked dead-on:

Blue Pelicans and orange Penguins, *The Pocket Oxford
    English Dictionary*;
Holmes and Poe, *The Universe*, the fading aura of an apple
    named *Discovery* –

I tried to extricate its itsy-bitsy tick of rind between one tooth
    and another tooth,
The way you try to winkle out the 'facts' between one truth
    and another truth.

Try to imagine the apple talking to you, tempting you like
    something out of Aesop,
Clenched about its navel like a fist or face, all pith and pips and
    sap

Or millions of them, hailing from the heavens, going *pom,*
    pom, pom, pom, pom
On the roof of the American Fruit Company, whose computer
    banks are going *ohm* and *om*.

They were trying to get down to the nitty-gritty, sixty-four-
    thousand dollar question of whether the stalk
Is apple or branch or what. The programme was stuck.

The juice of it explodes against the roof and tongue, the cheek
    of it.
I lied about the *Fablon*, by the way. It was really midnight
    black with stars on it.

THE NEW WORLD ORDER:
THE COLLAPSE OF COMMUNISM & ITS
CONSEQUENCES 1989–

The revolutions of 1989 were dubbed 'velvet' (with the exception of the Romanian), and they certainly proved to be soft-centred. After the euphoria, the problems unleashed were like those encountered whenever an empire collapses. For a brief period the phrase The New World Order was used without irony, but the outcome of the Gulf War (1991) and the civil war in Bosnia (1992–4) restored business as usual. The poets of Eastern Europe had been powerful figures in the resistance to Communism and some briefly figured in the new governments. In the scramble towards Western-style economies, pornography soon ousted poetry on the publishers' schedules and the poets largely fell silent or embraced chaotic postmodernism. In England and America, the Gulf War and Bosnia produced a great deal of poetry, some of it rising above the level of instant armchair indignation.

Charles Tomlinson

Prometheus

Summer thunder darkens, and its climbing
   Cumulae, disowning our scale in the zenith,
Electrify this music: the evening is falling apart.
   Castles-in-air; on earth: green, livid fire.
The radio simmers with static to the strains
   Of this mock last-day of nature and of art.

We have lived through apocalypse too long:
   Scriabin's dinosaurs! Trombones for the transformation
That arrived by train at the Finland Station,
   To bury its hatchet after thirty years in the brain
Of Trotsky. Alexander Nikolayevitch, the events
   Were less merciful than your mob of instruments.

Too many drowning voices cram this waveband.
 I set Lenin's face by yours –
Yours, the fanatic ego of eccentricity against
 The systematic son of a schools inspector
Tyutchev on desk – for the strong man reads
 Poets as the antisemite pleads: 'A Jew was my friend.'

Cymballed firesweeps. Prometheus came down
 In more than orchestral flame and Kérensky fled
Before it. The babel of continents gnaws now
 And tears at the silk of those harmonies that seemed
So dangerous once. You dreamed an end
 Where the rose of the world would go out like a close in music.

Population drags the partitions down
 And we are a single town of warring suburbs:
I cannot hear such music for its consequence:
 Each sense was to have been reborn
Out of a storm of perfumes and light
 To a white world, an in-the-beginning.

In the beginning, the strong man reigns:
 Trotsky, was it not then you brought yourself
To judgement and to execution, when you forgot
 Where terror rules, justice turns arbitrary?
Chromatic Prometheus, myth of fire,
 It is history topples you in the zenith.

Blok, too, wrote The Scythians
 Who should have known: he who howls
With the whirlwind, with the whirlwind goes down.
 In this, was Lenin guiltier than you
When, out of a merciless patience grew
 The daily prose such poetry prepares for?

Scriabin, Blok, men of extremes,
 History treads out the music of your dreams
Through blood, and cannot close like this
 In the perfection of anabasis. It stops. The trees

Continue raining though the rain has ceased
In a cooled world of incessant codas:

Hard edges of the houses press
On the after-music senses, and refuse to burn,
Where an ice cream van circulates the estate
Playing Greensleeves, and at the city's
Stale new frontier even ugliness
Rules with the cruel mercy of solidities.

'Prometheus' refers to the tone-poem by Scriabin and to his hope of transforming the
world by music and rite. – Author's note.
Kérensky: Alexander Kérensky (1881–1970) was Prime Minister in the Provisional
Government of Russia overthrown by the Revolution.
The Scythians: a poem by Alexander Blok which celebrated the Mongol hordes of
Asiatic Russia.

Miroslav Holub

The Third Language

It was empty
inside the head
and speechless.
People were neutralized
by statutory people.

And so it happened
that something like a disinherited idea
thought people up.

People from holes, people from houses,
people from cold storage, people from fly ash,
people from hot water
people from the conflagration of trees.

And suddenly they were one flash.
And suddenly it was Hora's
'at last'. People
came from everywhere, gathered,
went one way, equal to themselves,
identified with one another,
like stem cells from the bone marrow
of the idea.

The idea conjured up people
with three hands, people
with three colors above the gray dirt,
people with three languages,
Czech, Slovak,
and another one.

An uproar rose over the heads,
to the heavy, overcast sky.
It had no words.
It couldn't be bugged.
But they all understood.

The dictionary of the third language
lay in the square
and the newborn wind
was leafing through it. In this language
oxygen was oxygen
and a conic section passed through a fixed point
and intersected a fixed line.

A statutory man
in a Mercedes with a special licence plate
left without deciphering
the code of the third language.
He was mute.

Because too many people
for the first time in life
were really speaking.

Translated from the Czech by David
Young, Dana Hábová and the Author.

Hora: the Czech poet Josef Hora (1891–1945).

Jerzy Jarniewicz

Short History

It was in the Thirty Years War and
we went to ground under the debris
fearing
that we might be found by Wallenstein's
                                    mercenaries

When the great Hunt was on
we kept hiding in the cellars
fearing
that we might be found by the blond supermen
from Goethe's land

Today
we leave our rooms and walk the corridors
fearing that

nobody
will find us

Translated from the Polish by the Author.

Wallenstein: Albrecht von Wallenstein (1583–1634) was a Czech warlord who became commander of the Habsburg Empire's army during the Thirty Years' War (1618–48). He laid waste to much of Central Europe before being assassinated by officers of the Emperor.

Fleur Adcock

Summer in Bucharest

We bought raspberries in the market;
but raspberries are discredited:

they sag in their bag, fermenting
into a froth of suspect juice.

And strawberries are seriously compromised:
a taint – you must have heard the stories.

As for the red currants, well, they say
the only real red currants are dead.

(Don't you believe it: the fields are full of them,
swelling hopefully on their twigs,

and the dead ones weren't red anyway
but some mutation of black or white.)

We thought of choosing gooseberries,
until we heard they'd been infiltrated

by raspberries in gooseberry jackets.
You can't tell what to trust these days.

There are dates, they say, but they're imported;
and its still too early for the grape harvest.

All we can do is wait and hope.
It's been a sour season for fruit.

1990

Jo Shapcott

Phrase Book

I'm standing here inside my skin,
which will do for a Human Remains Pouch
for the moment. Look down there (up here).
Quickly. Slowly. This is my own front room

where I'm lost in the action, live from a war,
on screen. I am an Englishwoman, I don't understand you.
What's the matter? You are right. You are wrong.
Things are going well (badly). Am I disturbing you?

TV is showing bliss as taught to pilots:
Blend, Low silhouette, Irregular shape, Small,
Secluded. (Please write it down. Please speak slowly.)
Bliss is how it was in this very room

when I raised my body to his mouth,
when he even balanced me in the air,
or at least I thought so and yes the pilots say
yes they have caught it through the Side-Looking

Airborne Radar, and through the J-Stars.
I am expecting a gentleman (a young gentleman,
two gentlemen, some gentlemen). Please send him
(them) up at once. This is really beautiful.

Yes, they have seen us, the pilots, in the Kill Box
on their screens, and played the routine for
getting us Stealthed, that is, Cleansed, to you and me,
Taken Out. They know how to move into a single room

like that, to send in with Pinpoint Accuracy, a hundred Harms.
I have two cases and a cardboard box. There is another
bag there. I cannot open my case – look out,
the lock is broken. Have I done enough?

Bliss, the pilots say, is for evasion
and escape. What's love in all this debris?
Just one person pounding another into dust,
into dust. I do not know the word for it yet.

Where is the British Consulate? Please explain.
What does it mean? What must I do? Where
can I find? What have I done? I have done
nothing. Let me pass please. I am an Englishwoman.

The military jargon in this poem was all current during the Gulf War.
J-Stars: an aiming device in a pilot's visual display system.
Harm: Homing Anti-Radar Missile.

Linda France

Stateless

Tovarisch is a dirty word. Blue-pencilled
like an official secret. The built-in obsolescence
of perestroika, Leningrad, Space Station Mir.
My mother was so proud. Now Cosmonaut Krikalev
is just a repairman, Robinson Crusoe in overalls,
a hero for a country that doesn't exist.

When I was afraid of the dark, my mother
told me I could switch it on, like light.
And she'd show me the stars, families
of silver bears. Now I can't switch it off.
So many different shades of black,
clouds of stars and sewage. The only
lovely thing is earth, tantalising,
forbidden as a black-market apple.

First, the floating frogs kept us busy,
research. Then the quail chicks started
dying and everything went wrong like a joke
won't survive re-telling. I'm still
waiting for the punch-line: choke

on the glutinous food, reconstituted air.
Nothing like home. My family on TV
at the weekends: coloured postcards
I can't keep. I switch off the machine,
stare at its dark. Get back to my exercises.

I don't know if there'll be a party
when I come home: dancing, scarlet
in the streets, my name in the stars, medals
forged from melted missiles. Anything
would be better than what I don't know
already, everything I know about dark.

Cosmonaut Sergei Krikalev: sent into space in May 1991 to work on the space station
Mir. On 31 December the Soviet Union ceased to exist. For a while he was left suspended,
the authorities being uncertain what to do with him. When he returned, on 25 March
1992, he found himself in the newly independent state of Kazakhstan.

Ian McMillan

Bosnia Festival:
Your Full Guide by our Arts Reporter

At 10.00 a.m. mime show
by The Shuffling Headscarves.
Nothing much happens;
some shuffling, weeping.
Mimed weeping, that is.

At Midday, cabaret
in The Bread Queue
by The Arguing Headscarves.
Nothing much happens;
a feeble argument. Behind them
The Ducking Headscarves
are ducking the snipers.
The Shuffling Headscarves
mime weeping.

At three p.m. a one man show
by a man in a white suit
talking into a camera.
Nothing much happens.
The Shuffling Headscarves, The
Arguing Headscarves and The Ducking
Headscarves continue their act

which one critic described
as a lot of shuffling, arguing
and ducking.

There's so much happening.
There's almost too much to take in.
A kind of festival fatigue
comes over you: all these headscarves,
all that weeping, all those gestures.

Godot turned up last night, by the way,
in a headscarf, weeping.

The actors stood with their mouths open
like fish. Fish on a bloody slab.

Carole Satyamurti

Striking Distance

Was there one moment when the woman
who's always lived next door turned stranger
to you? In a time of fearful weather
did the way she laughed, or shook out her mats
make you suddenly feel as though
she'd been nursing a dark side to her difference,
and bring that word, in a bitter rush
to the back of the throat – *Croat/Muslim/*
Serb – the name, barbed, ripping
its neat solution through common ground?

Or has she acquired an alien patina
day by uneasy day, unnoticed
as fall-out from a remote explosion?
So you don't know quite when you came to think
the way she sits, or ties her scarf,
is just like a Muslim/Serb/Croat;
and she uses their word for water-melon
as usual, but now it's an irritant
you mimic to ugliness in your head,
surprising yourself in a savage pleasure.

Do you sometimes think, she could be you,
the woman who's trying to be invisible?
Do you have to betray those old complicities
– money worries, sick children, men?
Would an open door be too much pain
if the larger bravery is beyond you
(you can't afford the kind of recklessness
that would take, any more than she could);
while your husband is saying you don't understand
those people/Serbs/Muslims/Croats?

One morning, will you ignore her greeting
and think you see a strange twist to her smile
– for how could she not, then, be strange to herself
(this woman who lives nine inches away)
in the inner place where she'd felt she belonged,
which, now, she'll return to obsessively
as a tongue tries to limit a secret sore?
And as they drive her away, will her face
be unfamiliar, her voice, bearable:
a woman crying from a long way off?

Goran Simić

The Calendar

I heard the fall of a leaf from a calendar.
It was the leaf for the month of March.
The calendar belongs to a girl I know.

She spends each day checking the calendar
and watching her belly grow.
Whatever is in her womb
was nailed there by drunken soldiers in some camp.
It is something that feeds
on terrible images and a terrible silence.

What fills the images?
Her bloodstained dress, perhaps,
fluttering from a pole like a flag?

What breaks the silence?
The fall of the month of March?
The footstep of her tormentor – his face
the child's face, the face she will see
every day, every month, every year
for the rest of her life?

I don't know. I don't know.
All I heard was the fall of a leaf from a calendar.

Translated from the Serbo-Croat by
David Harsent.

Günter Grass

The Fortress Grows

The land lies fallow, food now for rooks and crows.
The moles proliferate and, as they'd never done,
suspect, along the fences strange dogs run.
We are to pay: in cash, and through the nose.

Because mid-European, wealthy and vulnerable,
fear sweated out its drafts for a defensive wall:
now as a fortress Novemberland seeks to be
safe from Black, Fellah, Jew, Turk, Romany.

As Eastern border Poland will serve again:
so fast we think of history, to our gain.
Building of castles has always been our special joy,
to raise the rampart, excavate the moat;
and against fortress megrims, dullness, gloom attacks
always a Hölderlin helped with poems in our packs.

Translated from the German by
Michael Hamburger.

THE WAY WE LIVE: EXISTENCE

Although Simone Weil's assertion that 'Every sentence that begins with "we" is a lie' has a great deal of force, contemporary life is so wired up – even before the coming of television, newspapers had created a mass consciousness – that, despite human diversity, it isn't idle to talk of 'how we lived then'. The poems here are poems of the collective life: stray observations and reflections emerging from the welter of experience. In 'The Quality of Sprawl' Les Murray defines the characteristic mood of our time: part anarchy, part insouciance, part sheer wackiness. Matters of health, political correctness, belief and the ironing board's blessing jostle companionably.

Kathleen Jamie

The Way We Live

Pass the tambourine, let me bash out praises
to the Lord God of movement, to Absolute
non-friction, flight, and the scary side:
death by avalanche, birth by failed contraception.
Of chicken tandoori and reggae, loud, from tenements,
commitment, driving fast and unswerving
friendship. Of tee-shirts on pulleys, giros and Bombay,
barmen, dreaming waitresses with many fake-gold
bangles. Of airports, impulse, and waking to uncertainty,
to strip-lights, motorways, or that pantheon –
the mountains. To overdrafts and grafting

and the fit slow pulse of wipers as you're
creeping over Rannoch, while the God of moorland
walks abroad with his entourage of freezing fog,
his bodyguard of snow.

Of endless gloaming in the North, of Asiatic swelter,
to launderettes, anecdotes, passions and exhaustion,
Final Demands and dead men, the skeletal grip
of government. To misery and elation; mixed,
the sod and caprice of landlords.
To the way it fits, the way it is, the way it seems
to be: let me bash out praises – pass the tambourine.

Bernard Spencer

Behaviour of Money

Money was once well known, like a townhall or the sky
or a river East and West, and you lived one side or the other;
Love and Death dealt shocks,
but for all the money that passed, the wise man knew his brother.

But money changed. Money came jerking roughly alive;
went battering round the town with a boozy, zigzag tread.
A clear case for arrest;
and the crowds milled and killed for the pound notes that he shed.

And the town changed, and the mean and the little lovers of gain
inflated like a dropsy, and gone were the courtesies
that eased the market day;
saying, 'buyer' and 'seller' was saying, 'enemies.'

The poor were shunted nearer to beasts. The cops recruited.
The rich became a foreign community. Up there leaped
quiet folk gone nasty,
quite strangely distorted, like a photograph that has slipped.

Hearing the drunken roars of Money from down the street,
'What's to become of us?' the people in bed would cry:
'And oh, the thought strikes chill;
what's to become of the world if Money should suddenly die?

Should suddenly take a toss and go down crack on his head?
If the dance suddenly finished, if they stopped the runaway bus,
if the trees stopped racing away?
If our hopes come true and he dies, what's to become of us?

Shall we recognize each other, crowding around the body?
And as we go stealing off in search of the town we have known
– what a job for the Sanitary Officials;
the sprawled body of Money, dead, stinking, alone!'

Will X contrive to lose the weasel look in his eyes?
Will the metal go out of the voice of Y? Shall we all turn back
to men, like Circe's beasts?
Or die? Or dance in the street the day that the world goes crack?

Gabriel Celaya

Great Moments

When it rains, and I go over my papers and end up
throwing everything into the fire: unfinished poems,
bills still unpaid, letters from dead friends,
photographs, kisses preserved in a book,
I am throwing off the dead weight of my hard-headed past,
I am shining and growing just as fast as I disown myself,
so if I poke at the fire, leap over the flames,
and scarcely understand what I feel while I'm doing it,
is it not happiness that is lifting me up?

When I hit the streets, whistling in sheer delight
– a cigarette in my lips, my soul in good order –
and I talk to the kids or let myself drift with the clouds,
early May and the breeze goes lifting up everything,
the young girls begin wearing their low-cut blouses, their arms
naked and tanned, their eyes wide,
and they laugh without knowing why, bubbling over
and scattering their ecstasy which then trembles afresh,
isn't it happiness, what we feel then?

When a friend shows up and there's nothing in the house,
but my girl brings forth anchovies, ham, and cheese,
olives and crab and two bottles of white wine,
and I assist at the miracle – knowing it's all on credit –
and I don't want to worry about having to pay for it,
and we drink and babble like there's no tomorrow,
and my friend is well off and he figures we are too,
and maybe we are, laughing at death that way,
isn't that happiness which suddenly breaks through?

When I wake up, I stay stretched out
by the open balcony. And dawn comes: the birds
trill sweetly in their heathen arabics;
and I ought to get up, but I don't;
and looking up I watch the rippling light of the sea
dancing on the ceiling, prism of its mother-of-pearl,
and I go on lying there and nothing matters a damn –
don't I annihilate time? And save myself from terror?
Isn't it happiness that comes with the dawn?

When I go to the market, I look at the nectarines
and work my jaws at the sight of the plump cherries,
the oozing figs, the plums fallen
from the tree of life, a sin no doubt,
being so tempting and all. And I ask the price
and haggle over it and finally knock it down,
but the game is over, I pay double and it's still not much,
and the salesgirl turns her astonished eyes on me,
is it not happiness that is germinating there?

When I can say: The day is over.
And by day I mean its taxis, its business,
the scrambling for money, the struggles of the dead.
And when I get home, sweat-stained and tired,
I sit down in the dusk and plug the phonograph in
and Kachaturian comes on, or Mozart, or Vivaldi,
and the music holds sway, I feel clean again,
simply clean and, in spite of everything, unhurt,
is it not happiness that is closing around me?

When after turning things over and over again in my mind,
I remember a friend and go over to see him, he says
'I was just now thinking of going over to see you.'
And we talk a long time, not about my troubles,
and he couldn't help me, even if he wanted to,
but we talk about how things are going in Jordan,
or a book of Neruda's, or his tailor, or the wind,
and as I leave I feel comforted and full of peace,
isn't that happiness, what comes over me then?

Opening a window; feeling the cool air;
walking down a road that smells of honeysuckle;
drinking with a friend; chattering or, better yet, keeping still;
feeling that we feel what other men feel;
seeing ourselves through eyes that see us as innocent,
isn't this happiness, and the hell with death?
Beaten, betrayed, seeing almost cynically
that they can do no more to me, that I'm still alive,
isn't this happiness, that is not for sale?

Translated from the Spanish by Robert Mezey.

Irving Feldman

You Know What I'm Saying?

'I favor your enterprise,' the soup ladle says.
'And I regard you and your project with joy.'

At Grand Forks where the road divides twice over,
the wet wooden squeegee handle poking out
of the bucket beside the red gas pump tells you,
'*Whichever* way – hey, for you they're *all* okay.'

The stunted pine declares from someone's backyard
you happen to be passing, 'I don't begrudge you
your good health. In fact, my blessing – you've got it, now.'

An ironing board is irrepressible.
'Your success is far from certain, my friend,
and still it's vital to my happiness.'

The yellow kernels in the dust, mere chickenfeed,
call out, 'We salute you, and you can count on us.'

We do not live in a world of things
but among benedictions given
and – do you know what I'm saying? – received.

Andrei Voznesensky

American Buttons

Buttons flash, buttons, buttons, buttons
shouting at the tops of their lungs
'Men are the ancestors of apes'
'Ronald Reagan is a lesbian'
'Fuck censorship'
'If it moves, fondle it'

GOD LIVES AT 18 PASTEUR ST.
REAR ENTRANCE PLEASE

I love Greenwich Village
with its sarcastic buttons.
Who's the shaggy one who showed up
cock & balls in dark glasses?
It's Allen, Allen, Allen!
Leap over Death's carnival,
Allen, in your underwear!
Irony is God today.
'Power to the People' is a holy slogan.

Better to stick your fingers in your mouth and whistle
than to be silent *booboisie*.

Button-stars of Bethlehem
on everybody's bottom,
mini-skirts on bellybuttons.

A wild girl agitator
winks from a dark corner
'Make love not war!'

Irony is God today.
Buttons flash over yawns.
The funnier they are, the more terrifying
And like bullseyes for bullets.

GOD HAS MOVED TO 43 AVENUE OF PEACE.
RING TWICE.

And above the Hippies, – above the Flood
like an ironic Cyclops
Time flashes its button-eye!

TIME,
Can I read what's written in your eyes,
rushing at me –
         growing bigger and bigger, like headlights?
Can I see through your antics?

O autumn with round leaves
O eight plates
tossed up by a juggler
                frozen for an instant in air,
as if a giraffe had run away,
                    and left its spots
                                    behind!

The giraffe retreats
with a sacred mushroom-button on its bottom:
'Make Love Not War'

Translated from the Russian by Lawrence Ferlinghetti.

Les Murray

The Quality of Sprawl

Sprawl is the quality
of the man who cut down his Rolls-Royce
into a farm utility truck, and sprawl
is what the company lacked when it made repeated efforts
to buy the vehicle back and repair its image.

Sprawl is doing your farming by aeroplane, roughly,
or driving a hitchhiker that extra hundred miles home.
It is the rococo of being your own still centre.
It is never lighting cigars with ten-dollar notes:
that's idiot ostentation and murder of starving people.
Nor can it be bought with the ash of million-dollar deeds.

Sprawl lengthens the legs; it trains greyhounds on liver and beer.
Sprawl almost never says Why not? with palms comically raised
nor can it be dressed for, not even in running shoes worn
with mink and a nose ring. That is Society. That's Style.
Sprawl is more like the thirteenth banana in a dozen
or anyway the fourteenth.

Sprawl is Hank Stamper in *Never Give an Inch*
bisecting an obstructive official's desk with a chainsaw.
Not harming the official. Sprawl is never brutal
though it's often intransigent. Sprawl is never Simon de Montfort
at a town-storming: Kill them all! God will know his own.
Knowing the man's name this was said to might be sprawl.

Sprawl occurs in art. The fifteenth to twenty-first
lines in a sonnet, for example. And in certain paintings;
I have sprawl enough to have forgotten which paintings.
Turner's glorious *Burning of the Houses of Parliament*
comes to mind, a doubling bannered triumph of sprawl –
except, he didn't fire them.

Sprawl gets up the nose of many kinds of people
(every kind that comes in kinds) whose futures don't include it.
Some decry it as criminal presumption, silken-robed Pope Alexander
dividing the new world between Spain and Portugal.
If he smiled *in petto* afterwards, perhaps the thing did have sprawl.

Sprawl is really classless, though. It's John Christopher Frederick Murray
asleep in his neighbours' best bed in spurs and oilskins
but not having thrown up:
sprawl is never Calum who, drunk, along the hallways of our house,
reinvented the Festoon. Rather
it's Beatrice Miles going twelve hundred ditto in a taxi,
No Lewd Advances, No Hitting Animals, No Speeding,
on the proceeds of her two-bob-a-sonnet Shakespeare readings.
An image of my country. And would that it were more so.

No, sprawl is full-gloss murals on a council-house wall.
Sprawl leans on things. It is loose-limbed in its mind.
Reprimanded and dismissed
it listens with a grin and one boot up on the rail
of possibility. It may have to leave the Earth.
Being roughly Christian, it scratches the other cheek
and thinks it unlikely. Though people have been shot for sprawl.

in petto: surreptitiously.

Sophie Hannah

Mountains out of Small Hills

Dogs are objecting to the word dogmatic,
the use of certain phrases – barking mad,
dog in the manger. Equally emphatic
are other species. Rats and snakes have had

enough of being symbols of deceit
and treachery. They say there's no excuse,
and there are fish protesting on the street
at being linked with alcohol abuse.

You couldn't taunt a coward nowadays
with 'scaredy-cat' or 'chicken'. Cock-and-bull
stories have been renamed. Nobody says
'God, she's a cow!' Nobody pulls the wool

over another person's eyes – the lambs
have seen to that. Nobody rabbits on.
Nor has there been a ramraid since the rams
petitioned parliament. We do not swan

around, get goosebumps; nothing gets our goat.
No cricket player ever scores a duck.
Once we were free with what we said and wrote.
Now we make do with swear-words. Bollocks. Fuck.

U. A. Fanthorpe

Resuscitation Team

Arrives like a jinn, instantly,
Equipped with beards, white coats, its own smell,
And armfuls of metal and rubber.

Deploys promptly round the quiet bed
With horseplay and howls of laughter.
We, who are used to life, are surprised

At this larky resurrection. Runs
Through its box of tricks, prick, poke and biff,
While we watch, amazed. The indifferent patient

Is not amused, but carries little weight,
Being stripped and fumbled
By so many rugger-players. My first corpse,

If she is a corpse, lies there showing
Too much breast and leg. The team
Rowdily throws up the sponge, demands soap and water,

Leaves at the double. One of us,
Uncertainly, rearranges the night-dress.
Is it professional to observe the proprieties

Now of her who leaves privately
Wheeled past closed doors, her face
Still in the rictus of victory?

David Craig

Operation

The condition (cancer) and the person (myself)
Reeled towards each other over the years,
Capsules slowly converging. Now they have docked –
'Raped!' the Soviet spacemen used to shout
As the new arrival fitted in.
                                              The surgeon
Is using homely words: 'We will take away
Everything except the nerves and muscles'
(That's sound, just what I would have done myself).
'The drains are rather a gamble, but presently
The lymph will find a new route through your body.'
His voice is cool, managerial, green eyes steady
Above the plump cheeks fledged with steely stubble.

Steady is good. I want him perfect – perfectly
Drawing his scalpel round below my armpit,
No tremor, no indecision, his focus keen
As a kestrel swithering over its prey, then stilled
As a cloud in Nevada, brain become all eye,
Sharpening and fining-down each grass-blade, wind-twitch,
Bee-shadow, mouse-breath, muscle-fibre, nerve-end,
Blood-vessel, vein-valve, lymph-gland, cancer-nodule . . .
The steel beak is sure. It feels and knows.
The hit is imminent. This programme cannot stop.
The invisible brain distils its brilliant drop.

Dennis O'Driscoll

In Memory of Alois Alzheimer (1864–1915)

I

Before this page fades from memory,
spare a thought for Alois Alzheimer,
called to mind each time

someone becomes forgetful,
disintegration vindicating
his good name.

II

His is the last image assigned
to the ex-President who has slipped
from public view; soiled sheets
give credence to his thesis;

his territory is marked out
by the track of urine
dribbled along the corridor
of the day-care centre.

III

Lie closer to me in the dry sheets
while I can still tell who you are.

Let me declare how much I love you
before our bed is sorely tested.

Love me with drooling toxins, with carbon monoxide,
with rope, with arrows through my heart.

James Fenton

God, A Poem

A nasty surprise in a sandwich,
A drawing-pin caught in your sock,
The limpest of shakes from a hand which
You'd thought would be firm as a rock,

A serious mistake in a nightie,
A grave disappointment all round
Is all that you'll get from th'Almighty,
Is all that you'll get underground.

Oh he *said*: 'If you lay off the crumpet
I'll see you alright in the end.
Just hang on until the last trumpet.
Have faith in me, chum – I'm your friend.'

But if you remind him, he'll tell you:
'I'm sorry, I must have been pissed –
Though your name rings a sort of a bell. You
Should have guessed that I do not exist.

'I didn't exist at Creation,
I didn't exist at the Flood,
And I won't be around for Salvation
To sort out the sheep from the cud –

'Or whatever the phrase is. The fact is
In soteriological terms
I'm a crude existential malpractice
And you are a diet of worms.

'You're a nasty surprise in a sandwich.
You're a drawing-pin caught in my sock.
You're the limpest of shakes from a hand which
I'd have thought would be firm as a rock,

'You're a serious mistake in a nightie,
You're a grave disappointment all round –
That's all that you are,' says th'Almighty,
'And that's all that you'll be underground.'

Carol Ann Duffy

Prayer

Some days, although we cannot pray, a prayer
utters itself. So, a woman will lift
her head from the sieve of her hands and stare
at the minims sung by a tree, a sudden gift.

Some nights, although we are faithless, the truth
enters our hearts, that small familiar pain;
then a man will stand stock-still, hearing his youth
in the distant Latin chanting of a train.

Pray for us now. Grade I piano scales
console the lodger looking out across
a Midlands town. Then dusk, and someone calls
a child's name as though they named their loss.

Darkness outside. Inside, the radio's prayer –
Rockall. Malin. Dogger. Finisterre.

BY THE LIGHT OF ORION:
SCI-FI & SPACE

On one way of reckoning, the Space Age came and went at the end of the Sixties with the moon landings, but this is likely to prove a mere taster for an era still to come. Space is an inherently poetic theme – the Sixties was the time for Sci-Fi poetry – and a tragic space failure, the annihilation of the Space Shuttle Challenger in 1986, spurred President Reagan to quote wartime pilot John Gillespie Magee's poem 'High Flight': 'O I have slipped the surly bonds of earth.' Although the Millennium is a purely arbitrary human construct and not a feature of the universe, it inevitably suggests a cosmic dimension.

Dorothy Hewett

Moon-Man

Stranded on the moon,
a librium dreamer in a lunar landscape,
the tabloids were full of your blurred, blown-up face,
the neat curled head, the secret animal eyes,
immolated forever in the Sea of Tranquillity.

I keep getting messages from outer space,
'Meet me at Cape Canaveral, Houston, Tullamarine.'
A telegram came through at dawn to the Dead Heart Tracking
    Station.
I wait on winter mornings in hangars
dwarfed by grounded crates like giant moths
  furred with frost.

Moon-pictures – you dance clumsily on the screen,
phosphorescent, domed, dehumanised,
  floating above the dust,
your robot voice hollow as bells.

The crowds queue for the late edition,
scan headlines avidly, their necks permanently awry,
looking for a sign, a scapegoat, a priest, a king:
the circulation is rising.

They say you have been knighted in your absence,
but those who swear they know you best,
assert you are still too radical to accept the honour.

They have sent several missions,
but at lift-off three astronauts fried,
     strapped in their webbing.
Plane-spotters on penthouse roofs
have sighted more UFOs.

Sometimes I go out at night
     to stare at the galaxies.
Is that your shadow, weightless,
     magnified in light,
man's flesh enclosed in armour,
suffering eyes in perspex looking down,
sacred and murderous from your sanctuary?

The first moon landing was achieved by the American Apollo 11 mission on 20 July
1969.

Katherine Frost

Space Shuttle

The first time I saw them
was in the Take-out. Buoyant,
pudgy as toys almost,
in their soft suits,
running and waving.

Grey on grey, their smiles
flickered out over
red chilis, green
and orange bhajia, purple
bhindi, nan.

Only what we knew
annulled hunger, or being
not much taken with space
programmes, for one tensecond
freezeframe stare.

At home they do it again.
In colour this time, in twenty-
six inch definition,
running and waving, smiles
toothy as a chatshow.

We watch, stung by clear
Florida sunshine, by their
unconquerable lack of
hindsight. Into the pointy
witchhouse they go –

shouldn't we call to them?
We watch. A seed too small
to quite believe in
trails its plume of down,
plummets to nowhere.

What comes next is hardly
probable, a trick
so casually astounding
we fail, time and again,
to catch the start

of it – Christa McAuliffe,
out of the airless, not
to be escaped nor fathomed
blue we are sure is
beyond our screens

out there – Christa McAuliffe
unfolds – remember those
hand-inked Japanese
toyflowers in water –
but burning – her own

hydraheaded thousand-
petalled chrysanthemum
sunburst, spiralling white,
cream, gold, sprawling
to scarlet – and oh, burning.

No newsflash can miss it.
We stare and stare and she
blooms and blooms. As if,
there, touching a switch
we have her, have it,

Under our hands, some kind of
map of the unthinkable.
Sex, childbearing are not
more private than what we
fancy trapped here.

'She won't have known a thing'
we comfort ourselves (we do
need comfort, reminded
of all that wholesome goodbreakfast
niceness, the way

everyone else's mother
always ought to be)
wondering, also in secret
and against ourselves,
had this then

become – why didn't we see
before – most elegant
of all solutions
to a teacher's lifetime of sums?
and what it is

to know what she knows,
what must we do to pull off
a sleight-of-self so
impeccable, such a deft
clarification?

(whites, golds, burning,
blurring to absolute,
as they will remembered,
fastidious contours ghosting
green at the rim
as ink will in water . . .)

Oh Tokyo-Rose, oh
siren of sirens now
how shall we ever stop you
calling our children?

On 28 January 1986 the Space Shuttle Challenger exploded seventy-two seconds from lift-off, killing the five men and two women on board. The catastrophe was caused by the brittle fracture of a rubber sealing-ring in very cold weather.

Gwyneth Lewis

From *Zero Gravity*

XII

Only your eyesight can be used in space.
Now you've captured the telescope, nebulae
are birthmarks on your new-born face.
The sun's flare makes a Cyclops eye
on your visor. The new spectrograph
you've installed in the Hubble to replace the old
makes black holes leap closer, allows us to grasp
back in time through distance, to see stars unfold
in nuclear gardens, galaxies like sperm
swirled in water, rashes of young hot stars,
blood-clot catastrophes, febrile swarms
of stinging explosions. But what's far
doesn't stop hurting. Give me a gaze
that sees deep into systems through clouds of debris
to the heart's lone pulsar, let me be amazed
by the red shifts, the sheer luminosity
that plays all around us as we talk on the beach,
thinking there's nothing between us but speech.

Hubble: the earth-orbiting Hubble Space Telescope was launched by the Space Shuttle
on 24 April 1990.

Adrian Henri

Galactic Lovepoem

For Susan

Warm your feet at the sunset
Before we go to bed
Read your book by the light of Orion
With Sirius guarding your head
Then reach out and switch off the planets
We'll watch them go out one by one
You kiss me and tell me you love me
By the light of the last setting sun
We'll both be up early tomorrow
A new universe has begun.

Edwin Morgan

The First Men on Mercury

– We come in peace from the third planet.
Would you take us to your leader?

– Bawr stretter! Bawr. Bawr. Stretterhawl?

– This is a little plastic model
of the solar system, with working parts.
You are here and we are there and we
are now here with you, is this clear?

– Gawl horrop. Bawr. Abawrhannahanna!

– Where we come from is blue and white
with brown, you see we call the brown
here 'land', the blue is 'sea', and the white
is 'clouds' over land and sea, we live
on the surface of the brown land,
all round is sea and clouds. We are 'men'.
Men come –

– Glawp men! Gawrbenner menko. Menhawl?

– Men come in peace from the third planet
which we call 'earth'. We are earthmen.
Take us earthmen to your leader.

– Thmen? Thmen? Bawr. Bawrhossop.
Yuleeda tan hanna. Harrabost yuleeda.

– I am the yuleeda. You see my hands,
we carry no benner, we come in peace.
The spaceways are all stretterhawn.

– Glawn peacemen all horrabhanna tantko!
Tan come at'mstrossop. Glawp yuleeda!

– Atoms are peacegawl in our harraban.
Menbat worrabost from tan hannahanna.

– You men we know bawrhossoptant. Bawr.
We know yuleeda. Go strawg backspetter quick.

– We cantantabawr, tantingko backspetter now!

– Banghapper now! Yes, third planet back.
Yuleeda will go back blue, white, brown
nowhanna! There is no more talk.

– Gawl han fasthapper?

– No. You must go back to your planet.
Go back in peace, take what you have gained
but quickly.

– Stretterworra gawl, gawl . . .

– Of course, but nothing is ever the same,
now is it? You'll remember Mercury.

Ivan V. Lalić

The Return of the Comet

Nearing once more, you drum through my soul,
Twofold anguish of a century
You stitch tight with your orbit
At either end, tailed fire, witnessed
Thirty times since the Aegean night
Herodotus may have seen you
And stayed silent;
     fire singing
Space as a training-ground for the skill
Of return at a given hour, the skill
Of some expected fidelity, venerated in legend,
Fire of a lover of the indescribable whatever
Awaiting you here and waving you off
Into the unplumbed abyss:
      to what
Do you return? And what do you stubbornly wish
To witness? He who wove you into a web
Of equations, gazing from the zero
Meridian into a *horror vacui*,
Measured a snake's skin,
Measured the direction and length
Of a line of footsteps in the sand,
       while you,
Fire, sing of the love of one who walks on sand.

(Who walks on sand, then stops
To light a fire of flotsam:
From the far shore, through the dusk,
The fire, distant, low over the water,
Is reduced to a point, a newborn star.)

But what you recognise, to what you return,
Is not known to the chronicler, obsessed with purpose.
Singing fire, what you will witness
On what might be your final return?

Translated from the Serbo-Croat by Francis R. Jones.

Louis MacNeice

Star-Gazer

Forty-two years ago (to me if to no one else
The number is of some interest) it was a brilliant starry night
And the westward train was empty and had no corridors
So darting from side to side I could catch the unwonted sight
Of those almost intolerably bright
Holes, punched in the sky, which excited me partly because
Of their Latin names and partly because I had read in the textbooks
How very far off they were, it seemed their light
Had left them (some at least) long years before I was.

And this remembering now I mark that what
Light was leaving some of them at least then,
Forty-two years ago, will never arrive
In time for me to catch it, which light when
It does get here may find that there is not
Anyone left alive
To run from side to side in a late night train
Admiring it and adding noughts in vain.

Poets are not prophets – when they write about the future they make the emptiness echo a little more resonantly. The Future, according to Les Murray, is 'the black hole/out of which no radiation escapes to us.' In 'The Numties', though, Robert Crawford boldly gives the unknown a plausible local habitation and a name. Not surprisingly the Book of Revelation has been dusted down for the Millennium and its rhetoric recycled by several poets. But the all-purpose poem-for-the-end-of-an-era was written in 1947, by Auden, 'The Fall of Rome'.

Sybren Polet

From *Self-Repeating Poem*

Coda

The year 2000. Peace. All Irishmen turn atheist. Peace.
All Americans turn socialist. Peace. All Calvinists
anarchists, all machinegun players harpsichordists. Peace.
– *Winning the war and getting killed for good.* (*Peace.*)

The year 2000. Peace. No maneater will still eat human flesh. Peace.
No one will die of precontaminated words and ideas. Peace.
– *Winning the peace and speaking a disabled language.* (*Peace.*)

The year 2000. Peace. Whites act as shadows for Blacks. Peace.
Animals act as shadows for angels, hangmen, angels. Peace.
– *Wearing sunglasses and closing one's eyes for good.* (*Peace.*)

The year 2000. Peace. Millions or nillions. Peace. OK or noK,
Gog and Magog, Krethi and Plethi. Ecocide or egocide. Peace.
– *Predicting what happened before, doing what's already been done.*
    (*Peace.*)

The year 2000. Peace. Hear & see: Mosammed read the Torahn
  together! Peace!
100 foreskins of Philistines. Peace. 100 plastic hymens. Peace.
– *Predicting what didn't happen, doing what's never been foreseen.*
  (Peace.)

The year 2000. Peace. No scatterbrained bull will honk twofooters
off the road anymore. Peace. No siren will wail. No artificial rooster
  crow,
no mama doll will cry. All men turn into psychiatrists. Peace.
– *Doing what's never been done, thinking what's never been thought.*
  (Peace.)

Millions or nillions. Peace. OK or noK, Gog or Magog, Krethi or
  Plethi. Peace.
All realists turn into utopians, all utopians into realists. Peace.
– *Thinking what's never been thought, doing what's never been*
  done. Peace.
Doing what's never been done. Peace. Doing what's ever been
  thought. Peace.

Peace. Peace.

Translated from the Dutch by Peter Nijmeijer.

John Agard

Millennium Bug

The bug threatens a domino-effect global collapse of computer
systems at midnight on 31 December 1999. Designed in the Sixties
with a two-digit number representing the day, month and year,
computers are unable to recognize a change of century which
requires four digits. Thus at the turn of the year 2000, the new
century will be 00, which computers will understand as 1900. And
the fear is it could lead to a Mad Max-type Armageddon.
                    – David Atkinson, The Big Issue, 20–26 May 1996

What do they expect when they heed not
   the dance of numbers?

Blunders and bloomers
   will be their undoing

bugs will flower in their computers
   for it is written a day will come

when the angel of mayhem
   appears in their IT systems

and demons disguised as digits
   trumpet the collapse of world markets

that trespass on the human soul
   and treat people as dispensable

and the millennium will toll
   its software Armageddon

and zero will be lifted high
   as the laughter of Galileo

and Pythagoras too will erupt
   at the mention of bankrupt

and the Devil alone
   shall sing in praise

   of the counting frame
     and runic rods
     and notched bone

Donald Hall

Prophecy

Your children will wander looting the shopping malls
for forty years, suffering for your idleness,
until the last dwarf body rots in a parking lot.
I will strike down lobbies and restaurants in motels
carpeted with shaggy petrochemicals
from Maine to Hilton Head, from the Skagit to Tucson.
I will strike down hang gliders, wiry adventurous boys;
their thigh bones will snap, their brains
slide from their skulls. I will strike down
families cooking wildboar in New Mexico backyards.

Then landscape will clutter with incapable machinery,
acres of vacant airplanes and schoolbuses, ploughs
with seedlings sprouting and turning brown through colters.
Unlettered dwarves will burrow for warmth and shelter
in the caves of dynamos and Plymouths, dying
of old age at seventeen. Tribes wandering
in the wilderness of their ignorant desolation,
who suffer from your idleness, will burn your illuminated
missals to warm their rickety bodies.
Terrorists assemble plutonium because you are idle

and industrious. The whip-poor-will shrivels
and the pickerel chokes under the government of self-love.
Vacancy burns air so that you strangle without oxygen
like rats in a biologist's bell jar. The living god sharpens
the scythe of my prophecy to strike down red poppies
and blue cornflowers. When priests and policemen
strike my body's match, Jehovah will flame out;
Jehovah will suck air from the vents of bombshelters.
Therefore let the Buick swell until it explodes;
therefore let anorexia starve and bulimia engorge.

When Elzira leaves the house wearing her tennis dress
and drives her black Porsche to meet Abraham,
quarrels, returns to husband and children, and sobs
asleep, drunk, unable to choose among them, –
lawns and carpets will turn into tar together
with lovers, husbands, and children.
Fat will boil in the sacs of children's clear skin.
I will strike down the nations, astronauts and judges;
I will strike down Babylon, I will strike acrobats,
I will strike algae and the white birches.

Because professors of law teach ethics in dumbshow,
let the colonel become president; because chief executive
officers and commissars collect down for pillows,
let the injustice of cities burn city and suburb;
let the countryside burn; let the pineforests of Maine
explode like a kitchenmatch and the Book of Kells turn
ash in a microsecond; let oxen and athletes
flash into grease: – I return to Appalachian rocks;
I shall eat bread; I shall prophesy through millennia
of Jehovah's day until the sky reddens over cities:

Then houses will burn, even houses of alabaster;
the sky will disappear like a scroll rolled up
and hidden in a cave from the industries of idleness.
Mountains will erupt and vanish, becoming deserts,
and the sea wash over the sea's lost islands
and the earth split open like a corpse's gassy
stomach and the sun turn as black as a widow's skirt
and the full moon grow red with blood swollen inside it
and stars fall from the sky like wind-blown apples, –
while Babylon's managers burn in the rage of the Lamb.

Les Murray

The Future

There is nothing about it. Much science fiction is set there
but is not about it. Prophecy is not about it.
It sways no yarrow stalks. And crystal is a mirror.
Even the man we nailed on a tree for a lookout
said little about it; he told us evil would come.
We see, by convention, a small living distance into it
but even that's a projection. And all our projections
fail to curve where it curves.

                                 It is the black hole
out of which no radiation escapes to us.
The commonplace and magnificent roads of our lives
go on some way through cityscape and landscape
or steeply sloping, or scree, into that sheer fall
where everything will be that we have ever sent there,
compacted, spinning – except perhaps us, to see it.
It is said we see the start.

                            But, from here, there's a blindness.
The side-heaped chasm that will swallow all our present
blinds us to the normal sun that may be imagined
shining calmly away on the far side of it, for others
in their ordinary day. A day to which all our portraits,
ideals, revolutions, denim and deshabille
are quaintly heartrending. To see those people is impossible,
to greet them, mawkish. Nonetheless, I begin:
'When I was alive –'

                         and I am turned around
to find myself looking at a cheerful picnic party,
the women decently legless, in muslin and gloves,
the men in beards and weskits, with the long
cheroots and duck trousers of the better sort,
relaxing on a stone verandah. Ceylon, or Sydney.

And as I look, I know they are utterly gone,
each one on his day, with pillow, small bottles, mist,
with all the futures they dreamed or dealt in, going
down to that engulfment everything approaches;
with the man on the tree, they have vanished into the Future.

Robert Crawford

The Numties

The parsnip Numties: I was a teenager then,
Collecting clip-together models
Of historical windsocks, dancing the Cumbernauld bump.

Satirical pornography, plant-staplers, nostalgiaform shoes
Were brochure-fresh. It was numty-four
I first saw a neighbour laughing in a herbal shirt.

Moshtensky, Garvin, Manda Sharry –
Names as quintessentially Numties
As Hearers and Bonders, duckponding, or getting a job

In eradication. Everything so familiar and sandwiched
Between the pre-Numties and the debouche of decades after.
I keep plunging down to the wreck

Of the submerged Numties, every year
Bringing back something jubilantly pristine,
Deeper drowned, clutching my breath.

Czesław Miłosz

And Yet the Books

And yet the books will be there on the shelves, separate beings,
That appeared once, still wet
As shining chestnuts under a tree in autumn,
And, touched, coddled, began to live
In spite of fires on the horizon, castles blown up,
Tribes on the march, planets in motion.
'We are,' they said, even as their pages
Were being torn out, or a buzzing flame
Licked away their letters. So much more durable
Than we are, whose frail warmth
Cools down with memory, disperses, perishes.
I imagine the earth when I am no more:
Nothing happens, no loss, it's still a strange pageant,
Women's dresses, dewy lilacs, a song in the valley.
Yet the books will be there on the shelves, well born,
Derived from people, but also from radiance, heights.

Translated from the Polish by the Author and Robert Hass.

Allen Curnow

Time

I am the nor'west air nosing among the pines
I am the water-race and the rust on railway lines
I am the mileage recorded on the yellow signs.

I am dust, I am distance, I am lupins back of the beach
I am the sums the sole-charge teachers teach
I am cows called to milking and the magpie's screech.

I am nine o'clock in the morning when the office is clean
I am the slap of the belting and the smell of the machine
I am the place in the park where the lovers were seen.

I am recurrent music the children hear
I am level noises in the remembering ear
I am the sawmill and the passionate second gear.

I, Time, am all these, yet these exist
Among my mountainous fabrics like a mist,
So do they the measurable world resist.

I, Time, call down, condense, confer
On the willing memory the shapes these were:
I, more than your conscious carrier,

Am island, am sea, am father, farm, and friend,
Though I am here all things my coming attend;
I am, you have heard it, the Beginning and the End.

W. H. Auden

The Fall of Rome

For Cyril Connolly

The piers are pummelled by the waves;
In a lonely field the rain
Lashes an abandoned train;
Outlaws fill the mountain caves.

Fantastic grow the evening gowns;
Agents of the Fisc pursue
Absconding tax-defaulters through
The sewers of provincial towns.

Private rites of magic send
The temple prostitutes to sleep;
All the literati keep
An imaginary friend.

Cerebrotonic Cato may
Extol the Ancient Disciplines,
But the muscle-bound Marines
Mutiny for food and pay.

Caesar's double-bed is warm
As an unimportant clerk
Writes *I DO NOT LIKE MY WORK*
On a pink official form.

Unendowed with wealth or pity,
Little birds with scarlet legs,
Sitting on their speckled eggs,
Eye each flu-infected city.

Altogether elsewhere, vast
Herds of reindeer move across
Miles and miles of golden moss,
Silently and very fast.

Biographies

DANNIE ABSE was born in Cardiff in 1923 to a Welsh-Jewish family. He served in the RAF before qualifying in medicine. He has pursued parallel careers as a poet and a practising doctor working in a chest clinic.

FLEUR ADCOCK was born in 1934 in New Zealand, spent the war years in England, and was educated at Victoria University, Wellington. She returned to England in 1963 and worked for many years in the Foreign Office Library. She has visited Romania several times and has translated the Romanian poets Grete Tartler and Daniela Crăsnaru.

JOHN AGARD was born in Guyana in 1949. He came to England in 1977, where he established a reputation as a mesmerizing performer of his often pungently satirical poetry.

ANNA AKHMATOVA (1889–1966) was one of the great Russian poets of the century and her name is always linked with those of Mandelstam, Pasternak and Tsvetaeva. She suffered grievously under Stalin's Terror. Her son was arrested in 1937 and 'Requiem' records the lives of those waiting for news of imprisoned relatives.

RAFAEL ALBERTI was born in 1902 in Cadiz. He attended a Jesuit school. In 1917 he went to Madrid intending to become a painter. He did paint throughout his life but he was predominantly a poet. After the defeat of the Republicans in the Spanish Civil War he went into exile, at first in Argentina and later in Rome.

YUZ ALESHKOVSKY was born in 1929 in Russia. He served four years in prison from 1950 'for violating military discipline'. He emigrated in 1979, eventually living in the USA. He performed his satirical poems to the guitar and 'Comrade Stalin' became enormously popular.

DICK ALLEN was born in Troy, New York, in 1939 and educated at Syracuse University and Brown University, where he met John Berryman. He is a lecturer. Several of his poems make dense collages of the turbulent American experience of the Sixties, contrasting them with the calmer Fifties.

LEWIS ALLEN (1903–86) was the pseudonym of Abel Meeropol, a poet, song-writer and political activist. 'Strange Fruit' was made famous by Billie

Holiday, who recorded it in 1939 and used to end her shows with it. Meeropol and his wife adopted the children of the Rosenbergs after their execution in 1953 for alleged spying.

MONIZA ALVI was born in Pakistan in 1954 and moved to England at an early age. Much of her poetry has a vein of bright fantasy as seen in 'I Would Like to be a Dot in a Painting by Miró'.

YEHUDA AMICHAI was born in 1924 in Germany and emigrated to Palestine in 1936. He fought in the British Army in World War II and in Israel's wars in 1956 and 1973. He is a poet of love and war.

MAYA ANGELOU was born in 1928 in St Louis, Missouri. She became famous for her first book of autobiography, *I Know Why the Caged Bird Sings* (1969), which tells the story of her early life: she was raped at the age of eight and became mute. Literature helped her to recover and she went on to study drama and dance and to work as a night-club singer, as an editor, as a coordinator for Martin Luther King, as an actress, and as a poet and writer. She was commissioned to write and read a poem to celebrate President Clinton's inauguration in 1992.

GUILLAUME APOLLINAIRE (1880–1918) was the pseudonym of Wilhelm Albert Vladimir Alexandre Apollinaris de Kostrowitski, the illegitimate son of a nomadic Polish woman and an unknown father. He was one of the leaders of the ferment in French artistic life before World War I, along with Picasso, Satie and Duchamp. He was the first to use the term 'surrealism' and his rootlessness was reflected in the artifice of his poetry, his multiple identities prefiguring postmodernism. He fought in World War I, suffering a serious head wound in 1916; nevertheless, he continued to write until his death two years later.

JAMES APPLEWHITE was born in 1935 in Wilson County, North Carolina. He teaches at Duke University. His work is much concerned with World War II and the technologies of that time, and how motorcars and piston-engined planes formed the hub of a whole way of life for many men.

LOUIS ARAGON (1897–1982) was born in Paris and joined Breton in the surrealist movement in 1919. He broke with surrealism and became a communist in 1931. During the war he simplified his style and became, through his work in the Resistance and his poems, the poetic voice of war-time France. In Louis MacNeice he met his perfect translator for the poem 'The Lilacs and the Roses', which is an elegy, not just for France, but for the whole world that passed away in 1939.

SIMON ARMITAGE was born in Marsden, Huddersfield in 1963. His first book *Zoom!* made an impact for its use of racy northern vernacular. He was a probation officer for some years and his work bristles with the argot of people living on their wits.

JOHN ASH was born in Manchester in 1948 and moved to New York in 1985.

His work is in the line of French and American avant-garde poetry and he is particularly influenced by the New York school of his almost-namesake John Ashbery.

JOHN ASHBERY was born in Rochester, New York in 1927. He studied at Harvard and has worked as an art critic and lecturer. Ashbery is a very influential poet whose own influences include French poetry and Wallace Stevens. The disjunctions in some of his poems can seem arbitrary but others mirror the complexities of late capitalist American society.

MARGARET ATWOOD was born in Ottawa, Canada in 1939. She is best known as a major novelist but she has always written poetry alongside her fiction, often exploring similar themes of the politics of male and female experience.

W. H. AUDEN (1907–1973) was born in York, the son of a doctor father and a mother who had been a nurse. He studied first Natural Sciences then English at Oxford. At the age of twenty-three he was recognized as the leader of a new generation of English poets and his varied and prolific output led him to be compared to Picasso and Stravinsky. He left England in 1939 and became an American citizen, only returning to live in England near the end of his life. Much of his work deals with the public themes of the twentieth century.

STANISŁAW BARAŃCZAK was born in 1946 in Poznan, Poland. He moved to America in 1981 to become a professor at Harvard. He is a noted translator and has been an important link between Polish and American poetry. His poetry of the Communist era exploited the wooden inflexions of official language.

ELIZABETH BARTLETT was born in Kent in 1924. She left school at fifteen and although she wrote poems from an early age, she only published her first book in 1979. She has worked as a medical secretary and in the home care service and much of her poetry is about people who are damaged in one way or another.

GOTTFRIED BENN (1886–1956) was born near Berlin; he practised as a doctor and his work added an element of clinicality to the Expressionist tendencies typical of German poetry at the time. He at first welcomed the Nazi era but by 1936 his work was banned for its degenerate tendencies.

LOUISE BENNETT was born in Jamaica in 1919. She is a champion of the Jamaican folk tradition. She worked for the BBC in London from 1945 to 1955 and has read and lectured all over the world.

JAMES BERRY was born in 1924 in Jamaica. He worked for a time in America before coming to Britain in 1948. The poems in *Lucy's Letters and Loving*, written in a patois very similar to Louise Bennett's, articulate the early experience of Caribbean immigrants in Britain.

JOHN BERRYMAN (1914–1972) was born in Oklahoma to a poor family. His father died of a gunshot wound in 1925, which was adjudged to be suicide.

Berryman's career was ravaged by alcoholism and he was forever trying on poetic masks. *The Dream Songs* are famous for their creation of an idiosyncratic, perkily morose persona.

JOHN BETJEMAN (1906–84) was born in Highgate and educated at Marlborough and Oxford. He began as a camp pasticheur but his interest in architecture, trades (his father was a cabinet-maker of Dutch descent) and English topography lends muscle to his best work. Whether satirical or plangent, his portrayal of the world of home counties suburbia in the Fifties is vastly informative about the era.

SUJATA BHATT was born in Ahmedabad, India in 1956 but grew up in America where her scientist father was working. She studied at the Iowa Creative Writing Program. She is married to a German and lives in Bremen. Sujata Bhatt's first language is Gujarati and she sometimes incorporates fragments of it in her poems, which explore the very wide range of cultures of which she has had first-hand experience.

ELIZABETH BISHOP (1911–79) was born in Worcester, Massachusetts. Her father died when she was eight months old and her mother suffered a breakdown, leading to Bishop being brought up by relatives from the age of five. She was the traveller poet *par excellence*: genuinely rootless, she made art out of detached and lonely places and a transient lifestyle.

PETER BLAND was born in Scarborough in 1934 and emigrated to New Zealand in 1954. Since 1968 he has lived mainly in England, working in theatre as a writer, director and actor. Displacement and cultural dislocation are key themes of his work.

ALEXANDER BLOK (1880–1921). Most Russian poets were sceptical of the Russian Revolution; Alexander Blok had a messianic temperament and at first he surrendered to the storm of change, his poem 'The Twelve' being the expression of that mood. His ardour soon cooled however and Trotsky said: 'Certainly Blok was not one of us, but he came towards us. And that is what broke him.'

RICHARD BLOMFIELD was born in Wimbledon in 1913 and has lived in Dorset for many years. He was educated at Bryanston and Queens College, Oxford. He served in the Army in East Africa. He has worked in advertising and public relations.

EDMUND BLUNDEN (1896–1974) was educated at Oxford and fought in World War I. He was decorated with the Military Cross. Blunden was a traditional English pastoral poet who managed to retain his country interests whilst not shirking the horrors of war. He was one of the first ecological poets.

DMITRY BOBYSHEV was born in 1936 and grew up in Leningrad. He studied chemical engineering and worked in the field of chemical weapons. His early poetry, including 'Upon the Launching of a Sputnik', was published in samizdat journals. He emigrated to the USA in 1979.

ALISON BRACKENBURY was born in Lincolnshire in 1953. She read English at Oxford and works in the family electroplating business in Cheltenham. In her poetry she often brings drama and lyrical depth to provincial lives.

MILLEN BRAND is a poet, novelist, screen-writer and editor. In 1975 he published *Local Lives, Poems about the Pennsylvania Dutch*, which included 'August 6, 1945'.

BERTOLT BRECHT (1898–1956) was born in Augsburg, Germany. He was the poet and dramatist of Germany's decadent years before Hitler and also one of Hitler's fiercest opponents. His work is noted for its pungent didacticism and his life for the inconsistency between his practise and his preaching: critics damn him for supporting Soviet Marxism, living in America (during the War), keeping his money in Swiss banks and exploiting his always large entourage of mistresses.

ANDRÉ BRETON (1896–1966) studied medicine and was highly influenced by Freud. In 1919 he made the first experiments with automatic writing, in collaboration with Philippe Soupault. He published the First Surrealist Manifesto in 1924. Surrealism became virtually a political party, from which members could be expelled, and during the Thirties many writers defected to the Communist Party. In 1935, a final schism occurred between the two bodies. Despite (or because of) this, Breton met Trotsky in Mexico in 1938.

ROLF DIETER BRINKMANN (1940–75) was born in Vechta, Western Germany. He became a primary school teacher in Cologne. He spent 1972–3 living in Rome. In England in 1975 for the Cambridge Poetry Festival, he was hit by a car in London and killed.

EDWIN BROCK (1927–97) was born in London. He was a policeman from 1951 to 1959 and then worked in advertising. His poetry is rawly direct in a way unusual amongst his generation.

JOSEPH BRODSKY (1940–96) was born in St Petersburg (then Leningrad), a city he revered. His father was a navy photographer and his mother a translator. He left school at fifteen and worked in a factory, educating himself by voracious reading. He was recognized as a gifted metaphysical poet when very young. Akhmatova gave him her blessing but he fell foul of the Soviet regime and was imprisoned for twenty months in 1964. Released, he was allowed to leave Russia in 1972, settling in America where he eventually came to write in English (as was the poem included here), adopting jazzy American inflexions. He was awarded the Nobel Prize in 1987.

GWENDOLYN BROOKS was born in Topeka, Kansas in 1917 and graduated from Wilson Junior College in Chicago. She became a professor at various universities. She writes of urban black life with a wide range of reference and a dispassionate objectivity.

ELEANOR BROWN was born in 1969. She is English but grew up in Scotland. She read English at York and was working as a barmaid at a north London

pub when she wrote 'The Lads'. She is one of the Nineties generation of
very gifted and confident English women poets with a strong satirical sense.

ERNEST BRYLL was born in Poland in 1935. A poet, playwright and novelist,
he was popular in the Sixties for alluding to suppressed topics in Polish
history. 'In a Fever' refers to the period of martial law following the banning
of Solidarity in 1981.

BASIL BUNTING (1900–85) was born in Northumberland, educated at a Quaker
school, and served six months in prison as a conscientious objector in World
War I. He met Pound in 1923 and became his disciple. He lived in Persia
for many years from 1939, having first been posted there in the RAF. During
the war he served in Egypt, Italy and Normandy before returning to Iran
where he became an MI6 spy until his expulsion by the nationalist leader
Mosaddeq in 1951.

PAOLO BUZZI (1874–1956) was born in Milan. He was Secretary in Chief of
the Provincial Government in Milan until 1935. He was a Futurist and
continued to celebrate machines and speed in his poetry throughout his life.

ERNESTO CARDENAL was born in Granada, Nicaragua in 1925. He became a
priest and founded the religious community of Solentiname in 1966. He
became a Marxist after a visit to Cuba in 1970 and in 1977 the community
was destroyed by the National Guard. Cardenal fled to Costa Rica and
returned in triumph in 1979 to become Minister of Culture in the Sandinista
government. He established poetry workshops throughout Nicaragua. The
Sandinistas lost power in 1990.

CIARAN CARSON was born in Belfast in 1948 into an Irish-speaking family. He
is a traditional musician as well as a poet. His poetry has been compared
to Paul Muldoon's for its sly narratives, with skittering allusions and deadpan
jokes.

C. P. CAVAFY (1863–1933) was born in Alexandria and spent the years from
nine to sixteen in England – English literature was an important influence
on him. He worked for most of his life in the Egyptian Ministry of Public
Works. A tormented and often lonely homosexual, Cavafy became the classic
case of a writer from the margins creating a world which becomes central
to a literary tradition.

PAUL CELAN (1920–70) was born in Czernovitz, capital of the Bukovina region,
formerly part of the Austro-Hungarian Empire but ceded to Romania after
World War I. There was a large German-speaking Jewish community in the
region, to which Celan belonged. His parents were killed in the Holocaust
and Celan spent the years 1942–4 in labour camps. He escaped death only
by chance. After World War II Czernovitz was transferred to the Soviet
Union and Celan emigrated to France. His work is linguistically innovative,
highly wrought and allusive. He committed suicide.

GABRIEL CELAYA was born in 1911 in Guipuzcoa province, Spain. He has been politically active, standing unsuccessfully as a Basque Communist Party candidate. In his poetry he has moved from an early surrealism through existentialism to postmodernism or 'posthumanism', as he calls it. 'Great Moments', however, fits none of these labels, being a straightforward, humanist poem.

HARRY CLIFTON was born in Dublin in 1952. He has lived largely abroad: in West Africa, where he taught, in Thailand, where he administered aid programmes for refugees, and in Italy and France. He is very much a poet of the new, restless, international mobility.

ROBERT CONQUEST was born in 1917 and educated at Winchester College, Oxford. He is famous as a sovietologist and his book *The Great Terror* (1968) is a standard work on Stalin's persecutions. In poetry he is best known for his anthology *New Lines* (1956) which established the Movement generation of English poets (Larkin, Wain, Davie, Amis, etc.).

WENDY COPE was born in Kent in 1945 and educated at Oxford. Many of her poems are parodies and when not parodying poems, she often sends up notions at large in the public domain, as in 'Engineers' Corner'.

JOHN CORNFORD (1915–36) was one of the young intellectuals who became totally engaged in the political struggle of the Thirties. He joined the Communist Party in 1935 and went to fight in the Spanish Civil War, where he was killed on the Cordoba front on his twenty-first birthday.

GREGORY CORSO was born in New York in 1930 to a poor family. He spent three years in prison for an attempted robbery. He was one of the original Beats and appeared alongside Ginsberg and Ferlinghetti in *Penguin Modern Poets 5*.

DAVID CRAIG was born in Aberdeen in 1932. He is known for his prose books about mountaineering. He teaches creative writing at Lancaster University.

ROBERT CRAWFORD was born in Scotland in 1959 and educated at Oxford. He is a poet, critic, Professor of English at St Andrews University, and one of the leaders of the Scottish literary renaissance of the Nineties. Besides Scottish matters, his work is often concerned with science, technology, the consumer society and postmodernism.

E. E. CUMMINGS (1894–1962) was born in Cambridge, Massachusetts. In 1917 he volunteered to serve in an ambulance team in France, where he was imprisoned for three months on a false charge. His work is famous for its typographical oddities (closedupwords, random/punctuation) and its whimsical charm.

ALLEN CURNOW was born in Timaru, New Zealand in 1911. He is the senior New Zealand poet now writing. His work is very varied, as the poems here show: one about the lifestyle of urban guerrillas of the 1970s; one a timeless lyric about time.

BOGDAN CZAYKOWSKI was born in south-east Poland in 1932. He was deported to the Soviet Union in 1940 and came to England in 1948, where he studied. Since 1962 he has taught Polish history and literature at the University of British Columbia, Canada.

FRED D'AGUIAR was born in London in 1960 to Guyanese parents and grew up in Guyana, returning to London in 1972. He worked as a psychiatric nurse before reading English and Caribbean studies at the University of Kent. He now teaches at the University of Florida.

KEKI N. DARUWALLA was born in 1937 in Lahore to a Parsee family. He has worked in the Indian Police and Diplomatic Service. His poetry deals with the many cultures that have shaped India, especially Hindu and Persian.

MAHMOUD DARWISH was born in Upper Galilee, Palestine in 1942. He and his family were forced to flee into Lebanon in 1948 but soon returned to Israel when his village was destroyed. In Israel he lacked papers and was often imprisoned between 1961 and 1969. In 1971 he moved to Cairo, where he wrote for the leading newspaper *Al Ahram*, and then in 1973 to Beirut to work for the PLO. He wrote extensively about the siege of Beirut in 1982 which resulted in the expulsion of the Palestinians. He was a member of the PLO Executive Committee from 1987 to 1993.

DONALD DAVIE (1922–96) was born in Barnsley, Yorkshire. He was a major critic and a leading member of the Movement. His attitude to the poets of the Thirties and their politics, the subject of 'Remembering the 'Thirties', was heavily influenced by his northern nonconformist upbringing.

C. DAY LEWIS (1904–72) was born in Ireland, of Anglo-Irish parents. He moved to England in 1905. In the Thirties he was heavily influenced in his social poetry by Auden, although after the war his true colours as a poet in the English pastoral tradition of Hardy and Edward Thomas became apparent. He was appointed Poet Laureate in 1968.

JAMES DICKEY was born in Atlanta, Georgia in 1923 and studied at Vanderbilt University. He has worked in advertising and as a lecturer. He served as a pilot in World War II and the Korean War.

KEITH DOUGLAS (1920–44) was born in Kent and educated at Oxford. He was the characteristic English poet of World War II as Owen was of the First. Mechanized war produced a tougher, more cynical approach, which was reinforced by Douglas's own temperament.

RITA DOVE was born in the industrial city of Akron, Ohio in 1952 and educated at the University of Tübingen, Germany. Many of her poems deal with the migration of black workers from the south to the north in mid-century. She has been Poet Laureate of the USA.

CAROL ANN DUFFY was born in Glasgow in 1955 and grew up in Staffordshire. Many of her poems use personas and she revived the use of monologue in English poetry. Her poems are often strongly political and she is in many ways the characteristic English poet of the Eighties and Nineties.

ROBERT DUNCAN (1919–88) was born in Oakland, California. His poetry was mystical, influenced by the Beats and the Black Mountain group of free-form poets. In the Sixties it also took a political turn through his passionate opposition to the Vietnam War.

DOUGLAS DUNN was born in Renfrewshire, Scotland in 1942 and worked for many years as a librarian, including a spell at Hull with Larkin. His first book, *Terry Street*, detailed the lives of a two-up-two-down street in Hull, territory that had never entered verse before.

PAUL DURCAN was born in 1944 in Dublin and studied archaeology and medieval history at Westport College, Cork. He made his name in poems that mocked Irish pieties and hypocrisies by cunningly exploiting vernacular language.

BOB DYLAN was born in Duluth, Minnesota in 1941, and grew up in nearby Hibbing, a declining iron-mining town. As an early disciple of the folksinger Woody Guthrie, Dylan came to fame in the folk revival of the early Sixties, but soon transcended folk music to become one of the most original and inventive writers of popular songs in the second half of the century. His lyrics blend blues and country vernacular diction, biblical cadences and surrealism to create poetry that is as distinctive as any written in this time.

RICHARD EBERHART was born in 1904 in Austin, Minnesota. He studied at Dartmouth College and Cambridge, England, and served in World War II as an aerial gunnery instructor in the US Navy.

ILYA EHRENBURG (1891–1967) grew up in Moscow. At school he was involved in Bolshevik activities. He emigrated to France in 1908, where he became friendly with Picasso, Léger and Louis Aragon. He served as a cultural courier between France and Russia.

IVAN ELAGIN was born in Russia in 1918. His name is a pseudonym for Ivan Vedikovich Matveyev.

T. S. ELIOT (1888–1965) was born in St Louis, Missouri but his well-to-do family came from Boston. He moved to England in 1914. Eliot became the most influential poet in English of the twentieth century, breaking with nineteenth-century traditions of English poetry, embracing French models, particularly Laforgue, and going back to the Metaphysicals for inspiration. His work defined Modernism for English poetry, and through it the modern world, usually in its most sordid manifestations, entered into poetry in a wholly novel way. *The Waste Land* is one of the few poems to define an era, although in later life Eliot dismissed its wider importance, calling it 'a wholly insignificant grouse against life ... just a piece of rhythmical grumbling'.

STEVE ELLIS was born in 1952 in York. He was educated at University College, London. He is Professor of English Literature at Birmingham University and has translated Dante.

D. J. ENRIGHT was born in Leamington Spa in 1920 and studied under F. R. Leavis at Cambridge. He spent many years teaching abroad. His poems bring a very dry irony to bear on exotic and dramatic subjects.

HANS MAGNUS ENZENSBERGER was born in Bavaria in 1929. He is the best-known German poet since Brecht, with whom he shares a didacticism and a clipped laconic voice. A wide-ranging public intellectual, Enzensberger has taken controversial public stands on the major issues of post-war Germany.

GAVIN EWART (1916–95) was born in London and educated at Cambridge. He published early as an Audenesque poet at the age of twenty-three but didn't publish another book until he was fifty. He then became prolific as a light-verse master, writing on virtually every subject under the sun. In many poems he used his light verse techniques to write serious and highly effective poems informed by an unsentimental humanism.

NISSIM EZEKIEL was born in 1924 to a Jewish family in Bombay where he has always lived. He is widely regarded as the first major Indian poet to write in English. Ezekiel's mixed background, being Jewish in India and writing in English, gives him an unusual and productive platform for writing poetry.

U. A. FANTHORPE was born in London in 1929. She was Head of English at Cheltenham Ladies College and then worked for many years as a hospital clerk, an experience which informed many of her earliest poems. She started to publish in 1978 and has since been prolific, sharing with Carol Ann Duffy the honour of having restored the monologue to poetic credibility.

IRVING FELDMAN was born in Coney Island, New York in 1928 and educated at Columbia University. His 'Lyrics, aphorisms, tales, psalms, prose poems, jokes and disquisitions range over the whole sad, funny backlot of modern life,' as the *Oxford Companion to Twentieth-Century Poetry* puts it.

JAMES FENTON was born in Lincoln in 1949 and educated at Oxford. He is notable as the only poet of his generation to follow a parallel career as a foreign correspondent, at first in Indo-China, particularly Cambodia, and later in the Philippines. His formal skill and intellectual range recall his mentor, Auden.

LAWRENCE FERLINGHETTI was born in New York in 1919. He was one of the original Beats and as publisher and owner of City Lights Bookstore and Publishing House in San Francisco, he published Ginsberg's *Howl* in 1956. Ferlinghetti is more influenced by European popular poets such as Prévert than were the other Beats. *A Coney Island of the Mind*, from which 'Sometime during eternity . . .' comes, was one of the biggest selling poetry books of the century.

DUNCAN FORBES was born in Oxford in 1947. He read English at Corpus Christi College, Oxford, and is now Head of English at Wycombe Abbey School. He lives in Reading.

LINDA FRANCE was born in Newcastle in 1958. She has worked in adult education and is the editor of the anthology *Sixty Women Poets*.

ANDRÉ FRÉNAUD (1907–93) was born in France. In 1940 he joined the army and was captured, escaping from a German POW camp in 1942 to join the Resistance. Most of the poems in his first book, *Les Rois Mages*, including 'House for Sale', were written in captivity.

ERICH FRIED (1921–89) was born in Vienna and came to England in 1938 where he lived, working in the German section of the BBC, until his death. He had a huge reputation in post-war Germany but was relatively little known in England during his life. Much of his work is intensely political and constitutes a primer in the politics in the twentieth century.

KATHERINE FROST was born in 1945 and grew up in London. She is a clinical psychologist.

ROBERT FROST (1874–1963) was born in San Francisco and settled in England in 1912 where he published his first book and met the English poets, especially Edward Thomas, who influenced him. He returned to America when war broke out. He became a farmer poet and America's most public poet of the century. He composed a poem for President Kennedy's inauguration in 1960 and was sent by Kennedy on a mission to meet Khrushchev in Moscow.

JOHN FULLER was born in Ashford, Kent in 1937, the son of the poet Roy Fuller. He is a fellow of Magdalen College, Oxford. Fuller is a virtuosic wit who in his later work has often applied his formal skill to an Audenian kind of civic poetry.

ROY FULLER (1912–91) was born in Failsworth, Lancashire. He trained as a solicitor and in 1938 he joined the Woolwich Equitable Society, where he remained, becoming a director in 1969. He was a prolific poet to the last and if he sometimes cultivated an old bufferish stance, he was an uncommonly cultivated and wise old buffer.

ELIZABETH GARRETT was born in London in 1958 and grew up in the Channel Islands. Her father is half French. She was educated at York and Oxford universities and has worked for the Bodleian Library and the Voltaire Foundation. Her poetry is traditionally lyrical and, as in the poem here, sacramental.

KAREN GERSHON (1923–93) was born in Bielefeld, Germany to Jewish parents. She came to England as a refugee in 1939, leaving her parents behind. She wrote many poems about the Holocaust and a prose book, *We Came as Children*, about the experiences of those who were given sanctuary in Britain without their parents, most of whom died in the Holocaust.

JAIME GIL DE BIEDMA (1929–90) was born in Barcelona and lived most of his life there. He was a critic and translator, fluent in English, and knew English poetry well.

ALLEN GINSBERG (1926–97) was born in New Jersey. He met the other emerging Beat writers in Greenwich Village and published *Howl*, his long poetic anthem for the Beat movement in 1956. He became the guru of the counterculture during the Sixties. His poetry takes Whitman's ecstatic embrace of the world into the twentieth century.

ELTON GLASER was born in New Orleans in 1945. He is a professor of English at the University of Akron, Ohio. He has said of 'Smoking' that the poem 'has no patience with the Puritan pieties of our time, this frightened and coercive age in which we too often find, as Shakespeare put it, "art made tongue-tied by authority".'

ALAN GOULD was born in Australia of British-Icelandic parents in 1949. He graduated from the Australian National University. He has worked as a teacher, a nuclear-physics technician and an agricultural labourer.

GÜNTER GRASS was born in Danzig in 1927 (then in Germany; it is now Gdansk in Poland). He worked as a draughtsman, sculptor, stage-designer, playwright, fought in World War II, and was captured by the Americans. His novel *The Tin Drum* (1959) made him famous. He is one of Germany's leading public intellectuals, and has had a long involvement with the Social Democratic Party.

ROBERT GREACEN was born in Derry, Northern Ireland in 1920. He has worked for the United Nations and as a teacher. His fictional persona Captain Fox allowed him the freedom to develop a rumbustious, irreverent strain in his poetry.

PHILIP GROSS was born in 1952 in Delabole, Devon. His father was an Estonian refugee and Gross has written about the Holocaust and the fate of the European refugees of World War II.

PAUL GROVES was born in 1947 near Chepstow and educated at Caerleon College in Wales. He was a teacher for many years. He is a versatile poet, adept at illuminating sad corners of modern life in often ingenious light verse.

DURS GRÜNBEIN was born in 1962 in Dresden, East Germany. He moved to East Berlin in 1985. He is the leading German poet of his generation. His austere rendering of contemporary life has something in common with Michael Hofmann, who has translated some of his poetry.

EUGÈNE GUILLEVIC (1907–97) was born in Carnac, Brittany. He is often known just by his surname. His poetry is very varied and experimental.

THOM GUNN was born in Gravesend in 1929. Initially bracketed with the Movement on the strength of the tight formality of his poetry, he moved to California in 1954 and adopted a freer style, warmly entering into the Californian lifestyle, especially its gay culture. He has written many poems about the AIDS epidemic.

IVOR GURNEY (1890–1937) was born in Gloucester, the son of a tailor. He was a composer as well as a poet and he had a deep love of the Cotswolds and the music of Elgar and Vaughan Williams. He served in World War I and was gassed at Ypres. On return to England he suffered a breakdown and spent the last fifteen years of his life in the City of London Mental Hospital. His poetry is more 'modern' than that of his peers despite his very English preoccupations. Gerard Manley Hopkins was an important influence on him.

BROTHER WILL HAIRSTON was a blues singer who flourished around 1956.

DONALD HALL was born in New Haven, Connecticut in 1928. He has been an influential editor, especially for his Penguin anthology *Contemporary American Poetry*. His long poem, 'The One Day', is remarkable for its quasi-biblical note of prophetic rage applied to the civilization of late twentieth-century consumerism.

MARK HALLIDAY was born in Ann Arbor, Michigan in 1949. He teaches at Ohio University. His work embraces the American flux, including a good deal of pop culture, and worries about the agonies of choice in contemporary consumer society with wit and charm.

SOPHIE HANNAH was born in Manchester in 1971. She published her first book at the age of twenty-four. She has made a name as a comic poet with an increasingly surrealizing touch, the latter marking her off from her mentor, Wendy Cope.

THOMAS HARDY (1840–1928) was born in Higher Bockhampton, Dorset. He is the only poet of the period who is also a major novelist. He did not publish poems during his career as a novelist and the poor reception of *Jude the Obscure* (1895) led him to concentrate on poetry in the latter half of his life. His great theme was fate: that Hardy should write the best-known poem about the sinking of the Titanic was another of the 'forefelt' conjunctions that so obsessed him.

TONY HARRISON was born in Leeds in 1937 to working-class parents. He became a classical scholar, a poet and a verse dramatist, working, uniquely amongst modern poets, for the National Theatre and television. Both his personal and public poems are highly politicized and his poems about the Gulf War led to him being sent by the *Guardian* as a poetic war correspondent to Bosnia. His long poem *v.* (1985), about the desecration of his parent's grave by skinheads, became one of the most controversial poems of modern times when it was made into a Channel 4 television film.

DAVID HART was born in 1940 in Aberystwyth, Wales and now lives in Birmingham. He has worked as an Anglican curate in London, a university chaplain in Birmingham, as drama critic of the *Birmingham Post*, and as an arts administrator. In 1998 he became the first Writer in Residence in a cathedral – at Worcester.

GWEN HARWOOD was born in 1920 in Brisbane but has lived since 1945 in

Tasmania. She has combined the careers of poet and music teacher and has written under many jokey pseudonyms.

SEAMUS HEANEY was born in 1939 in Mossbawn, County Derry, Northern Ireland, the son of a Catholic farmer. He went to Queen's University, Belfast and has lived in Dublin since 1976. In 1984 he was appointed Professor at Harvard and he was awarded the Nobel Prize in 1995. Heaney has written about the condition of Ireland from a deep historical perspective, finding parallels between the ancient Viking world of the preserved Bog people and present-day sectarian conflicts in Ireland.

ANTHONY HECHT was born in 1923 in New York City. He served in World War II in Europe and Japan. He is one of the most European of American poets, with a painter's eye for gorgeousness – but also a strong concern for the bleakest terrors of the twentieth century.

ADRIAN HENRI was born in 1932 and studied fine art at King's College, Newcastle. He was one of the trio of Mersey Poets in the Sixties with Roger McGough and Brian Patten. He is also a painter. He performed for three years with The Liverpool Scene, a jazz/poetry/rock group.

ZBIGNIEW HERBERT (1924–98) was born in Poland. He fought in the Resistance and afterwards studied law, commerce and philosophy. He is the most committed anti-Communist of the major Polish poets, and his work was little published in Poland before 1989. He became known in the West through the efforts of Al Alvarez, Daniel Weissbort and Ted Hughes during the 1960s. He is one of the writers famous for being expected to win the Nobel Prize but failing to do so.

MIGUEL HERNÁNDEZ (1910–42) worked as a goatherd as a child and was largely self-educated. He went to Madrid in 1934 and received encouragement from important poets, including Neruda, who was in Spain at the time. He fought as a Republican in the Spanish Civil War and was imprisoned towards the end. He spent two years in prison in Alicante and died of tuberculosis there.

DOROTHY HEWETT, was born in Perth, Western Australia in 1923. She has written novels and plays besides her poetry.

JOHN HEWITT (1907–87) was born and grew up in Belfast. From 1930 to 1957 he worked in the Belfast Museum and Art Gallery and from 1957 to 1972 he directed the Herbert Museum, Coventry. Much of his poetry deals with the position of his own Protestant community in Northern Ireland from a socialist and non-sectarian viewpoint.

NAZIM HIKMET (1902–63) is generally regarded as the major Turkish poet of the century. He spent a good part of his life in prison on political charges, the longest spell being from 1938 to 1950.

MICHAEL HOFMANN was born in Freiburg in 1957. His father was a noted German novelist. The family came to England in 1961 and Hofmann was educated at Cambridge. His poetry has a nervy, deadpan precision, especially when interpreting the signs and symbols of contemporary urban life.

DAVID HOLBROOK was born in Norwich in 1923. He has written social criticism and on education besides poetry, and has worked in adult education and university teaching. He has lived most of his life in Cambridge, home of one of the great centres of molecular biology, the subject of his poem 'The Maverick'.

JONATHAN HOLDEN was born in Morristown, New Jersey. He graduated in English from Oberlin College, Ohio in 1963. He is University Distinguished Professor and Poet in Residence at Kansas State University.

MIROSLAV HOLUB (1923–98) was born in Pilsen, Czechoslovakia. He had parallel careers as a noted immunologist and as a poet and writer. From 1968 to 1982 he was not allowed to publish in Czechoslovakia but he became well known abroad, especially in Britain and America. His work has very deep roots in European history and science. Of all the major poets of Eastern Europe, Holub was the one least affected by the changes of '89: his work was a battle against absurdity, a commodity to be found in all systems.

LANGSTON HUGHES (1902–67) was born in Joplin, Missouri. He was the first black artist to make a living solely from writing and also the first to write civil rights protest poetry. He also produced drama, fiction, and an autobiography. He consciously strove to catch the mood of the blues in his poetry.

TED HUGHES (1930–98) was born in Mytholmroyd, Yorkshire. His father was one of only seventeen survivors of an entire regiment wiped out at Gallipoli in World War I. He was educated at Cambridge where he met and later married Sylvia Plath. His raw nature poetry made an immediate impact when his first book appeared in 1957. Hughes belonged to the same radical dissenting tradition as D. H. Lawrence: like him, he saw everywhere primal energies being thwarted by polite society.

KATHLEEN JAMIE was born in 1962 in Renfrewshire, grew up in Midlothian, and now lives in Fife. She is a seasoned traveller and has written travel books about Asia. Her work is noted for its pugnacious and quintessentially Scottish brio.

JERZY JARNIEWICZ was born in Lowicz, Poland, in 1958. He is a lecturer in English at the universities of Łódź and Warsaw and is an editor of the literary journal *Literatura Nq Swiecie*. He has translated the work of several English poets, including Craig Raine.

RANDALL JARRELL (1914–65) was born in Nashville, Tennessee and moved between Los Angeles and Nashville in childhood. He graduated from Vanderbilt University in Nashville and made a reputation which survives till this day as one of the most trenchant of poetry critics. In 1942 he joined the US Air Force, failed to qualify as a pilot, and became a navigation trainer. He wrote many poems about the War which captured perfectly the mood of the big air bases.

ROBINSON JEFFERS (1887–1962) was an American isolationist who disapproved of America's engagement in World War II. His harsh and rather repellent philosophy did enable him to see some things others missed: for example, the corruption inherent in America assuming world leadership, or, as in the poem included here, the sanitizing effect of historical perspective.

LINTON KWESI JOHNSON was born in 1952 in Chapeltown, Jamaica. He came to London in 1963, where he studied sociology at Goldsmiths College. He has worked extensively with reggae musicians, and in 1980 founded LKJ records. He has been active politically in the south London black community and at one point joined the Black Panthers.

BRIAN JONES was born in 1938 in London. He is a teacher. His poetry of the Sixties and Seventies is particularly sharp on the colour-supplement lifestyle prevalent then. His work is due for a revival.

JENNY JOSEPH was born in Birmingham in 1932 and educated at Oxford. She has worked as a reporter, a pub landlady and an adult education lecturer. Besides poetry, she has written an experimental poem-novel and the philosophical prose pieces, *Extended Similes*. 'Warning' was voted The Nation's Favourite Modern Poem in a BBC poll of television viewers in 1996.

P. J. KAVANAGH was born in 1931 in Sussex. His father was a comedian who wrote sketches for the radio show ITMA. He fought in the Korean War and has worked in publishing, television and journalism. The death of his wife Sally, a year after their marriage, provoked some of his best poems and also the prose book *The Perfect Stranger*.

PATRICK KAVANAGH (1904–67) was born in Inniskee, County Monahan, Ireland where, initially, he followed his father as a cobbler and small farmer. He received no formal education beyond the age of twelve but he was already writing poetry then. In 'The Great Hunger' (1942) he wrote the epic poem of Ireland's most terrible human tragedy, the starvation of millions by the potato famine of the 1840s.

JACKIE KAY was born in 1961 and brought up in Scotland. Besides her poems, she has written plays, a biography of Bessie Smith and a novel, *Trumpet*, which won the 1996 Guardian Fiction Prize.

WELDON KEES (1914–55) was born in Nebraska and grew up during the Depression. He became a Trotskyite but art gained the upper hand: he was a jazz pianist, a journalist and film maker besides a poet. In 1955 his car was found near the Golden Gate Bridge but his body was never found. His reputation increased dramatically in the 1990s and something of a cult was erected around him. Several of his poems are written in the persona of Robinson, an enigmatic Chandleresque figure who has gripped the imagination of other poets, especially Simon Armitage.

GALWAY KINNELL was born in 1927 in Providence, Rhode Island, and studied at Princeton and the University of Rochester. He served in the US Navy in World War II then travelled widely before returning to the USA to teach at several universities.

RUDYARD KIPLING (1865–1936) was born in Bombay but educated in England. He returned to India where he worked as a journalist. He became a great public poet, with his harsh view of colonial and army life encapsulated in emphatic rhythms and colloquial language. His poem 'If' was voted the Nation's Favourite Poem in a BBC poll of television viewers in 1995.

CAROLYN KIZER was born in 1925 in Spokane, Washington, educated at Sarah Lawrence College and lives in Sonoma, California, and part of the year in France. She has said of 'Twelve O'Clock': 'I wanted the poem to be a piece of autobiography, to include everything – pathetically little! – that I had ever thought or heard about atomic physics and the use of the atomic bomb.'

RACHEL KORN (1898–1982) was born in Podliski, Galicia, Poland. She lived in Lvov till 1941 when she fled to Russia. She eventually emigrated to Canada. She always wrote in Yiddish.

NAUM KORZHAVIN was born in 1925 in Kiev. He studied at the Gorky Literary Institute. He was imprisoned in 1947 for writing flagrantly anti-Stalinist poems and spent eight months in prison and three years in exile in Siberia. He was allowed to return to Moscow in 1954, worked as a translator and was officially rehabilitated in 1956. He has a strongly disputatious and polemical streak, as is evident from 'Imitation of Monsieur Béranger'.

ABBA KOVNER (1918–82) was born in Sevastopol, Crimea. He grew up in Vilna where he was involved in the Zionist Youth Movement. When the Ghetto was set up in 1941 he joined the Jewish partisans and fought throughout the War. He emigrated to Israel in 1946. He has always written only in Hebrew.

MAXINE KUMIN was born in Philadelphia in 1925 and educated at Radcliffe College. She has written novels, short stories and essays besides poetry, and won the Pulitzer Prize in 1973. Her poetry is generally grounded in the natural world.

IVAN V. LALIĆ (1931–96) was born in Belgrade, Yugoslavia, where he worked as an editor. His work is very much in the Mediterranean tradition, showing an affinity with Greek poetry.

FRAN LANDESMAN was born in Manhattan in 1927 and has lived in London since the early Sixties. 'The Ballad of the Sad Young Men' comes from her musical *The Nervous Set* (1959), a parody of the Beat movement. The 'Ballad' and 'Spring Can Really Hang You up the Most' have become jazz standards.

PHILIP LARKIN (1922–85) grew up in Coventry and was educated at Oxford. He was a librarian all his life, for the last thirty years in Hull. He was the unofficial laureate of the shabby provincial England of the Fifties and Sixties, as well as being a personal poet of candour and grace under duress.

JAMES LASDUN was born in London in 1958. He now lives in New York where he teaches. He writes short stories as well as poems and his style is neo-Jacobean, at home in the decadent fleshpots of the Eighties and Nineties.

D. H. LAWRENCE (1885–1930) was born in the mining village of Eastwood, Nottinghamshire, the son of a coalminer and a mother who had been a teacher. Although better known for his novels and his philosophy of regeneration through sex, Lawrence's poetry has been influential (especially on Ted Hughes) for the darting way he captures the pulse of nature.

JOHN LENNON (1940–80) was born in Liverpool. His early songs were relatively uninteresting lyrically, but goaded by the bravura verbal feats of Bob Dylan and by the journalist Kenneth Allsop's remark that the language in his book *In His Own Write* (1964) was more interesting than his songs, he began to write songs like 'Norwegian Wood' with acerbic and carefully crafted lyrics. In 'A Day in the Life' (in which McCartney contributed the 'Woke up, fell out of bed ...' stanza) Lennon's love of newspaper ephemera produced results that have lasted.

DENISE LEVERTOV (1923–98) was born in Ilford, Essex. Her mother was Welsh and her father of Russian-Jewish descent. In 1948 she emigrated to the USA where she came under the influence of poets such as William Carlos Williams and Charles Olson. Her political stance, which grew from her spiritual convictions, came to the fore in her poems about the Vietnam War.

JOHN LEVETT was born in 1950 and works as a librarian in Kent. His poetry is notable for the way it incorporates polysyllabic technical language into formal iambic verse.

PRIMO LEVI (1919–87) was born in Turin to a long-established Italian-Jewish family. He lived in Turin all his life apart from the war years. He worked as a chemist before World War II, when he joined the Italian partisans. Captured and deported to Auschwitz in 1944, he survived, largely because he was able to work in the laboratory of the synthetic rubber factory attached to the camp. His account of Auschwitz and his return home, *If This is a Man/The Truce* is a classic, as is his chemist's memoir, *The Periodic Table*.

GWYNETH LEWIS was born in Cardiff in 1959. Her first language is Welsh. She was educated at Cambridge (first degree) and Oxford (D.Phil.) and spent three years in the USA, as Harkness Fellow at Harvard and Columbia. She is producer for the BBC in Cardiff. Her space poems were occasioned by the fact that her cousin is an astronaut.

ALFRED LICHTENSTEIN (1889–1914). Lichtenstein studied law. He was an early exponent of Expressionism, publishing one book, in 1913, before joining the army. He was killed in action.

LIZ LOCHHEAD was born in 1947 in Motherwell, Scotland. She is a playwright and performer as well as a poet.

PAUL MCCARTNEY was born in Liverpool in 1942. He is one of the century's great melodists and has written vivid narrative songs such as 'Eleanor Rigby', 'She's Leaving Home' and 'Penny Lane', which helped to make the pop lyric a force to be reckoned with in poetic terms.

ROGER MCGOUGH was born in Liverpool in 1937. In the mid-Sixties, together with Adrian Henri and Brian Patten, he created a new scene in poetry, with performances, sometimes involving music, which took their place alongside pop, folk and jazz music.

IAN MCMILLAN was born in 1957 in Barnsley and he still lives close by. McMillan has made a name as both a performance and a page poet. He has worked with performance groups, notably Versewagon, with Martyn Wiley and John Turner, which toured, giving street performances, and the Circus of Poets (same personnel). His work blends Northern grit and humour, surrealism and a canny knowledge of the postmodern condition of both art and life.

LOUIS MACNEICE (1907–63) was born in Belfast, the son of a Church of Ireland (Protestant) Bishop. He was educated at Marlborough College and Oxford. MacNeice met Auden as an undergraduate and their names were linked ever after. MacNeice adopted the stance of *'l'homme moyen sensuel'*, the average sensual man. He taught Classics, went to Spain, and worked for the BBC as a producer and feature writer from 1940 to his death. His long documentary poem, *Autumn Journal* (1939) is one of the most vivid records from the era of Munich.

DEREK MAHON was born in Belfast in 1941. He travelled widely in France, Canada and the USA, before settling in London in 1970 as an editor, journalist and writer of screenplays. He moved to Dublin in the Eighties. In his poems he has consciously inherited the mantle of MacNeice.

OSIP MANDELSTAM (1881–1938) grew up in St Petersburg. He visited Paris in 1907 and studied in Heidelberg. Mandelstam was a pure lyric poet, and 'The Stalin Epigram' was his one attempt at addressing the horror of the age. The poem led to his arrest in 1934; he was eventually freed, then arrested again, and he died in prison, having become demented from the treatment he received.

ERICA MARX (1909–67) was born in Streatham, London and educated at King's College, London. From 1941 to 1943 she was Commandant of the Women's Home Defence in Surrey.

GLYN MAXWELL was born in Welwyn Garden City in 1962 of Welsh parents. He has written verse plays and a novel besides poetry. Maxwell has found a style to mirror the artificial tabloid/soap opera world that grew up in the 1980s. He is much influenced by contemporary songwriters.

VLADIMIR MAYAKOVSKY (1893–1930) was born in Georgia. He joined the Bolsheviks in 1907 and was arrested several times before the Revolution for his political activities. He was the most prominent poet to serve the new regime and in the early Twenties he was a major exponent of the new art forms, both visual and literary, which briefly flourished in the revolutionary climate. His sprawling free-form stanzas have been influential on poets such as Yevtushenko, Voznesensky and Lawrence Ferlinghetti.

ARTYEMY MIKHAILOV's poem was published in a samizdat collection, *Poems from the Russian Underground*, in 1973.

CZESŁAW MIŁOSZ was born in 1911 in Szetejnie, Poland, to part-Polish and part-Lithuanian parents. He grew up in Vilna. He fought in the Polish resistance during World War II and from 1946 to 1951 he was a diplomat. He broke with the communist regime in 1951 and has lived in the West ever since, mostly in America, although he has frequently returned to Poland since 1989. He was awarded the Nobel Prize in 1980.

ADRIAN MITCHELL was born in 1932 in London, of Scottish descent. He has been a political performer since the Sixties and has tried to live up to his famous utterance: 'Most people ignore most poetry/because/most poetry ignores most people.' He has worked widely in the theatre and with music.

JONI MITCHELL was born in 1943 in Alberta, Canada. She studied art in Calgary then moved to Toronto where she began singing and writing songs. She is one of the most gifted of the singer-songwriters who proliferated in the Sixties. She is a painter and her work is more self-consciously artistic than that of most of her peers. She articulated the more romantic side of the Sixties and was equally at home in the Seventies.

EUGENIO MONTALE (1896–1981) was born in Genoa. From 1929 to 1938 he was director of the Italian Scientific-Literary Cabinet. After the War he worked for many years as music and literary critic of the leading newspaper *Corriere Della Sera*. He was awarded the Nobel Prize for Literature in 1975.

MARIANNE MOORE (1887–1972) was born in St Louis, Missouri. She lived with her mother all her life. She was one of the leaders of early American Modernism and she had an essayist's interest in animals, sport and gadgets.

EDWIN MORGAN was born in Glasgow in 1920. He taught for many years at Glasgow University. Morgan is one of the most varied and internationally orientated of poets. He has translated widely from Russian, Italian and several other languages; some of his translations appear in this book.

BLAKE MORRISON was born in Skipton, Yorkshire in 1950. He has been Literary Editor of both the *Observer* and the *Independent on Sunday*. Besides his poetry he has written a prose memoir, *When Did You Last See Your Father?* and a book about the killing of James Bulger.

ANDREW MOTION was born in London in 1952. He has worked as a poetry editor and is now Professor of Creative Writing at the University of East Anglia. He is also the biographer of Larkin and Keats.

EDWIN MUIR (1887–1959) was born on the Isle of Orkney. From 1921 he lived mostly in Europe, particularly Prague, where, with his wife, Willa, he translated Kafka.

PAUL MULDOON was born in Portadown, Northern Ireland, in 1951. He studied at Queen's University, Belfast, where he met Seamus Heaney and Derek Mahon. He worked as a producer for the BBC until moving to the USA in the mid-Eighties. He is one of the most influential poets of recent years, blending folk wit with sophisticated literary and anthropological allusions.

LES MURRAY was born in the village of Nabiac on the north coast of New South Wales. He grew up on his father's farm at Bunyah, in the same state, where he lives today. Murray's sensibility is unusual in poetry: celebrating the vernacular culture and aboriginal traditions of Australia, he has nevertheless, become one of the most influential poets in the world. His stance is epitomized by the lines, 'Some of us primary producers, us farmers and authors/are going to watch them evict a banker'.

HOWARD NEMEROV (1920–91) was born in New York City. He served in the Canadian and American airforces in World War II. He was US Poet Laureate in 1988–90. Nemerov resembles Frost in his ruminative voice and strong civic sense.

PABLO NERUDA (1904–73) was born in Parral in southern Chile. In 1927, he entered the Chilean consular service and served in Indo-China. He was in Spain as the Civil War broke out and was closely involved with the artists and radicals of Republican Spain. He became a senator in Chile in 1945 but in 1947 his Communist allegiance led him to go into hiding. He returned in 1950. When his friend Salvador Allende became President, Neruda went to France as Ambassador in 1971. In the same year he was awarded the Nobel Prize. He died very soon after the coup that toppled Allende's government.

VÍTĚZSLAV NEZVAL (1900–58) was the leading exponent of Czech surrealism in the inter-war years.

NORMAN NICHOLSON (1910–87) was born in Millom, Cumberland and lived all his life in the same house. He chronicled the life of this region where, until the 1960s, deep rurality and steel-making had co-existed.

PASTOR NIEMÖLLER (1892–1984). A Protestant pastor, Niemöller was one of the pillars of moral resistance to the Nazis, who imprisoned him for four years in solitary confinement but could not quench his spirit.

SEAN O'BRIEN was born in London in 1952, grew up in Hull and read English at Cambridge University. He belongs partly to a Hull tradition, with figures like Larkin and Douglas Dunn behind him, but his part-Irish background is important too. He is a critic and editor as well as a poet, and unusual in being committed both to style and politics.

DENNIS O'DRISCOLL was born in County Tipperary, Ireland in 1954. He was educated at Christian Brothers schools and works in the Irish Civil Service. He is a reviewer and critic of encyclopedic scope.

FRANK O'HARA (1926–66) was born in Baltimore, Maryland. He served in the US Navy (1944–6) and from 1951 worked at the Museum of Modern Art in New York. Like his friend and colleague John Ashbery, he was deeply involved in the New York visual art world at the height of its fame and world domination. His poems were almost a sideline, often dashed off in letters to friends which he refused to collect during his life: they capture the spirit of metropolitan dandyism and have been extremely influential, particularly on recent English poets like Simon Armitage. He died in an accident with a beach buggy on Fire Island.

ANDREAS OKOPENKO was born in Kaschau (Kosice) in Czechoslovakia to German parents. He was forced to leave in 1939 and settled in Vienna. He is a chemist by training and has written radio plays, a novel and short stories besides poems.

SHARON OLDS was born in California in 1942 but has lived most of her life in New York City. She is noted for her fierce and proud poems on female sexuality and her equally uncompromising poems on other aspects of family life and love.

WILFRED OWEN (1893–1918) was born in Oswestry. In 1911 he began work, under the influence of his evangelical mother, as lay assistant to the vicar in an Oxfordshire parish. He was brought to the verge of a breakdown by this experience and spent some time in France and worked as a tutor. He enlisted in 1915 and crossed to France in December 1916. He was injured and convalesced at Craiglockhart Hospital, near Edinburgh where he met Siegfried Sassoon. He returned to France, was awarded the Military Cross, and was killed leading his platoon. His poems had a profound and lasting effect, both on subsequent poets, and on the English conscience.

DAN PAGIS was born in the Bukovina in Romania in 1930, a member of the same community of German-speaking Jews as Paul Celan. In World War II he survived a concentration camp and emigrated to Israel after the War. He writes in Hebrew.

BORIS PASTERNAK (1890–1960) was born in Moscow. He was the son of the famous painter Leonid Pasternak and grew up in highly intellectual circles. He survived the years of Stalin's Terror but became embroiled in controversy over his novel *Dr Zhivago*, which won him the Nobel Prize in 1958 but also the condemnation of the Writers' Union. He was forced to decline the award. Pasternak is perhaps the most European of the great Russian poets of the century and his poems, although formally intricate, translate well.

TOM PAULIN was born in Leeds in 1949 and brought up in Belfast. Educated at the universities of Hull and Oxford, he has been a lecturer since 1972, at first at Nottingham and then at Oxford. He is critic and television pundit as well as a poet and he is also a powerful commentator on Northern Irish politics, with a deep interest in the tradition of radical dissent. He edited *The Faber Book of Political Verse*.

FERNANDO PESSOA (1888–1935) was born in Lisbon. His parents emigrated to Durban, South Africa, and he received an English education there. He returned to Lisbon in 1905, working as a freelance commercial translator whilst he developed an extraordinary poetic career. He assumed the personae of several completely different poets, each with a different biography and coherent poetic style and world-view. The persona of Álvaro de Campos was that of a Futurist, in love with machines and the pace and chaos of modern life.

GYÖRGY PETRI was born in Hungary in 1943. His bitter and scabrous indictments of the regime ensured that from 1982 to 1989 he published only in samizdat in Hungary, but his poems gradually became known in the West through the efforts of his translators, Clive Wilmer and his exiled compatriot George Gömöri.

JÁNOS PILINSZKY (1921–81) was born in Budapest. He was called up in 1944 and spent the last months of the War in German prison camps – an experience which changed his poetry. His poems of the camps are amongst the vital documents that speak with a human voice of total dehumanization.

ROBERT PINSKY was born in 1940 in New Jersey and educated at Rutgers and Stanford universities. He is a critic as well as a poet. His work is noted for its discursive tendency, allowing both argument and minute description. He was appointed US Poet Laureate in March 1977.

SYLVIA PLATH (1932–63) was born in Boston. After graduating from Smith College, she went to Cambridge, England, on a Fulbright scholarship, where she met Ted Hughes, whom she married in 1956. She had a record of instability and when Hughes left her and their two young children in 1962, the crisis produced a flurry of poems which made her name posthumously. She died by suicide.

SYBREN POLET (Sybe Minnema) was born in Kampen, Holland in 1924. In the early Fifties he lived in Stockholm and translated Strindberg and Swedish poetry. He is a restlessly experimental poet.

PETER PORTER was born in 1929 in Brisbane. He came to Britain in 1951. He worked for some years in advertising before becoming a freelance poet and critic. Auden is Porter's mentor and he is an incisive commentator on the emerging consumerist world of the Fifties and Sixties.

EZRA POUND (1885–1972) was born in Hailey, Idaho. When he was twenty-three he came to Europe, first to Venice and then settled in London where he quickly became an influential ringmaster of the emerging Modernist movement. In 1920 he left England, spending four years in Paris, and then settled in Rappalo, Italy. He became preoccupied with eccentric economic ideas and grew close to Fascism. He made broadcasts during the War on behalf of the Fascists, was arrested by partisans in 1945 and handed over to the Americans. His health broke down and he was found unfit to plead at his trial and incarcerated in an asylum from 1946 to 1958.

JACQUES PRÉVERT (1900–1977). Like so many French poets, Prévert was a surrealist in the Twenties but broke with them in 1929. He became a committed anti-Fascist but did not join the Communist Party. He wrote scripts for some of France's greatest films, especially Marcel Carné's *Les Enfants du Paradis* (1945). He also, with Joseph Kosma, wrote some of France's most popular songs, especially 'Les Feuilles Morts' ('Autumn Leaves'). These songs were performed by Juliette Greco and Yves Montand in the Fifties. His first book, *Paroles* (1947), made him the most popular poet in France.

AMRITA PRITAM was born in the Punjab in 1919. She was the first woman to receive the Sahitya Academy Prize, for her poems. She has edited a monthly literary magazine and lives in Delhi.

SHEENAGH PUGH was born in Birmingham in 1950 and read Russian and German at the University of Bristol. She has worked as a civil servant. She is also a translator and reviewer.

SALVATORE QUASIMODO (1901–68) was born in Sicily and trained to be a civil engineer. He was imprisoned by Mussolini for anti-Fascist activities. The war turned him from an hermetic poet into one of commitment. He was awarded the Nobel Prize in 1959.

RAYMOND QUENEAU (1903–76) studied philosophy at the Sorbonne. He began as a surrealist but broke with the movement in 1929. His output is enormous, of novels, essays, poems and *jeux d'esprit* such as *Exercises de Style*, the same passage described in 100 different styles, and *100 Million Poems*, in which single lines can be combined in almost infinite combinations by means of a simple ring binder.

CRAIG RAINE was born in Shildon, County Durham in 1944. His father was a boxer and he was educated at Oxford. His second book, *A Martian Sends a Postcard Home*, founded a new style, the Martian style, in which the world is described in startling metaphors as if seen for the first time. He was Poetry Editor at Faber from 1981 to 1991. He is now a Fellow of New College, Oxford.

ZSUZSA RAKOVSKY was born in Sopran, Hungary, in 1950. Her work combines a Western European élan with themes from the communist years.

VICKI RAYMOND was born in Victoria, Australia in 1949. She lived in Tasmania for thirty years and came to London in 1981 where she has worked as a financial clerk at Australia House. She has a witty, often quirky, and entirely independent voice.

PETER READING was born in Liverpool in 1946. He studied at Art College and worked for many years as a weighbridge operator at a feed mill in Shropshire. His work is notable for its extreme view of the behaviour of what he calls *Homo sap.* in the Eighties and Nineties.

JACQUES RÉDA was born in Luneville, Lorraine in 1929. He worked in aeronautics and publicity and then became a reader for the publisher Gallimard. He is an authority on jazz and a connoisseur of Parisian byways.

PETER REDGROVE was born in 1932 and studied at Cambridge. He is a prolific poet and a lay analyst, seeing his role as a preacher of sensual and spiritual awareness. The conventional boundaries between people and the inanimate often disappear in much of his work. In the poem included here, the animist verve is qualified by recognizable human pathos.

HENRY REED (1914–86) was born in Birmingham and educated at the University there. He worked in Naval Intelligence 1942–5, and then for BBC Radio during its golden period with figures like Dylan Thomas and Louis MacNeice. He published only one book of poems. 'Naming of Parts' is the best-known English poem of World War II and its brilliantly simple juxtaposition of bone-headed official procedures and the joys of life beyond the cramping present has been endlessly copied but never equalled.

CHRISTOPHER REID was born in Hong Kong in 1949 and educated at Oxford. His early poetry, of which 'The Gardeners' is an example, is notable for its minute precision of observation and a Wallace Stevens-like playfulness. He was Poetry Editor at Faber from 1991 to 1999.

ADRIENNE RICH was born in Baltimore, Maryland in 1929 and educated at Radcliffe College, Cambridge, Massachusetts. She has lectured very widely in the USA. She has been a leader of feminist poetics and politics.

MICHÈLE ROBERTS was born in London in 1949. Her mother is French. She is a Booker-short-listed novelist and also a broadcaster. She is one of the most original writers to emerge from the Women's Movement.

THEODORE ROETHKE (1908–63) was born in Saginaw, Michigan. His father, of Prussian extraction, was a market gardener. Roethke graduated from the University of Michigan and taught at various colleges. He was a romantic poet, influenced by Hopkins and Dylan Thomas.

PADRAIG ROONEY was born in 1956 in Ireland. He has taught in Paris and Bangkok and now lives in Rome. Besides poetry he has written a novel.

MURIEL RUKEYSER (1913–80) was born in New York City. She was very active politically and was a pioneer environmentalist.

CAROL RUMENS was born in London in 1944 and studied at Bedford College. She worked in advertising and has held several writing fellowships. She is an editor, anthologist and reviewer. Her poetry is notable for the range of its concerns: from London's suburbia, through Central Europe and Russia, to Northern Ireland, where she has lived on and off for the last few years. She has also written a novel and a play.

LAWRENCE SAIL was born in 1942 in London. He read French and German at Oxford and taught for five years in Kenya and then in Exeter until 1991. He directed the Cheltenham Festival of Literature in 1991.

TŌGE SANKICHI (1917–53) was born in Osaka and studied in Hiroshima. He was a victim of radiation sickness from the Hiroshima bomb. He wrote several poems about the Bomb which were published in his *Atomic Bomb Anthology* (1951).

CAROLE SATYAMURTI was born in 1939 and grew up in Kent. She lived in America, Singapore and Uganda before settling in London. She teaches sociology at the University of East London.

WILLIAM SCAMMELL was born in 1939 in Hampshire but has lived most of his life in Cumbria. He studied English as a mature student and worked in adult education until 1991.

VERNON SCANNELL was born in 1922. He served in the Army in World War II and has been a professional boxer. He is a popular craftsman poet with a sure touch for the tears of things.

DELMORE SCHWARTZ (1913–66) was born in Brooklyn, New York and graduated from New York University. He then studied philosophy at Harvard Graduate School – a tormented philosophizing is a feature of his work. His last twelve years were marked by paranoid mental illness.

JAROSLAV SEIFERT (1901–86) was born in Prague. He became a communist in 1921 and was expelled in 1929. During the War he became Czechoslovakia's unofficial laureate but the communist takeover in 1948 led him to withdraw from public life. He was an early signatory of Charter 77. He was awarded the Nobel Prize in 1984.

ANNE SEXTON (1928–74) was born in Newton, Massachusetts. Often bracketed with Sylvia Plath, she had several breakdowns and her poetry was often rawly confessional.

JO SHAPCOTT was born in 1953 in London and educated at Trinity College (Dublin), Oxford and Harvard. She has worked in the literature departments of the South Bank Centre and the Arts Council. She is the only poet to have won the National Poetry Competition twice, the second time with the poem included here.

KARL SHAPIRO was born in Baltimore, Maryland in 1913, the son of Russian-Jewish immigrants. He served in the South Pacific in World War II. Shapiro has been a notable editor and has taught at several US universities.

STEPHEN SHERRILL was born in Mooresville, North Carolina in 1961. His formal education began with a diploma in welding and went on to a degree in Fine Arts from the University of Iowa. A radio feature about the Katyn massacre inspired his poem.

JON SILKIN (1930–97) was born in London into a family of Labour lawyers. He started the literary magazine *Stand* in 1952 and edited it until his death. Jewish themes are a strong element in his work.

GORAN SIMIĆ was born in 1952. A Bosnian-Serb married to a Muslim woman, he and his family were trapped in Sarajevo during the siege from 1992 to 1994. His book *Sprinting from the Graveyard* is entirely concerned with the period of the War. He now lives in Canada.

LOUIS SIMPSON was born in 1923 in Jamaica to a Russian mother and a father of Scottish descent, and emigrated to the USA at the age of seventeen. He served in the US Army Airborne Division in World War II. After the War he took a Ph.D. at Columbia University and moved to Long Island, where he has taught.

BORIS SLUTSKY (1919–86). Slutsky grew up in Kharkov and studied in Moscow. He was wounded in the War. Although writing throughout the Forties, he did not publish a book during Stalin's life. His work is often brutally direct and coarse-grained.

STEVIE SMITH (1902–71) was born in Hull but lived her whole life from the age of three in the North London suburb of Palmers Green. She worked as a secretary in publishing until 1953. Stevie Smith became famous for her performances in which she sang out of key. Her poems similarly oscillated wildly in tone, being whimsical, arch, metaphysical and querulous by turns.

MARIN SORESCU (1936–96) was born in Oltenia, Romania. He worked for most of his life on newspapers and literary magazines. He travelled widely in the West and was visiting writer on the Iowa Writing Program (1971–2) and Visiting Writer in Berlin (1973–4). He was the coded fabulist of the communist era *par excellence*.

WOLE SOYINKA was born in 1934 in Nigeria and educated at Leeds University, where he met Tony Harrison, Geoffrey Hill and Jon Silkin, among others. He is famous for his plays, his poetry and his political role in Nigeria. He was jailed for two years in 1967 for supporting the secessionist province of Biafra. He was awarded the Nobel Prize in 1986. In recent years he has again fallen foul of the Nigerian authorities, having his passport removed.

BERNARD SPENCER (1909–63) was born in Madras, the son of a high-court judge, and educated at Oxford. Spencer straddled two traditions, beginning as an acolyte of Auden and MacNeice in the Thirties and becoming a British Council-sponsored Mediterranean poet of the Forties and Fifties. He worked in Greece, Egypt, Italy, Spain, Turkey and Austria. The three poems here are all fairly definitive poems on their respective subjects: allotments, money in the modern world, and a nostalgia for boats.

STEPHEN SPENDER (1909–96) was born in London and educated at Oxford, where he met Auden. He lived out the life of the concerned middle-class intellectual of the time, going to Spain to produce propaganda, flirting with the Communist Party, becoming a fire warden in World War II, editing *Encounter* until its CIA funding was discovered, becoming a fixture at International Congresses. His poems on express trains, aeroplanes and pylons helped to define the popular image of Auden, MacNeice, Day Lewis and himself as the 'Pylon Poets'.

WILLIAM STAFFORD (1914–93) grew up in rural Kansas and studied at the University of Kansas. He was interned in World War II as a conscientious objector. His poetry often deals with large public themes.

WALLACE STEVENS (1879–1955) was born in Reading, Pennsylvania and educated at Harvard. After a spell in journalism he studied Law and embarked on a career in company law, becoming vice-president of the Hartford Accident and Indemnity Company in 1934. Stevens is the role model for the poet who shuns the entirely literary life: 'It gives a man character to have this daily contact with a job,' he said. Strangely, this does not make his poetry down to earth, quite the reverse. Stevens is a poet whose poetry aspires to the condition of music and who creates delightful self-contained fictional worlds. He has been extremely influential, particularly on John Ashbery.

ANNE STEVENSON was born in 1933 in Cambridge, England, to American parents. She grew up in America and was educated at the University of Michigan. She returned to England in 1955, where she has lived ever since. In Britain she has been attracted by the Celtic world and the north of England as antidotes to the New England puritanism with which she grew up. 'The Spirit is too Blunt an Instrument' also reflects rebellion, against a sentimentalizing of the life process.

DOUGLAS STEWART (1913–85) was born in Eltham, New Zealand, and moved to Australia in 1938. He worked for twenty years as Literary Editor of the *Bulletin*. He wrote several verse plays.

WISŁAWA SZYMBORSKA was born in 1923 in Bnin, Western Poland. She was educated at Cracow. From 1953–81 she was Poetry Editor and columnist for a literary weekly. Szymborska's poetry mostly takes a curious and amused look at the spectacle of life. She often exploits contrasts between different registers of life, for example, the man who tomorrow will give a lecture on 'megagalactic cosmonautics' but for now has just come in in a bad mood and 'has curled up and gone to sleep'. She was awarded the Nobel prize in 1996.

JAMES TATE was born in Kansas City in 1943. He won the Pulitzer Prize for his Selected Poems and teaches at the University of Massachusetts. His poetry has a post-Ashberian playfulness.

DYLAN THOMAS (1914–53) was born in Swansea and after a brief period as a junior reporter he set himself up as a bohemian poet in London. First publishing in 1934, he looked rather like a Welsh surrealist. But the resemblance was superficial. Thomas was drunk on the sound of the Bible, Shakespeare and the cadences of Welsh speech. He had more in common with the neo-romantic artists of the Forties, and 'The Force That Through the Green Fuse' was an early expression of the 'organic' philosophy which was to become widely popular thirty years later.

R. S. THOMAS was born in 1913 in Cardiff. He grew up speaking English but taught himself Welsh and became a committed Welsh nationalist. He has been an Anglican priest all his life and most of his poetry is a tormented dialogue with God, with his parishioners often featuring as examples held up to the gaze of the deity. He has often written of science and he also has a series of poems about paintings.

RUTHVEN TODD (1914–78) was born in Edinburgh and educated at Edinburgh School of Art. He was an art critic and wrote several poems on artists such as Miró and Klee. His themes were very much those of the Auden generation and he resembles MacNeice in his combination of aestheticism and common-sense politics.

CHARLES TOMLINSON was born in 1927 in Stoke on Trent. He was educated at Cambridge. Tomlinson is an unusual poet: avowedly internationalist and modernist, but also very English in his meditations on landscape (in this he feels an affinity with the painting of Constable, about whom he has written a memorable poem). In 'Prometheus' his ambition is matched by the theme: an inquiry into extremes in art and politics. Written in the late Sixties, it has gained in power with the fall of communism.

ROSEMARY TONKS was born in London in 1932. She was expelled from school at the age of sixteen. Besides two books of poetry, she wrote three novels before disappearing from the literary map in the early Seventies when she converted to evangelical Christianity. Her poetry derives from the Baude-lairean notion of the *flaneur*, given to outrageous exclamation, and extrava-gant self-dramatization (compare Pessoa's 'Triumphal Ode' (p. 36) – a difficult pose that she pulls off with panache. In the Nineties there has been a revival of interest in her work by other poets.

MARINA TSVETAEVA (1892–1941) was born in Moscow, the daughter of a university professor father and a pianist mother. Her life was tormented in the extreme and her poetry is unique for its passion, scorn and tumultuous rhythmic movement. She followed her husband into exile in Paris in 1922. She endured extreme poverty and could not accommodate herself to the émigré world. She and her family returned to Russia in 1937 in the middle of Stalin's Terror. Her husband was shot, her sister and daughter were imprisoned, the latter serving nineteen years in labour camps. Tsvetaeva was evacuated in World War II to Yelabuga, near Kazan, where she hanged herself.

TRISTAN TZARA (1896–1963) was born Samuel Rosenstock in Moinet,

Romania. In 1915 he was sent by his parents to Zurich to complete his education. Here he quickly entered into the ferment of what was for a brief period the most dynamic centre of European culture. He initiated many of the outrageous phenomena that occurred at the Cabaret Voltaire, beginning in February 1916, and that became known as Dada. He went to Paris in 1920 and from this point wrote only in French. The Dada movement broke up in 1923 and Tzara became associated with Breton's surrealist movement though he did not join till 1929. In 1935 came another schism and he joined the anti-Fascist movement, though not as a communist. He was active in the Resistance.

JOHN UPDIKE was born in Shillington, Pennsylvania, in 1932. He was educated at Harvard and spent a year at the Ruskin School of Drawing in Oxford. He joined the staff of the *New Yorker* in 1955, a magazine he has written for ever since. Updike is best known for his novels, particularly *Couples* and his tetralogy of American life from the Fifties to the Eighties, the Rabbit novels. His poetry is the expression of a very wide-ranging and curious sensibility.

EVGENY VINOKUROV was born in 1925 in Bryansk, in the Soviet Union. He was an artillery section commander during the War and was stationed in the Carpathian mountains. He was Poetry Editor of the leading literary journal *Novy Mir* in the Seventies.

MAXIMILIAN VOLOSHIN (1877–1932) was born in Kiev, the Ukraine. He studied in Paris from 1903 to 1917, when he returned to Russia. He condemned the excesses of both sides in the civil war that followed the Revolution and his best work deals with that conflict.

ANDREI VOZNESENSKY was born in 1933 in Moscow. He studied architecture. America, in its modern aspects, is a huge inspiration to him and he has become very well known in the West. He was criticized by Khrushchev in 1963 but his work remained in print throughout the Communist years.

DEREK WALCOTT was born in 1930 on the island of St Lucia, West Indies. He received 'a sound colonial education'. He is a playwright as well as a poet and taught for many years at Boston University. He was awarded the Nobel Prize in 1991.

JOHN WHITWORTH was born in 1945 in Middlesex, grew up in Scotland, and was educated at Oxford. He has written topical and satirical verses for newspapers.

WILLIAM CARLOS WILLIAMS (1883–1963) studied medicine at the University of Pennsylvania where he met Pound. He practised medicine in the city of Paterson, the subject of his famous long poem of that name. Williams was the leader of an influential strand of American Modernism which, following Pound, eschewed formal rhythmic patterns. He adopted the credo 'no ideas but in things'.

KIT WRIGHT was born in Kent in 1944 and educated at Oxford. He is one of the most distinguished practitioners of the English tough-light-verse school: he writes for children, and has written poems that exploit traditional English humour, but many of his subjects are bleak: breakdowns, the plight of victims and underdogs.

ROBERT WRIGLEY was born in East St Louis in 1951 and educated at the universities of Southern Illinois and Montana. He has taught at Lewis and Clark State College in Lewiston, Idaho since 1977. He often wishes he were Oscar Peterson.

PETER WYLES' poem 'Aspects of the President' was first published in 1996. The form of the poem derives from Weldon Kees' 'Aspects of Robinson' (see p. 328).

W. B. YEATS (1865–1939) was born in Dublin; he moved to London at the age of two and back to Dublin at sixteen. His early poetry formed part of the Celtic Twilight with its concern for Irish myth and medievalized romance. His involvement in the dramas of Ireland's emergence from British rule gave his work new muscle. In 1899 he founded the Irish National Theatre and he became a senator of the new Free State in 1922. The 'rough beast . . ./ Slouches towards Bethlehem' from 'The Second Coming' is one of the century's most quoted texts.

YEVGENY YEVTUSHENKO was born in Siberia in 1933. He was rebellious as a child and was dismissed from school. His poetry was published early and he became famous with his poem 'Babi Yar' about the wartime massacre of Jews. He travelled very widely, reading his poetry, and his international fame protected him from persecution by the regime.

ADAM ZAGAJEWSKI was born in Lvov (then in Poland, now the Ukraine) in 1945. He studied philosophy at the University of Cracow and now lives in Paris. His poems have the glittering surfaces and overloaded detail of the obsessive exile.

Chronology of Events & their Poems

These are the dates of some events relating to poems in the anthology. It does not attempt to list comprehensively every event that is referred to in the book.

29 December 1901	Marconi's first transatlantic radio message	Joseph Brodsky, *From*: History of the Twentieth Century (A Roadshow), p. 2
17 December 1903	The Wright Brothers' first powered flight	Joseph Brodsky, *From*: History of the Twentieth Century, p. 3
30 June 1905	Einstein's paper on Special Relativity received by *Annalen der Physik*	Joseph Brodsky, *From*: History of the Twentieth Century, p. 4
5 September 1905	Portsmouth, New Hampshire, treaty ends Russo-Japanese War	Gottfried Benn, Foreign Minister, p. 215
15 April 1912	Sinking of the Titanic	Thomas Hardy, The Convergence of the Twain, p. 7
29 May 1913	Paris Première of *Rite of Spring* causes riot	Paolo Buzzi, Stravinsky, p. 420
28 June 1914	Assassination of the Archduke Franz Ferdinand	Joseph Brodsky, *From*: History of the Twentieth Century, p. 12
4 August 1914	England declares war on Germany	Wilfred Owen, The Parable of the Old Man and the Young, p. 13
24 December 1914	Christmas truce in the trenches	Paul Muldoon, Truce, p. 18
22 April 1915	Poison gas first used in war	Wilfred Owen, Dulce et Decorum Est, p. 14
19 December 1915	Alois Alzheimer dies	Dennis O'Driscoll, In Memory of Alois Alzheimer, p. 492

5 February 1916	First performance at Cabaret Voltaire, Zurich	Tristan Tzara, total circuit by the moon and colour, p. 21
24 April 1916	The Irish Easter Rising	W. B. Yeats, *From* Easter 1916, p. 231
28 May 1917	French troops mutiny	Erich Fried, French Soldiers Mutiny, p. 19
25 October 1917	The Russian Revolution	Jacques Réda, October Morning, p. 24
9 November 1917	Ernest Rutherford splits the nitrogen atom	Douglas Stewart, *From*: Rutherford, p. 452
11 November 1918	Armistice Day, First World War	Philip Larkin, MCMXIV, p. 22
31 July 1925	Mayakovsky arrives in America	Vladimir Mayakovsky, Brooklyn Bridge, p. 29
6 October 1927	The first talkie, Al Jolson in *The Jazz Singer*	Robert Crawford, Talkies, p. 427
29 October 1929	Wall Street Crash	Bertolt Brecht, *From*: Late Lamented Fame of the Giant City New York, p. 43
30 January 1933	Hitler comes to power	Eugenio Montale, The Hitler Spring, p. 58
16 May 1934	Mandelstam's first arrest	Osip Mandelstam, The Stalin Epigram, p. 66
6 December 1935	Erwin Schrödinger suggests the cat experiment	Gwen Harwood, Schrödinger's Cat Preaches to the Mice, p. 454
18 July 1936	Spanish Civil War begins	Louis MacNeice, *From*: Autumn Journal, p. 59
3 November 1936	The Jarrow March reaches London	Stephen Spender, Unemployed, p. 46
31 July 1937	Stalin orders the Great Terror	Anna Akhmatova, *From*: Requiem, p. 67
2 October 1937	President Trujillo of the Dominican Republic orders 20,000 deaths	Rita Dove, Parsley, p. 350
6 July 1938	Evian Conference on the reception of Jewish refugees	W. H. Auden, Ten Songs. I, p. 95

30 September 1938	The Munich Agreement	Louis MacNeice, *From*: Autumn Journal, p. 69
2 December 1938	First Kindertransport of Jewish refugee children reaches Britain	Karen Gershon, I Was Not There to Comfort Them, p. 98
1 September 1939	Germany invades Poland	W. H. Auden, September 1st, 1939, p. 74
16 June 1940	Fall of Paris	Louis Aragon, The Lilacs and the Roses, p. 77
22 June 1940	Vichy regime inaugurated in France	Jacques Prévert, The New Order, p. 83
29 December 1940	St Paul's escapes City bombardment	Ruthven Todd, These are Facts, p. 78
7 December 1941	Pearl Harbor	James Applewhite, News of Pearl Harbor, p. 81
4 August 1944	Anne Frank betrayed	Andrew Motion, Anne Frank Huis, p. 105
27 January 1945	Auschwitz liberated	Primo Levi, Buna, p. 104
13/14 February 1945	Bombing of Dresden	Durs Grünbein, Poem on Dresden, p. 88
8 May 1945	VE Day	Ivan Elagin, The last foot soldier, p. 91
16 July 1945	Test explosion of the implosion A-Bomb	William Stafford, At the Bomb Testing Site, p. 111
6 August 1945	Hiroshima	Tōge Sankichi, The Shadow, p. 113
10 August 1945	Japan surrenders	James Dickey, The Performance, p. 89
20 November 1945	Nuremberg Trials of Nazi war criminals start	Erica Marx, No Need for Nuremberg, p. 345
5 June 1947	The Marshall Plan	Dick Allen, Ode to the Cold War, p. 171
16 August 1947	Indian Independence	W. H. Auden, Partition, p. 143
4 October 1951	Henrietta Lacks dies and her cells are set to live for ever	Carole Satyamurti, The Life and Life of Henrietta Lacks, p. 465
5 March 1953	Stalin dies	Robinson Jeffers, Skunks, p. 213
25 April 1953	Watson and Crick publish DNA structure	David Holbrook, The Maverick, p. 464

22 September 1955	Commercial TV begins in UK	Howard Nemerov, A Way of Life, p. 409
26 September 1955	Debbie Reynolds marries Eddie Fisher	John Updike, The Newlyweds, p. 122
17 January 1956	Allen Ginsberg takes the pulse of America	Allen Ginsberg, America, p. 125
25 April 1956	Elvis Presley's first No. 1 hit, 'Heartbreak Hotel'	Thom Gunn, Elvis Presley, p. 123
14 June 1956	The neutrino discovered	John Updike, Cosmic Gall, p. 455
4 November 1956	The Soviet Union invades Hungary	György Petri, On the 24th Anniversary of the Little October Revolution, p. 136
5 November 1956	Invasion of Suez	Adrian Mitchell, Remember Suez?, p. 121
21 December 1956	Martin Luther King boards a bus in Alabama	Brother Will Hairston, Alabama Bus, p. 193
3 September 1957	Central High School, Little Rock, Arkansas, opens to black pupils	Gwendolyn Brooks, The Chicago Defender Sends a Man to Little Rock, p. 189
4 October 1957	Sputnik launched	Dmitry Bobyshev, Upon the Launching of a Sputnik, p. 138
2 November 1960	Penguin Books acquitted in Lady Chatterley Trial	Philip Larkin, Annus Mirabilis, p. 300
28 October 1962	Russians climb down over Cuban Missile Crisis	Paul Muldoon, Cuba, p. 167
22 March 1963	The Beatles' first LP	Philip Larkin, Annus Mirabilis, p. 300
22 November 1963	President Kennedy assassinated	Roy Fuller, From a Foreign Land, p. 176
14 August 1965	Watts Riot in Los Angeles	Maya Angelou, Riot: 60's, p. 195
17 January 1967	'4000 Holes in Blackburn, Lancashire', Daily Mail	John Lennon and Paul McCartney, A Day in the Life, p. 187
24 August 1967	The Beatles meet the Maharishi	Keki N. Daruwalla, Collage I, p. 148

31 January 1968	The Tet Offensive in Vietnam	Robert Duncan, Up Rising, p. 197
10 May 1968	French student uprising	Naum Korzhavin, Imitation of Monsieur Béranger, p. 185
16 January 1969	Jan Palách burns himself to death	Bogdan Czaykowski, Threnos, p. 139
20 July 1969	Moon Landing	Dorothy Hewett, Moon-Man, p. 495
14 August 1969	British troops called in in Northern Ireland	Seamus Heaney, Punishment, p. 234
15 August 1969	Woodstock Rock Festival begins	Joni Mitchell, Woodstock, p. 184
1 June 1972	Andreas Baader, terrorist, arrested	Allen Curnow, An Urban Guerrilla, p. 224
6 October 1973	Yom Kippur War between Israel and the Arab nations begins	Yehuda Amichai, *From*: Travels of the Last Benjamin Tudela, p. 204
7 August 1974	President Nixon resigns	Maxine Kumin, The Summer of the Watergate Hearings, p. 223
30 October 1974	Muhammad Ali regains the World Title from George Foreman	Wole Soyinka, Muhammad Ali at the Ringside, 1985, p. 435
17 April 1975	The Khmer Rouge enter Phnom Penh	Ernesto Cardenal, A Museum in Kampuchea, p. 226
31 July 1975	Miami Showband assassinated	Paul Durcan, In Memory: The Miami Showband, p. 237
25 December 1977	Charlie Chaplin dies	Yevgeny Yevtushenko, To Charlie Chaplin, p. 425
27 December 1979	Soviet Union invades Afghanistan	Adam Zagajewski, July 6, 1980, p. 168
5 June 1981	First medical report on AIDS	Thom Gunn, The Missing, p. 312
2 April 1982	Argentina invades Falkland Islands	Gavin Ewart, The Falklands, 1982, p. 380
23 March 1983	President Reagan launches the Strategic Defence Initiative (SDI)	John Levett, SDI, p. 170

28 May 1984	Police v. pickets at Orgreave Coking Plant	Sean O'Brien, Summertime, p. 382
15 November 1985	The Anglo-Irish Agreement signed at Hillsborough	John Hewitt, The Anglo-Irish Accord, p. 238
28 January 1986	Space Shuttle Challenger explodes	Katherine Frost, Space Shuttle, p. 496
9 February 1986	Halley's comet returns	Ivan V. Lalić, The Return of the Comet, p. 503
26 April 1986	Chernobyl reactor explodes	Michael Hofmann, 47° Latitude, p. 251
19 October 1987	Stock Market Crash	Jonathan Holden, *From*: The Crash, p. 280
4 June 1989	Tiananmen Square massacre	James Fenton, Tiananmen, p. 351
27 November 1989	Fall of communism in Czechoslovakia	Miroslav Holub, The Third Language, p. 470
11 February 1990	Nelson Mandela released	Wole Soyinka, Your Logic Frightens Me, Mandela, p. 355
24 April 1990	Hubble Space Telescope launched	Gwyneth Lewis, *From* Zero Gravity, p. 500
2 August 1990	Iraq invades Kuwait, precipitating the Gulf War	Jo Shapcott, Phrase Book, p. 474
1 May 1991	World Wide Web launched	David Hart, Angelica and Bob On Line, p. 412
31 December 1991	The End of the Soviet Union	Linda France, Stateless, p. 475
7 April 1992	Recognition of Bosnia by European Community signals war	Ian McMillan, Bosnia Festival: Your Full Guide by our Arts Reporter, p. 476 Carole Satyamurti, Striking Distance, p. 477
19 December 1996	Mystery of insect flight solved	Sheenagh Pugh, Bumblebees and the Scientific Method, p. 451
1 May 1997	Labour win General Election	Duncan Forbes, Downing Street Cat, p. 397
31 August 1997	Princess Diana killed	Adrian Mitchell, My Shy Di in Newspaperland, p. 398

| 17 August 1998 | President Clinton admits relationship with Monica Lewinsky | Peter Wyles, Aspects of the President, p. 396 |
| 31 December 1999 | Millennium Bug's time has come | John Agard, Millennium Bug, p. 506 |

APPLEWHITE: 'News of Pearl Harbor' from *A History of the River* (Louisiana State University Press, 1993), reprinted by permission of the author; and 'Iron Age Flying' from *Foreseeing the Journey* (Louisiana State University Press, 1983); LOUIS ARAGON: 'Little Suite for Loudspeaker. 1', translated by Rolfe Humphries, from *Aragon: Poet of Resurgent France*, edited by Hannah Josephson and Malcolm Cowley (Pilot Press, 1946); 'The Lilacs and the Roses', translated by Louis MacNeice, from *Collected Poems* by Louis MacNeice (Faber & Faber, 1979), reprinted by permission of David Higham Associates Ltd; SIMON ARMITAGE: 'Eighties, Nineties' and 'The Stuff' from *Zoom!* (Bloodaxe Books, 1989); JOHN ASH: an extract from 'Twentieth Century' from *Selected Poems* (Carcanet Press, 1996), by permission of the publishers; JOHN ASHBERY: 'Definition of Blue' from *The Mooring of Starting Out* (Carcanet Press, 1997), reprinted by permission of the publishers; MARGARET ATWOOD: 'A Women's Issue' from *Poems 1976–1986* (Virago Press, 1992), by permission of Little, Brown UK Ltd; W. H. AUDEN: extracts from *Letter to Lord Byron*, and 'September 1, 1939', from *The English Auden: Poems, Essays & Dramatic Writings, 1927–39* (Faber & Faber, 1986), and 'Funeral Blues', 'Partition', 'The Shield of Achilles', 'The Fall of Rome' and 'Ten Songs. I' from *Collected Poems* (Faber & Faber, 1991), by permission of the publishers; STANISŁAW BARAŃCZAK: 'These Men, So Powerful', translated by Adam Czerniawski, from *The Burning Forest* (Bloodaxe Books, 1988), reprinted by permission of the author and translator; ELIZABETH BARTLETT: 'Deviant' from *Two Women Dancing: New & Selected Poems* (Bloodaxe Books, 1995), by permission of the publishers; GOTTFRIED BENN: 'Foreign Minister', translated by Michael Hamburger, from *Destillationem* (Limes Verlag, 1953), by permission of the translator; LOUISE BENNETT: 'Colonization in Reverse' from *Jamaica Labrish* (Sangster's Book Store, 1966); JAMES BERRY: 'From Lucy: Englan' Lady' from *Lucy's Letters and Loving* (New Beacon Books, 1982), reprinted by permission of the author; JOHN BERRYMAN: 'The Dream Songs. 4' from *The Dream Songs* (Faber & Faber, 1993), by permission of the publishers; JOHN BETJEMAN: 'Executive' and 'Sun and Fun' from *Collected Poems* (John Murray, 1958), by permission of the publishers; SUJATA BHATT: 'Muliebrity' from *Brunizem* (Carcanet Press, 1988), reprinted by permission of the publishers; ELIZABETH BISHOP: 'Filling Station' from *The Complete Poems 1927–1979*, © 1979, 1983 by Alice Helen Methfessel, reprinted by permission of Farrar, Straus & Giroux, Inc; PETER BLAND: 'Lament for a Lost Generation' from *Selected Poems* (Carcanet Press, 1998), reprinted by permission of the publishers; ALEXANDER BLOK: an extract from 'The Twelve' from *The Twelve and Other Poems*, translated by Jon Stallworthy and Peter France (Eyre & Spottiswoode, 1970), by permission of Random House UK Ltd; RICHARD BLOMFIELD: 'Prélude à l'Après-Midi d'un Téléphone' from *Poetry Review*, Vol. 80, No. 1 (1990), by permission of the author; EDMUND BLUNDEN: 'Trench Nomenclature' from author and publishers; ROBERT CONQUEST: 'Guided Missiles Experimental Range' from *New and Collected Poems* (Hutchinson, 1988), © Robert Conquest, reprinted by permission of Curtis Brown Ltd, London, on behalf of Robert Conquest; WENDY COPE: 'Engineers' Corner' from *Making Cocoa for Kingsley Amis* (Faber & Faber, 1986), by permission of the publishers; JOHN CORNFORD: 'A Letter from Aragon' from *Understanding the Weapon, Understanding the Wound* (Carcanet Press, 1976), reprinted by permission of the publishers; GREGORY CORSO: 'Marriage' from *The Happy Birthday of Death*, © 1960 by New Directions Publishing Corporation, reprinted by permission of the publishers; DAVID CRAIG: 'Operation' from *London Review of Books* (22 January 1998), by permission of the author and publishers; ROBERT CRAWFORD: 'The Numties' from *Masculinity* (Jonathan Cape, 1996), and 'Talkies' from *Talkies* (Hogarth Press, 1992), by permission of the author and publishers; E. E. CUMMINGS: 'may I feel said he . . .' from *Complete Poems 1904–1962*, edited by George J. Firmage, © 1991 by the Trustees for the E. E. Cummings Trust and George James Firmage, reprinted by permission of the publishers; ALLEN CURNOW: 'Time' and 'An Urban Guerrilla' from *Early Days Yet: New and Collected Poems 1941–1997* (Carcanet Press, 1997), reprinted by permission of the publishers; BOGDAN CZAYKOWSKI: 'Threnos', translated by Adam Czerniawski, from *The Burning Forest* (Bloodaxe Books, 1988), reprinted by permission of the author and translator; FRED D'AGUIAR: 'El Dorado Update' from *Airy Hall* (Chatto & Windus, 1989), by permission of Random House UK Ltd; KEKI N. DARUWALLA: 'Routine' from *Apparition in April* (Calcutta, Writers Workshop, 1971), and 'Collage I' from *Under Orion* (Calcutta, Writers Worshop, 1970), reprinted by permission of the author; MAHMOUD DARWISH: an extract from 'Beirut' from *Sand*, translated by Rana Kabbani (Kegan Paul International, 1985), reprinted by permission of the publishers; 'We Travel Like Other People', translated by Abdulah al-Udhari from *Modern Poetry of the Arab World* (Penguin, 1986); DONALD DAVIE: 'Remembering the 'Thirties' from *Collected Poems* (Carcanet Press, 1990), reprinted by permission of the publishers; C. DAY LEWIS: 'Newsreel', 'The Tourists' and an extract from 'The Magnetic Mountain' from *The Complete Poems* (Sinclair-Stevenson, 1992), © 1992 in this edition, and the Estate of C. Day Lewis, by permission of Random House UK Ltd; JAMES DICKEY: 'The Performance' from *The Whole Motion: Collected Poems 1945–1992* (Wesleyan University Press, 1992); KEITH DOUGLAS: 'How to Kill' from *The Complete Poems*, edited by Desmond Graham (Oxford University Press, 3rd edition, 1998), by permission of the publishers; RITA DOVE: 'Parsley' from *Museum* (Carnegie-Mellon University Press, 1983), © 1983 by Rita Dove, reprinted by permission of the author; CAROL ANN DUFFY: 'The B Movie' from *Standing Female Nude* (Anvil Press Poetry, 1993), 'The Legend', 'Poet For Our Times' and 'Translating the English, 1989' from *The Other Country* (Anvil Press Poetry, 1990), and 'Prayer' from

Mean Time (Anvil Press Poetry, 1993), reprinted by permission of the publishers; ROBERT DUNCAN: 'Up Rising' from *Bending the Bow*, © 1968 by Robert Duncan, reprinted by permission of New Directions Publishing Corporation; DOUGLAS DUNN: 'The Clothes Pit' from *Selected Poems, 1964–83* (Faber & Faber, 1986), by permission of the publishers; PAUL DURCAN: 'In Memory: The Miami Showband – Massacred 31 July 1975' from *A Snail in My Prime* (Harvill, 1993), © Paul Durcan, reproduced by permission of The Harvill Press; BOB DYLAN: 'The Lonesome Death of Hattie Carroll' and 'My Back Pages', © Warner Brothers Inc, from *Lyrics 1962–1985* (Jonathan Cape, 1986), reprinted by permission of Special Rider Music; RICHARD EBERHART: 'The Fury of Aerial Bombardment' from *Collected Poems 1930–1976* (Chatto & Windus, 1976), by permission of Random House UK Ltd; ILYA EHRENBURG: 'Retribution', translated by Gordon McVay, from *Twentieth-Century Russian Poetry*, selected by Yevgeny Yevtushenko, edited by Albert C. Todd and Max Hayward (Fourth Estate, 1993), © 1993 by Doubleday, reprinted by permission of Doubleday, a division of Bantam Doubleday Dell Publishing Group Inc.; IVAN ELAGIN: 'The last foot soldier has already fallen . . .', translated by Vladimir Markov and Merrill Sparks, from *Modern Russian Poetry* (Mac-Gibbon & Kee, 1966); T. S. ELIOT: 'Preludes. I, II' and an extract from 'The Waste Land' from *Collected Poems, 1909–62* (Faber & Faber, 1974), by permission of the publisher; STEVE ELLIS: 'Gardeners' Question Time' from *Poetry Review*, Vol. 85, No. 4 (1995/6), by permission of the author; D. J. ENRIGHT: 'Apocalypse' and 'A Polished Performance' from *Collected Poems* (Oxford University Press, 1981), by permission of the author and Watson, Little Ltd; HANS MAGNUS ENZENSBERGER: 'At Thirty-Three', 'The Divorce' and 'Short History of the Bourgeoisie', translated by Michael Hamburger, and 'The Ironmonger's Shop', translated by the author, from *Selected Poems* (Bloodaxe Books, 1994), by permission of the publishers; GAVIN EWART: 'The Falklands, 1982' from *Selected Poems* (Hutchinson, 1996), by permission of Mrs Margo Ewart and the publishers; NISSIM EZEKIEL: 'The Patriot' from *Collected Poems* (Oxford University Press India, 1990), by permission of the publishers; U. A. FANTHORPE: 'Resuscitation Team' from *Standing To* (Peterloo Poets, 1982), by permission of the author; IRVING FELDMAN: 'You Know What I'm Saying?' from *The Best American Poetry 1997*, edited by James Tate (Scribners, 1997), by permission of the author; JAMES FENTON: 'God, A Poem' and 'In a Notebook' from *The Memory of War and Children in Exile* (Penguin Books, 1983), and 'Jerusalem' and 'Tiananmen' from *Out of Danger* (Penguin Books, 1993), by permission of The Peters Fraser & Dunlop Group Ltd; LAWRENCE FERLINGHETTI: 'Sometime during Eternity . . .' from *A Coney Island of the Mind*, © 1958 by Lawrence Ferlinghetti, reprinted by permission of New Directions Publishing Corporation; DUNCAN FORBES: 'Downing Street Cat' from *Poetry Review*, Vol. 87, No. 1 (1997), by permission of the author;

LINDA FRANCE: 'Stateless' from *Red* (Bloodaxe Books, 1992), by permission of the publishers; ANDRÉ FRÉNAUD: 'House for Sale', translated by Peter Forbes, from *Les Rois Mages: poèmes 1938–1943* (Editions Gallimard, 1977), © Editions Gallimard, 1977, by permission of the translator and publishers; ERICH FRIED: 'French Soldiers Mutiny – 1917', and 'Weaker', translated by Stuart Hood, from *One Hundred Poems Without a Country* (John Calder, 1987), by permission of the publishers; KATHERINE FROST: 'Space Shuttle' from *Poetry Review*, Vol. 77, No. 4 (1987/8), by permission of the author; ROBERT FROST: 'Acquainted with the Night' from *Selected Poems* (Penguin Books, 1990), by permission of the Estate of Robert Frost, the editor Edward Connery Lathem, and Random House UK Ltd; JOHN FULLER: 'Her Morning Dreams', 'Retreat' and an extract from 'Europe' from *Collected Poems* (Secker & Warburg), by permission of the author and publishers; ROY FULLER: 'Freud's Case Histories' from *Collected Poems 1936–1961* (André Deutsch, 1962), and 'From a Foreign Land' from *New and Collected Poems 1934–84* (Secker & Warburg, 1985), reprinted by permission of John Fuller; ELIZABETH GARRETT: 'Moules à la Marinière' from *The Rule of Three* (Bloodaxe Books, 1991), by permission of the publishers; KAREN GERSHON: 'I Was Not There' from *Selected Poems* (Gollancz, 1966), by permission of C. V. Tripp; JAIME GIL DE BIEDMA: 'In Mournful Praise and Memory of the French Song', translated by Timothy Baland, from *Roots and Wings: Poetry from Spain 1900–1975*, edited by Hardie St Martin (Harper & Row, 1976); ALLEN GINSBERG: 'America' and an extract from 'Howl' from *Selected Poems 1947–1995* (Penguin Books, 1997); ELTON GLASER: 'Smoking' from *The Best American Poetry 1997*, edited by James Tate (Scribners, 1997), by permission of the author; ALAN GOULD: 'South Coast Mechanic' from *Momentum* (Heinemann Australia, 1992); GÜNTER GRASS: 'The Fortress Grows', translated by Michael Hamburger, from *Selected Poems* (Faber & Faber, 1998); originally published in *Agenda*, Vol. 32, No. 2 (1994), by permission of the translator and publishers; ROBERT GREACEN: 'Captain Fox on J. Edgar Hoover' from *Collected Poems* (Lagan, 1995); PHILIP GROSS: 'A Breton Dance' from *Cat's Whisker* (Faber & Faber, 1987), by permission of the author; PAUL GROVES: 'Greta Garbo' from *Ménage à Trois* (Seren Books, 1995), by kind permission of the publishers; DURS GRÜNBEIN: 'Poem on Dresden', translated by Raymond Hargreaves, from *Young Poets of Germany* (Forest Books, 1994), reprinted by permission of the publisher and translator; 'Folds and Traps', translated by Glyn Maxwell, from *Falten und Fallen* (Surhkamp, 1994), by permission of the translator; EUGÈNE GUILLEVIC: 'Another War', translated by William Alwyn, from *An Anthology of 20th Century French Poetry* (Chatto & Windus, 1969); THOM GUNN: 'Elvis Presley' and 'The Missing' from *Collected Poems* (Faber & Faber, 1993), by permission of the publishers; IVOR GURNEY: 'The Bohemians' from *Collected Poems of Ivor Gurney*, edited by P. J. Kavanagh (Oxford University Press,

Godine, 1991; originally published in *Cimarron Review*, 1989), © 1991 by Jack Myers and Roger Weingarten, reprinted by permission of the publishers; MIROSLAV HOLUB: 'The Third Language', translated by David Young, Dana Hábová and the author, from *Poetry Review*, Vol. 80, No. 2 (1990), by permission of Ewald Osers on behalf of the author; 'Žito the Magician', translated by George Theiner, and 'At Home', translated by Ewald Osers, from *Poems Before and After: Collected English Translations* (Bloodaxe Books, 1990), by permission of the publishers; LANGSTON HUGHES: 'The Weary Blues' from *Collected Poems* (Knopf, 1994), by permission of David Higham Associates Ltd; TED HUGHES: 'Tractor' from *New Selected Poems, 1957–1994* (Faber & Faber, 1995), by permission of the publishers; KATHLEEN JAMIE: 'The Way We Live' from *The Way We Live* (Bloodaxe Books, 1987), by permission of the publishers; JERZY JARNIEWICZ: 'Short History', translated by the author, from *Index on Censorship*, 5 (1997), © Jerzy Jarniewicz, translation © Jerzy Jarniewicz, reprinted by permission of the author; RANDALL JARRELL: 'A Front' from *Selected Poems* (Faber & Faber, 1966), by permission of the publishers; ROBINSON JEFFERS: 'Skunks' from *Selected Poems of Robinson Jeffers*, © 1954 by Robinson Jeffers, reprinted by permission of Vintage Books, a division of Random House, Inc.; LINTON KWESI JOHNSON: 'Inglan Is a Bitch' from *Tings an Times: Selected Poems* (Bloodaxe Books, 1991), by permission of the publishers; BRIAN JONES: 'The Children of Separation' from *The Children of Separation* (Carcanet Press, 1985), reprinted by permission of the publishers; 'Stripping Walls' from *Poems and a Family Album* (London Magazine Editions, 1972), by permission of the author; JENNY JOSEPH: 'Warning' from *Selected Poems* (Bloodaxe Books, 1992), by permission of John Johnson (Authors' Agent); P. J. KAVANAGH: 'On the Way to the Depot' from *Collected Poems* (Carcanet Press, 1992), reprinted by permission of the publishers; PATRICK KAVANAGH: 'Epic' from *Selected Poems* (Penguin Books), by kind permission of the Trustees of the Estate of Patrick Kavanagh, c/o Peter Fallon, Literary Agent, Loughcrew, Oldcastle, Co. Meath, Ireland; JACKIE KAY: 'The Red Graveyard' from *Other Lovers* (Bloodaxe Books, 1993), by permission of the publishers; WELDON KEES: 'Aspects of Robinson' from *Collected Poems* (Faber & Faber, 1993), by permission of the publishers; GALWAY KINNELL: 'For the Lost Generation' from *What a Kingdom it Was* (Houghton Mifflin, 1960), © 1960, renewed 1988 by Galway Kinnell, reprinted by permission of the publishers. All rights reserved; RUDYARD KIPLING: 'The Gods of the Copybook Headings' from *Selected Poems*, edited by Peter Keating (Penguin Books, 1993); CAROLYN KIZER: 'Twelve O'Clock' from *Harping On: Poems 1985–1995* (Copper Canyon Press, 1996), by permission of the author; RACHEL KORN: 'Arthur Ziegelboim', translated by Joseph Leftwich, from *Poetry of the Second World War*, edited by Desmond Graham (Chatto & Windus); NAUM KORZHAVIN: 'Imitation of Monsieur Béranger', translated by Albert C. Todd,

W. S. Merwin, from *Selected Poems* (Oxford University Press, 1973), by permission of the publishers; ERICA MARX: 'No Need for Nuremberg' from *The Virago Book of Women's War Poetry and Verse*, edited by Catherine Reilly (Virago Press, 1997); GLYN MAXWELL: 'Sport Story of a Winner' and 'We Billion Cheered' from *Out of the Rain* (Bloodaxe Books, 1992), by permission of the publishers; VLADIMIR MAYAKOVSKY: 'Brooklyn Bridge', translated by Vladimir Markov and Merrill Sparks, from *Modern Russian Poetry* (MacGibbon & Kee, 1966), by permission of Harper Collins Publishers Ltd; ARTYEMY MIKHAILOV: 'Song about Crooks', translated by Joseph Langland, Tomas Axzel and Laszlo Tikos, from *Poetry from the Russian Underground* (Harper & Row, 1973); CZESŁAW MIŁOSZ: 'And Yet the Books', translated by the author and Robert Hass, 'Dedication' and 'A Poor Christian Looks at the Ghetto', translated by the author, from *Collected Poems, 1931–87* (Penguin Books, 1988); ADRIAN MITCHELL: 'My Shy Di in Newspaperland', 'Remember Suez?' and 'To Whom It May Concern' from *Heart on the Left: Poems 1953–1984* (Bloodaxe Books, 1997), © Adrian Mitchell, reprinted by permission of The Peters Fraser & Dunlop Group Ltd on behalf of Adrian Mitchell. Educational Health Warning! Adrian Mitchell asks that none of his poems are used in connection with any examinations whatsoever; JONI MITCHELL: 'Woodstock', © Warner Brothers Publishing, from *The Complete Poems and Lyrics* (Chatto & Windus, 1997), by permission of Random House UK Ltd; EUGENIO MONTALE: 'The Hitler Spring', translated by Maurice English, from *Selected Poems*, © 1965 by New Directions Publishing Corporation, reprinted by permission of the publishers; MARIANNE MOORE: 'Four Quartz Crystal Clocks' from *Complete Poems* (Faber & Faber, 1984), by permission of the publishers; EDWIN MORGAN: 'The Death of Marilyn Monroe' and 'The First Men on Mercury' from *Collected Poems* (Carcanet Press, 1990), reprinted by permission of the publishers; BLAKE MORRISON: 'Pine' from *Dark Glasses* (Chatto & Windus, 1989), and an extract from 'The Ballad of the Yorkshire Ripper' from *The Ballad of the Yorkshire Ripper* (Chatto & Windus, 1987), reprinted by permission of The Peters Fraser & Dunlop Group Ltd; ANDREW MOTION: 'Anne Frank Huis' from *Dangerous Play: Selected Poems* (Penguin Books, 1985), reprinted by permission of The Peters Fraser & Dunlop Group Ltd; EDWIN MUIR: 'The Horses' and an extract from 'The Good Town' from *The Complete Poems of Edwin Muir*, edited by Peter Butter (Association for Scottish Literary Studies, 1991), by permission of Faber & Faber Ltd; PAUL MULDOON: 'Cuba' and 'Truce' from *Selected Poems* (Faber & Faber, 1986), by permission of the publishers; LES MURRAY: 'The Dream of Wearing Shorts Forever', 'The Future' and 'The Quality of Sprawl' from *Collected Poems* (Carcanet Press, 1991), reprinted by permission of the publishers and Margaret Connolly & Associates/Literary Agents; HOWARD NEMEROV: 'Figures of Thought' and 'A Way of Life' from *Collected Poems* (University of Chicago Press, 1981), by by Peter Nijmeijer, from *Living Space: Poems of Dutch Fifties*, edited by Peter Glasgold, © 1979 by the Foundation for the Promotion of the Translation of Dutch Literary Works, reprinted by permission of New Directions Publishing Corporation; PETER PORTER: 'John Marston Advises Anger', 'Your Attention Please', 'A Consumer's Report' and 'Mort aux Chats' from *Collected Poems* (Oxford University Press, 1983), by permission of the publishers; EZRA POUND: an extract from 'E.P. Ode pour L'Élection de son Sépulcre' from *Personae: Collected Shorter Poems of Ezra Pound* (Faber & Faber, 1952), by permission of the publishers; JACQUES PRÉVERT: 'Picasso's Promenade' and 'The New Order', translated by Lawrence Ferlinghetti, from *Selections from Paroles* (City Lights Books, 1958), translation © Lawrence Ferlinghetti, 1958, 1959, by permission of the publishers; AMRITA PRITAM: 'Daily Wages', translated by Charles Brasch with Amrita Pritam, from *The Penguin Book of Women Poets*, edited by Carol Cosman, Joan Keefe and Kathleen Weaver (Penguin Books, 1979); SHEENAGH PUGH: 'Bumblebees and the Scientific Method' from *Id's Hospit* (Seren Books, 1997), by kind permission of the publishers; SALVATORE QUASIMODO: 'Man of My Time', translated by Edwin Morgan, from *Collected Translations* by Edwin Morgan (Carcanet Press, 1996), reprinted by permission of the publishers; RAYMOND QUENEAU: 'Crossing the Channel in 1922', translated by Edward Lucie-Smith, from *French Poetry Today*, edited by Simon Watson-Taylor and Edward Lucie-Smith (Rapp & Whiting, 1971), reprinted by permission of André Deutsch Ltd; CRAIG RAINE: 'An Enquiry into Two Inches of Ivory' and 'Insurance, Real Estate & Powders Pharmaceutical' from *The Onion, Memory* (Oxford University Press, 1978), by permission of the publishers; ZSUZSA RAKOVSZKY: 'Pornographic Magazine', translated by Clive Wilmer and George Gömöri, from *Poetry Review*, Vol. 85, No. 4 (1995/6), reprinted by permission of the translators; VICKI RAYMOND: 'The People, No' from *Selected Poems* (Carcanet Press, 1993), reprinted by permission of the publishers; PETER READING: an extract from 'Going On' from *Collected Poems: 2: Poems 1985–1996* (Bloodaxe Books, 1996); JACQUES RÉDA: 'October Morning', translated by Edward Lucie-Smith, from *French Poetry Today*, edited by Simon Watson-Taylor and Edward Lucie-Smith (Rapp & Whiting, 1971), reprinted by permission of André Deutsch Ltd; PETER REDGROVE: 'Old House' from *The Moon Disposes: Poems 1954–1987* (Secker & Warburg, 1987), by permission of David Higham Associates Ltd; HENRY REED: 'Naming of Parts' from *Collected Poems*, edited by Jon Stallworthy (Oxford University Press, 1991), by permission of the publishers; CHRISTOPHER REID: 'The Gardeners' from *Arcadia* (Oxford University Press, 1979), by permission of the publishers; ADRIENNE RICH: 'Living in Sin', 'After Twenty Years' and 'Artificial Intelligence' from *The Fact of a Doorframe: Poems Selected and New, 1950–1984*, © 1984 by Adrienne Rich. Copyright © 1975, 1978 by W. W. Norton & Company, Inc. © 1981 by Adrienne Rich, reprinted by permission of the publishers; MICHÈLE ROBERTS: 'Magnificat' from *All the Selves I Was* (Virago Press, 1995), by permission of Little, Brown UK Ltd; THEODORE ROETHKE: 'Dolor' from *The Collected Poems of Theodore Roethke* (Faber & Faber, 1968), by permission of the publishers; PADRAIG ROONEY: 'Pool' from *Poetry Review*, Vol. 87, No. 4 (1997/8), reprinted by permission of the author; MURIEL RUKEYSER: 'Alloy' from *A Muriel Rukeyser Reader* (W. W. Norton, 1994), © 1994 by William L. Rukeyser, reprinted by permission of International Creative Management, Inc.; CAROL RUMENS: 'Disco on the "Queen of Denmark"' and 'The Hebrew Class' from *Selected Poems* (Chatto & Windus, 1987), and 'The Freedom Won by War for Women' from *Unplayed Music* (Secker & Warburg, 1981), by permission of the author; LAWRENCE SAIL: 'Snooker Players' from *Out of Land: New & Selected Poems* (Bloodaxe Books, 1992), by permission of the publishers; TŌGE SANKICHI: 'The Shadow', *Poems of the Atomic Bomb*, translated by Richard H. Minear, from *Hiroshima: Three Witnesses* (Princeton University Press, 1990); CAROLE SATYAMURTI: 'Striking Distance' from *Selected Poems* (Oxford University Press, 1998), by permission of the publishers; 'The Life and Life of Henrietta Lacks' from *Poetry Review*, Vol. 86, No. 4 (1996/7), by permission of the author; WILLIAM SCAMMELL: 'The Act' from *Poetry Review*, Vol. 79, No. 4 (1989/90), © William Scammell, by permission of the author; VERNON SCANNELL: 'Autumn' from *Collected Poems* (Robson Books, 1993), by permission of the author; DELMORE SCHWARTZ: 'Tired and Unhappy, You Think of Houses' from *Summer Knowledge: New and Selected Poems 1938–1958* (Doubleday, 1959), reprinted by permission of Laurence Pollinger Ltd; JAROSLAV SEIFERT: 'Salute to the Madrid Barricades', translated by Ewald Osers, from *The Poetry of Jaroslav Seifert*, edited by George Gibian (Catbird Press), © 1936 Jaroslav Seifert, translation © 1998 Ewald Osers, reprinted by permission of the translator and publishers; ANNE SEXTON: 'For My Lover, Returning to His Wife' from *Selected Poems*, edited by Diane Middlebrook (Virago Press, 1991), reprinted by permission of The Peters Fraser & Dunlop Group Ltd; JO SHAPCOTT: 'Phrase Book' from *Phrase Book* (Oxford University Press, 1992), by permission of the publishers; KARL SHAPIRO: 'Auto Wreck' from *New and Selected Poems 1940–1986* (University of Chicago Press, 1987), © 1978 Karl Shapiro by arrangement with Wieser & Wieser Inc., New York, reprinted by permission of Wieser & Wieser Inc.; STEPHEN SHERRILL: 'Katyn Forest' from *The Best American Poetry 1997*, edited by James Tate (Scribners, 1997); JON SILKIN: 'Jews without Arabs' from *The Lens-Breakers* (Sinclair-Stevenson, 1992), by permission of Random House UK Ltd; GORAN SIMIĆ: 'The Calendar', translated by David Harsent, from *Sprinting from the Graveyard* (Oxford University Press, 1997), English versions © 1997 David Harsent, reprinted by permission of the publishers; LOUIS SIMPSON: 'I Dreamed that in a City Dark as Paris' from *A Dream of Governors* (Wesleyan University Press, 1959), © 1959 by Louis Simpson, by permission

Rogers, Coleridge & White Ltd, London, 20 Powis Mews, London WII IJN; TRISTAN TZARA: 'total circuit by the moon and colour', translated by Lee Harwood, from *Selected Poems* (Trigram Press, 1975); JOHN UPDIKE: 'Cosmic Gall', 'The Newlyweds' and 'Ex-Basketball Player' from *Collected Poems* (Hamish Hamilton, 1993); EVGENY VINOKUROV: 'Siberian Restaurant-Cars', translated by Anthony Rudolf and Daniel Weissbort, from *The War is Over* (Carcanet Press, 1976), reprinted by permission of the publishers; MAXIMILIAN VOLOSHIN: 'Terror', translated by Vladimir Markov and Merrill Sparks, from *Modern Russian Poetry* (MacGibbon & Kee, 1966); ANDREI VOZNESENSKY: 'American Buttons', translated by Lawrence Ferlinghetti, from *Nostalgia for the Present* (Doubleday, 1978); DEREK WALCOTT: 'A Far Cry from Africa' from *Collected Poems* (Faber & Faber, 1986), by permission of the publishers; JOHN WHITWORTH: 'Tinned Strawberries' and an extract from 'Careless Love' from *Lovely Day for a Wedding* (Secker & Warburg, 1985), reprinted by permission of the author; WILLIAM CARLOS WILLIAMS: 'At the Ball Game' from *Collected Poems, Volume 2: 1939-62* (Carcanet Press, 1989), by permission of the publishers; KIT WRIGHT: 'I Found South African Breweries Most Hospitable' from *Penguin Modern Poets, 1* (Penguin Books, 1995); ROBERT WRIGLEY: 'Torch Songs' from *Moon In a Mason Jar & What My Father Believed* (University of Illinois Press, 1998), by permission of the author; PETER WYLES: 'Aspects of the President' from *Poetry Review*, Vol. 84, No. 2 (1994); W. B. YEATS: an extract from 'Easter 1916' and 'The Second Coming' from *Collected Poems* (Picador, 1990), by permission of A. P. Watt Ltd on behalf of Michael B. Yeats; YEVGENY YEVTUSHENKO: 'The Angries', translated by Edwin Morgan, from *Collected Translations* by Edwin Morgan (Carcanet Press, 1996), reprinted by permission of the publishers; 'To Charlie Chaplin', translated by Albert C. Todd, from *The Collected Poems 1952-1990* (Mainstream, 1991), by kind permission of the publishers; ADAM ZAGAJEWSKI: 'July 6, 1980', translated by Renata Gorzynski, from *Tremor* (Harvill Press, 1987).

Every effort has been made to obtain permission from all copyright holders whose material is included in this book, but in some cases this has not proved possible at the time of going to press. The publishers therefore wish to thank those copyright holders who are included without acknowledgement, and would be pleased to rectify any errors or omissions in future editions.

Index of Titles and First Lines

Index of Poets

Index of Translators